Nepal in Transition
A Way Forward

Nepal in Transition

A Way Forward

Edited by

D. P. Tripathi

Chairman

Vichar Nyas Foundation
New Delhi

Vij Books India Pvt Ltd
New Delhi (India)

Published by

Vij Books India Pvt Ltd
(Publishers, Distributors & Importers)
2/19, Ansari Road, Darya Ganj
New Delhi - 110002
Phones: 91-11-43596460, 91-11- 65449971
Fax: 91-11-47340674
e-mail : vijbooks@rediffmail.com
web: www.vijbooks.com

ISBN: 978-93-81411-07-0

Price in India: ₹ 850/-
Price outside India: US $ 45

Printed in India
at Narula Printers

CONTENTS

INTRODUCTION

I have always held that Nepal is a special country to India for reasons more than one. Foremost, of course, is the cultural civilisational link that binds India and Nepal at the people-to-people level. The second most important reason is its strategic location in the Himalayas. Rest of the reasons comprising economic, social and political originate from people-to-people interaction facilitated by a 1500 km stretch of open border and political support/resistance to each other both at the government-to-government and grassroots levels. An unstable Nepal, therefore, is a wholly unwelcome situation, and that makes the current struggle for democracy in Nepal a matter of immediate concern to India.

The history of democratic evolution in Nepal has been uneven and protracted. The overthrow of 104 years of Rana rule in 1951 can be considered the first major landmark in this history when the cause of democracy was advanced. But it was followed by two other developments that pushed the cause of democracy backwards. In December 1960, King Mahendra staged a coup against the democratic system and its first elected government. He imposed a party-less Panchayat System to camouflage an active and assertive monarchical order. His successor, King Birendra was forced by popular resistance to seek renewed legitimacy for this system through a referendum by pitting it against the system of multi-party democracy. Questions about the 'free and fair' nature of the referendum held in May 1980 not withstanding, the party-less Panchayat system was endorsed in the referendum causing another setback to democracy.

The struggle for democracy however rebuilt itself to emerge victorious in 1990, when for the first time after 1960, the concept of popular sovereignty was accepted and a system of multi-party democracy under 'Constitutional Monarchy' was established. It was hoped that Nepal would now onwards evolve into a real functional democracy on the lines of Britain and such other constitutional monarchies. This however was not to be as the custodians of democracy could not keep their commitment to democratic governance and gradually surrendered their power to monarchy. In the meanwhile there was rise of Maoist insurgency since 1996. The character of Monarchy underwent a drastic transformation as a result of the 'palace massacre' in June 2001. Under the new King, Gyanendra and on the pretext of fighting Maoist 'terrorism', the active and assertive Monarchy re-emerged. On the lines of his father the late King Mahendra's coup, new King Gyanendra dismissed the elected parliament and representative government and took direct control of the polity on 1st February 2005. However, democracy re-triumphed with the success of *Jan Andolan-II* (Peoples' Movement-II) that brought not only all the political parties but also the Maoists and the civil society together, resulting eventually in the abolition of Monarchy and the establishment of a 'republic' in Nepal. This however has not made democracy stable and institutionalized as yet; there persists confusion and fragmentation of the coalition of forces that led the *Jan Andolan-II* to succeed.

The core objectives of the *Jan Andolan-II* were to bring the Maoists peacefully into the national mainstream and build with them the foundations of a vibrant, inclusive and stable democratic political order in Nepal. The history of democratic struggle in Nepal has been decisively and almost organically linked to a broader political consensus in Nepal and the convergence of this consensus with India's creative and supporting help. The way out from the present impasse in Nepal therefore lies in recreating the inclusive political consensus and re-harnessing India's constructive role in taking the agenda of restoration of democracy forward.

Nepal-India relations can no longer be understood through the conventional prism. The fast changing regional and international developments and trends such as the rise of ethnic, regional and non-ideological factors and their impacts on domestic and foreign policies have impacted bilateral relations. Since the old maneuverability does not exist to the extent as it was in the past, both India and Nepal are constrained to adjust to the new realities. Nepal's landlocked position and close economic interdependence with India does not allow Nepal to be fully creative in terms of policy decisions. Nor can China provide alternatives to it. The civilisational linkages are far too strong to be influenced by politics. Nepal's only option is to be more realistic in comprehending the emerging dimensions of regional and world politics as well as to adopt strong policy measures for internal development. Economically backward Nepal will only be a liability for India and China whose own developmental performances are strikingly different from others. Nepal's domestic stability, peace and development, and the maturity in thinking about the country and the people only assure its neighbours. Empowerment of people making them owner of the developmental processes and democracy would generate national confidence. But confidence should not be driven by empty slogans of nationalism. It must be understood that *rashtriyata* (Nationalism) is not necessarily anti-Indianism; it goes much beyond it. If the people are permanently reeled under poverty, start losing confidence in Nepal's intrinsic strength, abstract slogans of nationalism do not help them.

Any new decision to be taken cannot be unilateral in the given context, because only coordinated and cooperative policies to be pursued by both the countries would help them. I sincerely believe that instead of raising the issue of 1950 treaty every now and then, Nepal should now concentrate its energy on developing the country, institutionalizing democracy and making people confident of their future. Since domestic context of security has wider ramifications for bilateral, regional and internal security, chances of regime survival depend on socio-economic and political empowerment of citizens.

Placed in the strategic zone of the region, particularly between China and India, Nepal needs to play a more moderate and balancing role between the two neighbours. The location of Nepal which is physically integral to the Gangetic plain, the heartland of India, makes India more concerned about its security. Some concerns shown by India on Nepal's internal development is related to its own vital interest. And such concerns that focus on Nepal's peace, progress and stability and democracy cannot be construed as interference. Trust and confidence to be generated between Nepal and other countries, especially neighbours, alone can complement the efforts of development.

It is unrealistic to assume that these objectives could be accomplished in a short time span and through political quick fixes. Political transitions of this order take time, resources and all the necessary political skills of the political parties and the international community. Nepal has sufficient bases to develop and prosper. The present need is to identify such bases and mobilize them properly. Prudent and effective leadership with clear goals is essential for all parties involved to give a solid direction to the task of drafting a democratic constitution in order to put an end to the current situation of political instability and constitutional transition. I genuinely believe that Nepalese people have due aspiration for peace, they have high concerns for democracy and with the cooperation from the international community the political parties and the people of Nepal would be able to draft the constitution and complete the peace process and make the democratic revolution in Nepal beautiful and enchanting.

(D. P. Tripathi)

Excerpts from the unpublished Jail Diary of BP Koirala*

BP Koirala was an avowed and indefatigable champion of democracy and by far the tallest of all leaders that Nepal has ever produced.

The continued struggle for democracy in Nepal is his legacy. Here, we produce excerpts from his unpublished Jail Diary that show the agony and resolve of a political leader, ideas and ideals of a matured thinker and vulnerability and helplessness of a simple human being.

---

* BP Koirala : Bishweshwar Prasad Koirala

Bishweshwar Prasad Koirala

Born 8 September 1914, Varanasi;
education in Varanasi and Calcutta;
participated in India's Freedom Struggle:
arrested (1930), joined Congress Socialist Party (1936),
Organising Secretary of Bihar CSP (1937), arrested (1942);
Organiser, Nepal National Congress Party (1946);
started anti-Rana movement (1947);
started insurrectionary movement (1950);
Home Minister, Interim Government, Nepal (1950); merged his party Nepali National Congress with Nepal Democratic Party to make Nepali Congress (1949); Prime Minister, Nepal (1959-60); imprisoned in Nepal (1960) and released (30 October, 1968); self-exile in India (1968-76);
returned to Nepal (December, 1976); again arrested (December, 1976);
permitted to leave Nepal (June, 1977);
arrested on return to Nepal (November, 1977);
acquitted of treason charges (March 1978);
returned to public life (September, 1978);
under house arrest (April to September, 1979);
died on 21 July, 1982.

Jail Diary of BP Koirala

Explanatory notes in parenthesis are given to help readers locate the characters in BP Koirala's personal and political life - Editor.

January 1, 1967:

Made the usual New Year's Day resolution and drew a programme of work to be accomplished during the year. **This year will also be the seventh year of my imprisonment.** Want to make the year most productive. I have also drawn up a long list of books to read and to write. My health is on the whole good; there is no reason why I cannot work hard and particularly that is what I have resolved to do if my resolution endures.

January 2:

Thought of Prakash (Prakash Koirala, eldest son of BP Koirala) who has not been doing well in his studies. He is a very sensitive boy and has the makings of a leader. If he does not succeed in his studies, he will be thoroughly demoralized. I understand his difficulties, because I too had encountered them when I was a student. If I had been out, I would have been a great help to him. **He is paying the price for my idealism** - perhaps the pursuit of idealism entails a lot of sacrifice on the part of those who happen to be dependent on an idealist (who has, of course, made sacrifice himself).

January 3:

In my opinion at the **centre of man's problem is the problem of his freedom. He is born unfree, his lifelong striving is to be free.** Human activities philosophical and artistic, political and economic, social and scientific are his strivings in the quest of his freedom. I am deeply dissatisfied with the current spate of books which seem to forget this central problem (human) of freedom; that is why they appear so superficial to me. Modern man's young men's superficiality, his hollow activities (because they are not striving, but are a mere purposeless motion), his lack of idealism, are all due to his lack of interest in this central question. The great crime that is committed against man is the denial of freedom to him. **Those scientists (sociologists) who treat human beings as a species of animals are abettors of this crime.**

January 6:

Dr. Raj Bhandari examined me and found me okay. He cannot explain why I get occasional pain in my throat and nose. He has advised me to give up morning walk. Perhaps he thinks that cold has affected my throat. I have no intention of giving up my morning walk. It gives me pleasure to expose my face to the cold draught of the morning and to walk crunching over the frost hardened ground. I derive a sense of well-being and also a sense of adventure.

Talking of pleasures, I find them more in little things and petty sensations than in big ones. **Sex is too over pressing to be savoured as pleasure.** Sands, as they yield under pressure, prickle the soles of my feet playfully like a beloved. I like to rest in a tub of hot water; the drowsiness thus infused is akin to pleasure; to sleep over a clean bed; to feel beloved's breath somewhere on my body, warm and wet; fragments of music which tentatively floats and then disappears in the air. Sushila says that the greatest pleasure is just to watch children the way they have, the way they walk, the way they lisp, the way they spiel or giggle, they sleep, the way they play. She says that children do not over behave; they always play even in anger and sleep.

I read Mohan Rakesh's *Bandh Andhere Kamare.* Its language is on the whole good, but at places it takes on poetic quality which is the most unsuited to the tempo of the novel. Rakesh is a poet also perhaps the poet in him intrudes into his style and the language (which is out of place in a novel of this kind).

What does the writer want to say the story and the relationship of Harbans and Nilima? He takes us with them to all places, to all kinds of situations without telling us what the matter really is between them that prevents the understanding between this couple. Their frustration is not clearly accounted for in the novel.

January 9:

***Wey Din* by Nirmal Verma:** a much talked about novel in Hindi. I found it extremely disappointing though. Pale imitation of Hemingway (*Hemingway's The Sun Also Rises)* attempts at drawing picture of post-war atmosphere of frustration in Europe. There is not much of a story and the frustration that the writer wants to evoke is causeless, because he has not shown why there should be frustration in the life of the girl from Vienna too many signs and cryptic philosophical utterances do not constitute the cause of misery or frustration hence the story being a picture of unexplained unhappiness leaves the reader feeling cold. I did not like the prolific use of English words in the novel; it is a trick used in place of profundity to serve the purpose of profundity. The writer has proved that he has lived long years in Prague and knows the city and its sights, particularly its bars and dancing floors but he has overdone it when he starts writing about which street he went by or which bar he visited. We are not interested in the proper names of the streets and the city's other locations they are not necessary for the story. I also did not like his style of writing slipped sentences with too many dashes.

January 12:

I re-read *Saratbabu's Srikanta.* I had read it once when I was in school and had liked it then. I was in those days profoundly affected by his novels. But when I re-read *Srikanta* lately, I found it clearly dated. The things that struck me are his middle class values, which have become so outdated now that to take them seriously and sentimentally is only to provoke ridicule or at least disinterestedness. Love for a prostitute is not such a problem now because she is no more considered to be a fallen, unredeemable woman. Inspite of his clear sympathy for prostitutes and fallen women Saratbabu seems to suffer from a sense of prejudice for them or the society. Sexual or marital fidelity is another value which has lost its luster in the present social context but to which Saratbabu seems to be deeply attached. **Sexual conservatism is not necessarily a virtue, nor sexual liberation a vice by itself.** The glories of Saratbabu's projected womanhood emanate from this conservatism does not seem to conceive that sexually free woman can also be conservative. May be, when he wrote the novel, its sentiments were appropriate for the time but the drawback of this novel is exactly this topicality.

January 13:

After having written all my letters for this month, I feel vacant today. This happens at the end of every Nepali month, when I have to send out my letters for delivery. It seems I become too much involved emotionally as I write my letter, because, too full in mind are my dear ones that no sooner I am done with writing do **I become overwhelmed with loneliness.** Like disappearance of a powerful dream which, though a temporary experience, acquires vividness. It generates loneliness as if colours and light have disappeared from the scene, as if all the trees and streams, the hills and valleys, the blueness of the sky and its stars, the sun of the heaven all have vanished from the scene, leaving a vast emptiness in the centre of which I stand. I feel like weeping out of sheer loneliness. I also suffer from a sense of worklessness. There is nothing that I can lay my hands on, there is nothing that I can create. In the vast loneliness, it is not only the material world that loses its variety and colour, the world of the mind, too, loses the capacity of extolment and the ideas become gray mind and the world merge in the general grey here in my lonely hours. Worklessness - an attitude of mind which has lost its capacity for excitement - loneliness dulls the mind.

January 14:

Confusing reports on the happenings in China. What is this Red Guards movement? What does the conflict between Mao faction and Lin faction signify? Is army homogenous? If not, will not its participation in the conflict presage a civil war, a tradition and a recurring phenomenon of the Chinese history? Internationally, from the propaganda of Russia, it appears Russia is pro-Lin and anti-Mao; the rest of the world appears to be watching the situation with breathless expectation. The tone of Indian reporting reveals its anti-Mao lines. It appears only Russia is keenly interested in the outcome of the conflict - which means from that the point of view of Russian national interest, the victory of Mao would augur ill for Russia. Does it mean that Mao's policy is opposed to Lin's in the fact that Mao would like to escalate Chinese confrontation with Russia with implication that she would de-escalate its hostile policy towards India and USA? If so, the outcome of the struggle is of tremendous consequence to the world. **India does not seem to have grasped this implication.** The implication is that Mao's victory would introduce a period of easement in the relationship between China and India. USA will be a gainer against USSR; at present, the latter is gainer against USA as China confronts the latter.

January 16:

All the problems of man spring from this tentative character his middle position. That is why nothing explains him wholly; why all the contrary assertions about him in philosophy are valid; why there is both madness and method in him; why a normal man is sub-human; why there is this tension of existence in him; why he is most unsatisfied with life but is most reluctant to leave it. The current existential thought, the new philosophy (or the current vogue of this old philosophy), is due to the awareness of this middle position of man. **Science treats him as an animal (or even as particles of matter), idealism treats him as a God, and hence the peculiar philosophy of modern man, that is existentialism.**

Man's modernism, his selfishness, his egoism, his cruelty, his rapacity, his vanity, all his vices are human attributes, his "negative" qualities. But his selflessness, his charity, his generosity, his kindness, his nobility, his fellow feeling all his virtues are also human attributes, his "positive" qualities. Negative qualities are historical, reactionary and retrospective; positive qualities are creative, preferential and prospective. If man had only negative qualities, he would have remained an animal; if only positive, he would have already becomes God. He is neither, hence his puzzlement.

Man is not wholly an animal nor is he wholly a transcendental being. Man is the two beings animal and God. He is composed of a part animal and a part God, unseparately fused. There is no God in man; nor is there animal in him. He is a vanishing point between an achieved but now receding reality (the disappearing animality, that is, animal) and an unrealized but clearly glimpsed possibility (the approaching Godhood, that is unformed God).

January 19:

Gyaneshwari Gita, about which both Kishunji (Krishna Prasad Bhattarai) and Ram Narayan (Ram Narayan Misra) have very high opinion. Gyaneshwari once made a buffalo recite the slokas of the Vedas. GM (Ganesh Man Singh) thinks that both RN (Ram Narayan Misra) and KP (Krishna Prasad Bhattarai) believe in this story as true and terms them superstitious. GM himself believes in ghosts which he sees so often at night in the camp and believes that dreams are clues to future happenings. GM is not prepared to believe that any harm can come to him despite all the reports of cancer with which he is fatally down. I think this is superstition. But am I free from superstition? Is not trust in science some kind of superstition? Because **life is infinitely vaster than the explanation of it provided by science.** One should accept the verdicts of science with some skepticism, because they themselves are tentative, fragmentary, elementary and are relevant to a tiny area of human existence. To give more to science than is due is superstition in the reverse.

January 20:

My friendly critics had been telling me that my greatest political liability was that I did not know Nepal, and that therefore my method of work and my ideas were unsuitable and impractical. I have had enough time in prison to ponder over that criticism. Even Thuldaju (Matrika Prasad Koirala, the elder brother of BP Koirala) used to be contrasted with me and treated as a better example of political sagacity. I have never agreed with the analysts of my politics. I know I am not steeped in Nepal's history, which bores me no end and which I consider to be least educative, except as a horror story. I do not know the psychology of the various tribes and their social atmosphere. This I consider to be a liability. I am not one of those who would like to preserve the so-called special qualities of tribal communities and their culture and social colours (whatever they may mean) because we cannot have them and at the same time build up a society on modern lines. In one instance, I did not know the condition obtaining in Nepal as a matter of fact, the condition about which I think I was not aware of is not peculiar to the politics of Nepal. It obtains everywhere - where the chance of feudal dictatorship to emerge is present. **I did not know the mind of the**

King, because I thought he would not go against the present current of History. His dictatorship is feudal and reactionary and I know it; being against the spirit of the time and the progressive need of the country, it is only a temporary imposition like an incubus. If I did not understand such feudal mind I do not think I should be charged with not understanding the politics. My modern conception of politics did not come in the way of my building a sizeable party, which from every account was the best organized and most effective of all the parties in the country and of creating a democratic socialist atmosphere which stood us in good stead in the general election. As a matter of fact, I was so much in tune with the spirit of the time and had such an instinctive grasp of the mood of the people and their aspiration perhaps better than anybody and the king who is wrongly accredited with practical sense that the king had to give up politics and resort to arms. The king was against us in an admission of his political defeat. War is not politics, at least it is not the kind of politics which takes into account the moods of the people, their aspiration and their welfare and needs. Victory in a military war is conquest, not a political success. In such a military conquest, there is always an element of colonial suppression; a military victor always takes on the character of a foreigner. **Mahendra is once again a Prithvi Narayan Shah, a foreign conqueror and not an indigenous ruler.**

January 22:

Hope is a clever task master, who drives us voluntarily to our work; but pays in wages of mere pleasure. **Work through intervention of hope, is pleasure.** Through subtle intervention of hope our task is no more a duty it becomes a pursuit of pleasure. A compulsion of duty, through hope, is rendered into a voluntary pursuit of pleasure.

January 24:

Read in the paper that the King has appointed a committee to consider his draft of an amendment to the constitution. There is total secrecy as to the nature of amendment, draft of which has been sent by the King to the committee. Necessarily, there is a lot of speculation outside. I think the amendment contemplates mainly the enlargement of the executive authority of the Chief Minister who will most likely have the authority of a Prime

Minister. If it is so, there will be some other minor changes also allied with this basic one, namely (1) Ministry will be of cabinet type with collective responsibility; (2) Ministers to be responsible to Prime Minister; and (3) Ministry will be responsible to parliament.

January 25:

Leader is not merely a mouthpiece of a nation. He is also more importantly the directing brain of the nation. What is political sagacity?

My political opponents all have been vanquished except the King, who too, however, has lost to me politically. His victory over me has not been political, but military. My failure is that **I did not understand the role of army in the politics of Nepal,** otherwise I would have attempted at educating the army to make it an instrument of democracy or else would have tried to guard against its interference in politics.

"What the proprietorship of these papers is aiming at is power but power without responsibility the prerogative of the harlot throughout the ages." S. Baldwin, 1931 (said against Beaverbrook and others).

January 26:

I send for doctor at the slightest excuse and I am in the habit of consuming a lot of medicine. This is due to nervousness caused by long detention. There is a sense of lack of security, hence nervousness and hence the need and assurance of a medical man who is easily available to us here. The military doctors must be interpreting this imperative need of mine of medicine unsympathetically an old man's quest for health, as an evidence of malingering, as a trick to get medicine at no cost. Among us KP is least in need of medical attention. He does not take medicine unless he is bed-ridden, which he seldom is. His constitution is finest amongst us.

I read Krishna Chander's novel *"Ek Violin Samunder Ke Kinare."* Liked it, because of it being out of the usual style and an uncommon story, a mixture of myth and reality. The story, apart from its mythological order of Shiva granting a boon to one of his devotees, is a collection of disjointed events of fantastic, humorous, pathetic nature as if the writer did not care for the unity of the plot or the plausibility of the coherence of the structure of the story; yet they are held together by a theme like a thread throughout the story that despite human traits like love, an ancient man cannot live in a modern world and that such enduring questions lose significance with changes in social mores.

January 27:

Yesterday in a novel I read about love being both a theory and practice. I want to add: **Love is the only art that diminishes with practice.**

February 1:

When I review my political activities, I come to a startling conclusion - that **I am not a revolutionary, but a rebel.** My impatience with method and organization had been imputed to my mercurial temperament at best or at worst to my laziness of character. I had myself accepted this explanation of my incapacity for methodical work. But of late, I am coming to see myself in a better light. I am capable of hard work, and pursue my objective with a persistence that is almost tenacious and obstinate; otherwise I would not have been in politics, which has mostly brought flustering experience to me in the first place. I do not neglect to protect the interests that I have in my heart. I have also put in hard labour in such works as I am interested in. My hunger strike for 29 days is no evidence of my lack of steadfastness. During the last ten days, when every hour was an age and called for almost superhuman determination to hold on, I mostly came out successful in the test. During the election in 1958-59 I worked harder than anybody. Also, in organizing the Nepali Congress itself I can take justified pride that I came out successful. Nepali Congress is my creation, more than anybody's. Therefore, **I do not accept the charge that I am mercurial or lack steadfastness.**

February 3:

I cannot help being a rebel. This explains why I did not hold on to the control of the Mukti Sena after 1951 revolution, (Djilas thought that I was a fool to do so); Why I did not use it when I was turned out of the Government without ceremony in November, 1951 (Narendra Deo thought that I was again a fool); Why didn't military aspect of politics interest me? **Why did I not take trouble to build my base in Nepal's army when I had a chance (during my premiership)**; Why I did not build a secret organization;

Why, if I failed in these things, I am so singularly successful in open politics (vide election result) etc.

Perhaps I am too much of a democrat to be a revolutionary; and too much of a rebel not to be a democrat. Although I claim to have been influenced more by Marx than Gandhi, **I think, in reality, I am more influenced by Gandhi than Marx.**

February 4:

Jean Juarez speaks of creative hatred "la hairs creative."

Creative hatred is of different quality than a general hatred. Hatred as such is blind and has no larger aim than revenge. **Creative hatred is a kind of bitterness that drives you,** not to mere revenge which is contented once you have taken it, to a purposeful ideal the achievement of which will be a kind of revenge but of an entirely different order, i.e., creation of a situation in which hatred is not likely to be created at all. Hatred is personal; when it transcends and hitches itself to an ideal, it becomes bitterness.

Bitterness vs. hatred: Madalsa (a family friend) used to tell me that **a man in politics should not forget his injury.** Now I understand what she meant.

February 6:

What is the basic problem of the world today?

In my opinion, the basic problem is failure on the part of international leadership to get out of the rut of national thinking. The greatest stumbling block is the inertia of nationalism that hinders the emergence of genuine international outlook even among intellectuals who are supposed to be free from national obscurantism. If you take the world as a whole and the entire population as one single community, most of the problems will cease to be so dreadfully insurmountable. Poverty is not an international problem, because the international resources are so developed that if they are properly planned and utilized as one economic unit, there will be no poverty. Poverty is a specific problem, of undeveloped countries. It is not a global problem. The help rendered by developed nations to the underdeveloped ones is so minimal at present and so fragmented and unplanned that it has not been of much consequence towards the removal of poverty from the world. **Poverty cannot be wiped out unless the entire resources of the world are pooled together.**

February 8:

The most important political problem is the problem of democracy. The so-called conflicts between the capitalistic and the communistic states are only the present day expression of conflict of national interests. USA and USSR are gradually coming closer not in transcending their so-called national interests but in the outlook of their communal life and culture. What still differentiates between them is more or less of democracy in USA it is more, in USSR it is less.

February 11:

KP revealed the total disintegration of his personality psycho-pathetic symptom, when he started abusing the Major (commandant) of the camp in the vilest of terms. The provocation was, according to KP, that the Major had not conveyed his message to Gopalji (Gopal Prasad Bhattarai, brother of KP Bhattarai) for money. KP is in debt to the supply man, and the latter has stopped the supply of such items as cigarettes, soaps, nuts etc., to him. My offer to him that 'let me give you some money' has persistently been refused. Knowing his difficulties I feel that he should be helped, so I have kept my offer open to him. I do not want, however, to appear unwantedly generous. I want him to ask for money at least accept my offer of help in a spirit of friendliness to him. Since he is with me as co-prisoner suffering the same fate, I feel that simply out of common humanity he should be helped. I know that Gopalji and his people do not very much care for him, although he keeps the illusion that they are full of affection for him. Anyway the language that he used against the Major was so vulgar and in such a bad taste that I felt ashamed to hear it. Since he is in prison with me for the same cause, **I felt ashamed at the crudity and utter lack of taste in the man supposed to be my comrade.** Later on I felt unhappy because I did not intervene to stop KP from disgracing him like that. Even if he had not listened to me which he would not have I would have mitigated the humiliation to the Major by intervening. I predict that KP will go mad in the course of this year if he is not released.

February 12:

What is dignity? The word dignity is very commonly used to give a name to all kinds of qualities so commonly that it seems to have lost its specific attribution and is used to convey one approbation of somebody's conduct and behaviour. There is, however, an element of reservedness in one's behavior that easily lends itself the status of dignity. It is commonly supposed that a reserved man is a dignified man. I Completely lack reservedness; and when I am reserved I mostly seem so; essentially my reservedness is due to my diffidence. **Normally I am not reserved except when I am shy and diffident.**

GM says by way of criticism that I am really mercurial. He has chosen the word "mercurial" (because I am generally supposed to have mercurial temperament) because he did not want to give me offence by saying that I have no dignity. What he is dissatisfied with is my attitude to the army personnel, men of our guard company. I talk to them. He wants me to be reserved with them. That was the attitude of Thuldaju also, who once said that my action in accosting General Vijay (Vijay Shamsher, Foreign Minister and son of the Rana Prime Minister Mohan Shamsher) who happened to come up before us was "infra dig".My attitude of dignity is entirely opposed to theirs. I consider a studied attitude of indifference and hostility even towards your enemy as undignified. Moreover, **pose as a behaviour is the most undignified behaviour.** I have always held that GM is one of the greatest posers and actors in the political scene of Nepal.

February 14:

Interview Day: Mother, TP (Tarini Prasad Koirala, brother of BP Koirala) and Rosa (Rosa Koirala, wife of TP Koirala) came. I am very happy to see mother after such a long time. TP also looked better since the last interview. Govind (Govind Koirala), Dirgh Raj (Dirgh Raj Koirala), Govind's sons, Shilu and others had also come. I exchanged greetings with all of them through the wicket of the gate. **GM's wife gave me two types of pipe tobacco and a box of cigar.** Marshall Zulum Shakya and Dhrubaram were also there. On the whole I am pleased today. Sherchan's wife is however very ill. He is naturally very sad and gloomy. She appears to be affected by the lonely separation from her husband a tragedy which Nepal's dictatorship brings to individuals who are not prepared to bow down to the dictator. I have grown a liking for Sherchan (Yogendra Man Sherchan) and through him his wife who appears to be a very good girl. In the evening we took our food together. A kind of feast. GM's wife had brought some chen-chev in a net case. **On interview days I become causelessly tense with excitement.**

March 14:

The recent elections in India have brought about a tremendous change in the political picture of that country. The congress has lost power in eight states and in the centre it has been returned with sharply altered strength. The elections have produced surprising results also. What is of important consideration is the question whether the results have produced (l) more or less political stability and (2) strengthened the process of democracy. My first reaction is one of despair. The two questions stability and democracy have to go together, and if the former is weakened the reverse may not be true, that is, weakening of democracy may not necessarily lead to instability, it may rather lead to dictatorship. In any case, the change that the general elections have brought in India poses many questions and raises many doubts. The defeat of the Congress was necessary, but in the absence of alternative parties coming up to take its place, the weakening of the Congress is a dangerous development. Coalition politics would not prove successful in under-developed countries. Moreover, coalition can be effected only among such parties that have common approach to fundamental questions. There cannot be a coalition between the Communist Party and the Swatantrata Party or the Jan Sangh which have achieved some tangible success in the elections.

March 15:

Mother, TP and Rosa came to see me. Mother looked cheerful, which gladdened me. She has become thin, but looks healthy. Her energy and spirit at this age are stimulating, and I return encouraged after every time I see her. Madalsa had also come. I saw her through the wicket gate and exchanged a few words of greetings. It excited me to see her after such a long time. She has become rounded, soft like a typical Bhaktini. Radhaswami faith has done her good. Mother told me that she has gone a long way among the fellow devotees in the path of self-realization; when TP said that she was being considered for the exalted office of a guru of the sect, mother said that she was still below for that office. Mother showed me a photo of the present Guru, a lady, who looked in the photo charming and attractive.

May 16:

Interview Day: Sushila (Sushila Koirala, wife of BP Koirala), Shriharsha (Shriharsha Koirala, second son of BP Koirala), Manu (Shashank Koirala, youngest son of BP Koirala) and Baini (Bunu Koirala, sister of BP Koirala) came. I was happy, more so because I was surprised that they came without prior intimation. In anticipation, you begin enjoying an event even before it happens; and the event, when it comes, it loses some of its impacts of happiness. **The impact of happiness of an event which is not anticipated is all the greater on account of the element of surprise.** I was so happy that I could not talk coherently with them. As a matter of fact, when they had gone I felt I had not talked with the children at all. Most of the time I was taken up in inconsequential talks with Sushila Manu, a sensitive boy. He must have felt it. He remained quiet all the time. I am told he is doing well in his class. I exchanged a few words with Shriharsha. He looked grown up. Baini's health is also good. She looked charming. She was however shy with me. She is a very bad student but I was warned by Sushila that I should not refer to her failure in the examination because she would become unhappy. Prakash could not come because his examination is not yet over. I found Sushila, too, in fairly good health. She was cheerful too. I asked her if she was depressed. She said, 'No.' I asked about some political friends, she said that they were not frustrated. This is good news. What impressed me most was Sushila's confidence and cheerfulness. Her hair has become almost wholly grey and she definitely looks aged and weaker bitten but she was cheerful and confident.

TP said that Ramesh's (Ramesh Nath Pandey) movements were fishy. Sushila said that he had become self-important, that is all. He has had some recognition lately which has gone into his head. TP seems to think that the change in his behavior denotes something more sinister. TP said that Rudra Giri (Rudra Prasad Giri) has welcomed the recent arrest; it was a good and proper step he said on the part of the Government to arrest these undesirable elements. I am amazed at his volte face and brazen sycophancy. GM said that he wanted to earn a place in the ministry by flattery.

June 6:

Regular war has started between the Arabs and the Israelites. My sympathies are with Israel, although I admit that the Arabs are not without a case of their own. My sympathy for Israel is both emotional and rational emotional because the Jews have been a persecuted people whose suffering reached an unimaginable depth in the East Germany and Poland during the last war; rational, because once Israel has come into being as a result of the UN decision she has a right to exit, the right which is denied by Arabs. **Most of the problems associated with Israel versus Arabs would vanish once Israel's right to exit is accepted by the Arabs.** The Arabs at present are subject to the leadership which is either out and out feudal or demagogue dictators or military oligarchs. **Arabs are essentially emotional people, easily excitable who are being exploited by their leaders to maintain themselves in power.** It is therefore in their interest to keep alive the tension with Israel.

July 1:

I do not feel like doing anything. Is it psychological or physical? This condition of laziness is contrary to my temperament. **My usual state is one of restlessness and activities.** Since a few months I have been noticing a change in me I feel like losing. I have developed slothness. Along with this physical weakness, I am noticing some deterioration of my mind too. I cannot concentrate my mind on any subject for a long time my mind gets tired very soon. I have not the old alertness. My mind had never been quick, but it was active and inclined to make efforts; moreover, it was a clear mind. It took long to understand a thing, but it understood well. That is not how it is now. It gets bogged soon and is inclined to avoid hard and concentrated efforts. Is it old age? I should not think so, because such mental deterioration should not begin so early at my age (which is only 53 years). Is the life of the prison having its effect on me? If it is, then the deterioration has started all of a sudden.

Spent the day almost sleeping and dozing. I read a few pages of *Havelock Ethos.* **Sex is a subject that one can tackle even when the mind is so dull and unreceptive as is mine at present.**

July 2:

Read *'Father and Son'* by Turgnev. The novel was written more than 100 years ago, but the picture of the conflict of the two generations fathers and sons continues to be fresh and surprisingly up to date (even in the languages of the protagonists), although the social context has changed. This novel is not dated as the novels of Sarat Babu, whose appropriateness for the present time is very little. Moreover, the novel is not loaded with clustering details, which less competent artists resort to, to bring out the fullness of characters. The depth of the story is provided by alternative episodes and the characters have been developed with minimum details. There is neatness in the execution of the plan (scheme) of the novel.

But what does the writer want to convey through the character of Bezanov? Bezanov is before me in clear light but what I do not know is: what to make out of him? Is he an object of admiration and pity, or more admiration or more pity or is he, despite his energy, an ineffectual figure? Is he a ridiculous figure, a romantic young man, although he wants to pass off as a realist? Nihilism is it an ideal foredoomed to failure because it tries to impose itself on life, which does not tolerate any interference with it?

July 18:

Today I had an interview with TP and Nona (Nona Koirala, wife of Keshav Koirala). Bunu had also come but she could not interview me because the King refused to give permission. I saw her through the small gate and exchanged greeting. Sitara and Kamal had also come. Sitara has become quite charming she told me that she had stood first in her class and that she had won a wrist watch, which she showed to me. Kamal (Kamal Koirala, son of Matrika Prasad Koirala) was however shy. Bunu is enroute to Biratnagar to see mother, who had had a very serious attack of prolonged unconsciousness. TP told me that the doctor had at one stage despaired of her life. Saroj's (Saroj Prasad Koirala) wife Manju had also come with her little daughter.

I am concerned about mother's health. She is about 72. Although she has been keeping a good health and has always been active except when she was laid with asthma the age is against her. I cannot imagine an age-ridden incapacitated mother who has to depend on others for her personal work and needs. TP says that she is alright now. There was sudden loss of sugar induced coma which lasted for three hours. I lost father when I was in Jail. Perhaps I may not be with my mother when she will be dying. **I am her beloved son and her hero.**

August 4:

The current decade of the 60's during which we have been in prison has been a momentous period. Since our arrest much has changed on the national and international scene. The cold war tension between USA and USSR has considerably lessened, which has resulted in the undependability of these powers as friends of weaker ones. The USA image has been further eroded by the Vietnam war. England is definitely fading out as a world power, and her international position is pretentious rather than real. France is already faded out. In serious international matters both England and France are of no consequence. India's hollowness as a force in international politics even as a great power of Asia has been cruelly exposed. Its internal strength is still more minimal. China has emerged as a powerful state more powerful potentially than actually because of her military strength to which is added its capacity for nuclear war. **China is a great factor.** In Nepal, the King has succeeded in disorganizing liberal democratic forces although he has not done anything else. He has not built any viable political system there is vacuum in Nepal; and the change of peaceful progress towards democracy seems to have disappeared. The attractive one is Communism or radical democracy. **Radical democracy is distinct from liberal peaceful democracy.** It accepts violence as means to democracy violence of every political nature. It eschews restraints in political action. It concentrates more on the current urgency of demolition than on the future building of the society. There is an element of recklessness. It acts with fury, almost blindly but hoping that later day building process will take care of itself and that, ultimately, democracy will eventuate.

August 6:

Chauhan (Yashwantrao Balwantrao Chavan) Home Minister of India made a statement in the Parliament the other day, that India would not permit the Nepali residents in India to indulge in political activities against Nepal and the King. He also said that no Nepali paper would be permitted to be published in India which were of political nature and showed disrespect to the King. The statement reveals the weakness of India in her relationship with King's Nepal. I have never been very hopeful of India's effective role in Nepal, although I would very much like India to be effective in international relations. I want her also to be effective on the question of democracy in international context. But India is too weak and demoralized to play any effective role in international politics. **A weak state, like a demoralized individual, is prone to misunderstand its own interest and act adversely** to it. India is doing it in every field economic, social, political, at home and abroad. India is bankrupt and it would be a fatal mistake to depend upon her to be of any use to Nepali democrats.

August 28:

I have grown sentimental about children these days. It is not only my own children that I have become fond of. I seem to have developed fondness for all children in general also. It seems that the most important ideal that one can steadfastly adhere to is a child who needs to be loved, cared for and whose future one can dedicate oneself to. A child is a concrete ideal, whose present care and future well-being one can apply to without any doubt. **One cannot be sure of God; socialism may turn out to be a mirage; democracy a mere debate nothing. Nothing is as certain as a child** who demands immediate attention and who inspires me to sacrifice in the interest of his future. I want to be loved by all the children of Nepal.

September 17:

Received mother's letter informing that Shailaja (Shailaja Acharya) wants to marry Pradeep Giri. They are in love. They are postponing their marriage till my release.

I am glad of this news. Pradeep (Pradeep Giri) appeared to me to be a good boy, intellectual type, the type that would suit Shailaja, who herself is an intellectual type. I am only afraid that temperamentally she or he may not be a marrying type. **Intellectual types do not do well in a situation that a marriage is called upon to face.**

I received this letter after a long time. Mother seems to be too weak to write herself and therefore has this written by Bunu on her dictation. Bunu had come here, and has left with Kalpana (Kalpana Koirala, daughter of TP Koirala) for Pakistan.

September 18:

TP and Rosa came. TP told me that Pradeep Giri's people are not happy over his intended marriage with Shailaja's. Pinaki Babu also gave assent most unwillingly and only when Shailaja told him what he would do if she married a Muslim. Perhaps Pinaki Babu thinks that that would be the worst calamity and hence gave his consent to her marriage with a "sanyasi". But Shailaja is in trepidation, because she herself does not know if it would turn out to be a success.

I will write to her that she should marry and take the risk. But I am not permitted to write to her. Marriage is not love, because most loves we see in life or read in books are either virginal or adulterous. Marriage is, if anything, antidote of love. It is not company, because we can get company without marriage. **Marriage is a desire to own a person and be owned by him.** Marriage is thus a bondage and one who is not prepared to be owned cannot make a success of it.

September 21:

Received TP's letter which had been held up for a long time. The letter contained a remark the Government is vindictive towards the Koirala family which most likely had merited a most strenuous censorship. TP had been provoked into making that comment because of the release of others like SP, (Surya Prasad Upadhaya) VV (Vishwa Vandhu Thapa) who had lately been arrested for some anti-Government activities, while Girija (Girija Prasad Koirala, youngest brother of BP Koirala) was being kept in imprisonment since the last seven years.

TP writes that if we are all released, he would be the happiest in the world.

Would I be the happiest man if I am released today? No, in jail most of the time I am unhappy, and at times I suffer agonies of deprivation. But I feel that in the present political situation, which is so unfavorable to any democratic movement, the happiness of my release will be only temporary. I cannot be of any help to anybody outside and I cannot even be of help to myself. For a sensitive man like me who needs freedom and liberty more than anything else, jail is not always the worst place. Imprisonment is at least not an experience of humiliation; imprisonment is a kind of martyrdom and can be, in a way, a satisfying way of living. Man does not live by bread alone. I do not know. But I think **I would prefer death to life that has no other sustenance than bread.** In the present situation, I cannot even earn my bread without total dismemberment of my personality. Death is preferable to such existence; imprisonment is preferable to death.

January 1, 1968:

"Your real life is not behind but before you. It is the new year and not the old which is your opportunity." - Lyman Abbott

Apropos of Girija's hunger strike in the Nakhu jail about which there is a comment which is not opportune. Mother writes in her letter to me: **"Opportunity does not come to man from outside of his situation; he manufactures it out of his own situation.** Mother is full of pride for Girija who, she says, is a brave man. I myself was of the opinion that perhaps the hunger-strike was a mistake. But I now feel no action can be a mistake if backed by an indomitable will; Girija has decided to carry his will to the point of death.

January 4:

Means vs. End: Confusion on the issue because of analytical proneness of thinkers to treat them as separate and at times even contradictory entities. Proneness of intellect to analyze to dismantle an organic whole in order to study its separate parts as exclusive entities. If you give two names to separate parts of the same organic process, the logic of nomenclature will begin to put emphasis on the separate parts divided under separate names. Every human action is motivated by some objective or end or purpose; but every human purpose is also in its turn circumscribed by action directed towards it. End is a natural culmination of a process known as means. End is the last step, means is all the previous steps towards the last step. End is the last culminating action in a series of action, falling one after another in a natural sequence.

January 6:

Cannot justice be conceived something as social norm that slowly evolves a norm which society as a whole accepts in an imperceptible process of adoption? All social ethos have such social genesis. The real conflict in dictatorship arises because there is a clash between the dictator's order and the social norm (justice) that such order wants to supercede; that is, the conflict between what is good to the socicty and what is good to the dictator. A dictator wants to keep himself outside and above social justice.

Since justice in this sense is the ethical (moral) outgrowth of a collective conscience, which in its turn is built upon a social structure, it is perpetually in a process of adjustment to the change of social structure, i.e., Justice has to make appropriate adjustment to changes in social structure. In this sense morality is an evolving concept. **Rigid morality is unethical.**

I can no more be innocent habit of thought takes me away from it. When my mind works, it is seized with logic and I am a prisoner of thought. Why can't the shadow of a thing walk away from the thing? When I build my castles in the air, why must I always remember that such castles don't exist? Why shouldn't what exists in my dream also exist in reality? Shouldn't reality and dream intermediate each other? **I am so corrupted with the ways of truth that even my poetry is unredeemed of it; that even my fiction becomes a mere chunk of my life.**

"Happiness is virtue itself rather than a virtue's reward." Spinoza

February 10:

Marxist idea, that anarchism is a social condition of affluence, is the highest stage of Communism in which productive forces of the society are fully developed, hence anarchism has to wait for a historical period.

And Bakunin's idea is that anarchism has to wage its own revolution right now both for what the Marxist says economic development and man's freedom because, without this twin aim, economic revolution alone will bring about a greater tyranny on man.

In any case, anarchism is the slogan of the new revolution that is taking place in the developed societies. Gandhi is not being as extensively adopted by the new revolution because of (I) India's own image in the international world; (II) Gandhi's antipathy for machinery, etc. Mao's cultural revolution has an element of non-material ideal, hence he has an appeal among the new revolutionaries. **JP (Jayaprakash Narayan) has relevance in this higher type of revolution: his handicap is that he is an Indian and India has a very poor image in the outside world.**

February 11:

According to William Godwin, the established authority has no more right to regulate individual's action than to regulate his thought. The problem of freedom its dilemma lies in the fact that in any social organization some regulations (rule or code of behaviour), even if they are unbaked with the might of a state, are necessary. Even a game of cards has to follow certain rules which the players may change from time to time. But as long as a particular game is played, it must be played according to rules. We cannot conceive of such a state of total anarchism where each individual is free to behave as he chooses. State may wither away, perhaps it will; but some regulating authority, even if on ad hoc basis, will always be there, if only to serve as a road guide.

February 13:

Tulsi Giri once told me, "you are 50 years in advance of time. You have born 50 years before your time." **When I was the Prime Minster, the ambassador of Yugoslavia told me: "You have come into power perhaps prematurely."**

February 14:

TP and Rosa saw me on the usual round of monthly interview. Girija also saw me, but alone; even the army officers kept themselves away from the interview. They, however, kept us under observation by watching us from a distance. GP has said that he was working in agreement with Tarini Prasad for our release, which, according to him, depended upon reconciliation between the King and us. There is also compulsion of events that should lead to some understanding between us, he said. He felt that the King was also interested in the outcome of their efforts. As a matter of fact SP (Surya Prasad Upadhyay) has some kind of tacit support of the King. I expressed my doubt about the King's intention. I told GP that if the King really wanted reconciliation he could have released us without much ado. GP was with me for over an hour.

1. SP has got himself into this business on GP's instigation. It began a few months ago when SP was lodged in the same jail with GP.

2. When GP was assured by the PM and the commissioner that he would be released immediately after he broke his fast, he thought that it would help SP if he accepted the assurance of SP rather than the PM to break his fast.

3. SP has joined the Kisan Organization on the King's suggestion that the former must show by action that he was not against the monarchy. We would respond to his suggestion that the King should on his part show by act that he too was interested in democratic development of Nepal's politics. The chain of reciprocal relations must begin from SP, etc and hence SP joined the Kisan organization.

4. The King is prepared to amend the constitution to suit our requirements (King doing away with the tier system of election for the national Panchayat etc.).

5. **The King says that he is not under any pressure from outside. India is particularly in dread of him; hence she cannot even suggest anything to him. US have also lately given up putting pressure on him. China's pressure too is such that he can stand up to it. The King perhaps wants to convey to me that if he brings about change in Nepal it would be by his own volition and act, that is, the change will be again a royal gift.**

6. Communists are fast growing in the country and are entrenched even in Government departments. The King is aware of it.

7. My reputation is at the highest point at present.
8. Subarna ji (Subarna Shamsher) is frustrated, so one our workers who are in exile in India.
9. Subarna is isolated, because our workers feel that he has not succeeded in giving a lead to them.
10. Communal feeling is growing in Nepal: Flat nose versus high nose; Tarai versus Pahad; Parbate versus Newar, etc.
11. If the situation remains as it is, the Communists will take over the country within five or six years.
12. China's influence is fast growing.
13. **Morariji Desai has written to Koshu (Keshav Prasad Koirala, brother of BP Koirala) that he should try to work with the King and that India could not be of help to him (us).**
14. There is likelihood that we would be released in two batches - KP, Divan (Divan Singh Rai) and Sherchan in the first batch; GM and myself in the second. If things develop according to GP's effort of reconciliation, we would be released in course of four to five months.

Original attraction of Marxism is primarily due to the lacuna in the liberal thought which it attempts to fill up, by adding to the liberal ideology an economic conception of equality. Perversion of Marxism, which retains the humanism of liberal ideology in its original purity, which while adding some valuable contribution of its own to it, began with Lenin even before he came to power and was carried to horrifying extent by Stalin, who equated Marxism with mere economic development, thus destroying its kernel of liberal humanism.

March 15:

Interview with TP, Rosa and GP. **Shailaja had also come till the gate. She was too overwhelmed with emotion to exchange greetings with me.** GP said that his work on bringing about a rapprochement between me and the King was progressing satisfactorily. He said that a meeting between us would be arranged soon. He had gone to Calcutta to meet Subarnaji also, and he too had blessed the move of compromise by GP and SP. Subarnaji is not in good health. Three elements in Nepal's politics are opposing this compromise move: (1) individuals like Tanka Prasad, Tulsi Giri, etc; (2) Rashtriya Panchayat Parishad people who have developed vested interest in the present system; and (3) understandably, the Communists. GP would meet me again when the King returns from the tour on l4th of the current Nepali month, that is, 12 days hence. GP is very confident.

March 27:

Read in today's paper with horror that Sushma (Sushma Koirala, wife of GP Koirala) and her sister (Kumud) met with an accident of a very serious nature in Biratnagar as a result of the bursting up of a refrigerator in the school. They are in critical condition with third degree burn all over their bodies. Dr. Amkamo Kumar has gone there to attend to them on being called for assistance by the doctors of Biratnagar.

April l:

Received TP's two letters giving the details of the tragic accident that fell upon Sushma and Kumud. The details are gruesome. I am very unhappy today. The whole day I could not concentrate on anything; and at times I felt like I was suffocating and sinking. I remember Sushma who has been so full of life and so brave. She has been an adornment of our family. I remember her smiling face. Two months ago when she had come to see me at the jail gate, I had told her that it appeared as if she would not grow old and lose her youth and freshness; would never grow stale. She had smiled. I have already given up all hopes of her recovery, and even if she recovers, she will be woefully deformed, perhaps nothing better than a lump of flesh, which would be a tragedy worse than death. I am not thinking systematically today. The impact of the tragedy is stunning. I will get over it in course of time; but today it appears there is no remedy to such a tragic event; that time too cannot heal it. One thing is certain, a glory has departed; life has become poorer.

April 2:

Sushma passed away today.

April 5:

I read in today's paper that Sushma expired on Tuesday at 3pm. In his letter to me TP had held out a hope, however slender, that she might survive after all, despite doctors' anxiety, because she had rallied and had started taking nourishment and was conscious. The revival turned out to be the last flicker of the light before going out. A glory has departed from my life from the life of our family. We have become impoverished. She came into our family in 1960 as a bride in a romantic love. At that time I had thought that romantic love, having an element of impulsiveness, would not match for a steady relationship of understanding through stress and strains between her and GP. How radically mistaken I was. Our family is a happy family because its tribulation, which came thick and fast in the uncertain politics of Nepal in which I and GP in particular are involved, are shared commonly by all its members and thereby are converted into happiness, blessing and glory. Sushma joined this festival of suffering at once in such a spirit of identification with us as if she were a born member of the family. In jail I had thought that I had lost the capacity of sensitive reaction to tragic events. But today when I learn Sushma is no more I suffer acutely as if a lash of whip has cut into the raw spot my being. **I weep alone here in my cell. I am miserable today.** I want to believe that there is a soul which is deathless. I want to believe that the death has not touched with decay Sushma's soul.

April 6:

The report of Martin Luther King having been shot dead was broadcast. **The Americans have become a nation addicted to violence violence as an escape from the boredom of affluence and bareness of the ideal of more material progress.** Their culture appears to be skin-deep sensitivity of the nation lies in sensationalism; national spiritual content is lacking in their culture. The conception of their values is statistical; they have nothing to do with the personalities of the individuals except as numerical factors in the compilation of data. They have become dangerously impersonal so much so that human judgment is being replaced by mechanical reactions of computers. Intuition has no place in the thought content of the nation.

What is terrifying about America is that it has become the ideal of the world by virtue of its material prosperity and its technological prowess. It has become the leader of the world; hence the danger of its example and leadership. Agreeable in contrast are the Chinese who know at least knew till lately how to enjoy life to the maximum. **America is a geni of the fable that must be constantly put to work lest it should destroy the master.**

May 19:

On com ing out of the military prison I would like first of all to send out words of greetings to my countrymen, who have remained uppermost in my thought all the time that I was kept incommunicado from them. My greetings to innumerable democratic patriots also all those who had to undergo severe hardships some of whom had even to lay down their lives, consequent upon the royal coup of 1960. I also remember the individual officers and men of the army, my jailor for seven-and-a half- years, who in the discharge of their embarrassing duty did not fail to show courtesy and humanity to me, their prisoner.

My duty henceforth will be to unite and consolidate the democratic forces of the country that have been considerably disrupted and weakened in course of the last seven years and a half.

May 31

Taken to the hospital in the evening for x-ray examination of the intestine (barium). I had been on fast all day long and hence I felt I would faint during the examination. This has been my second outing during the long seven-and-a half years that I am in jail. In the hospital among doctors and nurses I felt the warmth of humanity. Therefore, although I felt very weak and exhausted on account of the journey and the medical examination that I was subjected to, **I became exhilarated with a dose of fresh human emotions** in the company of the doctors and the nurses. I was particularly filled with pleasure by small normal talks with the young nurse, who incidentally told me that the recipe of health is lot of food, lot of sleep and lot of carefreeness.

June 6:

Unscheduled interview with Sushila, children, TP, Rosa and GP. The officers withdrew after explaining that the interview would be private, without their presence. GP explained to me the political situation and development that are taking place outside. The interview lasted about an hour.

About Tulsi Giri there are two opinions, namely (1) that he is the King's man and (2) that he is China's man (his imprisonment is on account of his contact with China). As per the second opinion, SP's opinion conforms with this. But I think he is wrong. Tulsi is an instrument of the palace. His recent arrest was made in order to build him up as a political figure. King's illness is genuine, but the advice of the doctors on his arrival for three months rest is fake. TP thinks that it is not a political rest; that he is genuinely ill and that doctors have told him that he cannot survive beyond three more years etc.

June 24:

Received Sushila's letter, telling me that she would be leaving on Sunday. She writes that she is leaving Kathmandu with a heavy heart and with anxious mind about my health. She has written a sad letter. As a result of Subarnaji's statement and his offer of cooperation to the King on the latter's terms, she felt as others that we would be released soon. She writes that she even wrote to the King about the timorous growth in my intestine, but her letter went unacknowledged. I am myself very much worried about my health. I get constant pain in my stomach and back and near the region of testes. The pain has affected my psychology also; I have become gloomy. The idea of death has seized my imagination. I am not afraid of death; but to be uncertain about the seriousness of the disease that has affected my intestine whether the growth is benign or malignant is nerve-breaking. If I die that will be the end of me I will be no more to feel it. But I don't want too leave the world so soon, because I want to work for 15 more years after my release with vigor for my political cause, during which period our children will also have grown to manhood and settled in their different professions and occupations. The youngest among the children is Chetana (Chetana Koirala, daughter of BP Koirala) who is nine years old now. I want her to be 24 years old before I die. In Nepal's politics I have yet some role to play. If I am removed now from the scene, there will be no leader of the opposition to the despotic monarchy that reigns today. Communism may come ultimately, but I want to interpose a democratic system in the meantime between monarchy and communism. To be able to work for a cause is an exciting thing. Monarchy is entrenched today, but it is too anachronistic a system to be viable. **If capitalism can live in democracy, then I see no reason why communism cannot.** I want to live for another 15 years so that I may devote my last period of life to the cause of democracy and happiness of my people and thus make the period the most fruitful and satisfying.

Worry over my health is dominating my psychology to such an extent that I have become incapacitated for any intellectual work. I read only newspapers, magazines and light literature. I have started to attend the reading session in the morning in which Sherchand reads out passages from *western Philosophy*, a book written by Russell. This attendance does not entail much intellectual effort on my part. I superficially participate in the discussions that accompany the reading of the passages. Today's passage referred to the theological and philosophical ideas of Augustine. I have not been able to be clear about Augustine's ideas contained in the book. My difficulty is that I want to understand Augustinian ideas in terms of freedom which has been the quest of philosophy through ages. **The question as to who is supreme Christ or Caesar is not a mere theological question.** Christianity at that time was giving a fight in the interest of values which, according to it, could not come within the mischief of the sovereignty of the state. Even if moral questions were made non-religious the issue remains that part of Man's personal freedom is inviolate and therefore outside the jurisdiction of the state. The question is also relevant to the current discussion between monolithic state and pluralistic society.

I sometimes feel that if one has no religion, he must have the courage to take its place. A man without God has to have the courage to face trials and tribulations of life. Either God or courage. Sufferings of life are borne either with humility and surrender or with forbearance and stoicism. **Humility is the strength of the weak; stoicism is the pride of the strong. A sensitive man must have either the religious humility or the prideful stoicism.**

July 8:

In the evening at about six the prison commandant came inside with DIG,

Nar Narayan to ask Kishunji, Yogendraman and Divan to be ready at once with all their belongings packed. They were not told whether they were being released or transferred to some other prisons. Nar Narayan said that they would have to call at the commissioner. Our guess is that they would be released, but since they are being taken to the commissioner, they may be asked to sign some papers a kind of an undertaking to be of good behaviour. This they are not going to do.

July 9:

Feeling very lonely all day long. All India Radio announced the release of Tulsi Giri who had been arrested about some 80 days ago, but did not mention anything about the three comrades who left this camp yesterday perhaps they have not been released otherwise the All India radio would have mentioned it. May be they were released very late at night yesterday; the newsmen consequently missed it. GM and I discussed all the possibilities. GM feels that the King would now see us and discuss the political development with us. The release of three men from here was a prelude to a politic talk with us. I am not so sure although I am sure that they have been released, I am not sure that it is preparatory for a talk with us. I agree with GM that the King would now institute some kind of "National Government." As a matter of fact, I have been holding this view since a long time. When the time comes for the King to bring people into the Government he would like to dilute our influence by associating with it all kinds of diverse elements, like K.I. Singh (Dr. Kunwar Inderjit Singh), Tanka Prasad (Tanka Prasad Acharya) etc may be even Tulsi Giri, whom I have always considered to be a King's man. The fact that Giri was released so soon after his arrest on grounds of anti-national activities vindicates my point of view that Giri is an instrument of the palace.

July 10:

Two interesting items of news in today's papers: 1. *Dainik Nepal* mentions, referring to some authentic sources, that K.P., Yogendraman and Divan have been transferred to the Nakhu jail. We had never expected that they would be taken to Nakhu. We are intrigued. The Government should have had first ascertained from them (before they were taken out from here) whether there was any chance of their signing some kind of undertaking papers. From their general attitude the Government should not have expected that they had been morally weakened as a result of seven years and a half imprisonment and hence would be amenable to pressure. If anything, the long detention has morally strengthened us. Sometimes a thought occurs to me that may be we are being isolated here for some political purpose, for some kind of negotiation with us to be conducted with extreme secrecy. May be, therefore, the transfer of three of the comrades from here is a prelude to relaxation in the condition of imprisonment, although presently it has meant some kind of solitary confinement for us (now we are only two in this prison). 2. The Statesman (8th July) carries a statement from Subarnaji saying "let there be no doubt that we are not pardon seekers but Nepalese patriots who have always served their country well and shall continue to fight and die for their country. It is a refreshing statement - the only streak of light in the general gloom of despondency, sycophancy and chicanery. It has also served as a reply to those who felt that Nepali Congress offer of cooperation to the King was an abject surrender (GM held this view as against mine that the offer of cooperation is not a surrender). It has also served a notice to the Government that it should not expect from NC any further concession. Yesterday, PM Thapa (Surya Bahadur Thapa) made a statement which through its vagueness could be interpreted as a veiled demand that NC workers now living in exile in India must seek pardon individually.

Today's paper also carried the saddenise of Yogendra Man's father. He died of heart failure yesterday morning. I had seen him on the last interview day and had found him so emaciated and off-colour that I could not recognize him. He had been suffering from high blood pressure. High blood pressure seems to run in Sherchan's family. Yogendra Man used to be very much conscious of this fact and get his blood pressure checked every time a doctor visited the camp. Today he must be very sad in the new prison where he had yet no time to settle down to the new rhythm of life.

July 17:

Interview day: Mother, TP, Rosa and Girija came to see me. Bunu had just arrived in Kathmandu hence had not found time to seek permission from AM to see me. I exchanged greetings with her across the gate; her children were also there Tara and Bhai. Tara looked weak having just come out of illness. Bhai looked alright. Kaplana has also come from Lahore with them.

Mother, though thin and emaciated, was in good spirit. She said that she had an experience of physical collapse and sinking, she had found that death was not dreadful. She had an experience of peace and bliss when every one felt that she was dying and she herself was conscious of sinking into peaceful death. She had a vision, saw the light which mystics and her colleagues in the Radhaswami sect say is the vision of the Ultimate Being. It was a vision of great brightness which also filled her with peace and bliss. Mother will stay here for two or three months. Bunu has also come here for a long stay.

About my health my people seem to be in extra worry. The report on the growth of my intestine was sent to the doctors in Calcutta, Bombay and Patna. The unanimous opinion of them all was that the growth being located on an unusual place, it might not be benign turnover hence its immediate removal is urgently called for. GP has written to HM (His Majesty). TP thinks that in case I am released on medical grounds I will have to go to UK or USA for operation. As a matter of fact arrangements have already been made, hoping that I would be released soon.

I have a fear that the Government knowing the anxiety of my people would offer to release me on parole. To accept to be released on parole would entail some kind of an undertaking that during my freedom on parole I would not indulge in politics. I am not prepared to give any kind of undertaking, direct or implied but the Government's offer, if it comes to my people, would be extremely difficult to reject in view of the nature of my illness.

August 21:

Invasion of Czechoslovakia by Russia, Poland and Germany, Hungary and Bulgaria. I am upset and grieved. Czechoslovakia was introducing democracy lately which was a very encouraging sign for democrats all over the world. Invasion of a country by another does not affect me at all unless the purpose is to impose democratic system or totalitarian system - if former, I support such invasion (invasion of Hitler's Germany by the Allies etc); if latter I oppose it.

September 12:

Notice served extending our detention for further nine months. Deputy Commissioner came to serve the notice. The general was also there.

Economic development and Tyranny: There is a school of thought that tyranny is sine qua non of development without dictatorship there can be no economic development without Stalin USSR would not have developed.

Such thought is as superstitious as the one held in ancient and medieval period justifying human sacrifice to ensure success in a difficult enterprise. Recently, in Rajasthan a boy was sacrificed for unhampered completion of job at the site of a dam which was being constructed. The contractor who had taken the job of the dam construction behaved like Stalin the only difference between them being that the latter sacrificed millions and accomplished bigger construction jobs.

September 25:

In the hospital the whole day. Military hospital is an extremely dirty place, for a prisoner it is hell: it becomes both a hospital and a prison. Freedom is doubly curtailed as a patient and as a prisoner. After x-ray photos of my intestine ware taken (barium enema) I was again brought back to Sundarijal jail. I was happy to escape from the hospital. But the decision to send me back to the jail was taken suddenly; because till the evening the doctors were telling me that after the x-ray report and study of the plates they would make up their mind about further investigation which would necessitate my longer stay in the hospital. But even before the x-ray photos were taken in the evening (at 9pm) I was informed that I would be taken back to the jail immediately afterwards from the x-ray department.

October 5:

Mangalaji (Mangala Devi, wife of Ganesh Man Singh) came for a private interview with GM, lasting about two hours. SP wants to create misunderstanding through her between myself and GM. He told her that GP is playing a mischievous role and that I should not tell GM everything that GP tells me of his talks with the King. SP has created an impression with her that he is a powerful man on whose advice the King appoints his minister and that it was only in the case of Prayag Raj (Prayag Raj Subal) that the King did not listen to his advice and appointed Basudeva Dhungana from Graduates constituency a minister. He wanted her to convey to GM that I am trying to strike a bargain with the King and am prepared to give an undertaking for my release. It is to GM's credit that he reported to me all that she told him.

October 8:

Yesterday I had asked for a doctor (Dr. Mrigendra Raj). Today early in the morning Dr. Birendra Basnet came. I was told that Dr. Mrigendra Raj (Dr. Mrigendra Raj Pandey) was not available. Dr. Birendra said that I need not worry about the presence of polyp (about 40 centimeter up the colon). But it needs to be kept under observation. He suggested that I should pick up weight, he thinks I have been losing it drastically due to antibiotic treatment or other drugs that I have been taking for a long time in the past, the digestive system has become very much impaired.

October 7:

GP saw me today again. He had permission for three hours to talk but we talked only for 90 minutes that too because I knew that it would be perhaps the last private talk with him and hence I did not want to leave him. He had come to tell me that the King insists on my endorsing Subarnaji's statement and would not listen to my plea that I could not do it under duress. He said to him that unless I endorsed it the current talk should be treated as concluded. I told GP that I am perfectly clear in my mind that I cannot endorse it under duress.

According to GP the problem will be to hold our active workers under Subarna's leadership. They will be tempted to join the camp of Bharat (Bharat Shamsher), SS (Subarna Shamsher) or drift into the Communist camp. Other points: His tiff with the Indian Ambassador who thought that since Subarna acted in issuing the statement as the leader of NC I should not hesitate to endorse his statement as a loyal colleague.

GP told him that he had miserably failed diplomatically twice: (l) once when he got Subarnaji to issue the statement without prior commitment from the King that he would trespond to it; (2) then again this time by asking me to endorse Subarnaji's statement rather than insisting with the King for compliance on his part with his previous undertaking with him. Sengupta, Statesman's correspondent here, says that UK and USA are not in favor of our release. I cannot understand this.

I am very sad today. When I took leave of GP he was perturbed. I told him that they should be prepared even for my death in jail. On this note we bade farewell to each other.

I have been feeling that the King will try to bring about misunderstanding between GM and myself. We may even be separated for this purpose.

The King goes back upon all his commitments with GP who reminded him of this, upon which the King reportedly said let BP endorse Subarna's statement first, then he would reopen talk with me.

Apart from other things the whole question centers now round the King on whose words no one can rely.

Is there a murder plan to practically finish all political opponents? Refer Bhaktaram's son and the murder of Tej Bahadur (Tej Bahadur Amatya).

October 8:

The whole day I was in great agitation and infinitely sad. All sorts of ideas and thoughts are assailing my mind, and the total effect has been of utter mental confusion, agitation and sadness. The political problem is already there; even after eight years of imprisonment there is no prospect of the political situation easing and of our release. Subarna's offer of cooperation to the present system had raised hopes that the King, by responding to it, would ease the situation. They were false hopes; because now the King wants that I too endorse Subarna's statement. It was presumed when Subarnaji took the step that some action by the King would follow. The presumption was based on the King's statement in USA that our release depended upon Subarna's step, which means we are held as hostages for Subarna's good behavior. When he promises to behave, it now turns out that I too should also promise to behave. From here I conveyed to the King that I could not endorse his statement only because such endorsement would be interpreted as an abject submission on my part under duress. By not accepting this explanation for my not supporting Subarna from prison, the King seems to be motivated not by political considerations but by personal considerations. And here our problems comes; when one is impelled only by personal motives on political issues, it is impossible to reach any kind of political understanding with him. I agree with GM when he says that even if we support Subarna's move from here, the King will continue to sit tight as he did over Subarna's statement, there being no lever to put pressure on him to honour his word. The most unfortunate situation in Nepal's politics has been the utter lack of weight of the words of honour of the King, the most powerful individual in the Kingdom. This is the sinister aspect of the situation also.

The danger of Communist menace is increasing fast. If honourable understanding between the King and ourselves had been reached we could have tried to meet the challenge. If any body thinks that by submitting to the dictates of the King the Congress will retain its capacity to restrain the Communist, he does not understand the dialectics of the political situation. Our strength the strength of a democratic party is primarily based upon the image of righteousness, of selflessness, that it creates in the people's mind. We cannot be an effective force without that image. I am perfectly sure in my mind that by refusing to accept the term of the King and thereby risking the termination of the negotiation, which GP had been carrying on between the King and myself, I have at least ensured a possibility that we may be effective if a chance presents itself in future rather than lose everything at one stroke alone by appeasing the King and yielding to his obduracy. I think we have future, which I cannot jeopardize by anything that I do today to appease the King whose motives appear to me to be dishonourable.

Yesterday, although we had been given three hours for private consultation, I was too agitated to think over the problem that would be created by my refusal to accept the King's terms. Could I be sure of any commitment that the King makes to compel me to agree to his terms? The situation for us has turned worse.

GP has to be very careful now. I do not know how he will conduct himself in the situation. He is angry both with the King for his utter disregard to his own commitments, and with the Indian Ambassador for his muddle-headed intrusion in the negotiation. In the most trying situation that has now developed our workers may find communistic methods of work and its ideology very alluring. Even GP thinks he is now confronted with a big question.

All day long I have been thinking of GP. His position has become very difficult. He was not sure what he would do. What I regret is that I did not tell him words of consolation and could not advise him to be patient. I hope he will met JP as he once said he might and then go to Delhi too. Is there anything that can keep him busy for a few weeks so that he gets over the present sense of frustration and betrayal that the King's last minute insistence on my agreeing to endorse Subarna's statement has created in him? I am sad more because of him.

I have been remembering Sushila and other members of the family. They had been entertaining hopes of my release soon. They will be grievously disappointed. **Our financial position is also extremely critical.**

October 10:

Sent a message to GP asking him to be diplomatic and reasonable, not to annoy the King and India, not be on the wrong side of India and the King, to explain the position to Subarna and the workers honestly. I regret that I did not fully instruct Girija when I had the opportunity to do so at the last private interview with him. I was myself so greatly upset that I totally forgot that a very critical situation had now developed in which extreme caution, patience and political sagacity were needed. The King has the upper hand; therefore we cannot afford to annoy India although it has been mostly bungling in its dealings with the King. We, moreover, cannot afford to see the disintegration of the party which Subarnaji is holding together for some time. My strength depends upon the party remaining intact. It is here I have an apprehension that my not submitting to the King's demand to endorse Subarna's statement from jail may result in the effective party members losing confidence in Subarna altogether and veering round GP. I have taken proper care of my prestigebecause I know that if I go out with a loss of prestige, I cannot be effective in politics and will lose all the glamour and the political capital that I have built up by being in prison. But, sometimes, doubts assail me if I have not taken too much of care of my prestige at the cost of the party which might disintegrate as a result of continued political stalemate, which my acceptance of the King's demand would likely have broken. But here again, the question is: could I have trusted the King? If the King sat tight over my acceptance of his demand as he did over Subarna's offer of cooperation, then? I would have lost prestige without a corresponding gain.

I should have had discussed all this with GP, when I had my last private interview with him.

I feel very much concerned about my health too. I apprehend that perhaps I am suffering from some serious disease maybe cancer even which the doctors are not able to diagnose. I get constant pain in my stomach and lower region of the belly, there is occasional pain in the left testicle and on the tip of the penis. I have been getting constant pain on the back and the right shoulder. I constantly think of Sushila.

October 11:

It is no use regretting what I have done. What is done is done now. Today the newspaper carried the news that 45 men have been granted pardon by the King. Most of them were living in exile in India. I do not know if we have lost them altogether and if they will cease to be useful politically after they return home. Are we disintegrating? If I had accepted the King's terms, could I have stemmed this disintegration process? By holding on, have I rather ensured the integration of democratic forces on better and firmer foundation in the future? Those workers who could not hold on any longer had in any case been lost to the democratic cause whatever I might have done. Is it so? Is it not the chief quality of leadership to ensure that existing workers do not lose heart? After all, in future too I will have to build upon the people who have held on for long. I cannot afford to lose them. I should not have given them the sense of total frustration. I do not know anything. I am totally in dark, and I am not sure if my step has been correct.

But what has been done is done. I feel extremely unhappy, but now it cannot be helped.

Have I made Subarnaji's position untenable? Will we have to climb down still further? Seeking pardon from the King individually?

I have no faith in God. A living faith in him would have been a source of great moral strength to me today when I feel that I am totally without help. I think when great decisions are taken whose results are incalculable involving even life and death persons who are forced to take such incalculable decisions have to fall back upon some inner moral resources to sustain them. I lack those resources, hence my insufferable agony.

GM does not seem to suffer from this kind of mental agony. For one thing, he is fully convinced that even if we had accepted the King's terms we would not have been released and the situation would not have improved; rather it would have worsened by the evidence of our weakness. He is firmly convinced that the intention of the King was only to humiliate us. This conviction saves him from the sense of regret. I seem to agree with him, but I cannot build up such unflinching conviction in me and that is the source of my agony. The question presents itself to me repeatedly tragic miscalculation tragic for democratic cause and tragic individually for my dedication to this cause.

October 14:

After a week of agony and excruciating doubt about the correctness of my decision not to yield to the King's demand to support his system doubt because my decision, though made in response to the King's purpose, involves also the political status of Subarnaji, who as the acting president of our party and in consultation with his colleagues in India has categorically pledged to support the present system of Government and thus lends itself to the interpretation that I have repudiated his stand. I am now at peace with myself. I have written a letter to Sushila and Chetan, which too seem to have partly drained off my mental agitation.

My stomach gives me a lot of worries I get pain, almost constant; sometimes it is severe, otherwise it is a dull kind of pain. The pain in the intestine has considerably gone down, and its swollen rigidity that I could feel in the region of lower left abdomen is also lessened. But the stomach pain has increased. Ganesh Manji says that he would give up politics after his release, because democratic politics has no future so long as the King is there and the army remains as it is, oriented against democracy. I tell him that the situation is not so desperate for democrats and even if it is, we cannot but work for it, just as a doctor does in a desperate medical case he tries till the last. If GM's mind is set on this step, his political judgment is also likely to be affected by this decision. **A politician is a practical man who calculates the possibilities and on the basis of this calculation determines his course of action; he never deviates from the course set by the limits of possibilities.** If one decides to give up politics, his judgment need not be based on the calculation of possibilities, he may be impelled to take an extreme position, or he may decide to cut short his loss at once and retire without waiting for the possible gain that the future may bring to him. I am afraid GM's unyielding posture or his desperate political posture, that he creates in his thought for democracy, may be attributed to his decision to retire. What I mean to say is that the cause of his present political judgment is the firm decision that he has made with regard to his retirement from politics and not vice-versa, i.e., the cause of his decision to retire is not the desperate political situation in which he thinks he cannot be effective to the cause of democracy. If it is so, I will be gravely misadvised if I listen to GM's political views or be influenced by his rigid political stand.

By the way I told him today that my difficulty was that I considered myself to be a part of the democratic movement in Nepal and that I could not, therefore, afford to take a personal stand in politics.

October 18:

Interview with mother, TP, Rosa and Prakash. GP did not come here from Biratnagar. TP thinks that the negotiation with the King that GP was carrying on has been halted, and according to his calculation it may be resumed after some time. I asked him if friends were displeased with my decision of not endorsing Subarnaji's statement under conditions of stress, he said, "No. Why should they when you are not at faul?"

Mother is preparing to go to Canada with Bunu, where Zaki (Banu's husband) is being posted as counselor. Mother is finding it difficult to collect foreign exchange. She said that she might have to go to Canada alone because Bunu would have left before she collected enough foreign exchange. I was amazed at her sangfroid when she said that she would manage to reach Canada because the plane journey had made thing very easy.

October 29:

Sushila and SP came to see me. I make them understand that I would not endorse Subarnaji's statement from prison, and if released I will support it.

October 30:

Released in the evening with GM. A great press conference immediately after the release supporting Subarnaji's statement. GM did not attend the press conference saying that an endorsement of Subarnaji's statement immediately after release would detract from the unconditional nature of my release. I saw his point.

How I feel to be among my own men mother, Sushila, Bunu, Rosa, Girija, Tarini, Kalpana and others. A large crowd started collecting at our place immediately after I arrived there. Went to bed late at night.

October 31:

Awfully busy meeting groups of people throughout the whole day. I am overwhelmed by their warm sympathy. Young men in large number came to see me. It is a very encouraging development. **I am seeing general enthusiasm on my release all around.**

[BP Koirala was one of the outstanding leaders of South Asia. Sadly enough, he is yet to have a biographer of his match. As good luck would have it, his diaries and memoirs are in the safe custody of the Jawaharlal Nehru Memorial Museum & Library along with many reference materials. My dear friend Shri Pradip Giri helped us locate and choose from these materials. Shri Padam Bahadur Thapa, a senior Nepali Congress activist helped us immensely in the correction of names and contexts painstakingly. Think India is indeed indebted to these two comrades - Editor.]

Haridev Sharma

Interview with BP Koirala

We publish here parts of an Interview of BP Koirala which was conducted by the Late Haridev Sharma in Varanasi in the year 1975. The interview carries some very candid admissions and remarks of BP Koirala regarding his grooming in politics in India, his special relationship with the likes of Jawaharlal Nehru, Jayaprakash Narayan, Lohia and other luminaries of the Indian freedom Struggle, his meeting with Mahatma Gandhi as well as his entire political journey beginning from a political activist to becoming the Prime Minister of Nepal, the coup and his imprisonment, and the circumstances that led to his release in October 1968. Some excerpts:

Q: Tell us about your early life, and the influences to which you were exposed?

A: I was born in Banaras in 1914. My grandfather was doing *Kashibas. Kashibas* means, in old days generally people want to live in Banaras so that they may die there and attain *Moksha.* So my grandmother used to live there and to look after her, my mother was also here. That is how I was born there. When I was three years old, my father was exiled. I came along with the family. I did my matriculation from Banaras. I graduated from Banaras Hindu University in 1934. Then I went to Calcutta to study Law.

So my first influences were my parents, especially my father. My father was an idealist. He was not interested in worldly gains. He was interested in high ideals. And this was inculcated in our character that we should look after the needy, the poor, and fight for a worthy cause. So in the beginning, through him, I came under Gandhi's influence. But it was not very clear. It was only an emotional appeal of Gandhi.

Then I came under the influence of the terrorist movement. I joined the terrorist group in Banaras and was arrested also when I was only fifteen years old.

Then I came under Marxist influence. That was immediately after I did my Matriculation. In those days Meerut Conspiracy case was going on. So there was much news in the papers about that case. And there were one or two communists who recruited me and gave me lessons in Marxism, etc. I came under their influence. It was a very great influence because it was a big ridge for me from Gandhism to Marxism. So I retained the spirit of Gandhism also, but I accepted Marxism as a methodology not only as a methodology of understanding society but also about how society is to be changed and all that. This is how I came under the influence of Marxism. I think once we travelled from Bombay to Allahabad by the Bombay Mail and (S.A.) Dange was in the same compartment. It was he who told me about Marxism and then referred me to somebody in the (Banaras) Hindu University who used to give me lessons. His name was Deshmukh. We used to call him "Countrymukh." He was doing his Law and later on, perhaps, he started practicing in Nagpur. So I came under Marxist influence.

Q: Which year was this?

A: This was in 1938.

Q: Do you remember the Non-cooperation Movement in Banaras? What was the atmosphere then?

A: I remember two or three meetings. One was addressed by Gandhiji in which he exhorted people to boycott the government institutions. And I stood up and gave up my English studies and school, though it was a municipal School. And my brother was also there. He was at Dayanand High School. So we were the first to stand up and announce our decision not to continue in those schools. Secondly, in those days, there was Hindu-Muslim unity. There were two Muslim leaders: Shaukat Ali and Mohamed Ali. And I think both Shaukat Ali and Mohammed Ali came to Banaras and we pulled their carriage. They got down at Kashi station. I remember there was a huge crowd. Then there were processions and meetings which we used to join. I remember our first day at the Gandhi Ashram; now it has been converted into a vidyapith. In those days it was known as Gandhi Ashram. It was in the early twenties.

Then I also remember the Kanpur Congress of 1925. Sarojini Naidu was President. I remember that because I did not understand a word of her speech. But father had gone there and we also went there. There was great excitement, emotional excitement, without my being able to understand what they were saying. And I also remember that she spoke in English and that, too, very fast. So that is the impression I have.

Q: How was the Salt Satyagrha in Banaras?

A: There used to be processions every evening and some people used to come out of the processions and start preparing salt on the road, in front of the chowk, the police thana, and they used to come either from the (Banaras) Hindu University or from one of the Ghats and terminate somewhere in a meeting. So the evening used to be agog with activities. But there is not much that I remember.

Q: How did you come in contact with Jayaprakash Narayan and Lohia?

A: I came in contact with Jayaprakash Narayan's brother, Rajeshwar Prasad first. He was my class-fellow at Banaras; we used to call him Raju. We were studying together, and were staying in the same house. So one day Rajendra Prasad and Jayaprakashji came and stayed with him and I was introduced to them there. That was, I think, in 1933. And Lohia stayed with another class-fellow of mine, who used to stand first in the class. That is how I came in contact with him. But I was not very intimate with Lohia. I came closer and closer to Jayaprakashji.

Q: Did Lohia make some impression on you as an intellectual?

A: No. He was a bohemian. Jayaprakashji gave the impression of being a very organised, taciturn and not very keen to being very friendly; but Lohia was very friendly; and he was lean and thin. So he was more comradely rather than an intellectual. My impression of him was that he was a lively bohemian intellectual and a brilliant man, but not very organized. This is the impression that I have of him.

Q: What do you mean by saying that he was not organized?

A: He had no time for eating. He would drop in at any time of the day. He would not care whether you were writing or reading or engaged in serious work; he would drag you to the coffee house. Whenever he came to Banaras or Patna, he used to drop in and take us to the coffee house. Personally, I do not think he was a man of organization. He inspired personal loyalties rather than institutional loyalties. A man must be dedicated to him personally rather than to an institution. He himself was an institution, but he did not care to build up an organisation.

Q: Though you belonged to Nepal, why did you get interested in India's fight for freedom?

A: There were two reasons. One was, we were exiled from Nepal. When it became too hot for us to be in Nepal, we had to come to India. In India, we came in contact with the people of the revolutionary movement in Banaras and Bihar. That is how we started. And then ultimately we came to this conclusion that the liberation of Nepal or the democratisation of Nepalese system was not possible unless India got her freedom. In 1946, when we started the Nepali National Congress, one of our slogans was that unless India became independent there would be no democratic movement in Nepal, because ultimately it was the same power which was holding India in subjugation, and was preventing the liberalization or democracy in Nepal. So our struggle for democracy in Nepal and the Indian people's struggle for independence became a joint venture in our eyes. It was the reverse side of the same coin. Even today this is the discussion going on in our party. When we formed our party in 1947, I had said so and this is still my conviction. In those days, we had made India's independence a sine qua non for our movement. It was one of the planks for our platform. So now the so-called nationalists in Nepal take us to task for being more Indian than Nepali. But this is how, from our experience, we have come to this conclusion. We could not fight for democracy in Nepal unless India was independent.

Q: What are the books which have influenced your political ideology?

A: Lenin's *State and Revolution*, *What is to be Done* and *Imperialism, the Highest State of Capitalism*; Mehring's *Karl Marx*; *Plekhanov's 'Fundamental Problems of Marxism*; Bukharin's *A.B.C.* of *Communism* I consider this to be a very illuminating book. These were the most important books that interested me. There were other books also about which I cannot tell you off hand, but Lenin's *Imperialism, the Highest State of Capitalism* and *State and Revolution* influenced me the most. *State and Revolution* is a small book and not very high class, but still it interested me. I have not read much of Marx in the original except one or two pamphlets like the Communist Manifesto, etc. I have not read the original Das Kapital, only its interpretation by others.

Q: Now, over the years, do you think that you have outlived the influence of Marxism, especially the total view of life?

A: Yes, considerably. My conviction is that nobody has grasped the whole truth. Even the greatest thinker has only seen a part of the truth. Marx has had great influence on me. Even today, I am influenced by his methodology. It is not what he says in his conclusion as such but the method how to arrive at the conclusion; that economics plays a very considerable role in one's psychology in society. And again, how a revolution occurs and what are the forces that operate in society which ultimately culminate in a revolution. These are the original contributions: the economic interpretation of history.

Q: Why did you select Jayaprakash Narayan and Rammanohar Lohia for helping you in the formation of the Nepali Congress?

A: Whom could I go to? Firstly, I was working in the national movement here in India. So these were the people I came into contact with. They were in the socialist movement. Then I came into contact with other nationalist leaders also, but they had their own handicap; they were in the Government, so they could not help us directly. I first met Jawaharlal Nehru at the Meerut Congress with my problems; he had all sympathies with me but at that time he was Vice-President of the Executive council of the Viceroy. So he could not be of much help.

Q: What did he say?

A: He said: "I have all sympathy with you, but being in the Government we have to deal on a Government to Government basis with Nepal. So we cannot be of great help at this stage. Later on, when you build up your movement, we may be of help to you."

Then JP was free. When I told JP that Lohia was also helping me, he said: "All right, Lohia is quite competent and you take his assistance. Whenever you need my assistance, you can come to me."

Q: Now, what part did Lohia play in the formation of ...?

A: I think in the beginning he was the greatest help to us. We were inexperienced men from Nepal. I was the only experienced man because I had participated in the struggle here. I knew the tools of the organizations then, how to issue a statement, how to reach people, etc. But others were very raw. So it was Lohia who built us up, who advised us how and what statement to give, what was an opportune moment to issue a statement and on what lines. Then he also got Gandhiji interested in our movement. On the 28th January 1948, two days before Gandhiji was killed, I went with Lohia to meet him. It was he who introduced me to Gandhiji and I spend the whole day with him.

Q: Lohia was also with you?

A: Yes, we went there - Birla House - about 10 in the morning and left about 4-5 in the evening.

Q: What did he say?

A: Gandhiji said that he could be of no help to me: "When my own people do not listen to me, how can I expect the Ranas to recede; I cannot be of any help." These were his words. He was in a very frustrated mood. I told him that I did not come for any material help, but I wanted his moral support and blessings. Then he said: "You have my blessings. Wherever people fight for their rights or against oppression and tyranny, they have my support." I stayed there for the whole day.

Q: You had been associated with the socialist movement in India. Did you have any ambition of building up Nepal into a socialist state?

A: There are two models, I should say, of socialist society. One is given by Russia which is known as the Marxist model in which everything is owned by the state; the second is the Gandhian model which is quite contradictory to the first one. The state function is very limited in it, but it is also a socialist model. It will not be an exploitative mode; exploitation will have no place in it. In this system, there will be a small unit, in a co-operative alliance among themselves. The producing unit would be a family. So whatever is feasible for a family to produce, the Government will encourage that production, which means in a small village if they can produce electricity, it will be encouraged. As a matter of fact, we have explored the possibility of small hydro-electricity projects producing a few thousand kw or a few hundred kw of electricity operating in a particular area or in a small mill. We have explored the possibility in respect of Switzerland or Japan. So our aim was to build up independent families.

On what we wanted to do in the industrial realm, again our model was Switzerland. We do not have many important mineral resources, at least we do not know whether we have it or not. What we wanted to do was to manufacture some precision instruments like watches, balance, and even blades just as it is done in Switzerland. We had also invited some experts from Japan. This was our idea of the socialist model. It was not patterned after the Marxist model. It was, I should say, an agro-industrial socialist model, in which the Government would take an important part in encouraging the people or removing the obstacles here and there. But before introducing a socialist economy, you have got to have some abundance of material resources. This has been our feeling. In the party we discussed whether we should nationalise the land and expect the production to improve. We thought that it was not possible. So let us give each tenant the right to till the land. They would be responsible for giving rent to the Government, whatever the Government imposed as tax on land but the rest would belong to them. Then they would be induced to work hard on their piece of land.

Unless we build up economic resources, we cannot introduce socialism. And wherever socialism has been tried, it has been a perversion of socialism: It is in name in India or in Egypt or in other developing countries. It is not socialism. It is neither socialism nor freedom. They have lost freedom in the name of socialism, but they have not got the benefit of either.

Q: What were the features of your foreign policy, especially your attitude towards India and China?

A: I came to power at a very difficult juncture in the relationship between India and China. Since 1958 the situation had started deteriorating, and from 1959 it had come to a very explosive point.

You will be surprised to know that Jawaharlal Nehru had been too naïve. I used to discuss with him, even before I became Prime Minster, about the relationship between China and India. And he would not believe, he would not accept the argument that the conquest of Tibet by China would be a threat to India. He would not agree. He was too naive, because he felt that there would be no motive for China to be aggressive against India. He explained: "I think Chinese themselves are much too engrossed in their own problems, they would not be interested in a foreign adventure." That was in the early fifties.

When I became Prime Minister, the political situation had changed. Nehru came to lunch at my residence in Kathmandu. We had a long talk. I said: "The Chinese have always been imperialistic. They consider themselves to be the centre of the world, and now that the Communist regime, which has an aggressive ideology, is aligned with the basic imperialistic instinct of China desires to create trouble. The Chinese basically think the others are barbarians and they alone are fit to rule, and on top of that there is the existing Communist ideology. So the situation has worsened."

I used to tell him: "There is a state logic: A powerful and big state would never be content to remain within its limits. It has the logic of expansion. If there is trouble inside the country, then in order to divert people's attention, to make the people united under the leadership, they can go into foreign aggressive adventures. And if they are united and peaceful, then they have the resources to go into this adventure. So in any case, there will be a conflict. India also will not be content, if it is powerful or if it is not powerful." But he would not agree.

Q: How did the Chinese react to your government's stand on Tibet?

A: My difficulty was that my party had passed a resolution against the Chinese annexation of Tibet. We had passed it, after coining the words with Lohia and Jayaprakash. We did not give expression in strong terms, but still that was our idea, our party had passed a resolution. So I had apprehensions as to how the Chinese would take to this new development. But when I went to China and met the Chinese Prime Minister, they understood our position, so much so that they did not create any difficulty about our border problem.

The Mount Everest problem was smooth sailing. It was because the Chinese wanted to create the impression in the world that they were solving all the border disputes with every state on their border except India and the Soviet Russia, because both of them, according to the Chinese, were aggressive or had imperialistic ambitions.

So, with India we had the best of terms, although there was a faction in the Government of India which felt that I was becoming too friendly with China; they were not happy. This, I told Jawaharlal Nehru; I used to have private talks with him. He was satisfied. He understood my position. He said: "All right, I understand your point." So far as we were concerned we had no difficulty with either India or China. But there were some people in India who thought that we were nearer to China.

Q:How did you find Jawaharlal Nehru?

A: Personally?

Q: Yes, and also when you were the Prime Minister of Nepal?

A: My memory of Jawaharlalji is wonderful. In his relations with my family, my wife, and as I have told you, even in governmental matters, he brought an element of deep understanding, friendliness and a human touch. I will give one example. The problem that has been plaguing us almost since the British rule is about the trade treaty between Nepal and India. This problem has still not been solved. I thought I should discuss this with Jawaharlal Nehru, because the King was pressing for it for a long time. Fortunately or unfortunately, at that time the Indian Secretary who dealt with this was L.K. Jha. He was my class-fellow in Banaras. Now he is the Governor of Kashmir. He was not agreeable. Then Jawaharlal Nehru came in the morning. That day I was staying at the President's House, Rajendra Babu's house when he (Nehru) came. I told him about my difficulty. He said: "What is this problem? What can I do? I want to help you. In fact, you should build up yourself; if it helps you to create a nationalist image for yourself by taking us to task, you are welcome to do that, because we do not want to destroy your image as a nationalist." He was very affectionate. He was very considerate. But then I said: "My difficulty at present is this.

This thing has been pending for so many months and I am having this difficulty." He said: "Yes, I know that. But our difficulty is that so long as you are in the Government or anybody who is in power, is friendly to India, he will not misuse this treaty. But if any hostile government comes in power, it will misuse it. They will import goods from foreign countries, say Hong Kong, stamp it as made in Nepal, process it in Nepal and will take an advantage of the treaty and send it on to India. This is what the King's regime also did. This is what they did with the synthetic fibre, synthetic yarn, stainless steel utensils and blankets. They used to get Japanese synthetic yarn or material, and then process it in Nepal and send it on to India. But still, if that will create a favourable situation for you, I will ask my secretary to meet you". Then he, I think from there itself, contacted somebody and left. Then L.K. Jha came and saw me and said: "Yes, I have got clearance from the Prime Minister." That was typical of Jawaharlal Nehru.

Q: Any more personal memory?

A: There are many. Whenever I came to India on state visits, he used to treat me as a friendly guest. Once I paid a state visit. My wife was also with me. At that time my youngest daughter was a small child. Indiraji came and took the child during the ceremony at the airport. I was putting up at Hyderabad House. They came, they did not treat me like a foreign guest or a government guest but like a personal guest. Indiraji used to come to my wife and, many a time she took her for marketing. Once or twice, they went to an emporium also and bought some shawl or saree. It was like that. This was the personal touch. And when we left Delhi, a ceremonial send-off was given at the platform. I came back by train. A special train was arranged for us and all the compartments of the train even bathrooms were also inspected by the guards. So it was a very affectionate send-off as if a very special guest was leaving. It was not only the salute, the red carpet and all that which every head of the state and Government used to get, but there was special consideration for us.

Q: You seem to be very favourably inclined to Nehru?

A: We are very much grateful to Jawaharlalji for two reasons. One is, of course, personal. When I was on hunger strike, he saved my life twice. I told you that. I disagreed with him on some policy matters; we still continue to think that he was not a very committed socialist. He was not committed to anything. He was a pampered child of fortune, and he mismanaged on many fronts. He did not build up a bureaucracy attuned to the needs of the masses. I think the bureaucracy continues to be the same as given by the British government. But that is a policy matter. He was very gracious and our whole family is grateful to him because of his affection and consideration towards us.

Q: What were the other issues of disagreement between you and Jawaharlal Nehru?

A: As Prime Minister I had no differences with him. But before that, we had differences so far as Tibet was concerned. There was disagreement on the role of the Chinese. In the late fifties there was hardly any disagreement between us. But we differed on the pattern of economic development my opinion was somewhat different from his but we did not clash; there was no bone of contention. I thought that the model that Jawaharlalji had selected was Russia and I disagreed with his policy of preferring the communists more than the socialists. But as regards Nepal, there was not much difference except on the question of China.

Q: At what point of time your differences with the King started?

A: There was no point of time. The King never wanted a functioning democracy in Nepal. First of all, he diluted the commitment of his father. His father had committed that there would be a constituent assembly elected on adult franchise, and the King would be a constitutional head of the state. Now, he diluted that. He said that he would frame the constitution, and that the constitution would be his creation. Before he did that, he took an extensive tour of the country twice to ascertain the mood of the people, held meetings with big people people who count. And he came to the conclusion that he could safely hold the elections. Because according to his reports and personal contacts with the people in various areas that he had visited, no party would come in an absolute majority to be able to form the government. Secondly, he thought that people were not sufficiently politicalised, so they would not vote for the party, they would vote for the individuals with local arrangement. He thought that no single party would get a majority and that he would be able to play one against another and hold the government. That was his calculation and that misfired.

Q: Your success must have been a major surprise to the King?

A: He was shocked. We came with an absolute majority. Out of 109, we had 76. He did not invite me to form the Government for almost a month because he did not know what to do. So I went to the King and said: "In a situation like this, the King and the Prime Minister must see eye to eye on every issue. So if you have got any reservations about me, I will not seek election as the leader of the parliamentary party. Subarna Shamsher can become Prime Minister." Then the King said: "No, Subarna Shamsher is a very slow man. Who told you that I do not like you, or we have a conflict? You are a young man, I also want to contribute to the development of the country, we will be there together." There was this apprehension in Delhi also that perhaps I would be too independent and I was critical of India's unnecessary interference in our affairs. So I contacted Jawaharlalji. At that time he had gone for the inauguration of Kosi Barrage. I wrote a private letter to Jawaharlalji and sent it through D.P. Singh. D.P. Singh was a Member of Parliament then. Then Jawaharlalji said: "No. Anybody who is elected, we have to treat him with friendliness and sympathy. I have no choice, you are elected by the Party." So, I took care that Jawaharlalji was on my side as well as the King, but the King was not happy.

Q: How was the working relation between you and the King?

A: I gave all respect to the King. But I had to do my work. What happened was that the palace ceased to exist on the political side and the centre was transferred to the Central Secretariat. The Secretaries and the Prime Minister became more important than the King. Nobody went to the King; all petitions, demands, etc., Whatever they were, started flowing to the Secretariat, and that was too much for the King.

Then what he did was try and create a rift in the party. He wanted to purchase the party members; two very important members Tulsi Giri, the present Prime Minister, he was a very important member in our party, and Biswabandhu Thapa, the Chief Whip of the party went over to him. They started conspiring. The Chief Whip wanted to disrupt the party. That was the beginning. But they could not do anything, because the other political parties, the rightist parties, the Gurkha Parishad and the Communist Party in Parliament, they all said: "We will not permit you to be ousted; we will support you in any case, even if some of your own party members leave your fold." There were twenty-two members eighteen belonged to the Gurkha Parishad, and four to the Communists. So the King had to buy more than forty members out of one hundred and nine, which was not possible. So he could not succeed.

Q: Did he create difficulties for you?

A: Yes. He wanted to create difficulties about the land reforms, by putting ceiling on land. The landed aristocrats or the landlords, the *Kulaks* I should say, were against us. He asked them to create difficulties for us. So they came and gheraoed me; they started all kinds of trouble with processions, etc. But that too did not succeed. I invited them to a conference. I said: "You will have to lose the land. This is the best government that you are having because any other government will not only take your land but will take your head also. I am only taking your land. Ultimately they went away satisfied; moreover, they were not a political force, so they had no lever.

Q: What is the story of Yogi Narharinath? Why did you arrest him?

A: The King wanted to create problems for us by disrupting law and order situation, and for the very same purpose he enlisted the services of Yogi Naraharinath. His party was known as Karamvir Mahamandal. The King financed this group to create trouble for us. There were law and order disturbances in two or three districts. In one district it was a serious affair. The police had to open fire and eight people were killed. Then I started undertaking a tour, explaining our position. So that also failed. We arrested Naraharinath and caught hold of his papers and correspondences which had incriminating evidence of his link with the palace. I made a statement in the press at that time I was in Bombay for the Nepalese Students' Conference that Narharinath has been arrested and sent to Jail.

Q: The King was there in Nepal at that time?

A: No, the King was in England on a state visit. He had already decided to stage a coup. But he was apprehensive whether we would be able to retaliate, whether we had our men and arms. Unfortunately, we did not have; if we had even 500 men with arms, the King would not have dared take such action against us. It was due to the betrayal of the two members of our party not because they were siding with the King but, Tulsi Giri encouraged the King to take action by saying that we were not in a position to counteract. The King was apprehensive about our capacity to counteract by force.

Q: Perhaps there was some confusion over your getting arms from Israel?

A: I went on a state visit to Israel. I was interested in studying their military organization because I thought that their method, national construction, and the manner of their organisation was more suited to our context as we could not keep a big standing army. So if everybody was a soldier and could be pressed into service in times of need, then we would be saving a lot of money. That is why I was interested in studying it. Our pattern, our model of the army or navy was that of the British. The Indian model is the same. I thought it was most unsuitable for our country, and most unsuitable even for India. I thought we could change our military organization. So I had asked one of the officers, who was my bodyguard from the army, to study. He was deeply interested. Then he reported to me about what he saw.

I discussed this with their Defence Minister (of Israel). He took me around some of the army establishments, armament manufacturing units, and they presented me with a very powerful weapon, Uzi, which combines the range of a rifle with the efficiency of a stengun. So I thought it was very convenient. I think the German army was using the same weapon and also exporting them. They asked my bodyguard as to the number of men under his command for bodyguard duty at my house. He told them that it was about forty or forty-eight. So they gave fifty Uzi, and a special Uzi for me in an engraved wrapped box. When I came to Nepal, I told the King. He was alarmed. Every day he used to inquire whether the consignment had arrived. When it arrived, he got to know that it had. Immediately, he sent a man to take charge of the whole consignment, which means, there were fifty pieces; one was for me. He left that one in my possession, and the rest fifty he took away.

Q: How did the coup happen?

A: I had not foreseen it. The foreign correspondents and people were under the impression that we two people could not pull together, that the King wanted to take action against me. I argued that if that was so, why did he (the King) bring about this situation? He could have arrested me, but he did not; he could have brought Subarna Shamsher in, or he could have dissolved the Parliament, or called for fresh elections.

The day I was arrested, not a single leader of any party, such as the leaders and members of the Communist Party, the Gurkha Parishad and other parties or one single individual who had anything to do with politics, was outside the prison. All the Members of Parliament on whom the King could lay his hand were behind the bars. So it was not an action, it was not something what you call temperamental differences, that is what some of the American press had also mentioned temperamental differences between the King and the Prime Minister. It was not temperamental.

Q: Had he planned the whole thing?

A: He had been planning, even before the elections. When we used to discuss, he used to say: "If I cannot rule effectively, then what is the fun in being the King; why not declare Nepal a Republic, abolish monarchy." This is what he told me. He was a feudal, medieval King.

Q: After arrest, were you put in jail? What kind of treatment was meted out to you?

A: No, it was not jail. The CGS, that is the Chief of General Staff came to arrest me.

Q: You were addressing a meeting perhaps?

A: Yes, I was finishing the meeting. I had inaugurated a youth conference. Then, about 300 soldiers came, surrounded my meeting, and we were taken from the dais. I was told by the CGS that the King had asked him to arrest me. As a matter of fact, the man directing the operation came from the palace, Samer Raj who was guiding the operations and giving instructions to the CGS, but for the sake of appearance the CGS had been called. Major Geoffery was a friend of mine also. Actually, I was instrumental in making him the CGS, so he did not know what to do. He was fidgeting. He had been suddenly called to arrest all of us. So we were all arrested. We knew that something was going on. But somehow I did not expect that he would arrest me. I thought that I would be taken to the palace and the King would say that I have been shorn of power and that he was taking over, like that. But there were three to four thousand soldiers who came and took me to the army club and put me there. There was an army bungalow which was converted into an army prison. After six months I was transferred to the army prison. And the treatment was not bad, in the sense that there was respect for me. Army officers gave me full respect. The food was also good. For six months it was quite alright, that means whatever I wanted and whatever I needed I used to get. But after that I went on hunger strike, because they had kept me incommunicado; I had no contact with the outside world. I was not getting any paper; I did not have any reading material. No interview was allowed. I was completely kept in the dark. And for all the twenty-four hours a sentry was posted in my room, that means there was no privacy at all. The captain and the lieutenant, all of them used to be there all the time. Then there was a tent for latrine and toilet purposes.

After thirteen days of hunger strike, I was permitted, and thereafter I was transferred to the newly-constructed prison. The allowance was reduced from forty-five or forty rupees to seven rupees. But that was enough for me, at least at that time it was enough; I used to get some things from home also. So that was quite enough. The government started giving us newspapers published from Delhi and Calcutta. We started getting books from outside. After that I had an interview with the people. So on the whole, after that hunger strike, I started getting reading material, etc., which was not bad.

Q: What kind of books did you read?

A: All kinds of philosophy. I am interested particularly in philosophy and literature. I was not interested in political books. I read books on history, philosophy and literature, etc. In history I read all the volumes of Will Durant's *The Story of Civilisation* it is very interesting. In philosophy I have read Western as well as Indian philosophy, like Bertrand Russell's 'A History of Western Philosophy', and then in literature I read all Nobel Prize literature as well as ancient literature. I read some Sanskrit literature by Kalidasa. Then I read all the volumes of complete works of Swami Vivekananda. Like that. I was very selective.

Q: What factors led to your release?

A: My illness. I started losing weight and developing pain in the stomach. A friend of mine, who was also in prison, also developed pain. Later on, his case was diagnosed as cancer. He was released and he died. So the King perhaps thought that if I also developed the same kind of trouble, then it would be difficult, because a dead man would be more than a problem. Then, there was pressure from India also. But he had already withstood that pressure. At that time (James Harold) Wilson had also come to power in UK and had put pressure on the King. So the following April (1968) he started negotiations with my brother, GP Koirala. GP used to come with a piece of paper on which the King himself used to write. He used to ask me questions, and I used to answer. The King used to ask my bother as to what my reactions were on those questions. Then, ultimately, it was agreed that I should first meet the King, and if the agreement was reached then they would release me. In the meanwhile, my health had deteriorated to a considerable extent.

Q: Was there any condition of your release?

A: The King had put one condition that I must make a statement, supporting his system. Then Subarna Shamsher was the leader outside. He had issued a statement supporting the then system. It was suggested that I, too, support his statement. I said: "No, nothing from the prison; outside, of course, when I am a free man, I will decide." Ultimately negotiations broke down. JP was very worried because the King had said: "He had been in prison for eight years; I will keep him for another eighteen years." My family members became very perturbed because of my illness, because a team of doctors sent by the palace under the chairmanship of the royal physician had given a report which was alarming. So they had lost hope. My people and G.P. Koirala went to Patna, met JP and the latter advised my wife. Soon my wife went to Kathmandu. You know, the interview was only permitted once a month. So the King sent her to the prison to interview me. At the time of interview nobody, no officer was there. She told me about the situation that had developed. I said: "You should be prepared for the worst." Though the King was in a furious mood, I told her: "I am in prison and my statement given from prison would be treated as if I have made the statement under duress. I will not repudiate Subarna Shamsher's statement when I am a free person, but from the prison, I will not be able to release any statement."

Q: How was the release like? It must have been big news, both for you and the people outside?

A: My release was very peculiar. My people were told that I would be released in a day or two, and in the morning of 30th (October 1968) someone from the palace contacted my home in Kathmandu and informed that I would be released in the afternoon. I was not told. No one came and told me that I would be released. The press had also been told that BP would be released between 5 and 8 in the evening. So the international press was present there. A General came to the place where I was staying; I was preparing dinner and laying the table for Ganesh Man Singh and myself. He came to me and said: "There is an urgent call, I have come to tell you about that." I thought that I was being taken to the palace. But he didn't tell us where he was taking us. We thought that we were being taken to the palace. But ultimately he brought us to my brother's house. There was a big gathering; about sixty to seventy press correspondents were waiting. My sister had come from Pakistan, my wife and everybody was there. And I did not know that it was a new house constructed by my brother. He was also in prison for six years. The General said: "This is your house, you can go. Don't you know this is your brother's house? All the members of your family are staying here. The press has come to meet you." I said: "But you did not tell us that we were released. Have you released us or not?" He said: "We have only instructions that we should leave you here." In the meantime the press came; The Time correspondent, a girl I knew her before and others came rushing. I said: "No, we are still prisoners, I am not going to make any statement." Then they withdrew. After some time the General contacted the palace and then he came and said: "You are released." And then he left us.

Q: What happened afterwards?

A: When we went to the house, Surya Prasad Upadhyay had prepared a statement for me to be distributed to the press. I said: "But I have not seen the statement. He said: "Oh, this is nothing, in a general way, people have talked to you, the press people have seen you." I said: "No, I must see the statement before I make it." He wanted to force me into making a statement, which would have meant some kind of down fall for me. Then the press people came. I said: "You want some statement from me? All right, you will have to wait. I will have to talk to my people and then I will make a statement." So we, MG and myself, discussed. MG said: "No, I will not issue a statement because it will be misinterpreted." But I said: "I will make a statement." Then I drafted the statement. It was typed, and fifty to seventy copies were made. The press had to wait for two hours. Later on, I issued the statement. I simply said: "Subarna Shamsher has made a statement and being a colleague and having a democratic constitution, whatever decision he has taken, I must support him. So I endorse his statement. However, I will discuss with my colleagues and then I will give a statement." Subarna Shamsher suggested that I should make a statement then, but I said: "I will make a statement, but not today, because it would lead to some misunderstanding. So I will not issue the statement today." The next day, our leader MP Koirala made a statement and I endorsed that.

[We express our sincere thanks to Shri Padam Bahadur Thapa who did all the rigour to make available to us the manuscript of the interview from the Jawaharlal Nehru Memorial Museum & Library -Editor.]

SD Muni

Nepal's Democratic Evolution

Roles of Inclusive Consensus and India

Introduction

The history of democratic evolution in Nepal has been chequered and protracted. The overthrow of 104 years of Rana rule in 1951 can be considered the first major landmark in this history when the cause of democracy was advanced. But then followed two other developments that pushed the cause of democracy backwards. In December 1960 King Mahendra staged a coup against democratic system and its first elected government. He imposed a party-less Panchayat System to camouflage an active and assertive monarchical order. His successor, King Birendra was forced by popular resistance to seek renewed legitimacy for this system through a referendum by pitting it against the system of multi-party democracy. Questions about the 'free and fair' nature of the referendum held in May 1980 not withstanding, the party-less Panchayat system was endorsed in the referendum causing another setback to democracy.

The struggle for democracy however rebuilt itself to emerge victorious in 1990, when for the first time after 1960, the concept of popular sovereignty was accepted and a system of multi-party democracy under 'Constitutional Monarchy' was established. It was hoped that Nepal would now onwards evolve into a real functional democracy on the line of Britain and such other constitutional monarchies. This, however, was not to be as the custodians of democracy could not keep their commitment to democratic governance and gradually surrendered their power to monarchy. An additional disabling factor for democracy was the rise of Maoist insurgency since 1996. The character of Monarchy underwent a drastic transformation as a result of the 'palace massacre' in June, 2001. Under the new King, Gyanendra, and on the pretext of fighting Maoist 'terrorism', the active and assertive Monarchy re-emerged. On the lines of his father the late King Mahendra's coup, the new King Gyanendra dismissed the elected parliament and representative government and took direct control of the polity on 1st February, 2005. However, democracy re-triumphed with the success of *Jan Andolan-II* (Peoples' Movement-II) that brought not only all the political parties but also the Maoists and the civil society together, resulting eventually in the abolition of Monarchy and the establishment of a 'republic' in Nepal in 2007. This, however, has not made democracy stable and institutionalized as yet; there persists political chaos and serious fragmentation of the coalition of forces that led the *Jan Andolan-II* to success.

For any serious and comprehensive analysis of the evolution of democracy in Nepal and the landmarks achieved in this process of evolution, a number of varying contextual factors, personalities and political forces, both within and outside Nepal, may have to be taken note of. Such a comprehensive and intensive analysis is not intended here owing to the constraints of time and space. There have however been two factors that consistently played a decisive role in the advancement or set back to democracy, i.e., The nature of inclusive political consensus in favour of democracy within Nepal and the role of India. It may also be kept in mind here that the struggle for democracy in Nepal has, until 2006, been against feudal institutions and forces. The nature of democratic struggle after 2006 has been radically altered as it has become a struggle for institutionalization and consolidation of democracy. There are theoretical possibilities of the Monarchy staging a come back or the Maoists going back to jungles to fight the next round of their 'peoples' war' to thwart the evolution of democratic order in Nepal. But these possibilities look remote and some what unrealistic, notwithstanding the occasional claims of some of the respective proponents of these options.

End of the feudal order

The anti-Rana uprising was a manifestation of the growing unrest at popular level against a decadent feudal order. Early protests raised during the nineteen-thirties could be suppressed as the level of awakening at the peoples' level was poor and there was still the British Empire in place in India to provide a protective umbrella to the Ranas. The situation however changed during the late forties when the British rule folded out from India and the civil uprising in Nepal against the Ranas became broad-based. A mark of inclusive consensus to fight the Rana rule was evident in the democratic struggle that was led by the Nepali Congress (NC), the newly established Communist Party of Nepal and the old democratic warriors who had come forward to challenge the Ranas under the banner of Praja Parishad during the 1930s. The indication of mass support for the struggle could be seen in the popular agitation sparked off by the strike in the Biratnagar jute mill. India got directly involved by organizing the flight of King Tribhuwan and his royal family through the Indian Embassy in November 1950 to Delhi to bless the anti-Rana revolt. The Rana system was thrown out, but only a compromised democratic process could be initiated. India's strategic priorities dictated it to go only step by step, gradually in facilitating institutionalization of democracy in Nepal. Success in the march towards democracy could be achieved only to the extent of minimum mutual acceptance between India and the inclusive Nepali political consensus.

There was no Nepali inclusive political consensus when King Mahendra staged his coup in December 1960 to dismiss a representative government and an elected parliament. In the process of preparing this coup, King Mahendra had not only wooed the leaders of the ruling Nepali Congress and others like Vishwa Bandhu Thapa, Tulsi Giri and Rishikesh Shah, but also the sections of Communist Party like those led by Kesarjung Raimajhi, on his side. Thus he had succeeded in fragmenting and isolating the principal domestic stakeholder of democracy, the Nepali Congress. As a result of this internal political disintegration of the democratic constituency within Nepal, he could withhold the Indian pressure for the restoration of democratic system and the elected government. To contain India's pressures he was greatly advantaged by the support of the US and Sino-Indian tensions on the border dispute which precipitated a serious military confrontation between Nepal's two Asian neighbours in October 1962. His emissary Rishikesh Shah as a foreign minister had succeeded in ensuring Chinese security guarantees against India barely a fortnight before China opened fire on India. On October 6, the then Chinese defence minister said that any threat to Nepal would be considered a threat to China. This forced

India to accept the supremacy of King Mahendra in Nepal and compromise on the objective of building democracy. In the face of Chinese threat, Indian leadership chickened out on the cause of democracy in Nepal. The critical significance of the role of internal inclusive political consensus and India's support in the sustenance of democracy in Nepal can be made by arguing that if the former had not been fragmented, King Mahendra could not have staged his coup and had India continued to support the struggle for democracy led by the ousted Nepali Congress ignoring the security imperatives of Sino-Indian conflict, the King would have not been able to hold for long.

The autocratic system of assertive monarchy imposed by King Mahendra in 1960-62 lasted for the next thirty years and democratic order could be reinstated under constitutional monarchy only when the inclusive political consensus in favour of democracy within Nepal coincided with India's support. Nepal's first *Jan Andolan* was driven by this convergence. It was led by the Nepali Congress but actively supported by the Madhesh groups, the Communist party of Nepal- United Marxist Leninist (UML) and all other communist groups including the Maoists. India's relations with the royal regime in Kathmandu had seriously soured during 1988-89 on account of break down of the bilateral trade treaty and Nepal's efforts to procure Chinese arms. Rajiv Gandhi, the then Prime Minister, refused to relax pressure on Kathmandu on these issues knowing very well that internal public pressure for political liberalization was building on. The leaders of the successive political dispensation in New Delhi ignoring the pretext of 'non-interference' by the government, openly joined Nepal's peoples' movement for democracy to ensure its success. The visit of political leaders from the then ruling Janata Party like Chandra Shekhar and Subrahmanyam Swamy to Kathmandu to lend support to the movement for the restoration of democracy in January 1990 may be recalled. These leaders were also supported by other major Indian political parties, the Communists as well as the Congress, with the exception of Bhartiya Janata Party (BJP). Monarchy obviously could not stand against the combined political pressure of internal Nepali political consensus and the pressure from India.[1] The Panchayat System collapsed yielding to the restoration of multi-party democracy under Constitutional Monarchy of 1959-60.

Challenge of building democracy

It was, however, unfortunate that the restoration of democracy brought about by the success of the *Jan Andolan-I* could not be brought to its logical conclusion in the form of institutionalization of democratic processes and consolidation of democratic norms and culture. Blame for this must be shared by the two major parliamentary parties, the NC and UML which became pre-occupied with the politics of power and patronage that weakened democratic institutions and allowed the ever willing Monarchy to usurp most of the effective authority. Challenge to the restoration of democracy also rose from the rise of Maoist agitational politics and insurgency since 1994. Senseless and excessive use of force by the parliamentary parties' led governments against the Maoists proved to be counter productive as it swelled the ranks of the insurgents and made them more determined and aggressive in the pursuit of their political goal through the 'Peoples' War'. King exploited the internal conflict to weaken and discredit the political parties by not only refusing the use of army against momentum the insurgents but also by providing them with patronage. Insurgency gained momentum at the cost of democratic processes and institutions. India remained indifferent to this democratic erosion in Nepal, firstly due to frequent governmental changes and then due to the illogical bias of the NDA government (1998-2004) towards Monarchy. The crisis of 2005-2006 in the form of the King's direct take-over and the response to this crisis in the form of *Jan Andolan-II* were the culmination of a decade of political chaos and failure of governance in Nepal.

It was again the convergence of the internal inclusive political consensus with the support of India that made *Jan Andolan-II* successful. After radical transformation in the character of Monarchy following the palace massacre of June 2001, the new King Gyanendra divided and marginalized political parties. While he partially succeeded in this strategy between 2002 and

---

[1]See for details; S.D. Muni, India's Foreign Policy: The Democracy Dimension, Foundation Books, Cambridge University Press-India, New Delhi, 2009, pp.60-64.

2005, his drastic move to take over power under his direct command in February 2005 proved to be counter productive. This move alienated international community and brought together not only the parliamentary parties in the form of a Seven Party Alliance (SPA), but also bridged the gap between the Maoists and the parliamentary parties in their common resolve to fight autocratic feudal order. This resolve was enshrined in an understanding concluded between the Maoists and the SPA on November 22, 2005 in the form of 'Twelve Point Understanding'. India extended its support to the process of building inclusive consensus in favour of democracy at various levels of civil society and masses, political parties and the government. Intellectuals, Academia and media took the lead and the political parties forged a united front led by the young activists like D.P. Tripathi of the Nationalist Congress Party, Sita Ram Yechury of the Communist Party (Marxist) and Digvijay Singh of the Congress Party to support the struggle for democracy in Nepal. At the governmental level, efforts were made initially to dissuade the King from persisting on his dictatorial course even in the name of fighting the Maoists' terrorism, but when the King not only ignored these persuasions and tried to blunt India's efforts by invoking the China card, no other option was left for New Delhi but to lend support to the struggle for democracy. Government of India facilitated the conclusion of 'Twelve Point Understanding' between the Maoists and the parliamentary political parties of Nepal and extended moral support to *Jan Andolan-II.*[2] India tried to save Monarchy and even some residual powers for the King through its good-offices with the King on April 21, 2006 to help *Jan Andolan-II* reach its culmination. But the anti-King sentiment unleashed by the peoples' movement was so strong that India had to succumb to the ground reality and eventually endorse Nepal as a Republic.

The Republic of Nepal, imbibing the spirit of *Jan Andolan-II* is still far away from being established on firm institutional basis even after nearly five years of the success of the *Jan Andolan-II.* There is a deadlock in Nepal's political dynamics after the April 2008 elections to Constituent Assembly.

---

[2]I have discussed the details of India's role in Nepal's Jan Andolan-II in my 'Bringing Down the Maoists from the Hills: India's Role", in a Volume on 'Nepal' being published by the Cambridge University Press, under the editorship of David Malone etc. (Expected in 2011).

The peace process has come to a stand-still, the constitution making is extremely tardy with the critical issues of devolution of power (federalism) and the form of governance (Presidential or Parliamentary) are still to be addressed seriously. There are clouds of political uncertainty and anxiety hovering over the Nepalese people with troublesome prospects of a presidential rule, an army takeover or street agitations and civil strife if the Constituent Assembly fails to adopt a Constitution and complete the peace process before its extended term comes to an end on May 28, 2011.

Political stalemate and the way out

What has gone wrong? We must go back to the two critical factors of inclusive political consensus and India's role to seek an answer. The convergence between these two factors that have been underlined in our foregoing narrative of struggle for democracy in Nepal has been shattered as neither an inclusive political consensus exist in Nepal nor does India's priority seem to be on the restoration of democracy and stabilizing peace in Nepal. The erosion of the political consensus that drove the *Jan Andolan-II* was set in motion as soon as the results of the Constituent Assembly elections were out. None of the major political parties, nor even India and the international community expected this outcome which brought the Maoists as a major force on the front. These results made the Maoists complacent and the two other major political parties, the NC and the UML insecure vis-à-vis the Maoists. Under the pressure of unfolding tensions and anxieties between them, the informal power sharing arrangement between the Maoists and the NC to endorse the NC President G.P. Koirala as the first president of the Republic of Nepal broke down. The Maoists were not even prepared to share the defence portfolio with the NC in lieu of presidency. The NC on its part did not transfer power to the elected Maoist representatives for three months and that too after deciding to sit in opposition in violation of the spirit of interim constitution that underlined the need for consensus until the completion of the peace process.

The remaining part of the *Jan Andolan-II* consensus broke down when the UML and the Madhesh parties parted company with the Maoists forcing them to resign on the question of sacking the then army chief General

Katawal in May 2009. Since then Nepal has drifted into non-governance and political discord among the major political formations. The breakdown of consensus is on power sharing arrangements, not on the principles and dimensions of the re-structuring of a new state in Nepal, which are no less formidable. The major political parties are also cheesed off by the Maoists on their reluctance to deliver on the promises of the integration of their armed Peoples' Liberation Army (PLA) cadres, dismantling of the instruments of political coercion like the Youth Congress League (YCL) and the return of illegally acquired properties during the insurgency period. The Maoists have also alienated the international community and India on the issues of PLA, YCL, sacking of the army chief and holding of illegal properties. The power sharing virus has crippled the major political parties not only externally but internally also. Each of the major political parties, the Maoists, the NC, the UML and the Madhesh groups, stands internally divided on the issues of who should lead and who should be placed where in the party hierarchy. The internal conflicts within the parties are not letting them take a firm and rational position on any of the issues of national significance which in turn is hindering broader consensus among the political parties on such issues. The UML leader Jhal Nath Khanal has publicly admitted this. [3]

The international community and India had supported the *Jan Andolan-II*. In the interest of Nepal's peace process and a new constitution, the international community, particularly India, should have ensured that consensus-based power sharing arrangement did not breakdown in August 2008 when the NC decided to sit in the opposition and the Maoists-led coalition came to office. However, rattled by the victory of the Maoists, their obstinacy on the issues of presidency and defence ministry with the NC, India watched aimlessly and latter became a party to polarization in Nepali politics just to keep the Maoists out of power. India's apprehensions vis-à-vis the Maoists also sprang from the fear that the Maoists may facilitate China's greater assertion south of the Himalayas. There were too many Chinese delegations visiting Nepal to India's disliking during the short

[3] See http://www.nepalnews.com. December 12, 2010, I underlined the point of intra-party fragmentation on power sharing in my interviews in Nepal Dailies, The Kantipur (November 27, 2010) and Kathmandu Post (November 29, 2010).

period of nine months when the Maoists were leading the Nepali government. This has also resulted in India willingly or otherwise contributing to the fragmentation of other political parties as well, especially the Madhesh groups.

The core objectives of the *Jan Andolan-II* were to bring the Maoists peacefully into the national mainstream and build with them the foundations of a vibrant, inclusive and stable democratic political order in Nepal. It is unrealistic to assume that these objectives could be accomplished in a short time span and through political quick fixes. Political transitions of this order take time, resources and all the necessary political skills of the political parties and the international community. We have also seen in our discussion that the history of democratic struggle in Nepal has been decisively and almost organically linked to a broader political consensus in Nepal and the convergence of this consensus with India's creative and supporting help. The way out from the present impasse in Nepal therefore lies in recreating the inclusive political consensus and re-harnessing India's constructive role in taking the agenda of restoration of democracy forward. The first step towards that would require addressing of the differences within and outside the political parties on the basis of democratic principles and norms of power sharing. Accordingly, the Maoists being the largest group in the Constituent Assembly will have to be brought in to lead a coalition, but for that the Maoists will have to demonstratively assure all others that they will give up the politics of coercion and violence for ever. The Maoists will also have to accept the concept of democratic power sharing as they do not enjoy absolute majority in the Constituent Assembly. If this is not done, the vision of an inclusive democracy in Nepal would remain as distant as ever.

Narahari Acharya

Challenges of Nepal's Democratic Transformation and Nepali Congress

Nepal is undergoing a grave phase of transition, confusion and uncertainty. A constitution could not be drafted within the appointed two years. A number of issues that had to be solved before the drafting of constitution are yet unresolved, and are getting complicated. Even when the additional duration for the Constituent Assembly remains a mere six months from now, the constitution drafting process has not been given momentum. Political parties are persistent in their stands. They have not been able to find ways to convince people who are furious with the political parties and hopeless about the future of the country.

The Nepali Congress party, which was established in 1946 with a major agenda for democratic transformation of Nepal, is standing amidst tough challenges. The fact that the communist parties have been gaining popularity for the last few decades, has added to the challenges for Nepali Congress which has been recognized as a democratic party on ideological/ philosophical grounds. Through the last Constituent Assembly elections, the Nepal Communist Party (Maoist) has emerged as the single largest party in the Constituent Assembly. Apart from that, the number of the Nepal Communist Party (UML), which came into democratic process with the People's Movement of 1990, and the existence of other communist parties make the total number of representatives of communist parties to 60 percent in the Constituent Assembly.

Given the role played by the Nepali Congress in the history of Nepal's democratic movement, the fact that Congress is becoming narrower looks quite unusual, but there are some solid reasons to this.

Odyssey of Nepali Congress's struggle

The founders of the Nepali Congress, who were influenced by the Independence Movement of India, did not only lead during the movement for uprooting the 104 year long Rana regime, they were also able to present Nepali Congress as a symbol of a complete socio-economic transformation. As a result of this, the Nepali Congress put forward a host of fundamental socio-economic agendas following the decade after the 1950 Movement. During this period, the first elected government led by B.P. Koirala implemented many of these agendas as its programmes. The monarchy, which was re-established following the end of the Rana regime, did not want to remain under the constitution. Also, due to the sympathy and support of an influential faction of the Indian establishment to King Mahendra, who wanted to present himself as a Hindu emperor, the king was able to subject the Nepali Congress to military control.

Afterwards, the Nepali Congress led all kinds of democratic movements that were launched against the autocratic monarchy. As a result of the final People's Movement launched by involving different factions of the Communist party, the autocratic rule under the direct leadership of the monarchy came to an end in 1990. A multi-party democracy including a constitutional monarch was established. In the parliament formed after the Movement, while the Nepali Congress received a comfortable majority, the factions of the Communist party became the second and the third biggest parties. This had not only changed the political structure of the parliament formed after thirty years, but also signalled that the Nepali people aspired for a socio-economic transformation. The Nepali Congress could not decode this signal seriously. The elected government formed after 1990 could not bring solid programmes of socio-economic transformation. Moreover, even in the duration of twelve years, there had been no efforts on the part of the Nepali Congress for any kind of political-constitutional improvement and revision to address the changing aspirations of the Nepali people brought about by the establishment of democracy and opening up of the society. In fact, in 1990, the then constitution was prepared within a short duration of three months with a motive to shortly end the transitional period and take the country into general elections immediately.

The necessity of political strengthening and provincial restructuring was felt then itself. But, then, these issues had not been considered in detail because of the rush. Later, the leadership of the Nepali Congress did not pay heed to the voices raised from inside and outside the party. Thus the bases for strengthening new democracy were kept at bay. On the other hand, as the king and the palace had been feeling stripped off their rights, they were waiting for failures and shortcomings of the political parties. As a result, the rise of the Maoists and the activity of the king grew against the then political system. That resulted in the obstruction of democratic processes. Elections for local bodies could not be held, parliamentary election was halted.

The People's Movement of 2006 took place with a massive participation of the Nepalese people. In fact, the Movement was a result of a resistance programme of seven parties including the Nepali Congress and the 12-point understanding with the Maoists. The Movement was basically launched for abolishing the then monarchy which had been proving itself anarchic time and again. However it had not vented its dissatisfaction only against the monarchy. It was also an expression of total disagreement of the violent nature and activities of the Maoists. Moreover, it was against the tendency of status quo and indecisiveness prevalent at the leadership level of political parties including the Nepali Congress. In fact, the Movement was directed towards positive and progressive changes which would bring about comfort and prosperity in the lives of the people of Nepal. It was also for the dignity of the Nepalese people and for national glory. The political parties probably did not, in time, understand the depth of all these messages of the Movement. As a result, because of ideological confusion and lack of far-sightedness, the achievements are now in shambles. At this moment, there is a need of a thoughtful, cognizant and leading democratic force, which could take control of, and give an outlet to the situation. The Twelfth General Convention (2010), which was held recently in Kathmandu, was expected to give a new life to the Nepali Congress, which would also ensure the fulfilment of this necessity. But, this expectation, too, does not seem likely to be fulfilled easily.

Democratic transformation of the Maoists

World history shows that it is the democrats who launched the first ideological and practical struggles against monarchy. Therefore, a republican structure is the brainchild and creation of the democrats. But in Nepal, there is a misconception among many that the concept of a republican system was begun by the Communist party. A fair seven decades before the Communist Manifesto (1848) was written, the democrats had established a republican system in the United States of America and France. It was the democrats who led the struggle for abolishing the Russian monarchy (Czarism). The establishment of a republican India was the result of the peaceful non-cooperation Movement led by Mahatma Gandhi. Likewise, a republican system was established in China, under the leadership of the democrat leader Sun Yat-sen. But in the later phase, because of several shortcomings and mistakes within the democratic Kuomintang party, the Communists came to power under the leadership of Mao Tse-tung, and the republic took the form of a Communist rule. In Nepal, it was the Nepali Congress who first raised an organized and institutional voice against both the Shah monarchy and the Rana oligarchy, the dynastic and feudal form of governance. Military, religious, single-party (Communist or otherwise) autocracy are the defective forms of a republican system. A constitutional monarchy is not a political philosophy or ideology, but a compromise between the king and the democratic leaders. Democracy is the soul of a republican system. In fact, it is only the republican system that can give completeness to democracy. The philosophical-ideological identity of the Nepali Congress is a republican system with democratic values.

Communists have considered struggle and violence as synonymous to each other in philosophical terms. And it was not unusual for the Maoists to believe in the same ideology. But it was not a long-lasting ideology. Certainly, the Nepalese Maoists showed their enthusiasm in the struggle. They spread some fresh dreams. Specifically, they mobilized youth and women. They also brought the Dalits and marginalized groups to the forefront. But even among such circumstances, what is to be noted is that there should be a cooperation between sense and thought for the transformation of a country and its individuals. This aspect was completely absent in the Maoist party. This problem occurred because the Maoist party was formed based on the ideological-philosophy of a single-party autocracy. So, the party still has its ideological differences with the concept of multiplicity, the very basis of democracy. At present, this has been a major ideological distance and difference between the Nepali Congress and the Maoist party. Because of their differences with the concept of multiplicity, the Maoist's commitment in different agreements seems to be weak and artificial on ideological terms. Moreover, as seen in terms of behaviour and activities, the Maoists are not inclined to showing a democratic path to their cadre. Even at present, during the training conducted for the cadre level, senior party members were inclined to indoctrinating the juniors with the psychology of motiveless ill-defined revolt and war. On the other hand, in front of the international community, the party is orchestrating its commitment to follow capitalism that ensures socio-economic transformation.

Therefore, the democratization of the Maoist is a primary issue, which is also a major aspect of the ongoing peace process. The Maoist has not yet freed themselves from the wartime militant attitude and methods. Recently, at the extended meeting (21-27 November 2010) held in Palungtar, Gorkha (the election constituency of Dr. Baburam Bhattarai), they expressed similar mindset. This has resulted in the Maoist not being able to take correct and solid initiative in the constitution drafting process, even after having emerged as the biggest party in the Constituent Assembly elections. But the Nepali Congress also needs to take up its responsibilities, after bringing the Maoist party into the democratic process. So, the Congress should take some policy level initiatives in certain fields, i.e. rather than taking rigid stances for conventional democratic structures, in certain circumstances, the Nepali Congress should take initiative to adopt a new structure or form of governance which ensures progressive socio-economic improvement with a firm commitment to global democratic values. Moreover, this should be the major basis on which the Nepali Congress establishes its communication and relationship with the Maoist. Only by paving this road can we ensure a convenient journey for Nepal's democratic transformation.

Stance of Nepali Congress on fundamental issues of the constitution

In the present state of affairs when a new constitution is being drafted with the restructuring of the state, it is necessary for the Nepali Congress to have a straightforward policy on two major issues, which are, form of the system of governance and state formation. Even there, the Nepali Congress needs to focus on securing fundamental bases on which stands firm a democratic constitution. These bases are: human rights inclusive of individual freedom, periodic election in a multiparty environment ensuring voting rights for all adult citizens, free and effective judiciary, rule of law, free press, accountable/transparent and inclusive form of governance.

What will be the structure of the state at the centre? Who will be more powerful, the President or the Prime Minister? What will be the form of election for the President? What will be the nature of Prime Minister's election? How many chambers will the parliament consist of? What will be the nature of hierarchical division in the state administration (military, armed police force, civil staff and Nepal Police Force) and judiciary? Nepali Congress needs to come up with clear standpoints on these issues, and open a space for discussion and agreements with all other parties, political (including Maoists) and otherwise.

Direct election of an executive head

Nepal shall be transformed from monolithic and centralized state to a federal state through state restructuring. Thus, because of pragmatic and other perspectives, the British parliamentary system (Westminster Model) does not seem appropriate for Nepal. Certainly, the British parliamentary system has remained the priority of Nepali Congress. But inside Nepali Congress, there has been a discourse regarding direct election of the Prime Minister as the executive head. This has become an issue of formal discourse after the elections to the Constituent Assembly (2008). Moreover, based on the homework done by 25 NC and CA members, an independent motion has been presented in the CA committee for deciding the governance structure, regarding the direct election of the Prime Minister. Therefore, while the Constituent Assembly is still in the process of deciding on a model of governance, it will be appropriate to search for newer options. Even among the Western democratic states there exists many variants of democracies. These countries have developed models of governance according to their own needs and experiences. South Africa has a unique parliamentary system which consists of an executive head elected by the parliament as President, but does not have a Prime Minister. Spain has a constitutional King, but the Prime Minister (executive head) is called the President. Although the British Westminster model has been regarded as the classical parliamentary system of governance, different countries have adopted their own kinds of revised and progressive parliamentary systems. So, all countries have done their own unique experiments. There is no uniformity in the models of the parliamentary system. In fact, the British parliamentary system seems appropriate for establishing democratic practice where there still is the provision of a constitutional monarch. This system has been useful in other such countries which have the provision of a constitutional monarch. This has been a compulsion in countries like India which have close ties with Britain. Even for India, which has been striving to emerge as a world superpower, the provision of direct election of the executive head has already become a political necessity.

Direct election of the prime minister will be a new experiment not only in Nepal but also elsewhere. One such practice was adopted in Israel a few years ago under different circumstances. In Nepal's case, the lesson learnt and the experience gained while practising the Westminster model during 1991-2004 have remained at the background of this concept. Because of a weak Prime Minister and a series of abnormal and non-transparent dissolution of the parliament, even Nepali Congress, while in position, has been unable to secure governmental functioning and stability. It is not that the abolition of monarchy automatically brings about parliamentary stability. As we have experienced during two years in the Constituent Assembly, even after the formation and dissolution of two governments and having voted several times for a third, we are lingering in a complex situation of indecision. Apart from that, this concept is based on the assumption that, for our country which shall adopt a federal system with provincial structures, if the Presidential election could equitably represent the nation's multiple identities, and if the direct Prime Ministerial election could ensure the participation of the entire nation, it would in turn ensure governmental stability and efficacy. The necessity of emotional integrity of the proposed federal Nepal and result-oriented and practicable governance has further provided the pragmatic and ideological foundation for such a system. In this system, when the party nominates its candidate for the Prime Minister, it should be decided not through units like the parliamentary board consisting of limited people, but through internal election held in broadly represented units like the General Convention or the General Assembly.

In this context, issues have been raised on what would happen if the current provision of an Executive President is to be retained. Definitely, the presidential system also fulfils several expectations what would otherwise be expected from the directly elected Prime Minister. Moreover, the provision of a directly elected President would help reduce the expenditure and do away with the dual relation of offices, thus making an environment for the President to work independently. But when we adopt the directly elected executive presidential system, we will have to take into consideration the communal, linguistic, cultural plurality and social differentiation. Otherwise, we can not establish a constitutional provision which represents plurality at the highest office of the nation, which is expected of the federal system. For example, we can compare between the ongoing practices in the USA and India. Even in the USA, where there is a legacy of an executive presidential system for over two hundred years, they have elected their first Black President only recently. But they have not yet been able to elect a woman President. But in India, we can see the representation of nine different identity groups from among the eleven presidents so far. Second, because of inefficient execution of the classical parliamentary system, the developing countries have seen the rise of authoritarian tendency, military intervention, and totalitarianism through an executive President with military background.

There is a dual basis on which the executive presidential system can check such a situation. The president can, keep vigil on the constitutional values in the capacity of the constitutional head of the nation, and also on the Prime Minister on moral grounds. The parliament can also establish a provision of supervision on the allocation of the budget and the nomination of the executive head of the state through its committees or through direct channels. In fact, in democracy, a high emphasis is laid on the structure of an accountable government. The directly elected Prime Minister is accountable to the people who elected him/her on the one hand, and to the parliament on many aspects including governance, personal activities and behaviour. In this way, even when the Prime Minister is free and capable of fulfilling his/her duties and promises; we can make him/her bound and systematized by the structure of dual accountability. In the traditional parliamentary system, even when the parliament (legislative council) elects the Prime Minister, the constitutional compulsion for the Prime Minister (head of executive council) to make decisions according to the whip, establishes the tradition of the legislative council, in practice, being under the executive council. That is why, there is the possibility of an independent character of a parliament (legislative council) under the directly elected prime ministerial system. Thus, only with the provision of a directly elected prime minister along with a constitutional President can we ensure the fulfilment of fundamental gaps inherent in the presidential and the traditional parliamentary systems. It is necessary to provide a secure base of democratic governance for a society like ours which has not yet grown out of traditional feudal thinking and customs. Moreover, it is equally necessary to maintain executional stability and effectiveness for economic growth to happen. Thus, here are the major characteristics of a directly elected prime ministerial and indirectly nominated presidential system.

- An executive head with a direct mandate from the people, and directly accountable towards the Parliament and the people
- A solid medium of executive stability and effectiveness
- The Prime Minister as a symbol of a democratic national integrity and action in the federal structure
- An independent legislative official unconstrained by the whip released by the head of executive council
- A comfortable arrangement between polarization and balance of power between the executive and the legislative councils.
- The President as an institution that ensures the customary representation of communal and regional plurality

The basis of state formation

In the discourses and proposals regarding the structure of federalism, some have emphasized on regional structures, some on ethnic while others have emphasized on linguistic identities. What, in fact, should be the number of autonomous states? What should be the basis of their formation? Should they be based on mutual dependency or complementarities? What should be the basis for distribution of resources and treaties/agreements? How to keep the state from division? How to establish understanding between all parties? These are the questions whose answers we should seek to form our basis of state formation.

Because of Nepal's geographical structure, nature of habitation, and communal and linguistic plurality, it is not possible, scientifically and practically, to form a state on only one basis. It should be taken into consideration that the demand for federalism in Nepal is raised for bringing the state and the government closer to the people. Therefore, even if the linguistic-cultural or communal identity can become a major basis for determining the number, name and territorial division of the states, it can not be the one and only basis for doing so. It is also necessary to give equal emphasis to the foundations which are capable of providing stability and smooth running to the states after their formation. Steady resources and economic infrastructure are the fundamental requirements of an independent and autonomous state.

In Nepal, the demand for federalism is an attempt to establish the identity, representation and reach of the citizens, as a means to eliminate inequality and imbalance. But, in view of the geographical structure and the condition of habitation in Nepal, it seems necessary to determine state division keeping in mind the concept of a multi-cultural state. Its major function is to emphasize that wherever one is living, he or she belongs to the same place. While determining a name for any state, together with fulfilling the expectations of the dominant cultural groups, it becomes necessary to take into consideration the plurality inherent in it. It is best to name a state according to the choice of the majority of the nation. Experts argue that it becomes practicable if the constitution demarcates the territory and settles the number of states, and leaves the provincial legislative body to determine its name. Certainly, security issues of the communities and cultures in minority can become sensitive with the area and name of the state. Therefore, regarding the issues of naming of the state, the Constituent Assembly should search for factual basis and determine a democratic, judgmental process. Moreover, even after a constitution has been passed regarding the naming of the states, it would be appropriate to establish a provision that if the provincial parliament deems it necessary to alter its name, it can pass a resolution for alteration and propose before the federal parliament, and if the federal parliament in turn passes it with a two-third of its majority, it shall then be altered. Regarding this issue, the committee's report, submitted to the Constituent Assembly, has also presented some alternative suggestions. Disintegration of the nation is the foremost among anxieties expressed regarding the formation of an autonomous state. The Nepali Congress should have a policy of formation of states in such a way in which the anxieties of the people are addressed.

It is necessary for the constitution to have a detailed list clarifying the structure of government in the village and municipality, its working area and a clear distribution of power division. In fact, only when the local government becomes strong and empowered by the constitution, can the advantages of federal governance reach the citizens. Nepali Congress needs to deeply understand these issues and also act responsibly to take them further towards fulfilment. It seems appropriate to restructure the existing local bodies on the basis of their number, appropriateness and field of authority to form an effective village or municipal government.

The structure of socio-economic transformation

The foremost objective of the Nepali Congress is development and prosperity of the nation. In its 1946 Manifesto of Mass Revolution, the party had declared:

> The Nepali Congress will not be satisfied only by political improvement. It will also enhance the nation economically and ameliorate the economic status of its people. Through an economic perspective, the present social system of Nepal is highly unjust. The entire power of the society is lost in discrimination between the rich and poor. In the kind of nation Nepali Congress plans to construct,

> the society will have no place for exploitation. That is to say, the haves will not be allowed to do injustice over the have-nots on mere strength of their riches. The Nepali Congress wishes to revamp the whole society on the basis of equality and justice.

But unfortunately, even after six decades of the 1950 Revolution, Nepal could not determine its politico-constitutional structure. Several other nations, however, gave a momentum to socio-economic transformation amid political strife. It could not happen in Nepal which is unfortunate. According to the World Bank's Global Development Report published last year, the average annual per capita income of Nepal is 350 dollars only. Even all other south Asian nations have better per capita income as compared to that of Nepal.

Over the past 20 years, among the two big neighbours of Nepal, India has an annual economic growth of 7/8 percentage, whereas China has accelerated it to 10/12 percentage. Nepal, situated amid these two growing economies of the world, has an annual economic growth rate of around 3 percentage over the same period of time. Nepal wasted 10 years of time in internal armed conflict instead of taking advantage from the propinquity of growing neighbours. Even today, statistics show the average life expectancy of Nepalese to be 65 years but it may be even less in reality. The literacy rate of the people is also around 65 percentage. Health condition is so substandard that hundreds of rural population die simply due to diarrhoea. Health related manpower produced with huge investment is heading abroad and not to the rural areas.

Challenges for economic development

The supreme responsibility of national development rests on political leadership. It should be able to acknowledge necessary means and resources for development and successfully mobilize them to give momentum to the development of the nation. When Singapore got its independence in 1964, the then Prime Minister Lee Kuan Yew gave a transition to his nation from third world to the state of first world within 30 years through maximum utilization of the people, airport and seaport, which he thought were the only resources of his nation with possibilities. The political leadership of Nepal till date does not seem to have understood that Nepal is enriched with natural resources and laborious people and carries with it the possibility of being counted among the rich countries of the world.

Nepal has been unable to achieve necessary progress, inspiration and excitement in the fields of agriculture, industry, education and health because of the implementation of plans and policies indicated by other countries instead of conducting development programs according to the need of the nation. The nation could not achieve desired change as these sectors lacked serious group research, program and its proper implementation. The ignorance of leading political parties of Nepal towards economic development, lack of concern and a kind of neutrality, are the major reasons behind this.

The leaders of political parties should possess the strategy of inspiring people through unblemished, simple and limpid lifestyle. A developing nation is like a family striving to achieve economic enhancement. A step of inspiration to people for hard work would be to let them experience the control of unnecessary government expenditure, prioritizing qualification on every type of appointment and present objective and justifiable verdicts. The public services like education, health, transportation, communication are other sectors through which people can be inspired by making them contrived, regular and effective as far as possible. Road sanitation, timely repair and maintenance or an instant remake in case of damages are other sources of public inspiration in our context. An environment of trust can be created among people through such simple looking ideas. No sector can speed up development when it lacks faith in its leadership.

Priority Sectors

Nepal is endowed with innumerable amount of natural beauty and resources. Here lies many possibilities of development due to the presence of snow clad mountains, hills, panoramic Terai landscape, several rivers, forests, habitat of birds and animals. We, thus, are in need of such leadership that can utilize land, water, forests, medicinal herbs and human resources with clear vision of development and an ability to congregate national consensus, for its successful implementation.

In view of the geographical positioning and structure of Nepal, there are five sectors we can rely on for economic development, which are: tourism, water resources, agriculture, education and health sectors. Moreover, there are three such areas of research for which Nepal can be the centre of attraction from all over the world. These are, Military University (with focus on issues regarding peace corps), research institutes on mountaineering and on high Himalayas. Since India and China constitute the highest population of the world and their economic growth is also on the rise, these countries have seen a rise in the number of middle and high class rich people. Nepal is the closest destination for them and therefore, Nepal's tourism industry does not need to seek customers elsewhere, if it can attract only one percentage of the total population of each of these countries. Similarly, Nepal, being rich in water resources, has a possibility of producing 83000 MW of hydroelectricity but we are bound to face load shedding. Internalizing this fact, our development policy should attempt to attract cheaper and accessible investment as expected in the development of water resources. But, because of the unmotivated national leadership that we have as of now, all signed and future treaties of hydro power development, specifically with India, are prey to strife. For this, we have to build a consensus with India concentrating on the national benefit of Nepal. We need to have clear policies and programs and a firm determination for their implementation. Hydroelectricity is not the only way to utilize water resources. We are in specific need of a national policy for the use of water resources also in sectors of drinking water, irrigation and industry. Nepali Congress can begin making a difference prioritizing such matters of national policy.

Even today, agriculture is the backbone of Nepal's economy. Nepal also has traditional and native experience in this sector. Environmental diversity within a small landscape is a very important circumstance for agricultural research. Agriculture-related university curriculum should include Nepal's traditional experience. Solid steps are essential for the development of other sectors near to agriculture such as animal husbandry, milk production and proper national and international market for the finished products. We should also come forward with well planned and managed herb production in the higher mountainous range as an agricultural programme.

We should also concentrate on the fact that agricultural products with special quality, produced in exquisite climate of the hills and the Himalayas and specially produced through composts can get market not only in our neighbouring countries but also in other countries like Singapore, Japan, Korea and even European nations. Thus this sector should be encouraged with priority to avail oneself of the possibility of national as well as international market.

We usually tend to forget the issue of land management while talking about the development of agricultural field. Though there are many talks about revolutionary or scientific land reform, it has not been able to exceed the election manifesto. In fact the situation strongly demands policies of land management and its utilization. When several complications regarding absent land ownership, tillers right to land and proper policies on ownership with programmes for distributing land to the landless are yet to be resolved, new problems are arising. For a nation like ours, which is transforming into a federal state, we should have clear stances about the classification of land, rights of the state on it, and on whom rests the rights to final decision on land - the centre, the province or both. In reality, the land policy of a developing nation like ours should be the responsibility of the centre and the major issue of land management should best be the responsibility of both the centre and the federal states/provinces.

Many of us still think that development is possible only through foreign aid. These beliefs must be changed for the development of the nation. Nepali Congress, intending to change these perceptions should forefront programmes related to national policy making and its implementation. We certainly may not be able to work with all infrastructures of development with our own means, resources and attempts, but still, we must categorize national projects into two parts. We should have the determination to accomplish a few specific projects through national competence. It strengthens our self-confidence and capability. It also speeds up development at its own pace. It acts as an inspiration to the future generation. This way, our development process gets a passage to all fields like production, export, tourism, energy, fundamental physical infrastructure and the service sector.

Effective foreign policy

In the past, Nepal has adopted different kinds of foreign policies in different circumstances. Presently, Nepal does not have any existential danger from any foreign power. But, still, the country feels insecure. Why? What is the priority of the current foreign policy? How can we fulfil the present need of internal socio-economic development of the nation and make it more effective and result-oriented. Nepali Congress can formulate an effective foreign policy for Nepal with an extensive research as answers to the aforementioned questions.

The nation cannot escape a fearful psychology of insecurity unless it is socio-economically stable and prosperous. The nation could not achieve proper socio-economic development, even after 240 years of national unification. This subject is thus of primary importance to both internal and foreign policy of Nepal. Internal policy and foreign policy are two parts of co-ordinated national policy. This consciousness should direct our foreign policy.

Even in the changed context after 1990, Nepal could not maintain a comfortable relation for the benefit of the nation with her two neighbours, specifically with India (as complementary in prioritizing socio-economic development). Thus, the socio-economic condition of the nation could not be much different from that of the Panchayat Regime. Several sectors of co-operation with India such as trade deficit, border security, treaties, Bhutanese refugees, water resources remained raw. There is a need to stimulate policy and diplomacy to solve them in a trustworthy and responsible manner. Similarly, China is our next significant neighbour, forward on a journey towards achieving economic and other power and thereby becoming a super power. New prospects of relationship are developing with China as well. With the passage of time, China will not only acquire economic liberalism but also shall have possibilities of inclining towards political leniency.

It is more essential for us to have a clear stance regarding Nepal's role in the United Nations. While sending peace corps to the peace keeping mission of the United Nations is a major contribution of Nepal, the acceptance of the role of United Nations Mission to Nepal (UNMIN) is its immediate compulsion. In such a circumstance, we should have clear standpoints on Nepal's expectations from the UN.

The Nepal-Britain friendship dates a long way back, and Britain's army still have the Gurkha Battalion. Britain is also among Nepal's donor nations. At the same time, Nepal has friendly relations with the USA, the world super power. Therefore, our country needs to be clear on its policies on how to co-operate with these nations to withstand the national challenges. We should also have clear conceptions about Japan, Germany and the whole European Union on several fields of co-operation in development, human rights and environmental issues.

Nepali Congress should also have a clear stance regarding Nepal's standpoint on regional organizations like BIMSTEC and the World Trade Organization. There exist challenging questions on how Nepal can enhance its national benefit through such regional and worldwide organizations, which obviously requires a realistic, practical and clear perspective.

Nepal, being situated between two emerging super powers has very significant relationships with its neighbours. Our relationships with these nations also define and guide other international relations. This is our geo-political reality. Our internal development attempts, food security and issues related to security and peace are also affected by our relationship with our neighbours. This has remained true in the past, and has been crystal clear in the context of the world structure of the 21st century.

The closer we are with some one, more are the strands of inter-relationships and complexities. It is true in case of nations as it is among people. Thus, more than internal affairs, the major political parties should engage in regular discussions regarding common minimum policy and programmes on foreign relations, and establish an understanding on strategies to achieve them. There needs to be a national understanding on how we perceive our neighbours and establish an affable, cordial and strong relationship with both of them. If any decision maker acts lightly in a surge of excitement or without acquiring proper knowledge of the time and situation, the nation might lose its respect and achievements earned, sparing decades of time.

In the present context, it is necessary for not only the Nepali Congress but all other parties to have clear standpoints on the priorities of Nepal's foreign policy and should establish a common understanding on the issue. We feel that the priorities should be as mentioned below.

> Nepal does not only have geographical proximity with India but there also exist economic, social, trade and security related ties. Therefore we should create common concept of economic development with co-operation on the banking sectors. It should formulate common policy and program to enhance all types of economic relations in a practical basis of bilateral and regional level.
>
> Nepal's relationship with China is also extending in a multidimensional way. The growth of trade has also emphasized such expansion. We should extend our relationship keeping in view this kind of growth. We can establish cooperation in the banking sector. We should come up with common goals and programs to expand all sorts of economic relations in bilateral or regional level on pragmatic basis.
>
> Extend Nepal's role in the United Nations making it more task-oriented.
>
> Coming up with better-managed and effective policies regarding the participation in peace corps.
>
> Extend fruitful relations with Nepal's donor nations including USA, UK, Germany, Japan, and member nations of the European Union.
>
> Maintain a purposeful role in regional organizations like SAARC, BIMSTEC.
>
> Improve practical and fruitful relations with gulf nations, Malaysia, Singapore and South Korea where Nepali workers are increasing

Conclusion

Nepal has sufficient bases to develop and prosper. The present need is to identify such bases and mobilize them properly. There is no reason for Nepali youths, who are recognized as hard working and faithful, to be incapable of developing this beautiful nation enriched with abundant means, resources and diverse climate at the same time. For this, hard working, faithful, prudent and effective leadership with clear goals is essential for all parties and the nation. Nepali Congress should emphasize on giving a solid direction and leadership to the task of drafting a democratic constitution and help to put an end to the current situation of political instability and constitutional transition. Moreover, it is the necessary charisma of the leadership of Nepali Congress to maintain harmony and liberal values within the internal organization of the party and foster a political culture of cooperation and understanding. This type of leadership can rightly face the challenges of Nepal's democratic transformation and maintain minimum understanding within the internal sector while establishing maximum co-operation at the external level.

Anand Swaroop Verma

Interview with
Pushpa Kamal Dahal 'Prachanda'

Pushpa Kamal Dahal 'Prachanda' is the Chairman of the Unified Communist Party of Nepal (Maoist). The Constituent Assembly elected Prachanda as Prime Minister of Nepal on 16 August 2008. He was sworn in as Prime Minister on 18 August 2008. Prachanda resigned from the post on 4 May 2009.

Q: After the Gorkha plenum it was widely reported that on the question of Party Line there are three mutually diverse views and, that the differences are so intense that the party is on the verge of a break up. What is your comment?

A: For a scientific and revolutionary party it is quite natural to have debate and discussion within it. Moreover, the impact of the current political stalemate in the country is getting reflected in the party forum also; but it is natural. In such circumstances there is nothing wrong in feeling concerned about the future of the party and the revolution in the country and have discussion and debate over it. We consider it a positive development. In the history of Nepal, it was for the first time that party cadres participated in debate and discussion on such a large scale. In the Gorkha plenum there were altogether 7000 people comprising party cadres and leaders who took part; the plenum continued for seven days and concluded very successfully with a meaningful conclusion. It is a matter of great pride for a mass based party like ours. The apparent risk involved in this type of experiment can be taken only by a party which has a scientific and revolutionary ideology. The decision taken at the end of this plenum, of making a combined proposal out of the proposed three, was also a big achievement. It is largely due to this exercise at the plenum that a resolution could be successfully adopted i the central committee meeting. The plenum has proved to be a great asset in suggesting ways to do away with the sense of uncertainty and despair prevalent in Nepal today and provide direction for the future. We have given more strength to the party on the basis of fresh initiative and reasonable attitude.

Q: But you would agree that on the question of principal contradiction there are sharp differences between the views taken by Baburam Bhattarai and others. Could you sort out the differences in the central committee meeting ?

A: Definitely, this has been the main issue of debate in the party's plenum, and as per the directive of the plenum the final resolution adopted by the central committee makes it absolutely clear that on the question of principal contradiction there is a change in the stand as compared to the one taken earlier. It has been said in the resolution that the vested interests represented by the Indian monopolistic capitalism and the Nepalese domestic reactionism comprising the brokers, bureaucratic capitalism and the feudal elements are alike and have converged. The two are united against the people of Nepal and the Nepalese Nationalism due to their own vested interests. This is the view that was adopted by the central committee though some comrades continue to differ on this. We will continue this debate by following Lenin's principle of freedom of expression and unity of action and this will not create any problem in the party. When we talk of the alliance between the two strange forces Indian monopolistic capitalism and Nepali reactionism some believe that we have declared India or the Indian ruling class our main enemy. This kind of interpretation is absolutely wrong. We have not identified Indian government as our main enemy. The vested interests of the Indian and the Nepali ruling classes are now alike and therefore the two are united against the people of Nepal. But our focus of attack will be Nepali reactionism this has been made abundantly clear in the resolution. But there are some who have started creating confusion by spreading the canard that the Maoists have launched offensive against India. They are instigating people by creating this wrong impression in the minds of the people that we are trying to create trouble whereas our intention is not malafide. We will fight against the increasing Indian intervention but we will continue to target the internal Nepali reactionism, this I would like to make very clear.

Q: Keeping this in mind do you think that the process of restoration of peace and making of constitution would not be disturbed or these will continue smoothly?

A: No, there won't be any stopping of these processes. The plenum and the central committee have categorically said that we will try our level best till the end to bring the peace process to a meaningful end and work for making a people oriented constitution. On these issues there is no difference of opinion in the party. But the fact of matter is that the Nepali reactionary elements are continuously trying to disrupt the peace process and disturb making of the constitution. The Indian monopolistic capitalism or a section of the Indian ruling class is also keen to ensure that the peace process in Nepal does not succeed. They are working hard for this. Therefore, the danger has increased today. So, in order to defeat the design to disrupt the peace process and making of the constitution, people of Nepal will have to be organized and prepared for a movement. Our emphasis is this. But sometimes people get confused and feel that the Maoists would dissociate themselves from the peace process and also not participate in the drafting of the constitution. This is absolutely incorrect. We are committed to taking the peace process to a successful conclusion and also to ensure completion of the drafting of a people oriented constitution. But the reactionaries feel that if the peace process succeeds the strength of the Maoists in Nepal would further increase, and if the present constituent assembly succeeds in making a constitution the credit would go to them as one third of the strength of the assembly is constituted by the Maoists alone. And, they also fear that in the election that would follow the promulgation of the constitution the Maoist may get two third majority. Therefore, the reactionaries and revisionists want to disturb this whole process. This is part of a big conspiracy that is going on in Nepal. We want to say that we should launch movement and organize people against this conspiracy. The Maoists have made utmost sacrifices to have a people oriented constitution. The slogan for the constitution was given by the Maoists. How can we ignore the task of making the constitution? We are rather more concerned about this but in order to expose and defeat their conspiracy, the people have to be mobilised to come to the street and launch movement. In our party there are some who are interested in preparing the constitution even by making compromises with the Nepalese reactionaries and Indian ruling class. I believe this kind of act would be insulting to national honour and people's emotion. This would be a kind of surrender of national sovereignty. This is not going to benefit either the people of the country or the Nepalese nationality.

Q: It means that you want to complete the drafting of the constitution and organizing people's movement simultaneously?

A: Yes, both the works will continue simultaneously. We will try to successfully complete the peace process and also prepare people for movement to defeat the sinister design against Nepal.

Q: What is the view of your party and those of other political parties in Nepal regarding the UNMIN (The United Nations Mission in Nepal)?

A: Though the responsibility of formulating policy and taking decision regarding peace process rest with the political parties of Nepal, the UNMIN has predominantly been associated with the peace process right from very beginning. The role of the UNMIN has been clearly defined with regard to the broad parameters of the peace process, monitoring of arms and ammunition, interim constitution and a number of other important agreements. Now, when the UNMIN leaves Nepal, these agreements will have to be redefined and appropriate amendments will have to be made. Therefore, the stand of our party is that the tenure of the UNMIN should be extended for another five months, i.e., up-to the coming May (May 2011). This will help in preparing a positive environment for pushing the peace process in the right direction and leading it to an acceptable conclusion. But the government has announced that the tenure of the UNMIN has been extended only till the 15th of January and that this is the last extension. It means the government wants to say a goodbye to the UNMIN after that. Discussion is going on over this issue and we have discussed it with other political parties, too. Although Nepali Congress and CPN (UML) have not made their position clear over this issue, the Security Council has already been informed that extension of UNMIN (till Jan 15) in Nepal is for the last time. We are going to write a letter to the Security Council with a request to make appropriate arrangement and atmosphere for extending the term of the UNMIN for another 5 months. If it is not possible, then we can look for an alternative proposal and send it to the Security council. If the term of the UNMIN is not extended then in its absence a political office and a team of observers of the Security Council should function in Nepal to do the follow up action with regard to the peace process and keep the Security Council updated about it.

B.C. Upreti

Society in Nepal
From Tradition to Transition

Nepal a small country in the southern slopes of the great Himalayan ranges had been an authoritarian, monarchic and Hindu state for long. It was only in May 2008 that the monarchic system was abolished and Nepal was declared a republican state. The country has also been declared a secular state and in the context of the recent political transformations in the country the Hindu identity of the state and the society has lost its relevance, at least in theoretical terms in the context of the emerging Nepalese state and society. The centralized authorization political order represented by the hereditary Shah rulers and the aristocratic Rana rulers nearly for hundred years and Hinduism became important factors in the evolution and growth of society and culture in Nepal. Even after 1950 when Nepal embarked on the path of modernization and development the basic determinants of the Nepalese society remained almost the same.

The evolution of the modern society of Nepal may be considered since the foundation of a unified kingdom of Nepal in 1769 by the Gurkha King Prithvi Narayan Shah through a military expedition. The sustenance of a unified kingdom out of numerous small tribal principalities that were rival to each other and the Newars of Kathmandu valley was not an easy task. It required a structured social order and a sustained social support base. It was not possible with the existing social order as it was not only multi-structured but highly conflictual as well. Therefore the sustenance of the monarchic rule also required a unified social order. It was thus the evolution of state was closely knitted with the evolution and growth of society. The society was broadly termed as the realm (desa) and it was under the possession of the king. The structuring of the society thus followed the wishes and requirements of the monarchy.

The geographical factors also played an important role in the growth of society and culture in Nepal. The ecology influenced the growth of social norms, behaviour and patterns of life and attitudes. The deep valleys and isolated regions had given shape to different patterns of society. The unification of the kingdom of Nepal also led to the homogenization of different socio-cultural patterns. It may also be pointed out here that the migration of people both from the north and the south added to socio cultural diversities. However, the cultural influences from the south remained dominant as it gained royal patronage and the open border played an important role in socio-cultural assimilation. Nevertheless, the diverse geographical patterns also led to the growth of diverse cultural patterns as well. Thus the Parbateye culture which represented the royalty and the socio-political elite of the hills had clear cut geographical boundaries.

It is in this background that this paper seeks to highlight some of the core issues relating to the evolution and growth of Nepalese society and culture.

The tribal set up

Before unification Nepal was inhabited by different tribal groups that had migrated to the hills from the north and the east at different points of time which were basically marked by socio-economic backwardness. They had their cultural norms, customs and religious practices. These tribal societies lacked dynamism and they remained confined to internal cohesion.[1]

Most of the tribal groups belonging mainly to Mongoloid and Tibetans origins lived in well-defined tribal boundaries. Some of the important tribal groups were Magars, Gurungs, Tamang, Murmis, Khambus, Yakhas, Sunwars, and the Newars of Kathmandu. The Tharus and Danwass were the two important tribal groups in the Tarai region.[2]

---

[1]For a detailed description see, Ram Niwas Pandey, Making of Modern Nepal, Nirala, Delhi,1997.

[2] Dor Bahadur Bisht, The People of Nepal, Ratna, Kathmandu, 1967.

These tribal groups failed to provide a cohesive social set up although there were certain similarities in terms of social order.[3] For instance, each tribe had its own hierarchical order at the top of which was the tribal chief who in most cases happened to be the head in the lineage. Next to him was the priest who also held this position on hereditary basis. He was responsible for performing all sorts of rituals and was the most popular person. Next to them were peasants, hunter, artisans, etc. But the social institutions, social ceremonies and rituals were different among different tribes.

These tribes lived in a primitive social order under a hostile environment; they were small in scale and ethno-centric based on the principle of kinship.[4] Their vertical and horizontal mobilizations were least. Apart from social and political barriers, the environmental barriers were also important in this regard.

These tribal communities began to exhibit some sings of adaptation and change with immigration into Nepal particularly from the South. Hinduism was introduced in Nepal by the Lichchavi rulers. However, it had little influence over the local tribal traditions; only a minority had begun to observe the Hindu rituals. Nevertheless, it was the entry of the Hindu religion in the hills of Nepal that became a factor in social awakening; the entry of Buddhism into Nepal further enhanced this process. The Mahayana Buddhism came to Nepal during the 7th century AD which had tremendous influence on some communities. But, as in the case of Hinduism, Buddhism also underwent significant changes in Nepal. These two religions got localized and customised significantly both in form and sprit under the local tribal social customs and rituals. It paved the way for changes among the tribal communities. However, as stated earlier, it was not possible to evolve a unified social order under the tribal political set up. This process began only with the unification of the kingdom of Nepal in 1769.

Foundation and growth of society

The modern state of Nepal came into existence in 1769. Before this, Nepal was divided into several small principalities. There were forty six small

---

[4]R. S. Chauhan, N. 3: 16-20.

[3]R.S. Chauhan, Society and State Building in Nepal, Sterling, New Delhi, 1989:1-16.

states in the east and the west of the Kathmandu valley known as Basis and Chaubisi states, representing different ethno-religious groups and communities. These apart, there were tribal states of Kosi and Gandaki basin, the Newar rulers of Kathmandu valley and the Sens of Palpa. Prithvi Narayan Shah, a ruler of the Gurkha principality, took up a military adventure and defeated the rulers of various principalities. He then founded the Kingdom of Nepal in 1769. King Prithvi Narayan Shah was conscious of the fact that the new Kingdom was founded by a forced unification of diverse ethno-cultural groups that were inimical to and fighting with each other for their existence. It was indeed a matter of great consideration that these principalities had been brought together through a military power alone on a long-term basis. There was a need to evolve a socio-cultural milieu that would bring about and consolidate a monolithic social order in Nepal. There was also a need to evolve a strong socio-religious base for the King.

Before the advent of the Shah rulers the tribal societies were divided into different clans and numerous tribes existed in Nepal. These tribal societies were not monolithic and they had diverse forms and systems.[5] King Prithvi Narayan Shah tried to define the state in religio-cultural terms.[6] It was declared by the King that all the land resources of Nepal automatically came under his possession and control. The land was identified as Desa (the country) and the people as Realm. The King was projected as the sovereign lord with the proprietary authority over both. He was accorded a religious basis and was declared as the incarnation of Lord Vishnu which accorded him the right to rule the Desa and realm both. Thus, the King was projected as sovereign over the land, the protector of his subjects and the territory and the source of all aspirations, rules and traditions.

King Prithvi Narayan Shah adopted a multi-dimensional approach in order to build a strong and unified Nepalese society and state. He followed a stratified hierarchical model for the society based on the Chaturvarna Hindu caste system. The Brahmins and the Kshatriyas (Rajputs) were accorded top places in this hierarchical order. They were called Tagadharis

[5]R.S. Chauhan, N. 3: 20-23

[6]Richard Burghart (ed.), The Conditions of Listening, Essays on Religion, History and Politics in South Asia, Oxford University Press Delhi, 1976: 226-259.

who had the authority to wear the sacred thread and perform religious rituals. Next in the hierarchy were the Matwalis. The Matwalis were divided into two categories - non-salvageable Matwalis and salvageable Matwalis. All the ethnic groups were classified under these categories. On the whole there were four varnas and chattis jats (Thirty six castes). Jung Bahadur Rana further classified them in his Mulki Ain of 1854.[7] King Prithvi Narayan and his successors though accepted cultural diversity, they never recognized cultural rights of these communities. They were not given the opportunity to articulate their rights and demands.[8]

The social set-up thus evolved had Brahminic supremacy. As a result, the Brahmins acquired social prestige and also gained supremacy in politico-economic and administrative fields. The Kshatriyas (Thakuris) had the next place in the social hierarchy. They got positions in the royal palace. They were the protector of the royal authority. As a result they enjoyed power, privileges by the King and hold over land. Thus, the fundamental conceptions about social groups were centripetal and hierarchical. [9]

What is important here is that in the hierarchical social order of Nepal, it was Brahmins and Thakuris of the hill region who were accorded positions of power and privilege. This sowed the seeds of regional disparities as well because it were the Brahmins and Thakuris of the hill region who became the repository of the hill culture. Henceforth, identification with the hill culture and caste hierarchy became important in determining power and prestige of various social groups.[10] The people of Tarai were encouraged to follow the hill culture.[11] They resented it and consequently they got dissatisfied and felt being discriminated. Thus, there was no identification

---

[7] A. Hoffer, The Caste Hierarchy and the State in Nepal: A Study of the Mulki Ain of 1854, Wegener, 1979.

[8] Prayag Raj Sharma, The State and Society in Nepal, Historical Foundations and Contemporary Trends, Himal Books, Lalitpur Nepal, 2004:212.

[9] David N. Gellner, "Ethnicity and Nationalism in World's only Hindu State" in David N. Gellner, (ed.), Nationalism and Ethnicity in a Himalayan Kingdom, The Politics of Culture in Contemporary Nepal, Harvard Academic Publishers, Amsterdam, 1997:4.

[10] Ramakant & B. C Upreti, "Regionalism in Nepal", in Ramakant (ed.) Regionalism in South Asia, Aalekh, Jaipur, 1980: 138-160.

[11] For details see, Frednick H. Gaige, Regionalism and National Unity in Nepal, California University, Berkeley, 1975.

of the people of Tarai with the state. The differences between the hill and the Tarai people provided a negative definition for the Nepali national identity.

The Sḥah rulers used Hindu religion as a source of legitimization.[12] They started a process of Hinduaization in order to form a monolithic society. The non-Hindu tribal communities were motivated as well as forced to accept Hindu religion. They were categorized under the Hindu hierarchical caste order. All tribal people were placed at the lowest ebb of this social order. A policy of compensation and accommodation was also followed in order to bring non-Hindu communities within the fold of Hinduism. The Magars were allowed to wear scared thread as recognition to the services that they had rendered to the Palace. King Prithvi Narayan Shah said, "I am the King of Magrant." It was indeed an emotional attempt to assimilate Magars. The Gurungs were also rewarded for the services rendered by them to the Gurkha rulers. Autonomy was also given to Limbus for sometime.

The monarchy accorded protection to Hindu temples and shrines. Crime was graded on the basis of caste and punishment was fixed accordingly. The Brahmins were excluded from capital punishment. Thus, Brahminic supremacy became hallmark of Nepali state and society.

A unified religious and cultural policy was pursued. Nepal was given the status of a Hindu state. King Prithvi Narayan Shah said, "Yo Asli Hindustan Hao" (This is the real Hindustan). The Gorkhali or the Khas Kura was designated as the language of Nepal in the form of Nepali.

The Mulki Ain of 1854 promulgated by Jung Bahadur Rana said earlier was the first attempt to provide a legal framework to the state and the social order.

The four main ingredients of state were defined as Rajan, Rajya, Praja and Sthiti (social order). It also accepted the hierarchical social order. The state was to define this hierarchy and it was the main arbitrator in caste-

---

[12]John Whapton, "Political Identity in Nepal: State, Nation and Community" in David N. Gellner (ed.), N. 9: 43-44.

related matters.[13] The Shah and the Rana rulers adopted the policy of consolidation of the tribal areas. Once the tribal rulers were defeated Brahmins and Kshatriyas were sent in these areas to take up the local administration in their hands. Land was confiscated from tribal landlords under the Kipat land system and it was redistributed to Brahmins and Thakuris under Raikar, Birta, Guthi and Jagir systems. New settlement of the high caste people in the tribal areas was encouraged. A large number of high caste Brahmins and Thakuris became absentee landlords in these areas. Thus, the indigenous people were exploited under the new system. The policy of patrimonial rewards and punishment continued. Thus a patrimonial state and society emerged in Nepal. The hierarchical relations became dominant in the society

It is clear that the Nepali rulers followed a policy of forced cultural unification of different ethnic groups. Efforts were made to bring various tribal groups, belonging to the Mongoloid racial stock, under the fold of Hinduism. It served dual objectives of social and political order.[14] The institution of monarchy was a rallying point between the high caste Hindus of the hill and the other ethnic groups. It may also be pointed out here that the Nepali rulers deliberately kept various communities isolated and underdeveloped. Actually, the ruling elite wanted to lay down a foundation of a unified model under the framework of Hinduism. Obviously, no efforts could be made towards the socio-economic uplifting of backward communities, assuming that it would generate consciousness among them, ultimately being detrimental to the authoritarian rule of the monarchy and the Ranas. The state thus emerged in Nepal had been viewed by scholars as a predatory Hindu state. [15]

The concept of purity

The concept of purity was observed strongly in order to maintain social order, status, duties and legitimacy. Thus the concept of purity became a part of the social order and social practices. The concept of purity had different dimensions. The society was divided into three categories in terms

---

[13]See A. Hoffer, N. 7.

[14]Harka B. Gurung, Social Demography and Expression, New Era, Kathmandu, 1998:88.

[15]Hanka B. Gurung, "State and Society in Nepal" in David N. Gellner (ed.), N. 9: 465-472.

of purity:

1. Those groups which would accept water from each other and no purification was required.

2. Those groups from whom water could not be accepted but any purification was not required on touching them.

3. Those groups from whom water could not be accepted and purification was required on touching them. This concept of 'Choi Chitto holno parne was observed very strongly and is still prevalent in traditional hill families.

The women had to live in separate 'out houses' as a part of purification during the days of monthly cycle or till a certain time period after giving birth to a child.

As a part of purity, each year before Dashara (Desain) The King dealt with all the criminal cases so that the society could be purified.

Those Nepalese who visited India or elsewhere had to undergo purification after returning to their homeland. They had to take bath for 14 days. It was believed that the King also would have done sins during his reign, so after his death the Brahmin who would perform his death rituals would share some of his sins; so after the rituals were over he would be termed as Demon Brahmin and he would be asked to leave the realm. It was also a part of the concept of purity.

King and the realm: state-society relations

The Shah rulers tried to define the realm (domain) in terms of social relationship. It was considered to be necessary in order to establish social order and forge social integration. King Prithvi Narayan described his kingdom as heaven of four varnas thirty six castes. The centre of King Prithvi Narayan's realm was the temple of Bhawni and the cave of Guru Gorakhnath. But after unification he recognized all the centres of religious importance and treated them as equal.[16] The relations of hierarchy were

---

[16]Richard Burghart, N. 6: 231-232.

also observed between realms. The concept of equivalence was also observed in different realms. For instance, a Maithili Brahmin visiting the hills would not take water from a hill blacksmith as the hill Brahmins would not do that. But a hill Brahmin visiting Tarai would accept water from a plains blacksmith as the Maithili Brahmin would do that.

On the whole the Shah rulers tried to establish that the realm was an auspicious system of social relationships so that the monolithic concept of the society could be strengthened. The King had the proprietary authority within the realm.[17] Within the realm the caste system provided an auspicious order of the social universe.

The Parbateye culture

The broader Hindu culture drawing influences from local customs and rituals and other religious traits particularly Buddhism acquired the shape of a Parbateye culture, which received royal patronage under the Shah rulers and later the Rana rulers. In geographical terms the Parbateye culture was obviously confined to the hill areas of Nepal and the Kathmandu valley in particular. It is difficult to state whether Parbateye culture was a composite culture. But it is a fact that it developed under the royal patronage and hence it acquired dominance and superiority. The Parbateye culture or the Parbate was considered to be the repository of the Nepali culture.

The Parbteye culture was in sharp contrast with the Madhesi culture which represented the plain Tarai region of the country. Strangely the same caste groups of the Tarai region were not considered part of the Parbateye culture hence not repository of the Nepalese culture. In fact Madheshis itself was an inferior and derogatory term used for the people of the Tarai region. It seems that since the Parbateye culture was closely knitted with the Kathmandu based power structure, therefore the high caste people who also formed the power elite did not want entry of others into the power structure. In fact it became an essential prerequisite for entering into the power structure to be representing the Parbateye culture. It was obvious that the people of Tarai remained excluded from the framework of the Parbateye culture. This distinction led to the growth of two distinct

---

[17]Francis Hamilton, An Account of the Kingdom of Nepal (Reprint), New Delhi, 1971.

patterns of life, values and cultures in Nepal though both had the similar broader cultural framework but distinguished politically. The people of Tarai had much more socio-cultural interactions with the neghbouring Indians. Hence, they were considered to be more near to India. As such they lacked confidence within the power structure of Nepal. Since the power elite also represented the social elite being at the top of the social order, the people of Tarai could not become part of the Parbateye culture. The geographical barriers also played a significant role. The open border between Nepal and India and the entirely different socio-economic and geographical set up helped the hill people in using the geographical variations as a tool for the consolidation of their hold over power.

The cross border socio-cultural linkages and its impact

The socio-cultural linkages between India and Nepal are a unique feature of the bilateral relations between the two counties. The growth of Hinduism in Nepal brought this country closer to India socially and culturally. In fact, in socio-cultural terms there is hardly any difference between the two countries except that the Hindu religion and culture remained more intact in Nepal in comparison to India primarily due to Nepal's lesser exposure to the outside world. The Shah rulers had often claimed that Nepal was the real Hindustan. Although it was a statement made by King Prithvi Narayan Shah in order to strengthen the Hindu philosophy of kingship, yet it also dignified the status of Hindu religion and culture in Nepal.

The migration of people from India to Nepal, the pilgrimage, etc. also contributed to the socio-cultural assimilation between the two countries. It may be observed that the two regions developed intimate socio-cultural linkages. In fact Tarai was considered as a cultural extension of India by the Kathmandu based ruling elite and therefore a secondary treatment to the people of the region. Nevertheless, the fact remains that it is difficult to differentiate the cultural landscape of the Indo-Gangetic plains of which Nepal Tarai forms a part. The socio-cultural patterns remained the same on both sides except those of the tribal groups in Nepal Tarai such as Tharus etc.

The Gurkha rule over the Kumaon and Garhwal since the middle of 1790's till 1815 brought the hill areas of western Nepal close to the Indian hills. Although the socio-cultural connections between the Kumaon and Doti in Nepal had been age old and developed in a natural way, the Gurkha rule gave recognition to the high caste Kumaon Brahmins in the royal court and the cultural exchanges became deeper.

The open border has been a major source of continuation and strengthening of socio-cultural connections between the two countries. Nepal's larger exposure to India and the migration relations between the two countries helped in strengthening the socio-cultural landscape of Nepal due to commonalities in religious and cultural terms.

Modernization, development and patterns of social change

The political change in Nepal marking a shift from traditional authoritarian to liberal democratic order also opened ways and means for the mobilization of the traditional social order. As pointed out here the traditional social dynamism of Nepal was closely related with the intimate interaction between state and society. The monolithic character of the society, pre eminence of the Parbateye culture and their supremacy began to be questioned once the traditional political order began to be changed. The opening of the Nepalese society to the outside world, the development of the means of transportation and communication, growth of liberal democratic values, institutions and political superstructures, expansion of modern education, expansion of trade and commerce, increased emigration and immigration created an environment for vertical and horizontal mobilization in the society. It is true that the impulses of change in the society were weak and urban-centric, but there was a change in the traditional social order of the country, particularly in the context of its adaptation to outside socio-cultural forces. However, the continuation of the political dominance of the traditional elite, the continuation of the upper class dominance in the power structure and Nepal's persistence as a Hindu state also underlined continuation and dominance of the traditional social order.

After 1950 and more specifically after 1980, resentment against the traditional social order began to grow. The Mongolian ethnic groups and the Madhesis which had been depressed communities traditionally began to resent against both the Brahminic supremacy and the hill respectively.

The main issues of contention were:

1. Monolithic character of the Nepalese society as propagated by the traditional power elite. It was being argued that the Nepalese society was multistructured and the ethno-regional identities had to be recognized properly.
2. The people of Mongolian origin began to organize since 1979 in order to assert their distinct ethno-cultural identity.
3. The people of Tarai began to resent against the socio-cultural, linguistic and political domination by the hill people.
4. The status of a Hindu state.
5. Upper caste domination in the political structure of the country had continued despite the dawn of democracy in the country.

In fact, the democratic order that came up in the country failed in reducing the upper caste domination in politics, administration and army. Thus it remained exclusive in nature. Hence demands were raised for an inclusive democracy.

All these factors became highly significant in the context of the emerging political situation in the country in the 1990s. Although demands were being raised from different sections of the society for the restructuring of the Nepalese society, it was the Maoist insurgency which gave a framework to these issues. The Maoists realized the discontent within the Nepalese society and raised the issue of restructuring and transformation of the society within a new political framework and inclusive democracy.[18] With the abrogation of the institution of monarchy and declaration of Nepal as a secular state, some changes within the broad framework of the Nepalese society are possible. It is equally important that the plural character of the Nepalese society in terms of beliefs, values and practices is a complex issue and would take its own course.

---

[18]See for details, B. C. Upreti, Maoist Insurgency in Nepal, Kalpaz, Delhi, 2008; B. C. Upreti, Nepal: Transition to Democratic Republican State, Kalpaz Delhi, 2010.

To conclude, it can be observed on the basis of the above brief discursion that Nepal's transition from a tribal social set up to a structured hierarchical social order was closely linked with the unification of the kingdom of Nepal and the evolution of the modern Nepalese state. The centralized authoritarian rule described the broad parameters the Nepalese society and allowed it to function and grow in a direction that would help consolidation of the authoritarian power structure. The state and society were closely interlinked. The society defined in terms of the realm remained subservient to the interest of the authoritarian power structure. The society obviously remained static to the core.

After 1950 a gradual change occurred in the social order. However, the foundation of hierarchical social order and the Brahmanic supremacy was so strong that it has continued despite Nepal's quest for modernization, development and democracy. However, in the context of the present political transformation in the country the issue of social transformation has become prominent. It is quite possible that certain broad parameters of social reordering and change are drawn. However, transformation of social norms and values may take its own course.

Pradeep Gyanwali

The Nepalese Peace Process
At the Brink of Crisis

New challenges

The high peak of political enthusiasm in Nepal is going down as the hope and aspirations among the people are fast evaporating. The common people in Nepal were jubilant exactly 5 years ago when the 12-Point Understanding was signed on November 7, 2005, which had opened the door for the historical Movement of April, 2006. They were celebrating the end of a decade long violent conflict that took the lives of almost 17 thousand people 4 years ago, when the Comprehensive Peace Agreement was being signed on 5 November 2006. The following two years were also spent on the preparation for Constituent Assembly elections and the celebration of the establishment of a republic. Those days were full of optimism. But now, the energy, excitement and hope brought about by the Movement, Peace Agreement and the Constituent Assembly Elections seem to be disappearing rapidly. There is dissatisfaction, disappointment and dejection among the people of Nepal.

There are ample reasons for this dissatisfaction. According to the constitutional provision, a new constitution had to be promulgated on or before the 28th of last May (2009). We failed to meet that target, and even when half of the additional one year is over, a concrete structure for drafting the constitution is still not visible. The peace process that had to be completed within six months of the Constituent Assembly (CA) elections, the integration and rehabilitation of the Maoist combatants are still kept at bay. After over six months of Prime Minister Madhav Nepal's resignation, a new government is yet to be formed. People's aspirations with the epoch-making change have been shattered the state of affairs is not quite up to the mark on issues related to poverty alleviation, creation of employment opportunities, overall socio-economic development, justice to victims of conflict and governance. The index of corruption and impunity is negative. There have arisen voices of communality, religiosity and regionalism in the Nepalese society which was otherwise popular for social harmony and pluralist culture, and these have created tension in the society. And, as if unaware and indifferent to the suffering of the nation and people, the leaders of some political parties seem very hungry for power, thus distancing themselves from the spirit of the Movement. It is but natural for such a situation to create dissatisfaction and hopelessness among the people.

Is the Nepalese peace process possibly heading towards failure? Is the Constituent Assembly becoming irrelevant? Is Nepal turning into a failed state by not being able to effectively manage post-conflict situation? Is the instability of Nepal giving rise to regional conflict, posing danger to the security of neighbouring countries? These questions are bothering not only the Nepalese politicians but also the international friends who are concerned about Nepal and wish to see permanent peace, viable democracy and people's prosperity in this tiny republic.

However, it would be a mistake to conclude that the peace process will fail, constitution will not be prepared and Nepal will be a failed state, by just looking at the present state of affairs in Nepal. Nepalese people have due aspiration for peace, they have high concerns for democracy and there is ample patronage from the international community as well. Moreover, our fundamental social fabric is so deep rooted that it is not easy to destroy it at somebody's will. In spite of various limitations, the Nepalese political parties have, in the past, been able to address these issues in the last minute. So, it is unlikely that the Monarchy will find it easier to reestablish itself. Similarly, even if the Maoists pass the agenda for a "people's revolt" in their manifesto, it is not easy for them to go back to the violent conflict. But, the prolonged transitional period, addition of unexpected challenges, and shattering of people's hope for change and trust on leaders are matters of utmost concern. The biggest strength of democracy lies in the continuous trust and support of the people. If the same is weakened, democracy loses its strength to save itself from the attacks of its adversaries.

Where did we fail?

While signing the 12-Point Understanding in New Delhi, political parties stood on a new ground. After realizing the futility of the eleven years long violent conflict and the impossibility of a militant takeover of the state, the Maoist party had committed that it would join the mainstream by shunning violence and accept democratic norms and values. On the other hand, the mainstream political parties had consented to go for a republican system by doing away with Monarchy and to promulgate a new constitution. In other words, the 12-Point Understanding was arrived at on the democratization of the Maoists and progressive liberalization of other parties.

The movements of 1951 and 1990 were attacked within a decade of their establishment. The main reason was that both these Movements ended up in compromises with the monarch, and fresh bid by the monarch to reestablish an autocratic regime by discarding the boundaries of constitutional monarchy both the times. The other crucial reason for its failure lay in limiting the democratic experiment within formal political rights while neglecting the socio-economic and cultural rights of the people. Likewise, the differences among revolutionary parties before the institutionalization of democracy and the opportunistic efforts made by the monarch to get advantages of this division within revolutionary parties was yet another reason which gave serious setback to democratic experiment. Then, we had promised not to repeat those mistakes in history.

The unity among seven parties and the Maoists made it possible to lead the peaceful Movement, sign the Comprehensive Peace Agreement within six months, bring the Maoists in the Interim parliament and the government, conduct the elections to Constituent Assembly which had been prolonging for sixty years and establish a federal democratic republic in a peaceful manner. That was a very swift, successful and exemplary period of peace process.

But the election for Constituent Assembly had an impact on many things. The Maoist came to the wrong conclusions that feudalism had ended along with the abolition of Monarchy, that it was replaced by the "comprador-bureaucratic capitalists," and its representatives, the parliamentary parties, had become the enemies of revolution. That conclusion led the Maoist to the extent of cutting off relations with the erstwhile collaborators like CPN (UML) and Nepali Congress. The same conclusion excited the Maoist to speak of "dragging Girija Prasad Koirala - presidential candidate - out of Baluwatar," and to deceive Madhav Nepal by rejecting him only an hour before the deadline for application of candidacy for the same post. Certainly, other parties might have become adversaries of the Maoist because of their unexpected loss. But the inevitable unity between revolutionary forces for the management of transitional period and preservation of the achievements became fragmented because of the Maoist's wrong perception. We failed to give a novel message by unanimously electing the first president of the Republic of Nepal.

In spite of the Maoist's betrayal, CPN (UML) proposed to them to form a government as the Maoists constituted the largest party. But that government could not become a national consensus government because Nepali Congress, the major democratic party, remained in the opposition. Even then, had the Maoist wanted to use that opportunity to lead the peace process towards meaningful conclusion, history would have recognized the party as the "Hero." But the Maoist gave a false definition to their triumph. It interpreted the mandate given to them by the people as a legitimization of its past activities, and as a license to do whatever they liked. The Maoists failed to realize that the people had given this mandate to them in the hope of establishing peace. They did not focus on completing the peace process, integration and rehabilitation of combatants and then transforming themselves into a civilian party and clarifying the suspicions. In spite of gaining the confidence of the army and working towards healing the scars of the conflict, it began to act randomly, which resulted in the downfall of its own government. The cold relation that developed between the Maoist leadership and the army, and the lack of trust in the Maoist by other parties still survives.

The period of one and a half years following Prachanda's resignation was not utilised for maintaining peace process and drafting of the constitution. From the beginning, the Maoist were engaged in activities like blockade, and in leaving no stone unturned in defaming Madav Nepal's government. "Puppet", "operated by foreign remote", and "illegitimate" - these are some of the representative tags given by the Maoist to the Madhav

Nepal Government. The government was formed according to the constitutional provision with a majority in the parliament. But Maoists challenged the legitimacy of the government and tried to topple it unconstitutionally, and they also tried to establish the party's supremacy in the name of "civil supremacy". Because of all these activities, we lost more than a year in vain.

Challenges of Constitution drafting

Drafting a Constitution through Constituent Assembly is not an easy task. In procedural terms, it is a long, complex and expensive process. It is not easy to include different layers of people's aspirations into a single manifesto satisfying all and drafting a constitution with the ownership of the people. We have also seen examples of the failure of Constitutional Assemblies in several nations.

In procedural terms, the major challenges before drafting a constitution are - how to include the highly disputed voices of people, how to coordinate with the communal, linguistic and regional issues ignited by political interests, to make them work for national interest, and how to promulgate a constitution within the additional duration (of which only five months remain). Mainly, the sensitive issue of formation of the structure of federalism seems to be the most complex. But the most important question is - what kind of a constitution will we prepare? Do we accept pluralism or not? Do we need to have a limit so far as number of party is concerned or adopt a competitive multi-party system? Whether we need an independent judiciary or not? Do we give space for the constitutional provision of opposition in the system of governance or not? Do we recognize the rights related to an individuals property or not? Do we take communality as the basis of federalism, or do we create mixed communal units? There are disputes on some of the fundamental issues of drafting the constitution. These issues determine whether our constitution would be democratic or autocratic in intent. On many of these issues, the Maoists and the other parties have opposite views. By opposing pluralism, advocating for limited multi-party system, rejecting the independence character of judiciary, political system without the provision of an opposition, and proposing a communal state, the Maoists have put themselves on the side of an autocratic system.

Some parties seem to be anti-liberal on several issues related to socio-economic rights. But even then, the Constituent Assembly has prepared a draft proposing epoch-making rights for education, health, shelter, employment, clean environment, social security and justice, also gathering consensus on the socialist bent of the future economy. If the Maoists come forward with a positive attitude on the above mentioned issues of democracy, we can be assured of a progressive and democratic constitution. If we accept the universal laws of democracy and gather consensus on the intricacies of social justice, the dispute on the form of governance will be solved easily. Again, the major question is, whether the peace process is completed in time and a fearless environment is prepared for promulgating a constitution. Because, we know that a constitution cannot be promulgated under the shadow of a gun . It will not be of any significance to promulgate a constitution in a state of conflict.

The knot of the peace process

The intention of the 12-Point Understanding and the Comprehensive Peace Agreement to keep both the armies under the supervision of the United Nations or any international organization until the completion of Constituent Assembly election was to keep the Constituent Assembly election away from any kind of fear and shadow of an armed force. Its intention was not to keep the presence of two parallel armies in the nation up to indefinite future. It is true that the Maoists' armed presence even in the Constituent Assembly election had a serious negative impact, and there have now arisen arguments that it was a mistake to let the rebel party to take part in the election with arms. Even if it seems right when looking back at the process taken then, it was not possible to go for the election after completing all the due procedures. We should consider the fact that there was also the monarch at the time. But the peace process should have been completed after the Constituent Assembly election.

The peace process has some major important aspects. The first and most important issue is the integration and rehabilitation of Maoist combatants. Second, provide justice to the victims of conflict by constituting a Truth and Reconciliation Commission and Commission for Investigation of the missing people. Third, implementation of the past commitments, especially the return of properties seized during the conflict, creating an environment for the displaced to return home, demobilization of the paramilitary structure of Young Communist League (YCL) and putting an end to violent activities, and an assurance to execute political activities in a fearless environment. Fourth, democratize the Nepal Army. And fifth, end all kinds of communal, linguistic and class discriminations to address the bases of conflict, and establishment of social justice.

Meanwhile, a new military act has been passed, and thus the Nepalese army has come under civilian control. By presenting itself on the side of transformation, the army is winning the hearts of the people. This is an important achievement regarding the democratization of the army. It is not that there are no problems that remain to be solved. This is also a continuous process. Likewise, the process of forming a discrimination-free society to end the bases of conflict has also begun. This is also is not an issue that can be solved overnight. But the progress in the area of issues related to the implementation of past commitments, bringing the perpetrators of serious crimes committed during the conflict to books, an overall integration and rehabilitation of the Maoist combatants is not satisfactory. This is mainly because of the Maoists.

A new consensus between the seven parties was reached upon in June, 2008, in which it was clearly mentioned that the integration and rehabilitation of the Maoist combatants would be completed within six months of the formation of a new government and that the state would take no responsibility regarding the combatants. Pushpa Kamal Dahal 'Prachanda' became the Prime Minister following the agreement. He had got an important opportunity to complete the issue of the combatants, because he was at once the president of the Special Committee for Integration, supreme commander of his own military branch and de-facto chief of the national security units. But within the duration, he failed to make any progress on this count; instead, he tried to play foul with the army. This has a role behind the other parties' lack of trust in the Maoists.

Meanwhile, the Maoist has been requested several times to bring the combatants under the control and supervision of the Special Committee, classify them in different camps for voluntary exit, integration and rehabilitation, and end the double security system. The democratic forces have often proposed that, once these tasks are completed and the Maoists consent to follow a dependable timetable for taking the peace process to a close, they may lead a new government. But, though the Maoists show their commitment to the peace process in front of the international community, they are dilly-delaying in formally separating the combatants from the party and transforming the party into a violence-free civilian party.

It is in no way beneficial for the Maoist and for that matter for any other party to keep the 19 thousand combatants in the camps for a long time in an uncertain future. If the dissatisfaction explodes from within, it will bring complexities to the Maoist party itself. But the Maoist is using such a sensitive issue a a "bargaining chip" and thus complicating the peace process itself. Today, the most important task is to keep emptying the camps by freeing those willing for a voluntary exit with a "golden handshake", providing those willing to rehabilitate with opportunities like education, skillful training or employment and thus helping them get rid of the combatant life and return to social life, and integrating those combatants, who meet the criteria, in the security units. But the Maoist is delaying the task by coming up with different excuses time and again.

In the blue hall of Baluwatar, Prachanda has promised , time and again, to the late Girija Prasad Koirala and other leaders: "As soon as you all decide to go for a republic, I will unilaterally dissolve the Maoist army." Today, the nation has seen the abolition of Monarchy, declaration of a Republic and emergence of the Maoist as the biggest party through election and form a government. But the Maoist army continues to survive and flourish.

Complications of power sharing

Generally, peace process, drafting of the constitution and power-sharing are distinct issues. It is not necessarily that there is always a consensus on governance, but even between differences, there is a possibility of consensus regarding peace and constitution, given that the stakeholders are open hearted. But in the case of our nation, peace process and power-sharing have been made integral to one another. Before the combatants were confined in the camps, we brought the Maoist in the parliament, an interim government included the Maoist even before the UN verified the combatants, and we, the unarmed political parties, competed with the armed party in the election. Was it right or wrong to do so - it is for history to decide.

As is already stated above, the Maoist had got an historical opportunity to bring all the forces together and take the transitional period towards completion, which it missed. Also, if the Maoists had supported the attempts of this government on the issues related to peace and constitution, we would have moved far ahead. The hollowness of the Maoist claim that Madhav Nepal was the crux of all the problems, that his resignation was a panacea and all the problems would be solved within two hours of his resignation, has already been proved false. Formation of a national consensus government is the best way out. But this is possible only when the Maoists rid themselves of other parties' suspicions by transforming the party into a civilian party free of arms and combatants, or accepts the leadership of other parties before certain important tasks of the peace process are completed. Do you always need to be told that you should take off your shoes to enter the Pashupatinath temple?

Maoist dilemma

The CPN (Maoist) represents that school of the Nepalese Communist movement which considers violence to be the necessary means of revolution and the dictatorship of the proletariat to be the ideal of the state. Driven by the same ideology, the Maoists began an armed insurgency in 1996, the 6th year of the introduction of multi-party system in Nepal. Then, the Manmohan Adhikari government, while successfully executing its popular reform programme, had established the fact that a maximum of service could be done for the benefit of the people even by following a democratic process. In this environment, raising arms was nothing more than ultra-leftist logic. The Maoist claim that it had to raise arms against the repression of the then government is nothing but a false argument. In fact, the Maoists were inspired by Mao's formula that "state power comes through the barrel of a gun," the extremist philosophy that "everything except war is illusion" and the false ideology that "there can be no Communist party without an army."

However, that ultra-leftism was able to spread all over in a short span of time. By exploiting the division between democratic forces, the indirect complicity of the Monarchy, exploitative policy of the external forces, and the dissatisfaction of the people, the Maoist kept on expanding the extent of violence and brought about a kind of tremor throughout the nation. But with the passing of time, their limitations began to surface - a militant triumph over the state seemed impossible, people affected by violence came up with counter-attacks, internal dispute of the party widened, and the vicious circle of violence seemed unending. Exploitation of an external land for violent activities became difficult. Collaboration with the then king Gyanendra could prove unsuccessful. All these reasons compelled the Maoist to come to the peace process.

The Maoists have gained a lot after joining the peace process. They constitute the largest party in the Constituent Assembly and have also led a government. The external forces that announced "Red Corner Notice" are now themselves ready to lay red carpets for the Maoists. But what is unfortunate about the Maoists is that, They do not believe in their own commitments to peace and democracy - the same commitments which helped them become an acceptable force in the international circle. The Maoists cannot free themselves from the fetish of violence and autocratic ideology which had nearly swept them off the shore. Swinging like a pendulum between the ballot and the bullet is the biggest problem of the Maoist.

At the moment, the Maoists are debating over the manifesto of the extended meeting. Their leaders seem to have major differences on several issues. The party hardliner Mohan Vaidya is not happy with the fact that the party is undergoing a peace process - he believes that by accepting the concept of a democratic republic the Maoist party would be no better than a Rightist party, and he advocates for a direct "peoples' revolt" rather than the peace process and drafting of a constitution. Dr. Baburam Bhattarai is in favour of attempting at completing the peace process and the constitution drafting process and forming a government till the last moment, and argues that the party should go for a "mass rebellion" only if these alternatives prove to be impossible. And Prachanda seems to be quite in a mess while, on the one hand, he is busy alluring Mohan Vaidya that a revolt is a necessity, he is, on the other hand, instigating Bhattarai with the three "S"sarkar, sansad and sadak (government, parliament and street). Prachanda has stated in his manifesto the "the struggle of sovereignty against Indian expansionism" has become (our) prime focus. Likewise his conclusion is this process will not lead to peace and drafting of constitution. It is necessary to get rid of this process, but that should be done dexterously. However, despite their differences over "when" and "how" of the process, all three Maoist leaders come to the same conclusion - a peoples revolt is necessary.

A self-contradictory policy of the Maoists has pushed the Nepalese peace process towards complexities. On the other hand by involving the combatants, who have principally come under the Special Committee for the Integration of Combatants, in meetings and by classifying them in the following of one leader or the other, the Maoists have further contributed to the suspicion upon itself.

International factors

Because of her distinctive geopolitical situation, Nepal has been the centre of international concern for quite some time now. This concern has accelerated since the beginning of the armed conflict. Peace and stability in Nepal can give solace to both China and India. It is quite natural for the two giants to become conscious of any development in Nepal. China would expect that there be no game from Nepal's side to add to the trouble in its sensitive region Tibet. India would appreciate that its 17 hundred kilometers of open border with Nepal is not misused in favour of its enemy. We need to take concerns about the sensitivity of the two neighbours and give them assurances. Their roles in Nepal's peace process are of great importance. The United States of America and Europe would also play an important role in Nepal's peace process.

Nepal and India have a very special relationship. These two countries are bound together by deep social, cultural and economic relations and mutual interdependence. But there are complexities. While Nepal experienced a dominating attitude from some Indian leaders/rulers with typical British colonial mentality, India complains that some factions in Nepal have misused the open border to operate criminal activities against them. Anti-Indian attitude has also become the basis of "nationalism" for some of the political forces. Several uneven treaties, huge trade loss, border encroachment, flooding along the border regions because of the dams built unilaterally, and selfish attitude for maximum use of hydro resources are some of the problems Nepal is facing from India. Cross-border crime has become the common problem of both the countries.

It has already become necessary to define Nepali nationalism in the present context. Criticism of any nation cannot become the basis of our nationalism. We can strengthen nationalism by identifying our own nation's interest, while strengthening national unity and developing an equal and respectable relationship with the friendly nations based on mutual benefit. The unity between democracy and national forces can become the basis for nationalism.

After having to step down from the government, the Maoists are now trying to raise the issue of "national sovereignty". The Maoists have concluded that the fight against India has become their major concern because, India is "hatching a conspiracy" not to let the party lead the government despite it being the largest party. For the same, lately, it is collaborating with the monarchist parties in the name of "nationalist front". Prachanda has explained this in his manifesto presented in the extended meeting. His ideological conclusion of the "Nepalese revolution to begin from class struggle and end in national struggle" is sure to add complexity to the Nepalese politics. In the meantime, he has also tried to involve China in Nepalese politics and play the "China card" which was already used in the past. However, China has clearly stated that it would not interfere in Nepal's internal affairs and suggested the Maoists to strengthen the unity with other democratic forces and improve its relationship with India. After returning from Shanghai Expo, Prachanda has expressed his willingness to engage in a different level of talk with India, and also stated that a strategic cooperation should be established between Nepal, India and China.

UNMIN is outgoing on the 15th of January. However, UNMIN could not keep itself out of disputes within its stay in Nepal. Its "gentleness" seemed to be misused by the Maoists in different contexts. Meanwhile, if the Maoist combatants did not come under the control of special committee in the true sense, and the arms could not be managed, UNMIN's outgoing could create a state of void. To make sure that this juncture does not prove to be one which brings more complexity to the peace process, the democratic forces of the nation as well as international friends should seriously take heed of the situation.

What will happen next?

What will happen to Nepal in the days to come is a big question that deserves attention of media, political analyst and international friends of this tiny republic. The Nepalese peace process was not as simple as we thought it was. At several points of times, the peace process depended on the "mood" of the late Girija Prasad Koirala and Prachanda. And we neglected several tasks that had to be done tc institutionalize the peace process. We need to take lesson from the history.

The future of the Nepalese peace process depends, to a large extent, on the future policies and behaviour of the Maoists. They represent 38 percent of the total members in the parliament, and even in technical terms, it is impossible to draft a constitution without their support. And, it is one of the two stakeholders of the peace process. If the Maoists don't behave, the Rightist status quo-ist forces who do not want change, may find it easier to organize with the excuse of the Maoists. Because of the politics of identity fostered among masses, there will appear tension on communal, linguistic, cultural and religious issues. As anarchy keeps growing, Nepal may be pushed backwards, closure to a failed state. In such a situation, Nepal may become an open field for international forces to play their power game. In other words, we are at the crossroads.

As the mood and the Manifesto of the Maoist leadership suggest they seem to be in a dilemma. They know that it is impossible to triumph over the state through an armed struggle. But then they do not want to transform their party into a civilian party free of violence. They know that a dictatorship of any form cannot sustain. But they are hesitating to adopt the universal ratification of democracy. They know that it is impossible to move forward by prohibiting the democratic forces like CPN (UML). But, rather than winning the trust of the democratic forces, the Maoists seem to be ready to collaborate with the followers of the ex-monarch. They know that their anti-India "struggle for national sovereignty" will lead them to nowhere, but they do not stop crying loud. This same dilemma of theirs has been the main obstacle in creating an environment of trust with other parties and in taking their cadres on the way towards democratic transformation.

If there are practical difficulties in the management of the combatants, who were earlier given arms along with false dreams, the other parties should obviously help them get over with the problem. If the Maoists suspect that they will be kept isolated and deceived after they are free of the combatants and arms, the other parties should give them assurances. The democratic alliance should not be used as a front to keep the Maoists isolated. But if the peace process is used as a strategic programme, as a "temporary stoppage in the way to establishing a people's republic", it is a grave issue.

Recently, in Brazil, Dilma Rousseff won the presidential election. The triumph of the ex-militant Dilma was the reinstatement of the democratic and socialist norms begun in Brazil by Lula. In Nicaragua, even if Ortega had to stay out of power for a decade, people have brought him once again to presidency. In Venezuela, the craze for Hugo Chavez is still growing. The attempt of Che Guevara, who shunned all the amenities of Cuba to sow the seeds of revolution in Bolivia, was finished forty years ago, but Morales has established a new example by running a leftist government in a democratic method and by winning the hearts of the indigenous people in Bolivia.

On the other side, the "Shining Path" of Peru, which was once regarded as the model of a Maoist struggle, is now in a devastated state. The same Gonzalo, who discarded the government's call for talks, is now living within the confines of a jail. Such is the condition of the Filipino Jose Maria Sison who was once the leader of a powerful Communist party with 27 thousand militants. After neglecting anti-Marcos democratic movement, he is also fast moving towards regression. In Burma, Aung San Suu Kyi has become the icon of anti-Junta struggle, but the Communists, who once declared half of the nation's land to be a freed region, are nowhere to be seen at present.

The meaning of the above examples is that the leftist and socialist movement has now taken a new wave at present. Those leftists, who believe in the power of the people, believe in the peaceful transformation of the society and are ready to move ahead through democratic methods, are getting success in their attempts. But the faction that considers violence as a necessity and supports one-party system in the name of dictatorship of the proletariat is declining fast. The relevance of socialist norms and leftist leanings has grown high at present - but that is possible only through a democratic process.

Which path will the Nepalese Maoists take now? There is enough space for them if they transform themselves democratically. People have many complaints against the present democratic forces. The Maoists can take that free space now. But if they try to walk a different path, they will push themselves and the nation towards crisis.

The problem cannot be solved only by reacting on the thoughts or actions of the Maoists or by identifying oneself as an adversary of the Maoists. The democratic forces should become serious on this matter. Nepal is moving forward through the process of an epoch-making transformation. The Maoists have only encashed on people's dissatisfaction and aspirations for change. Whether the Maoists transforms themselves or not is one thing, but we cannot weaken the issues of radical changes. The democratic forces should be able to hold this flag of transformation. It will be a deception to the people if the achievements like republican setup, democracy, federalism, social justice and secularism are tagged as unnecessary just for the sake of criticizing the Maoists.

Nepal has paid an expensive price for the conflict. Now we are not in a position to pay more. People have a strong will for peace, want for democracy and thirst for prosperity. At a time when the neighbors are moving forward towards fast economic development with ten percent economic growth rate, Nepal cannot afford to remain a poor island in the whirlwind of conflict and be drowned by political instability.

Anand Swaroop Verma

Interview with Baburam Bhattarai

Baburam Bhattarai is a senior Standing Committee Member of the Politburo of the Unified Communist Party of Nepal (Maoist). He was elected to the Constituent Assembly from Gorkha in 2008 and became Finance Minister in the Cabinet formed after the election.

Q: After the Gorkha plenum it is believed that the party is virtually on the verge of collapse. It has been reported by the media also that the three mutually contradictory proposals advanced by the three leaders in the plenum are indicative of the fact that breakup of the party is imminent. What is your comment on this?

A: After the Gorkha plenum our party has rather emerged stronger because, according to the Marxist philosophy, class struggle, or internal struggle or struggle between schools of thought is integral and endless. It keeps on evolving. So far as class struggle is concerned, it has matured sufficiently. There have also been satisfactory developments in the aftermath of the 10 years of People's War and several people's movements. The internal struggle or the struggle involving the two opposites keeps going on in a dynamic party. The party would cease to survive the moment this internal struggle comes to an end. In order to break the impasse in our party, we openly encouraged this democratic exercise in the plenum. This helped a lot in sharpening the ideological and political outlook of the party. Therefore, the impression that the party is on the verge of a break up is indeed a canard. In fact, the plenum has helped us in making the party stronger and united to take up the unfinished challenges of the Nepalese revolution in the days to come.

Q: But the party could not identify its main political agenda regarding the course of struggle ahead or the principal contradiction in Nepal, etc. What is the difference between your proposal and those proposed by others?

A: First of all, we must understand that a plenum has a limited mandate. It merely plays the role of an advisory body for the extended meeting of the central committee. The democratic exercise in the Gorkha plenum has created a solid ground for taking important decisions about the future. We will discuss and debate over the issues that have emerged in the plenum and give them a formal shape following further debate and discussion on it in the general body meeting and the party congress. To immediately execute the decisions taken regarding the ideological and political issues by the plenum is not advisable. This decision should be taken further at the level of the party congress. In the plenum we have identified our agenda. Let us understand it this way. So far as the difference between our resolution and those of others is concerned, there are two-three things that must be kept in mind. First of all, how to protect, utilise and further develop the surviving Marxist philosophy of today? On this vital issue there is difference of opinion amongst us. Marxism is a dynamic philosophical science. This does not merely explain the world, but it tends to change the world as well. If the world is in transition, then Marxism as a science will have to be understood in terms of dynamics of transition, and in doing so Marxism will also be further shaped , reshaped and enriched. How to interpret and develop Marxism in the 21st century is a matter of great debate amongst us. So far as imperialism is concerned, there has been marked difference in the character of imperialism after the days of Lenin and particularly after World War-II. It is now known as globalised imperialism. We are examining the difference between the strategies and policies of the People's Revolution. Now, in a semi-feudal and semi-colonial exploitative country like ours, the role of nationalism and class war are important issues. We have been debating over whether to give prime importance to nationalism or class war (internationalism). We had debates also on the nature and character of the Nepali revolution. Although the spirit of revolution is internationalism, its format is national. It is a well known Marxist understanding. However, the Nepali revolution has a different context. We have debated over all these issues. On these issues, comrade Prachanda, comrade Kiran and I have expressed our opinions and it was debated in the plenum. We will discuss it further and give a final shape to it in the party congress. Following Lenin's principle of freedom of discussion (speech or expression) and unity of actions, we will keep working together while debating. This is the message of the plenum.

Q: Is there any decision over the political strategy to be adopted to break the deadlock in Nepali politics ?

A: Following the spirit of constitutional assembly, we have to give a proper shape to the democratic achievements made during ten years of People's War. At the same time we will keep working for completing the task of People's Revolution. These are the two important lines that we have decided to adopt after debate and discussion. This, we believe, is in the better interest of Nepal. If we look at the international communist movement we find that when peoples war reaches the level of strategic offence, it indulges in capturing of power at the centre. This is what happened in China. Should we also choose the same path? This is the classical communist pattern but we believe that we will have to do something different in the context of Nepal. Here the equation between the internal and external forces is not the one as elsewhere. Looking at this angle we have decided to complete the task of People's Revolution after reaching the stage of strategic offence with the help of the Constituent Assembly which is the epitome of bourgeoisie democracy. We have decided to follow this route as the situation in Nepal is different as compared to other countries. For example, the situation in the neighbouring India is also different from Nepal. Therefore, our model cannot be applied there. The fundamental difference lies in the fact that we have been victims of the absolute Monarchical regime in Nepal for the last thousands of years. Therefore, the capitalist in Nepal is also impotent here and is incapable of completing the task of democratic revolution and so we have to encourage the common people and the working class to go ahead and take the lead in launching People's Revolution in Nepal. That is why we have demolished the Monarchy under the leadership of the working class and succeeded in obtaining the largest number of seats in the Constituent Assembly. We must try to get the democratic rights of the people through the Constituent Assembly and continue to struggle for other kinds of rights. This would be more practical and useful in the context of Nepal. This is our point of view, and we want to do away with the ongoing political stalemate in Nepal with the help of peaceful means and constitutional methods. But at the same time, we have to build the pressure from below, i.e., at the of street level. Unless and until people come forward and struggle, the struggles launches only from above will prove futile. Even Lenin said that at the stage of democratic revolution we can institutionalise the democratic values only by pressurising from above and from below. We can attain our objective only when the struggle is launched both from above and from below. We have already talked about the struggle at the level of the street, Parliament and the government. The poor peasants, exploited farmers, downtrodden, women and the tribals must be organised for the struggle on the streets. This is the main strategy of our struggle and if this struggle is supported by the Parliament and at the level of the Government, it will produce dividends.

Q: Is there an alternative to People's Revolution also in the agenda?

A: In fact, the principle of social evolution itself contains the elements of quantitative as well as qualitative changes, and this takes the form of revolutionary changes. According to dialectics, this is (social change or social revolution) a continuous process and to reach at a certain stage of quantitative change, qualitative change is a must. This higher stage of change is called a revolt or a revolution. Therefore, nobody can stop this. When and how it will take place may of course be debated. The fundamental rights of the people to revolt, to act for metamorphic change in the system or to act for revolution cannot be denied.

Q: What is the nature of the principal contradiction in Nepal? Is it Indian expansionism or a combination of feudalism and internal local reactionism?

A: The two have intermingled. Nationalism and people's rule are two separate issues today. Nationalism can be used to fight against imperialism and expansionism while people's democracy and rule can be employed to counter the feudal forces and democratic capitalism. In a country like ours, these are the two issues related to Peoples Revolution. However, the two cannot be equated because, to identify the principal contradiction means that people will have to attack it by every means. Which factors should be given prime importance in preparing a revolutionary strategy is an important question. I understand that, in Nepal, even after the demolition of Monarchy, some forces of feudalism still survive. Because the army, bureaucracy and judiciary, which constitute the three pillars of a country, are yet to be democratised. These are still dominated by the feudal forces which have to be reformed. The economic relations and production relations are still semi feudal in nature. So far as land relations are concerned, feudal relations continue to dominate. People's Revolution cannot be completed unless and until we make a revolutionary change in land relations and alter the surviving production relations. It means that the main agenda of Nepali revolution is against the feudal forces in Nepal. This will be followed by a war against imperialism and expansionism sponsored by the Indian ruling classe. So far as the question of principal contradiction is concerned, I sincerely believe that unless and until we demolish internal feudal forces, unite the exploited working clase and strengthen the common people, we cannot stand against the forces operating from outside. Therefore, the appropriate strategy would be to first resolve our internal problems and then counter the external intervention. I understand that the internal feudal relation is the principal contradiction. It is a different thing that they are being externally supported by the Indian ruling classe.

Q: Who are the friendly forces supporting your ideology? Whom do you visualize as friends in your struggle?

A: We will have to carry on with only those forces who are willing to support revolutionary changes, are in favour of empowerment of women and emancipation of Dalits, tribals and the other sections of the exploited lot. Only by taking them together can we can hope to successfully complete the works of People's Revolution. We know that the Indian ruling class is unnecessarily intervening in our affairs. Therefore, Nepali Nationalism has to be strengthened in order to unite the common people against the intervention of the Indian ruling class. In the absence of matured nationalism and unity among the masses, it is unrealistic to think of effectively countering intervention of the Indian ruling class. If we forget this fact, we may lose our democratic achievements.

Q: Will the struggle in the future be peaceful?

A: Of course! We the Marxists believe in peaceful struggle and from our side we always follow this principle till the end. But if the reactionary forces attack us, then we are forced to counter them and for that eventuality, we should always be prepared. Violent attacks have to be countered by violent means.

Q: When would this ongoing political impasse end? Do you foresee the possibility of associated dangers?

A: Look, if this impasse continues till 28th of May, then there is an imminent threat to the Constituent Assembly. It can be dissolved. In that case, the peace process will also come to an end. Following these developments, there will be threat to democracy, federalism and secularism and other kinds of achievements. Therefore, we want to end this deadlock and protect our democratic achievements.

Q: Then you are left with no time now?

A: Yes, because the leftover tenure of the UNMIN is only one month now. Once it leaves, the take of Army integration will be kept in cold storage. Apart from this, now, there is no time left for drafting of the constitution. If these two works are not completed, the peace process will also be jeopardized.

Q: It is apprehended in a certain circle, that once the UNMIN leaves, there will be presidential rule in the country and with the help of the Army, there will be massive attack on the Maoist. Do you foresee such kind of danger?

A: This apprehension is there for the last one and half years. There is an attempt to implement reactionary agenda by isolating our party which played a leading role in the Nepalese Revolution and succeeded in emerging as the biggest force in the Constituent Assembly. This act is being sponsored by the reactionary forces from within and outside; they have united against us. But this is part of the class struggle. They are meant for that. The revolutionary forces will have to chart out a strategy which can defeat their intention. Therefore, we want to fight against them with the help of the old parliamentary forces, consisting of the Nationalist, the Leftist and the pro-people sections. We will have to stand against the danger of Army rule in Nepal and the rule of the Nationalist reactionaries. If we fail to counter and check them, we are likely to lose our democratic achievements and the parliamentary forces will also have to pay dearly. I don't understand as to what kind of benefit the Indian ruling class is going to get if Nepal goes back to the old route. If the peace process and making of constitution are broken and revolt and armed struggle takes place again, as in the case of Afghanistan, it will have a devastating impact on India also. Therefore, the Indian ruling class should also extend its support in completing the peace process and making of the constitution. I fail to understand why they are not doing this and are hell bent upon isolating the Maoists.

Q: The People's War, followers by the elections to the Constituent Assembly and the formation of the Government led by the Maoists all these achievements of your party were supposedly against the wishes of India and the US. But after the Katwal incident, your partys popularity has gone down and India seems to have an upper hand. What was the reason?

A: It is not possible to give right answer to this question. But if you look at the present situation in the world, you will realise that the role of the imperialist and expansionist forces has become more important. They are more powerful now and therefore they cannot be ignored. Thus, in order to demolish the Monarchy in Nepal, the 12 Point Agreement that we had prepared had the tacit support of the Indian ruling class, though India was not directly involved in it. But, realising the growing strength of the Maoists in Nepal, the Indian ruling class had anticipated that we can take over the power in Kathmandu. And this led them to formulate a strategy of trying to co-opt the Maoists in the system by initiating democratic principles. We also thought that there is no harm in trying the alternative way out if we succeed in attaining fundamental change in Nepal. This was the common meeting point between them and us. Till the time of elections to the Constituent Assembly, they were probably under the impression that the we would not emerge as powerful a force as we are today, and that they would be in a position to guide and keep us under their control. But after the election, we emerged as the most powerful force in the Assembly and they became alert and started making strategy to corner us. It is precisely in this process that the Katwal incident took place. We cannot forget the fact that India is a big and important power of the South Asian region. In India also, the common people are struggling against the exploitative policies of the Indian ruling classes. Being a communist, I would like to side with the down-trodden and the exploited masses. Despite all these, the strategic position of Nepal is such that we feel the need of sustaining the ongoing diplomatic relation with our biggest neighbour, that is, India. So if we look at it from this perspective, there is a dual relation of struggle against and of alliance between us and the Indian ruling class. Our friends are not willing to understand this. We want that there must be a check on the wrong policies of the Indian ruling class towards Nepal. When we talk to the Indian ruling class, it must not be misinterpreted.

Q: Is there any danger of split in the party?

A: Not at all. There is no such danger. Yes, a debate is going on in the party on this issue. In a revolutionary party like ours, there should be open debate and discussion and that we are doing. There is nothing to worry about this. This will rather strengthen the party.

Q: Is there any personality clash between Prachanda and you?

A: This is absolutely wrong. There is no personality clash. We have been working together in the same committee for the last twenty years. There is a difference in our way of thinking. There is difference of opinion on the question of revolutionary strategy and praxis. There is no personal clash.

Q: Is the decision taken in the meeting at Chunwang also being questioned as to, whether it was wrong or right?

A: Look, when it was decided, comrade Kiran and Comrade Gaurav were imprisoned in India. Therefore, they and some others had some difficulty in understanding under what circumstances we had decided to do this meeting. But in the party circle, it is accepted that the decision was right. Had we not come through Chunwang, a Peru like situation would have emerged. In that eventuality, we could have sacrificed our achievements of the last ten years. It is due to the decision of the meeting at Chunwang, that we have safeguarded our achievements and have reached up to the present level.

Q: Has the decision taken at Chunwang been accomplished or it is still incomplete?

A: At Chunwang, we decided that we will establish a democratic republic after the elections to the Constituent Assembly. Subsequently, the bourgeoisie forces would try to limit us merely to parliamentary democracy and we the representative of the working class people would like to convert this into a People's Republic. Parliamentary Republic is a common term. The leader of Nepali Congress and Nepal Communist Party (UML) are trying to give it the form of an old bourgeoisie republic. We want that our republic to be a new one where the rights of the large number of common exploited people, castes, religions and genders be safe and secure. This also is our idealistic imagination.

Bimal Prasad

Jayaprakash Narayan and Nepal

A number of Indian socialist leaders actively participated in the struggle for Democracy in Nepal. Jayaprakash Narayan - popularly known as JP- was one of the most inspiring among them. He had a great passion for freedom and democracy not only in India, but in other neighbouring countries including Tibet and Nepal. JP as a national statesman stood for end of monarchy and rule of law and democracy because of his personal passion for it. The other personal element behind his soft corner for democratic movement in Nepal lay in his personal association with the legendary Nepalese Congress leader Late Bisheshwar Prasad Koirala, who was also referred to as BP in his own country and elsewhere. BP Koirala who was spearheading a movement against the rule of the Ranas in Nepal was very closely associated with the Congress Socialist Party of India led by Jayaprakash Narayan. In fact, BP was once arrested in Banaras during the Quit India Movement of 1942. In 1946, BP Koirala was also elected as the Joint Secretary of the Socialist Party in Bihar which provided him an opportunity to come closer to JP. Koirala had a very charming personality and so had JP, both came closer.

BP formed the Nepalese Congress and became the foremost leader of Democratic Movement in Nepal which was fighting against the Rana Oligarchy. The Rana dynasty was founded by the one Mr.Jang Bahadur, leading to Rana autocracy. It ruled the Kingdom of Nepal from 1846 until 1953, reducing the Shah monarch to a figurehead and making Prime Minister and other government positions hereditary. The Rana dynasty developed into a powerful family clan . The family formed a close alliance with the Shah dynasty through marriage and business alliances. The Ranas were staunchly pro-British, and assisted the British during the Sepoy Rebellion in 1857, and later in both World Wars. In 1923 the United Kingdom and Nepal formally signed an agreement of friendship, truth, and law, in which Nepal's independence was recognised by the UK. Under the British Raj, the Ranas were acclaimed and given much prestige. Under the rule of the Ranas Democratic Freedom was not known in Nepal. The emerging pro-democracy movements and political parties in Nepal were critical of the Rana autocracy. JP openly supported this movement which also involved the use of arms. He (JP) was so keenly interested in the end of Rana regime that he arranged supply of arms through Burma. Aung San, father of Burmese democracy icon and Nobel Peace laureate Aung San Suu Kyi, was very close to JP who helped in arranging arms for the movement of Democratic rule in Nepal. Aung San was a Burmese revolutionary, nationalist, and a founder of Communist Party of Burma He was instrumental in bringing about Burma's independence from British colonial rule but was assassinated six months before its final achievement. He is recognized as the leading architect of independence, and the founder of the Union of Burma. Aung San is still widely admired by the Burmese people, and his name is still invoked in Burmese politics to this day. However, It was the veteran socialist leader and a former CM of Odisha, Late Mr. Biju Patnaik, who brought these arms to Nepal. Thus in the early 1940s, while the anti-British movement was intensified in India, the movement against the Rana regime gained momentum in Nepal. Jayaprakash Narayan, Rammanohar Lohia, and many other Indian leaders took active part in the movement against the Rana in Nepal. Jayaprakash Narayan and Rammanohar Lohia were arrested and imprisoned in Nepal. Because Krishna Prasad Koirala had allowed JP to hide in his home, he was arrested in Morang and was put in Kathmandu Jail, where he subsequently died in 1944. In order to escape the Ranas, on November 6, 1950, King Tribhuvan left the palace with his family and took shelter at the Indian Embassy. As Prince Gyanendra who was merely three and half years old then was left behind at the palace, the Rana declared Prince Gyanendra as the King on November 8, 1950. On November 10, 1950, India sent two airplanes to bring the King and his family to India, and King Tribhuvan left Nepal with his family. Following this Nepali Congress declared armed struggle against the Rana rule. On February 12, 1951 the Rana, Nepali Congress, and India Government agreed for what is referred to as "Delhi Samjhauta". Accordingly, King Tribhuvan returned to Nepal on February 15, 1951, and declared democracy in Nepal ending 104 years of the Rana rule on February 18, 1951.Thus, The movement against the Rana achieved some success. Following that king Tribhuvan became the King of Nepal and MP Koirala (BP's brother) became the PM.

However, tension developed between the brothers -BP and MP. BP Koirala was more charismatic leader but because of the intervention of the then Prime Minister of India, Pt. Nehru, MP became the Prime Minister of Nepal. JP was never guided by personal considerations in politics or in other sphere of public life, therefore he brought the Koirala brothers closer again.

In 1955, King Tribhuvan was succeeded by his son king Mahendra who proved to be a man of greater ambition. In the new regime the politicians were marginalised with powers centralised in the king. However , in course of development King Mahendra was forced to call a general election in 1959. This was the first general election in the history of Nepal. . In this general election the Nepali Congress swept the poll. Out of the109 elected seats it captured 74 . And , following this historic victory in 1959 General Elections, BP Koirala became the first Elected Prime Minister of Nepal. But unfoıtunately, it did not last long. B.P could hold this office merely for 18 months. His charismatic personality and his personal acquaintance with the leaders and head of the states in India and China and at the United Nations during his foreign visits were apprehended by the king. This finally culminated into a clash developed between him and king Mahendra. The ambitious King was put him behind the bar. JP wrote a letter to king Mahendra and personally visited Nepal to seek the immediate release of BP. Koirala. King's supporter in Nepal were so annoyed with this act of JP that they demonstrated against him, but he was determined.

After he was released, BP Koirala came to India and continued his struggle against the King in Nepal. JP was with him on this score but Nehru as prime minister of India had some very strong reservations . He was not in favour of the Indian soil being used against the King of Nepal which in the opinion of Nehru was a foreign sovereign nation. JP wrote two strong letters to Nehru expressing his displeasure over his attitude. JP argued that to support a democratic movement which is struggling for the end of dynastic rule in foreign nation is just and natural. I remember when I raise this issue with JP during an interview with him in 1978 and asked, "Recently you asked the King of Nepal to release Shri BP Koirala. How do you defend this in view of the fact that Nepal is a sovereign country and it is an accepted norm of international relations that one country should not interfere with the internal affairs of another?" His reply was, " Well that applies to leaders of government, not to a person like myself who does not hold any office in the government. I have been a fighter for freedom all my life and for me, National frontiers are of no significance. If freedom is in peril, anywhere I, as an humble citizen of this world, have a right to raise my voice. India and Nepal are close neighbours and I cannot just shut my eyes to what is happening there simply because Nepal is another country." My this conservation with JP is part of a book on him, whose title was suggested by the Loknayak himself.[1]

During Emergency rule of 70's in India, the then Prime Minister Mrs. Indira Gandhi even asked BP Koirala to go back to Nepal. Like her father Pandit Jawaharlal Nehru , she as prime minister did not approve BP's intervention into internal affairs of Nepal while operating from India. But in certain quarters it is still believed that her objection was more because of BP Koirala's close association with Jayaprakash Narayan, who was leading a movement against Emergency in India. JP also advised Koirala to go back. After Emergency, when Janata Party came to power in 1978, it was the party president Chandra Shekhar -former Prime Minister - who very forcefully spoke in favour of democratic rule in Nepal in Indian Parliament and outside. Thus, the movement for the establishment of Democracy in Nepal which was supported by greater Indian socialists like Jayaprakash Narayan has a rich memorable past which continues to inspire many in India and outside even today.

---

[1]Prasad, B (edt.) (1978). A revolutionary's quest: Selected writings of Jayaprakash Narayan.

Pushpesh Pant

Many Nepal, Many India

Much before I learnt that Nepal was a landlocked Kingdom, the only Hindu nation in the world and Kathmandu was its Capital I was aware of Doti, a remote region in western Nepal in Mahakali anchal. This is where all the Dotiyals came from who comprised majority of the labour force employed by the Indian Veterinary Research Institute in Mukteshwar where I grew up as a child in the early 1950's. They lived in coolie lines constructed by the British and performed all tasks that involved hard physical labour - carrying heavy loads, chopping wood, fetching water, tending to cattle etc. Ironically, few had any knowledge of their country besides a vague idea that their sovereign was Paanch Sarkar, the Maharaja of Nepal who ruled their lives. They were totally ignorant of the fact that the Gorkhas had ruled this tract of land not very long ago.

The Dotiyal identity was very different from the gorkhas who were employed as supervisor 'mates'. They spoke their own dialect and practiced a religion that was more animistic than orthodox Hinduism. Their priests were Dhamis who multi-tasked: discharging shamanistic duties of an extortionist when required, maintaining accounts of wages, loans and debts, arbitrating disputes, house breaking new recruits. The community was broadly divided among the so called upper castes maljaatiya and others. Suffixes to their names were indicative of the caste status - Mohaniya Sunar, Kashi Luar were exceptions, most made do with abbreviations like Nautiya, Dhauliya and Kalu. What needs to be underlined that the Dotiyal though hailing from Nepal were not treated as foreigners - they were lumped together with other impoverished and illiterate Pahari people living in remote villages cut off from civilization in Kumaon. Residents of Danpur Patti for instance or those from Kali Kumaon also walked for a week to reach Almora (the district headquarter) or Mukteshwar. For generations Doti has had much closer contact with adjacent Indian territories to the west than with regions of Nepal lying to its east. Just the river kali separates the two countries in Uttarakhand and is easily spanned by rope bridges. At places like Jhulaghat all weather bridges have made crossings much less hazardous. The man made political border remains blurred and the frontier fuzzy. Shauka tribal trans-Himalayan traders are denizens of a twilight zone who have easily melted into India and Nepal almost at will. But all this was learnt much later. What one imbibed unforgettably in that idyllic innocent childhood was that 'people living on the other side of the river' were not enemies or aliens, they were just like us and in some cases relatives by blood or marriage.

Baitadi shone just a stone's throw away with its stone-slated roofs reflecting the sunlight and the playful clouds creating a patchwork of shadows on its terraced fields didn't take too long to move over to our side of the river.

II

There were a number of fellow students from Nepal when I joined college in Nainital in 1961. They distanced themselves from compatriot Dotiyals who eked out a living as porters, dandi bearers and rickshaw pullers. It was impossible to remain blind to the class divide. This is not to suggest that India then appeared as a more egalitarian society free from deprivation and inhuman discrimination but the parts of the country directly ruled by the British had certainly rid themselves of a feudal mindset to a large extent and the process had continued apace after independence. The behavior of Nepalese classmates to elders in the family, and those perceived as superiors was different - much more reverential.

A class mate later became for a brief term in office the prime minister of Nepal; another rose through ranks to hold office as deputy governor of Nepal Rashtra Bank and a member of the Election Commission. A senior with brilliant academic career closely related to our principal and joined the foreign service in Nepal and served as ambassador to the UN and Foreign Secretary. The scions of middle class families were acutely aware of the shortage of educated manpower in Nepal and the opportunities awaiting there. They looked forward to availing these and planned accordingly. They claimed and were recognized as scheduled tribes as Indian citizen and once had obtained the required qualification could and did acquire Nepalese citizenship. This was the time when I first realized that Nepal and India were two separate entities and however close and cordial our relationship may have been, there could be a conflict of interests and some of us have would have to make difficult choices in future.

The Sino-Indian Border War in 1962 turned out to be the time of reckoning. Nepal, till then a steadfast friend of India, uncomplaining and dependent, taken for granted by insensitive Indians - both in government and business - decided to remain strictly neutral. King Mahendra who had succeeded Maharaja Tribhuwan was beginning to assert an independent role and had introduced basic Panchayati form of democracy in Nepal. This did not find favour with Indian government who had never hidden their sympathies for Nepali Congress and the Koirala brothers. Panchayat system, it feared would mean the end of constitutional monarchy and destroy the multi-party system. The irritants that had remained submerged surfaced suddenly and multiplied. The conflict in national interests was stridently highlighted. Increasing Chinese presence in Nepal as aid workers and the warm welcome they received was viewed apprehensively by India. Nepal started opening embassies in different countries and criticizing the 'unfair' treaty of 1950. The following decade was full of tensions, diplomatic crises and unpleasant exchanges.

I was extremely fortunate to find an erudite and wise Nepali teacher and make friends with this brilliant young Nepali at the time when I moved to Delhi in 1965 to the Indian School of International Studies. This saved me from falling into the trap of 'patriotic' defense of Indian national interest vis-a-vis Nepal and helped me broaden my mental horizon beyond Doti. Prof. Ishwar Baral had recently returned from London and was close to the Nepali Congress. Earlier he had studied in Banaras. Well versed in Sanskrit he was familiar with the work of Gumani a celebrated Kumaoni poet of 18th-19th century. Though he himself belonged to the terai region, he had great affinity for the hills and hill people. Dr. Baral shared very generously with me his personal memories full of priceless insights into the lives of Nepalese in India encompassing in a fantastic sweep the crescent from Patna to Pithoragarh, blending magically space and time. He was a walking-talking encyclopedia who had inherited a vast body of traditional knowledge that Nepalese Brahmins were privy too and had enhanced this with the riches gleaned from an English education. A person with refined taste he had spent most of his adult life as an exile in India. He was awarded a scholarship by the palace as a promising young scholar but had become a persona non grata when he fell under the spell of BP Koirala and was drawn to Nepali Congress. A person of refined literary tastes and old world charm he was something of a misfit at the School of International studies. How one wishes that he were better utilized there! But I digress. Baral Sab was the one who sensitized me to the dazzling diversity - geographical, ethnic, cultural and political. Nepal was and is and always will be much more than Doti plus Gorkhaland. It is home to Magar, Tamang, Limbu, Rai, Newar, Sherpa, Madhesia and many more. It has as rich a Buddhist legacy as its Hindu inheritance. Though it was recognized as a monarchy for most of the 20th century but some members of its educated elite had been closely involved with India's freedom struggle and had forged close ties with Indian Socialists. BP was seen as a Nepali Nehru and Chandrashekhar was a Koirala family friend. All this is common knowledge for all Nepal experts. But it is perhaps important to recall this shared past for the benefit of young Indians. It is important not to forget that like India different parts of Nepal have a distinct personality and Indians as well as Nepalese have images of each other primarily based on 'what they have experienced where'. Those who interacted with poets and writers, scholars and political activists obviously treated each other as peers. For them stereotypes - the Ugly Indian, Marwari or Sarkari and the dependable and dependent at the same time 'Bahadur' did not matter. But for the majority of people in both nations life was lived in black and white; it had no gray shades. What is equally significant is that Nepal meant much more to people in Almora-Pithoragarh, Gorakhpur-Deoria, Patna-Banaras, Sikkim-Darjiling than it did to those far removed from the neighbour in the plains, peninsula or the coastal belt. In past few years distances have shrunk and technology has homogenized life style at least in urban settlements. Satellite based television transmission has created a dangerous illusion that we are eye witnesses to events unfolding near and far and that this vicarious personal contact renders redundant any need for historical study or exercising sociological imagination. Memories of 'Many Indias and Many Nepals' are fading fast.

III

Years later, in the early 1990's, while shooting a documentary I spent a fortnight in east Champaran in Bihar. We were repeatedly invited by our local host to cross the border and visit Nepal. He was very enthusiastic about escorting us to a 'foreign land' without a passport. The temptations offered were duty free shopping and imported beer and other alcoholic beverages. We crossed over to Birganj and that's when I discovered that Nepal next door was (or at least appeared) richer than 'our' Indian side. Electric supply was meager and erratic in Betia and elsewhere, roads were full of potholes and abject poverty glared at you on the face. People were grossly malnourished, ill clad and seemed resigned to their sad state. Birganj bustling with energy and its roads lined with dazzling shops presented a picture in contrast. Prosperity of its residents was visible. Most of the day time population comprised frenzied Indian tourists who were on an unabashed shopping spree Chinese umbrellas, fountain pens, cameras, textiles and toys. This was before the economic reforms and liberalization in India that dismantled the customs regime. Birganj, at that time, appeared a poor man's Singapore, Hong Kong or Dubai. When a friend accompanying us asked how he could carry the heavy duffel bag loaded with contraband stuff back home, he was reassured that the customs personnel on both sides of the border were quite accommodating and delivery could be arranged at a small consideration. What was interesting was that most of 'residents' we came across were Nepali speaking Indians, very few Nepalis who returned home via this entry point could be spotted making purchases. It was clear that they had already done their shopping in India. Later that evening our host shared with us the secret that much of the imported "phoren" stuff in this town was actually 'made in Ludhiana' and only marked 'made in China'. This 'gateway town', like many other settlements on Indo-Nepal border, was obviously catering primarily to tourist traffic.

What was striking was that here, despite all the talk about 'blurred international boundaries' and 'fuzzy frontiers' the mental divide between India and Nepal was sharply marked and the place had a very different ambience from that at the Jhulaghat or Mahendranagar. Access may have been easier but obviously there was no palpable sense of kinship between the people. Ironically, the Indians didn't seem embarrassed about poverty and squalor and lack of development on 'this side'. All that mattered was that an affordable playground was available. They seem to be taking a perverse pride in showing off their 'ownership'. Much later, when traveling in and around Gorakhpur and Deoria one had a strong sense of déjà vu when once again the highlight of the trip was touted as an excursion into Nepal-Maharajganj and beyond.

IV

Sikkim circa 1980's was very different from either Jhulaghat or Birganj. Here Nepalese were the Kings. Lepcha-Bhutia, the original inhabitants of the Bemyul Dzong had steadily dwindled in population ever since 'annexation' of the Himalayan kingdom by India and Nepalese had emigrated in large numbers from neighbouring Darjiling and eastern Bhutan. With large numbers in their favour they have easily succeeded in dominating electoral politics. This is one state in India where people of Nepalese origin are not playing subservient or subordinate roles. Sikkim is adjacent to West Bengal where for decades past the demand for an independent Gorkhaland has been shrilly articulated. At times the agitation has become violent, and assumed secessionist overtones, openly flouting the sovereignty of the country and holding the tea estates into ransom. Motor vehicles plying in the region are forced to pay illegal toll and taxes, quite a few sympathizers to the cause sport Gorkha Land number plates. The state governments and the Central government have considered discretion the better part of valour and have treaded with extreme caution, bordering on timidity. They have tried to cope with the challenge by keeping the negotiations open and holding out the promise of autonomy short of independence.

Two things need to be highlighted in this context. Darjiling and the territories around it were ceded by Nepal to the British after the Anglo-Nepal War in 1816-17. Many in Nepal continue to look at this tract of land as their own and fuel irredentist fantasies of 'Greater Nepal' focused on these. Recently, when the then foreign secretary of India Shiva Shankar Menon visited Nepal he was greeted with black flags by youngsters demanding that India return the territories that the British had seized and annexed from Nepal. Shyam Sharan, another senior Indian diplomat on a tour of Nepal also had to cope with a similar irritant.

What has made the matter more sensitive is that the Gorkhaland agitation was spearheaded by an ex-Indian army serviceman- Subhash Gheshing. This has lent a scary edge to the problem that if the situation is mishandled it could easily get out of control and breed disaffection amongst a large number of serving and retired Nepali soldiers. Nor can it be forgotten that Nepali immigrants have been a constant source of worry for Bhutan. Their influx is perceived as threatening by the Bhutanese who feel that the alien way of life of these people belonging to a different ethnic stock is altering the demographic profile of their country and if not checked can make Bhutanese culture extinct. What has mattered worse is the increase in violent crime in districts where Nepali population is concentrated. Long time Nepali residents, some of them for generations, on the other hand have complained of victimization and violation of human rights. The UN has taken cognizance of the problem and is also sensitive to the apprehensions of Bhutan. Refugee relief has been accorded priority.

Nepal for the past two decades has been in the throes of a Maoist rebellion. The insurgency directed against an oppressive, unbridled monarchy led to large parts of Nepal falling under the control of insurgents. In the disturbed circumstances 'security' threats real or imaginary distorted the perception of mutual relations between neighbours - India, Bhutan and Nepal. (The Maoist uprising, it may be recalled, had originated in Jhapa - eastern most region of Nepal; Naxalbari where the Maoist insurgency had ignited in 1969 isn't very far from the junction of Assam, West Bengal and Sikkim. Anti-Indian insurgencies have simmered endemically in the north eastern states of Nagaland, Mizoram, Manipur and more recently in Assam. This is what makes it imperative that the Gorkhaland issue is not allowed to blow up and is defused. Relations with Nepal in the eastern India have a totally different complexion than in Uttarakhand or Uttar Pradesh.

V

Problem with many Indians is that suffering from a time warp they remain blind to far- reaching changes that have taken place in Nepal. South Block has remained sadly blinkered and still can't turn its gaze away from Durbar

Marg in Kathmandu. Nepal has abolished monarchy and doesn't particularly identify itself as a Hindu nation. It is keen, and understandably so, to assert its separate identity. Obviously, Hinduism or Buddhism isn't enough to sustain a mutually beneficial relationship. Nor can popular culture necessarily provide the corner stone. Bollywood has moved a long way from the days of Mala Sinha. Gone are the days when picture post card images of Pokhra and song and dance sequences shot against breathtaking scenery in Nepal a la Devanand's Ishq Ishq Ishq and Jewel Thief could enthrall royal audiences and ensure enduring cordial relations. Stereotyped images in Hindi films, in any case seem to have provided irritants rather than an emollient. Depiction of the Nepalese as gullible goof or a drunkard hasn't gone down well with Nepalese. There have been times when a ban on Indian films and television channels has been demanded and unofficially imposed.

By the end of the 1960's it was clear that the Americans were not and couldn't win the war in Vietnam. The hippies descended on India in large number. The younger generation was disenchanted with their own government and social culture. Indian-Nepalese societies beckoned them. Kathmandu became the Mecca for the lost 'beat generation'. The drop outs made parts of the Nepalese Capital their own. Easy availability of marijuana, cheap accommodation and leisurely pace of life in the lap of beautiful Himalayas attracted foreigners like a strong magnet. This was when areas like Thamel grew and acquired a reputation-not always enviable-as 'Freak Street'.

Nepal, long closed to the world outside except adjoining regions of India, was suddenly exposed to a diversity of alien influences and repeatedly jolted with cultural shocks. Young Nepalese learnt to speak not only English fast but also acquired a saleable smattering of French and German. Catering to the needs of backpacking tourists inspired self taught entrepreneurs to provide these services'. This is not the place to review and analyze the impact of this on Nepalese society or to comment on how this has created, serious problems of uneven regional development and adversely impacted on environment; suffice it to note that this experience unleashed a powerful tide of rising expectation at the same time unveiling options other than India where a better future could be explored. This was the time when young Nepalese began to migrate for study or employment to Japan, Germany, the USA and the UAE. With passage of time the Diaspora assumed a critical mass. Free from any nostalgic baggage, this post-Beat generation articulated its aspirations very different from their parents. India, was next door but more distant destination appeared both more accessible and hospitable. They didn't have to cope with the problem of being treated as stereotypes or the 'Big Brother' syndrome.

While youngsters in Nepal were being drawn to other foreign countries, and beginning to view the world forsaking the Indian prism, in India too, the 'image' of the Nepali was changing. For generations, Nepali-Gorkha had always been considered the epitome of loyalty and selfless service but involvement of a number of rootless Nepali domestic servants in heinous crime- shocking gruesome murders, burglary, drug-trafficking and flesh trade dealt it a severe blow. After a spate of news items appeared in the Capital's press almost overnight all illiterate, impoverished Nepali became 'suspects'. No one had the time or inclination to examine the provocation or complicity of Indian partners in crime.

This suspicion was, most unfortunately, fuelled unwittingly by the Indian government, who was about this time getting concerned about the Maoist threat spilling over from Nepal into India. It was believed, by law enforcement agencies that even hitherto law abiding guest workers could in changed circumstances be tempted or coerced to harbor outlaws from 'home'. Employers were advised to undertake proper surveillance and police verification was encouraged.

Perhaps it needs to be added that this hostility was not directed ethnically against only the Nepalese. Other immigrants like those from Bangladesh- most of them illegal-have suffered because of such targeting. Nor have Indian citizen lacking proper documentation like ration cards, voters ID from Rajasthan, Orissa, UP and Bihar have had to suffer humiliation due to insensitive statements of the administration.

Till the 1960's the ambition of most Nepali youth born in villages didn't extend beyond recruitment in Indian Army. Those belonging to middle class families coveted 'seats' in Indian medical and engineering colleges. Those with right political contacts sought to ensure admissions through recommendations of Indian Embassy or the external affairs ministry. All this changed dramatically in the next two decades. Nepalese have always been exceptionally footloose and intrepid travelers. Once away from home they are not deterred by long distances, arduous journeys and tough working conditions. One comes across them literally from Ladakh to Cape Cameron.

I vividly recall a chance encounter with a pleasant young taxi driver named Bharat in Mumbai who shared his dreams of soon 'moving over' to Qatar/Dubai to earn enough money fast to buy his own car and run it as a taxi in Kathmandu. Then, there was this teenaged domestic drudge who was saving up to pay a labour agent who had assured him that he could be employed as a tandooriya in some restaurant abroad and was always pouring over a Rapidex English teacher to learn spoken English. Uma, who used to work with us had her brother working as a guard in Sharjah and had sent enough money back in just three years for his parents to buy some land and build a nice house in the village. She constantly nagged her husband to follow in his footsteps!

Whole wide world today beckons young Indians and Nepalese but there are times when one is reminded that both find it difficult to part ways even if pleasantly. Emotional bonds are no less compelling than strategic or commercial imperatives. One chilly winter morning when I was walking around the square in Patan the disheveled guide surprised me with his bilingual fluency and knowledge of history and culture that he was encapsulating and communicating brilliantly. When he joined us for tea I discovered that he was a Nepali born and brought up in Dehradoon and an Indian citizen who had migrated to Kathmandu in 'search of a better future when he failed to get gainfully employed 'there'!

Hari Kishore Singh

The Political Impasse in Nepal
Implications for India and South Asia

The ongoing crises in Nepalese politics is a direct by-product of the failure of democratic forces in providing good governance after the abolition of Monarchy. The then government in Nepal had agreed to abolish Monarchy as part of a deal to persuade Maoist former rebels to rejoin the interim administration. As per the deal, Nepal was agreed to be declared a republic after a general election and a new Constituent Assembly. The Maoists had pulled out of the government earlier, demanding an immediate end to the monarchy. The deal was signed by Nepal's main parties, including the Maoists. The six-party ruling alliance and the Maoists said in a joint statement: "Nepal will be a federal democratic republic nation and the decision will be implemented after the first meeting of the Constituent Assembly." With the abolition of Monarchy, the Himalayan nation of Nepal became the world's newest republic, ending 240 years of monarchical rule. But, however, after the abolition of Monarchy, the Nepali Congress and the Left failed to give an effective government which was sabotaged by the Maoists who were out to grab total power in Nepal. This has led to the present impasse in Nepal.

Nepal, Like India, is not a homogeneous country. It is broadly divided into three physio-graphic areas: the Mountain Region, the Hill Region, and the Terai Region. All three parallel each other, from east to west, as continuous ecological belts, occasionally bisected by the country's river systems. These ecological regions were divided by the government into development sectors within the framework of regional development planning. These three geographical regions--Himalayan (mountains), Hill, and the Terai (flatlands once covered by forest) are divided administratively into 5 regions, 14 zones, and 75 districts, where regional commissioners heads each region, while chief district officers head the districts to look after the day-to-day administrative matters, maintaining law and-order, and coordinating works of the field agencies of different ministries.

There are diverse elements contending for their respective share in the power structure and economic development. One such prominent element contending for share in power and development in Nepal is the three geographical areas mentioned above. Any solution to the longstanding problem in Nepal lay in resolving the conflicting interest between these regions.

There is a caste angle, too. For majority of the people living in the territorial boundaries of the modern Nepali state, especially after the promulgation of the National Code or Muluki Ain in 1854 , the caste system has been a major determinant of their identity, social status and life chances. As in India, here, too everyone was organized in terms of their relative ritual purity into the four broad varnas of the classical Hindu caste system: the Brahman, priests; the Kshatriya, kings and warriors; the Vaisya, traders and businessmen; and the Shudras, peasants and laborers , with an additional group technically "outside" the caste system because of their ritually defiling occupations which rendered them "untouchable" by others. Since 1950, the power structure at the mass level in Nepal has been dominated by the Brahmins; all political parties including the Nepalese Congress and the Maoists have Brahminical leadership. The concentration of leadership in the elitist Brahmins is yet another crucial reason for the current impasse. In the last two decades there has been awakening in the terai area leading to the rise of Madhesia Movement. People belonging to various groups which constitute Madhesi have asserted themselves and now occupy important places in the power structure including the presidency. The backbone of Madhesi Movement is constituted by the OBC factor which has to be adjusted properly in the new power structure in order to satisfy their aspirations and ego. The Terai region of Nepal is the long strip of the plains of Nepal adjoining Indian territory inhabited by the Madhesis, an ethnic group of Nepal of Áwadhi, Maithili and Bhojpuri descent. They form 35% of the Nepalese population. Despite their sizeable population, they have long been discriminated as second class citizens of Nepal in terms of job opportunities in administration and in representation in political set-up; this, despite the fact that the Madhesis and the Terai region make an overwhelming contribution to Nepali's economy, in both agriculture and industry. The Madhesi political turbulence that recently surfaced in Nepal can be said to be also a spillover of the new political dynamics that the Nepalese Maoists imposed on Nepal through their armed insurgency and their recent back-door entry into Nepali' political space, of upsetting the status quo. The Madhesis too seem to be asking for a change of status-quo in the discrimination that they have suffered so far.

Thus, Nepal's ethnic and linguistic diversity, coupled with the sheer physical barriers that have discouraged the construction of a dense nationwide transport and communications network, continue to pose severe challenges to the country's development .In addition, the social cleavages originating in the caste system continue to obstruct the welfare of the vast majority of people in Nepal. Once a means of controlling scarce labour resources as well as preserving social order, these intricate divisions now prevent most of the country's citizens from contributing to national progress as well as raising their own living standard.

The Maoists, who had shown a tilt of accommodation during the Movement against Monarchy, failed to abide by their commitment after dethroning of King Gyanendra and abolition of Monarchy in Nepal. Because, after the elections to Constituent Assembly, they did not agree to the election of Girija Prasad Koirala as the first president of the Republic. This was taken as a betrayal of the consensus that had emerged during the movement against Monarchy. The former premier had played a pivotal role in the peace process, Nepal's transition to democracy and bringing the Maoists into the mainstream politics. Koirala was instrumental in the signing of the 12-point agreement between the then Maoist rebels and seven political parties in November 2005 in New Delhi, which was aimed at toppling monarchy and restoring democracy in the country. After this, Maoists joined the mainstream politics in 2006, ending the decade-long armed conflict that left some 16,000 people dead. Girija Prasad Koirala was the universally acclaimed leader of Nepal and he richly deserved to be the first president of Nepal. It was Koirala who had proposed the motion to abolish monarchy through voting during the first meeting of the Constituent Assembly on May 28, 2008, which was endorsed by an overwhelming majority of the

601-member House.

But the lust for power and glory in the Maoists led by K.D. Prachanda spoiled the story and led to the present chaotic situation. In June 2008, a group of leftist intellectuals met the Maoist Chairman Prachanda at his residence in Naya Bazaar. During the meeting, they said that Prime Minister Girija Prasad Koirala should not be made the first president of the country. The intellectuals urged the Maoist chairman not to reach any understanding on electing Nepali Congress President GP Koirala the country's first president, as he does not "reflect people's wishes". "We have not changed our official stance. People's mandate as expressed through the CA polls is against making Girija Prasad Koirala the first president," one of the leftist participants reportedly quoted Prachanda as telling them.

For the South Asian region, this anarchy in Nepal is a matter of great concern and this is truer for India because of its unique strategic geographical location. Nepal is very important for India. It acts like a buffer state between India and China with whom we fought a humiliating war in 1962 and we cannot remain a silent spectator to the development in this tiny republic, especially more when there is a Maoist rule. In the long stretch of India's borders with Tibet, the Chinese hold is broken only by Nepal and Bhutan. Nepal, therefore, keeps Chinese military presence away from India for a stretch of hundreds of kilometers. Culturally, the fact that Nepal is predominantly a Hindu nation the cannot be ignored by secular India, as Indian Hindus comprising over 80% of India's population have a special attachment to it. Nepal is rated as one of the poorest countries in the world and India has been the main benefactor of Nepal as it has been providing substantial aid to Nepal.

Peace and stability in Nepal is in the larger interest of the south Asian region. The Nepalese capital, Kathmandu, offices the headquarters of SAARC, which includes countries like India, Pakistan, Bangladesh, Nepal, Bhutan, Sri Lanka, Maldives and Afghanistan. Founded in 1985, SAARC is an organization dedicated to economic, technological, social, and cultural development emphasizing collective self-reliance. SAARC is supposed to be the nodal agency for economic development of member countries which inhibit a large chunk of humanities. Approximately, 150 crore people inhibit this area. The SAARC region has natural potential for development. If it is properly developed, it will become more prosperous. Perpetual trouble and political instability in Nepal is likely to cause tremor in the neighbouring country like India and in other member nations of the SAARC. One major danger faced by many of the SAARC nations is the challenge posed by terrorism of diverse kind. During the recent past India has been a major victim of terrorist activities. And the territory of the troublesome Nepal is reportedly used in conspiring terrorist activities in India. According to one assessment, "India has become the victim of another kind of terrorism from its neighbour, Pakistan. It is economic terrorism in printing and circulating counterfeit Indian notes. The Pakistani intelligence agency, ISI's role in printing and circulation of fake Indian currency notes has never been a secret...The ISI has been using Pakistan International Airlines (PIA) to transport counterfeit currency to its conduits in Nepal, Bangladesh and Sri Lanka. The modus operandi of the ISI was revealed by two Nepali counterfeit currency traffickers who were arrested by Thailand police sometimes back. During interrogation, the accused disclosed that they were working for a prominent Nepali businessman. The fact that Nepalese territory is being used by Pakistanis to smuggle counterfeit currency is well known." (emphasis added)

It is, therefore, a great tragedy that Nepal continues to struggle through political crisis. The lack of understanding and confidence between the two major members of the SAARC countries, India and Pakistan, also adversely affect the political development in Nepal. Hopefully, a good sense prevail among major power players in Nepal and they settle down in the larger interest of people of the Himalayan Republic.

Lok Raj Baral

Nepal-India Relations
Formal Treaty and Beyond

Countries' relations are not guaranteed by formal treaties alone. Many other factors and determinants shape inter-state relations. Nepal-India relations are no exception to such natural and compelling factors. Even with the formal security treaty, Nepal's geo-political situation imposes certain guidelines that can hardly go against either of the two neighbours. Nepal's policy therefore needs to be balanced despite being too close to its southern neighbour. The emerging regional and international politics have further shrunk Nepal's options forcing it to be more prudent to pursue a correct policy towards its neighbours. It does not mean that Nepal's overarching relations with India stands on equal footing with China despite the latter also being the next door neighbour. Such nuances and realities of India-Nepal relations have also been appreciated by China since it established diplomatic relations with Nepal. Recently, Chinese leaders, as in the past, were reported to have suggested the Nepali Maoist leaders including the Chairman of the party, Prachanda, that they should develop good relations with India. Geographical situation and functional interactions with the Southern neighbour have contributed to extensive and deep relations between Nepal and India.

Nevertheless, dealing with Nepal-India relations is not an easy ask. Half of their relations are characterized by informalities. It is always deep and extensive covering all areas such as civilizational commonalities, historical background, demographic identity (with north India), physical Structure of Nepal and its compulsions, economic interdependence, emerging geo-politics and its linkages with global politics, open border and its own dynamics and some of the most significant aspects of bilateral relations. The 1950 Treaty of Peace and Friendship encapsulates some of such fundamentals. Most important aspects covered by the Treaty are recognition of Nepal as an independent and sovereign state; mutually agreed security relationship; economic aspects, and people to people relations through the open border within which many things mentioned before are included. Prior to the signing of the Treaty, the then Prime Minister of India Pt. Jawaharlal Nehru had repeatedly spoken of the international status of an independent nation and policy of non-intervention in that country's internal affairs. Moreover, dead against as he was for forging alliances with other countries, he said that though India would not tolerate "any invasion of Nepal from anywhere... It is not necessary for us to have a military alliance with Nepal.[1]" Nehru had even repudiated the view of a leading politician, then hell bent on overthrowing the Rana regime, that Nepal and India could forge a joint Defence and Foreign policy. Such an expression came as a strategy to create a distance between the Indian government and the fledgling Rana oligarchy. Even the treaty of Sugauli (1815-16) had recognized Nepal as an independent country with which the victor (British) concluded the treaty, and later the 1923 Treaty further clarified the international status.

The 1950 Treaty was also an extension and modification of the former treaties in order to update the relevance of closer relations between the two. However, there has been a difference between the 1950 Treaty and the Treaty of Sugauli in one respect. The former was concluded between the victor and the vanquished; the latter was the product of mutually agreed parties for fulfilling the objectives of the two countries. Both the countries were prompted by their common threat perceptions of the coming of Red China in Tibet. The worldwide panic created by the rise of Communism in general and South of the Himalayas in particular led the three Himalayan Kingdoms (Bhutan, Nepal and Sikkim) to move closer to India. So the Clause Two of the 1950 Treaty attaches the importance of informing each other of "any serious friction or misunderstanding with any neighbouring state likely to cause any breach in its friendly relations subsisting between the two Governments." The Letter accompanying the Treaty is more explicit in explaining it stating that "neither government shall tolerate any threat

[1] See Jawaharlal Nehru's speech delivered in Parliament on March 17,1950 in Avtar Singh Bhasin, ed., *Nepal-India,Nepal-China Relations volume 1* (Delhi: Geetika Publishers, 2005), p.84

to the security of the other by a foreign aggressor. To deal with any such threat, the two Governments shall consult with each other and devise effective countermeasures.[2]"

Relating to the security aspect of the treaty, the issus of imports of arms, ammunition or warlike material and equipment for the security of Nepal have been addressed. But the Letter specifies this provision in Clause Two stating that such import of arms could be done by using the territory of India. Later, in 1965, it was agreed that in case India was unable to provide arms and ammunition, the US and the UK could fulfill the Nepali requirements in consultation with India. The Nepali side, however, interpreted the clause differently in 1989 when India objected to the import of arms and other weapons from China without consulting India. The royal government argued that since these arms came from the North and not through the territory of India, no question of violation of the treaty could be raised by India. Yet, the spirit of the Treaty and the accompanying letter allow Nepal only to import through the territory of India.

Another major component of the Treaty relates to the national treatment to be given to the peoples of both the countries. In participation in trade and commerce, movement and other privileges of similar nature, no discrimination would be made between the Nepalis and Indians. Article VII states: "The Governments of India and Nepal agree to grant, on a reciprocal basis, to the nationals of one country in the territories of the other the same privileges in the matter of residence, ownership of property, participation in trade and commerce, movement and other privileges of a similar nature." Regarding the development of natural resources or of development of industries etc., Nepal was/is required to give preference to the Indians.

Controversy over the Treaty

The 1950 Treaty is assailed as an unequal treaty as well as a framework for continuing the age old ties existing between the two countries. Criticisms that come from the political parties or from the so-called rashtravadis are based on some of these grounds:

---

[2] Text of the Treaty and Letter. Ibid. pp. 94-96.

- The treaty has outlived its utility and hence the abrogation or renewal of it;
- It has put a slur on Nepal's independence and sovereignty and needs to be changed;
- It is security-related treaty putting Nepal under the umbrella of India;
- The emergence of China and Nepal's formal diplomatic relatio with it and India makes it irrelevant for Nepal, for China is no longer a threat. It therefore nullifies the "special relation" as emphasized by India.
- It has threatened the existence of the country by allowing free movement of peoples across the border;
- Indians have been much benefited than the Nepalis; India is a big country where Nepalis figure as drops in the ocean, whereas Nepal is a small country, where the influx of Indians into Nepal would outnumber the Nepalis thereby posing a threat to the existence of the country itself.
- It is also argued that by granting citizenship certificates to as many people as possible without sound verification and in a haphazard manner was wrong. The open border might have been used by the people coming across the border.
- Tendency to encourage Indians to dominate the Nepali economic activities is also not fair.

The positive side of the treaty is no less significant and realistic. Some of the arguments made in favour of the treaty are:

- The 1950 Treaty has not diluted Nepal's independence, sovereignty and territorial integrity. On the contrary, Indian recognition of this aspect was/is more explicit even prior to the signing of the treaty.
- Nepal's physical location facing south and greater inter-connectedness between the two countries has imposed certain

constraints on Nepal. The structure of security relationship goes back to 1816 and 1923 and to other mutual arrangements made by the two countries. The recruitment of Gorkhas (Nepali) into the British and Indian armies has given impetus to close relation between Nepal and India. Moreover, Nepali youth population to be recruited into or retired from the Indian army themselves do not agree to end the treaty relations unless Nepal would develop its economic capacity to provide them gainful employment. Given the situation in the country, there seems to be no employment opportunities for those aspiring youth.

- The same logic can be applied to the poor people of Nepal who find easy access to the Indian job markets. In each adverse situation, these poverty-stricken Nepalis make beeline for going to India. Since no in-depth study has been done or survey made for finding the actual numbers of Nepalis in India, it is assumed that more than 6-7 million Nepalis are in India. Alluding to this dimension of Nepal-India relation, more than forty years ago, Myron Weiner, while writing a paper on the Political Demography of Nepal, remarked India as a "safety-valve [3]" for Nepal. Has Nepal developed economic capability for employing them within the country? Has not the 1950 treaty that entails open border regime helped maintain Nepal's security? As internal security is increasingly becoming more important than external threat, it has indeed salvaged Nepal from its multiple crises.

- It is said that it is an imposed treaty as the Ranas were dictated by India to stem the threat of Communist China. But it can safely be said that any realistic ruler of Nepal would not have ignored this fact. If any one would have rejected the Indian offer for renewal of old relations in view of the new geo-political reality, he/she would have been a naïve in dealing with foreign policy.

- The North Atlantic Treaty Organization continues today even after the collapse of communism. On the contrary, most of the East

---

[3] Myron Weiner, "The Political Demography of Nepal" in *Population and Development 2* (Kathmandu: CEDA, 1971).

European states, then satellites of the Soviet Union or even present Russia, are moving closer to the NATO or the European Union. So it was a timely decision taken by the Rana rulers. How pragmatism worked when King Mahendra, the author of the so-called "Nepali Rashtrabad", continued the treaty. Although the Rana rulers were pushed to the wall by both India and the anti-Rana forces while concluding the treaty, the domestic political dynamics needed to be isolated from the changed regional environment.

- The argument that the Ranas on their own might have tried to please India for prolonging their regime, but that alone did not make points in the changed context. Even after the signing of the treaty, India put pressure to democratize the regime by going too far for holding election to a constituent assembly as well as for starting the era of party politics.
- The Indians view the 1950 treaty as unequal for them and the manner the Nepali politicians raise this issue is not based on reality. For Nepal it has become one of the issues for political mobilization and politicians use this strategy when they are short of issues. Observations made by some scholars that Nepalis would be the sufferer by the annulment of the treaty deserve to be examined in order to find a better perspective of the treaty. For, Nepalis are the principal beneficiaries in education, health and employment sectors in India,[4] let alone the recruitment of Nepalis into the Indian army.
- Symbolically also, Nepal's international status has never been compromised. Nor have the policy decisions taken by Nepal on various bilateral, regional and international issues ever been strongly challenged by India. Nepal was much ahead of India while establishing diplomatic relations with Israel and other countries. Pakistan which was/is a bête noire for India fluttered its flag in Kathmandu in the late 1950s. Nepal's independent approaches

[4] For a defferent interpretation of the 1950 Treaty, see Uddhab Pyakuel," Rashtiyatako Kasima 1950 Treaty (1950 Treaty in the Context of Nationalism), *Kantipur*, February 24,2010

to international issues validate that the 1950 treaty is not at all a hindrance to Nepal's development. Both in symbol and substance, Nepal occupies an important place in the comity of nations.

Then where does the problem lie? Can Nepal develop fully without the treaty? Is India the only factor for all its problems? Can Nepal pursue an insular policy towards India in order to be fully independent? Some of the Indian experts have often cautioned Nepali leaders against opening the "Pandora box" [1950 Treaty] without taking into account the entire gamut of bilateral relations. Muchkund Dubey, former foreign secretary of India and a scholar, has stated:

> In my view, the review or revision of the Treaty is not a priority issue in Indo-Nepal relations. There are other issues---like water resources, economic development of Nepal, imparting strength, resilience and stability to the democratic process in Nepal etc., which deserve priority attention. I am afraid , undertaking a review of the Treaty would open a Pandora's box [that] will cloud all other important issues and may adversely affect relations in the medium run if it is not handled properly. And given the emotive character of the issue of the review of the Treaty, it is not at all going to be easy to come out unscathed from the review[5].

It seems that the 1950 Treaty has been dragged into controversy since its signing in 1950. As Rose has also remarked that "demands for revision of the treaty were voiced almost immediately after its ratification, and the Ranas were accused of 'anti nationalism' for having accepted the treaty [6]". Most critics, especially "the Rashtrabadis" and the some Left parties, have often joined the chorus against it without however offering an objective analysis for its abrogation; some critical points mentioned before are short of practical solutions.

Internal politics and India-Nepal relations

Another factor that often gives rise to controversy in Nepal-India relations

---

[5] See in Particular, Muchkud Dubey, " Some Reflections on India-Nepal Relations" in Lok Raj Baral, ed., *Looking to the Future; India-Nepal Relations in Perspective*

[6] Leo E. Rose, *Nepal: Strategy for Survival* (Delhi: Oxford University Press, 1971), p. 187

is Nepal's domestic politics. Any country's foreign policy is indeed an extension of internal politics. If a country is well governed and is politically stable, economically sound and socially more or less cohesive, its external relations are accordingly shaped. Depending on its overall capacity and requirements prescribed for being a power --- weak or strong--- a country has to determine its role in the comity of nations. Nepal, for instance, has its own limitations due to its geopolitical and geo-strategic situation between India and China. Since the formation of the present modern Nepali state, Nepal has had been interacting with its southern and northern neighbours in a variety of ways sometimes acting as a belligerent power by adopting the expansionist line; sometimes it had to shrink its role by being a vanquished in war, and at times trying to play one neighbour against the other. However, since the conclusion of the Treaty of Sugauli in 1815-16 with the British-Indian government, its relation with the southern neighbour was stabilized. And it continues today despite the emergence of the PRC in 1949 and even after the coming of China to Tibet. The 1950 Treaty only reinforced the security, economic and political relations with India although Nepal-India relations have undergone stresses and strains when Nepal tried to redefine "special" relations vis-à-vis its two neighbours the opening of Kathmandu-Kodari road and India's uneasiness with Nepal's expanding relations with China becoming a matter of great concern to India and the Nepali rulers trying to maintain a balanced triangular relation.

If one tries to examine Nepal-India relations within a large historical canvas, internal political dynamics seems to have played an important role in the bilateral relations. In 1950, India played a middle way policy for introducing democratic change by adopting the strategy of continuity and change. Politically, democracy became a driving force when all the contracting parties agreed to a Constituent Assembly to be duly elected by the people of Nepal. It was also the acceptance of popular sovereignty in a country that was under the traditional Shah and Rana rule for centuries. Ironically, the deal could not last long as the Delhi compromise subsequently turned out to be an unholy alliance between the three contending forces the King, the Nepali Congress and the Ranas. So, within a short period, all the three forces parted company taking divergent lines and sidelining the issues of democratic development. And India also entered into the controversy when its leaders started showing their preferences for parties and leaders. Nehru's personal letter to King Tribhuvan in 1951 shows that he preferred M.P. Koirala to B.P. Koirala (the two step-brothers) as the latter, in Nehru's view, was more radical than the former. Nehru wrote:

> I do not think that B.P. Koirala would be the right choice as Prime Minister. Any such appointment would weaken the Government instead of strengthening it. B.P. Koirala's tendency to concentrate powers in his hands would be encouraged and he would tend to become more and more autocratic.[7]

Anti-Indian sentiment was thus sown soon after the overthrow of the Rana rule. Even the Nepali Congress that got tacit support of the government of India for making the anti-Rana movement a success was divided due to both internal political conflicts and India. So King Tribhuvan, who was considered till then as democratic, started taking back all powers in his own hands declaring that Nepali tradition and custom allowed him to do so. King Tribhuvan's successor, Mahendra, further consolidated royal power until all the parties accepted him sovereign empowering him to give a constitution as a royal gift. All the so-called revolutionaries thus succumbed to the Royal power and accepted the Constitution in 1959 under which the first election to Parliament was held. And that too was terminated by the King when he staged a coup against the elected government on December 15, 1960. Indian official reaction came only after three days, on December 20, when Prime Minister Nehru referred to the royal step as a "set back to democracy".

Nepal-India relations were not smooth even during the elected government that was in power only for eighteen months. BP's effort to maintain a balance between China and India was not appreciated by the Indian media and the government. Nehru's unilateral declaration in 1959 that any attack on Nepal would be taken as an attack on India did not get a favourable response from his Nepali counterpart when Koirala said that no threats had come from any quarter, nor could India take any action without Nepal's request. It could be guessed that one of the reasons for King Mahendra taking over power was his calculation that India,

7 A.S. Bhasin, op.cit, p. 192

notwithstanding Nehru's rejection of the coup, would not take any precipitate action against his action, while China kept quiet on the issue. Subsequently, reconciling to the royal regime, India started cultivating relations with Nepal and became the largest donor in the late 1960s. Yet, the internal politics continued to become a pinprick in Nepal-India relations. During the 1990 and 2006 anti-regime movements, India became a key factor for change.

Continuity and change

The duality in Nepali neighbourly policy was more pronounced since the 1960 coup. On the one hand, King Mahendra was using China as a countervailing force against India until both Nepal and India improved their strained relations. The hit and run activities carried out by the Nepali Congressmen from Indian bases had also made Mahendra and his lieutenants paranoid with the alleged support to the anti-regime elements then condemned as "anti-nationals". Eventually, both China and the King used each other for enhancing their respective interests. Mahendra took a bold decision, obviously to the chagrin of India, by opening up the Himalayan route allowing the Chinese to construct a road linking Tibet with Kathmandu. Ridiculing Indian criticism, the King said that if communism didn't travel on a mule, how could it come on a taxi?

In hindsight, it can be said that from Nepal's point of view, the diversification policy was not wrong. Given the emerging trends in regional and international politics and with both China and India becoming economically prosperous and strong, Nepal's past step to be closer to China, without however creating problems for India, should be made beneficial for Nepal's own development. Yet, Nepal-India relations often become hostage to irrational behaviours of Nepali political elites who find fault with India when they themselves become incapable of handling bilateral relations.

Nepal's parameters of foreign policy remain basically the same but variables are adjusted when the need arises. By so doing, it also becomes expedient for scoring certain immediate objectives which are not necessarily guided by the larger interest of the nation. But these intervening factors also play. The same strategy used by King Mahendra in 1961-62 vis-à-vis

India and China didn't work in the 1989 and 2005 when King Birendra and King Gyanendra tried to emulate their father's game later. Birendra's decision to import Chinese arms without consulting India backfired following Indian unilateral decision to terminate the Treaty of Trade and Transit and the fall out of it in the form of Indian support for restoration of multiparty system in 1990. Nor did China replace India for supply of goods and petroleum or by providing massive economic aid during the crisis. It demonstrated that China had its own limitations and even calculations that might have prevented it from coming out fully in aid of the beleaguered royal regime in 1989. It also proved that India-Nepal relations are incomparable with any other power including China. And Nepal's landlocked position facing South and severe constraints imposed on it by geography and other factors cannot be seen in isolation.

King Gyanendra's proposal for membership of South Asian Association of Regional Cooperation (SAARC) to China after India proposed Afghanistan in the November 2005 Dhaka Summit did not go well with the King's policy. Discretely showing its annoyance to the King, who had already become a bete noire following the latter's decision to impose a state of emergency in Nepal on February 1, 2005, India was allegedly unhappy with the King's move for bringing in China in the SAARC. Whether it turned out to be one of the principal reasons or not for shifting Indian attitude towards the royal regime, the royalists do not fail to attribute it to the end of monarchy in Nepal.

Monarchy, which had been perceived by foreign powers including the Chinese as a stable reliable institution, was no more so; nor had other parties been able to impress on Nepal's foreign friends. Thus, it was natural that the foreign powers, in particular India, the US, the European Union and China, became active in Nepal. During the Maoist insurgency, all these powers didn't hesitate to supply arms and other kinds of support to the Royal regime. But India and other Western powers discontinued such military and political support urging the King, who had fallen from grace after his decision to take all powers into his hand, to open dialogue with dissidents. Considering it as a setback to the democratic process, India and the Western powers had withheld military support to the regime. Yet China didn't join others and continued its own type of relations with the Palace.

Nepal-India relations can no longer be understood through the conventional prism. The fast changing regional and international developments and trends such as the rise of ethnic, regional and non-ideological factors and their impacts on domestic and foreign policies have tried to reshape bilateral relations. The role of smaller states to manage both national and international trends has also shrunk in recent years. Since the old maneuverability does not exist to the extent as it was in the past, Nepal is constrained to adjust to the new realities. Nevertheless, some key elements seem to constantly engage Nepal in defining its relations with India. They are: political, economic, socio-cultural , strategic and perceptual.

Nepal's landlocked position facing the Southern neighbour and close economic interdependence (dependence?) does not allow Nepal to be fully independent of policy decisions. Nor can China provide alternatives to it. The civilizational linkages are strong that can hardly be influenced by politics. Sometimes, the religious issue gets politicized as it happened while changing the priests of the Pashupatinath temple. Political parties both in India and Nepal seem to overplay such issues. Nepalis are by comparison more flexible to delve into the depth and height of Indo-Nepal relations, but the obscurantist elements on both sides of the border try to manipulate them to score their own interests.

The security relations between Nepal and India are not likely to be fundamentally different in the future. Nepal's attraction is being increased due to its strategic location where each big and powerful country wants to set its foot. So the foreign policy pursued in the past would not suffice to manage active power players; nor will Nepal's conventional wisdom and strategy be relevant to the changed context. Nepal's only option is to be more realistic in comprehending the emerging dimensions of regional and world politics as well as to adopt strong policy measures for internal development. Economically backward Nepal will only be a liability for India and China whose own developmental performances are strikingly different from others.

Nepal's domestic stability, peace and development, and the maturity in thinking about the country and the people only assure its neighbours.

Empowerment of people making them owner of the developmental processes and democracy would generate national confidence. But confidence should not be driven by empty slogans of nationalism. It must be understood that rashtriyata is not necessarily anti-Indianism; it goes much beyond it. If the people are permanently reeled under poverty, start losing confidence in Nepal's intrinsic strength, abstract slogans of nationalism do not help them.

Any new decision to be taken cannot be unilateral in the given context, because only coordinated and cooperative policies to be pursued by both the countries would help them. In my opinion, instead of raising the issue of 1950 treaty every now and then, Nepal should now concentrate its energy on developing the country, institutionalizing democracy and making people confident of their future. Since domestic context of security has wider ramifications for bilateral, regional and internal security, chances of regime survival depend on socio-economic and political empowerment of citizens.

Placed in the strategic zone of the region, particularly between China and India, Nepal needs to play a more moderate and balancing role between the two neighbours. The location of Nepal which is physically integral to the Gangetic plain, the heartland of India, makes India more concerned about its security. Some concerns shown by India on Nepal's internal development is related to its own vital interest. And such concerns that focus on Nepal's peace, progress and stability and democracy cannot be construed as interference. It also needs to be noted that Nepal's landlocked position and close economic interdependence (dependence?) does not allow Nepal to be fully independent of policy decisions. Nor does it allow playing one neighbor against the other. Trust and confidence to be generated between Nepal and other countries, especially neighbours, alone can complement to the efforts of development.

Similarly, China's major concern is Tibet to which the Nepali side needs to be serious. Now with the enhanced regional and global power position of India and China, strategic dimensions are likely to be more complex for Nepal. How China is increasingly showing its concerns over Nepal's internal and external developments has been vociferously raised by visiting Chinese dignitaries and its representatives in Nepal.

It is also witnessed that perceptions rather than substance make the elites of Nepal and India unnecessarily hypersensitive. The psyche that India is the key factor for bringing about changes either in the government or in regime make Nepali politicians both jittery and grateful at the same time depending on the conditions in which they react. Lack of culture of empathy thus gives rise to distrust on both sides. The Indian side should not also be prejudiced against certain parties and Individuals or governments taking into account the changed internal political dynamics of Nepal. If political parties are fragmented and weak, it would be difficult to deal with small groups and individuals. But political parties of Nepal too, regardless of their backgrounds and orientation, should try to be more mature and objective in dealing with neighbours and other powers. Casualness with which relations are conducted would be only suicidal for the country.

It seems that difficult days are ahead for Nepali policy makers. Internal situation is in a mess with the major parties responsible for bringing about a radical change quarreling for no substantive reasons. Economic, regional, ethnic and governance crises are looming large indicating no concerted effort to resolve them. If Nepal fails to maintain a minimum level of development keeping its own house in order by consolidating representative institutions, its aspirations to be an independent and sovereign nation would also be undermined. Above all, minimum level of consensus among the major political forces, internal development, peace and stability are the prerequisites for a sound foreign policy. And a policy based on objective analysis and pragmatism alone would be able to deal with neighbours and other powers, now active in Nepal.

Rishikesh Shaha

Monarchy in Nepal : Where does it go from here?

We reproduce here an article of the Late Rishikesh Saha, former Foreign Minister of Nepal and a celebrated human rights activist. The article had first appeared in Think India, Vol.2, No.2, pp.1-14 (1990) Editor.

From 1846 to 1950, Nepal was autocratically ruled by the hereditary Prime Ministers of the Rana family who, by eclipsing Royal authority, had enjoyed a veritable monopoly of political power in the country for a period of 104 years. However, the Rana rule in the last phase during the late 1940s proved utterly incapable of providing the kind of foresight and statesmanship demanded by the changed environment both domestically and externally. The system of hereditary Prime Ministers was dealt with a fatal blow by the armed insurrection started by the Nepali Congress Party in the autumn and winter of 1950-51 with the covert blessings of the King Tribhuvan and the connivance of the Government of India. Apart from allowing the Nepali rebels and insurgents to use Indian territory as a base for their activities, the Nehru Government continued to recognize and support King Tribhuvan even after he had been formally removed from the throne by the de facto Rana Government and flown to India by a special Indian Air Force plane for his safety. The 1951 political change restored the King to the position of a constitutional monarch and brought the beginning of democracy to the people.

The traditional concept of legitimacy based on birth and the sword and the familial core of politics underwent modification only after the political 'revolution' of 1951 which abolished the Rana family oligarchy, and obtained the monarch's commitment to constitutional rule. But during the period between 1951 and 1960, constitutional concepts and democratic sentiments could not be fully realized despite the attempts of the modernizing political elite to introduce some of the legal and political forms of democracy in Nepal.

General elections were held in 1960, but the first ever elected government which resulted remained in office for only eighteen months. The Royal Takeover of 15 December 1960 amounted to the restoration of the kind of monarchical rule that had prevailed before: 1846 and the concept of popular legitimacy based on universal adult suffrage was subverted, before it had time to gain respect and sanctity, by the doctrine of royal supremacy. The Crown was once again regarded, in theory and in practice, as the source and dispenser of executive, legislative and judicial authority.

King Mahendra's Political Innovations

King Mahendra, a master tactician, used considerable skill to avoid emphasizing certain aspects of his political system. To justify his dissolution of Parliament and to present his subsequent practices in a favourable light, he attempted to create a cultural myth about the Panchayats to support claims of legitimacy by royal authority. He put forward a vigorous plea that his 'democratic' Panchayat system with its roots in the soil of the country was better suited to the socio-psychological climate of Nepal than parliamentary democracy, which was 'alien to its tradition and genius'. The Panchayats, however, had never in the past functioned as regular units of local self-government and had been at best councils of elders drawn from a particular caste to conciliate minor disputes relating to caste matters. In support of his climate-and-soil theory, King Mahendra furbished the Panchayats on a model of traditional polity that basically derived its authority from the spirit of reverence for hierarchy based on seniority and age in a caste ingrained society.

King Mahendra's Panchayat system was in practice a means of exploiting, under the garb of 'tutelary democracy', the age-old Nepali tradition of unquestioned obedience to autocratic authority of any kind. Mahendra took great care to avoid the impression that his Panchayat system had, in practice and theory, discarded the basic democratic tenet that power belongs to the people. He professed faith in the concept of popular sovereignty by emphasizing in public the principle of decentralization. He did not, however, make it clear whether or not decentralization implied in actual practice gradual diminution of his royal powers and prerogatives.

He also was never tired of repeating in public that his Panchayat system was basically democratic. When for the first time in the Panchayati decade King Mahendra, in 1968, appointed a Cabinet on the recommendation of his Prime Minister Surya Bahadur Thapa, he appeared to be handing power back to the people, as though he had only temporarily held it in trust for them. The concept of holding royal power is also amenable to interpretation in terms of modern constitutional and democratic practice. But all this did not deter King Mahendra from ruling directly without any Prime Minister from mid-April 1970 to mid-April 1971. The only plausible explanation for this state of affairs is that the King did not wish to appoint any Prime Minister other than his own favourite, Kirti Nidhi Bishta, who had been Prime Minister in 1969 and was finally returned unopposed to the National Panchayat in 1971. The conclusion seems warranted that what King Mahendra really sought to accomplish was to retain intact his position as the traditional custodian of absolute authority and the source of all legitimizing powers.

King Birendra's Concept and Practice of Monarchical Rule

King Birendra Bir Bikram Shah Dev, who succeeded his father, the late King Mahendra on 31st January 1972, had clearly stated his position on the question of the ultimate source of political authority in Nepal in his written answers to questions submitted by a correspondent for a press interview, published in the American weekly, Newsweek, on 10 September 1973:

Q. *Can you imagine Nepal ever becoming a constitutional monarchy such as Britain is?*

A. My country is a constitutional monarchy because my government and people are governed by dharma, a system drawn from the Hindu religion. The King cannot change this value system. Therefore he too is governed by the ethical code. According to this code, the King lives and has his being only to protect the people, to dispense justice to them and punish the wrongdoers. Indeed the King embodies the collective identity of the people and, as desired by his people, it is he who grants and amends the constitution.

Q. ***How do you feel about being looked upon as God?***

A. It is not a question of how I feel about it. There are local customs and traditions. This relates to our religious background. I have responsibility (under the Vedic scriptures) to protect the people against injustice. The concept of God is there among the people.

The obvious implication is that the interests of the King and the people are one and indivisible. Independentl of the King, the people, as individuals or as a body, cannot have any wishes or interests of their own. Both the King and his subjects are bound by the very same ethical code, which compels the latter to merge their individual selves into the King, and the King himself is powerless to change this value system.

However, the real rationale of the Panchayat system is politically personal rather than ideological or traditional. It is based on a tutelary and teleological concept of democracy which simply assumes that the Nepali people are not prepared to practise self-government. The source of all political authority, the King has the sole and ultimate responsibility to decide what is best for his subjects, politically and otherwise.

Kingship in Vedic and Sanskrit literature

Since King Birendra has referred to dharma, a system drawn from the Hindu religion, it will not be out of place here to look briefly into the nature of the Hindu religion and the connotation of the word dharma, in the context of the royal statement. Hinduism is not a religion in the accepted sense of the word because it has neither an established church nor a corpus of codified doctrines and practices. What passes for Hindu religion in popular parlance is, in short, the body of thought and speculations, rituals and practices comprising different periods of the cultural development of a people from the early Vedic age to the present time.

In the Vedic period kingship was not hereditary and the magician-kings of the time were elected on the basis of their skill in performing magical feats, such as causing rain and stopping it by the incantation of mantras or words of revelation. Even later, at the time of the Buddha, monarchy was not hereditary and kings were elected for fixed periods. The Buddha's father, himself, was one such elected king. There seems to have been a strong republican tradition in the southern part of today's Nepal and the adjoining Indian plains, as indicated by the republics of the Sakyas and the Lichchavis. The republican trend in the Hindu tradition was, in due course of time, submerged under the imperial tide characterized by the rise of the Nandas, the Mauryas and the Guptas.

The literal and derivative meaning of the word dharma, is 'that which sustains', and implies nothing more than a collective sense or mutuality of rights and duties which sustains a society. The rights and duties of the monarch and his subjects are defined in the ritualistic, metaphysical and speculative literature of the earliest times such as the Vedas, the Brahmanas, and the Upanishads, in the popular epics such as the Ramayana and the Mahabharata, and the eighteen Puranas, and also in the latter-day Dharmasutras and Dharmashastras, which served as legal and social codes. The concept of rights and duties of the king and his subjects seems to vary with the time in which a particular kind of literature appears. Nowhere in the Hindu tradition do we come across anything that approximates the model of a modern constitutional monarch who does not enjoy any effective powers and who, therefore, is absolved from all blame. In the Hindu tradition the king enjoyed powers but the people could always hold him to account for errors of omission and commission. Even regicide is recommended in extreme cases, and the killing of King Behn, notorious for his oppressive measures, is celebrated as an event in Hindu religious literature.

Countries have different ways of authenticating or legitimizing the authority of rulers. Such authentication involves religious beliefs, sacerdotal functionaries, and the power relations between the ruling house and sacred institutions. Religion in Nepal has always been used as a handmaid of politics. Even the apparently powerful institution of royal preceptor, equipped with the arbitrary power of dispensation and excommunication, was always used in Nepal to legitimize the acts of the powers-that-be. King Mahandra did away with heredity as the basis for the appointment or selection of royal preceptors by promulgating a royal ordinance which made the office open to competition among all qualified persons of the Brahmin caste who fulfilled certain qualifications or conditions.

Despite the epithets referring to the Nepali King in the official panegyrics as Giriraja (lord of the mountains), Chakrachudamani (crest-jewel of the wheel), Nara-Narayana (God among men) historically, the Kings of Nepal in the past never considered themselves to be gods. They did not claim descent from gods as some other rulers, such as the emperors of China and Japan, did. The Kings of Nepal merely regarded themselves as the seekers of the blessings of God or the recipients or beneficiaries of God's favours. It was only after effective ruling power had passed into the hands of the three times Shri Rana Maharaj-cum-Prime Ministers that the title of five times Shri Maharajdhiraj was applied to the kings. The bearer of the title began to be referred to ironically as an incarnation of Narayana who, like the image of this god at Budhnilakantha in Kathmandu, did not act on his own or speak to the common people but was, all the same, worthy of veneration by them. The Ranas so contrived to exalt the majesty of the king that he became immobilized, or at least unable to act independently. After B.P. Koirala became the first ever elected Prime Minister of Nepal following the 1959 general elections, King Mahendra is reported to have said to him in casual conversation once: 'B.P., as I am still young and energetic, I would not like to be just a Narayana, reclining on the bed of water at Budhanilakantha.'

The attempt to exploit the ruler's ties with the Hindu religion for blatant political purposes is as recent as the post-1960 period of King Mahendra's rule. Before that Nepal, in pursuit of the declared goals of the 1951 revolution, such as the representative Westminster model of parliamentary monarchy or democracy and secularism, always emphasized officially the lack of religious discrimination in its tradition. The 1962 constitution of Nepal characterized Nepal as a Hindu state for the first time, even at the risk of incurring the displeasure of non-Hindu minorities. King Mahendra was motivated by a political desire to exploit the Hindu sentiment in India to combat the pressure the Jawaharlal Nehru Government was putting on him to adhere to the secular democratic tradition ushered in by the 1950 revolution in Nepal. Again, the practice of issuing royal messages of goodwill, not only to Nepali Hindus but to all Hindus in the world, initiated by King Mahendra and followed by his son and successor, King Birendra, is another example of a conscious intent to use religion for political purposes. The Shah kings had never in the past professed to be religious leaders or heads of the church like the rulers of Great Britain and had been content with their role as the protectors of religion in keeping with the old Kshatriya tradition. The concept of traditional legitimacy in Nepal was primarily based on this arbitrary claim, backed up by the ruler to use physical force to compel obedience. This concept of kingship was reinforced by the Hindu view of the nobility of birth, resulting from meritorious action in a previous life and sanctified by custom.

Tradition of Rule by Peremptory Command

During the period from 1769 to 1846 and also from 1960 to the present day the kings of Nepal have ruled in practice as well as in theory. Their command has been found to override the existing laws and the decisions of the courts of law in actual practice. Their exercise of authority may be best characterized as rule by 'hukum' or peremptory command, which has been patrimonial rather than feudal.

Jung Bahadur Rana, the founder of the system of hereditary Rana Prime Ministers his which prevailed in Nepal from 1846 until 1951 with the kings as mere figureheads, claimed to have obtained peremptory command for himself and his progeny. The Hukumi Shasan or rule by peremptory command of the Rana Prime Ministers continued up to the beginning of 1951.

After 18 February 1951, following the 1950-51 political revolution, the King regarded at least in theory his own right to rule by peremptory command not withstanding his public commitment to abide by constitutional arrangements to be made in due course by a Constituent Assembly directly elected by the people. And again after Nepal's first general elections were held in February-April 1959, according to the terms of the 1959 constitution promulgated by King Mahendra himself, the King retained the emergency power to dissolve the elected Parliament and rule by peremptory command. He soon made use of this power and dissolved the first ever elected Parliament in Nepal on 15 December 1960. He thus continued the tradition of rule by peremptory command under the cover of 'the party less democratic Panchayat system' with all powers vested in himself.

The spirit in which King Birendra introduced the second constitutional amendment in 1975 could be best understood and analysed in the light of his own novel concept of constitutional monarchy, which was said to have been derived from a certain aspect of Hindu dharma or religious code of conduct and which was not the usually accepted one in which both the King and his people derive their rights and responsibilities from a constitution which can be changed at any time by the required majority of the votes of the people or of their representatives in popularly elected national legislatures. His theory of constitutional monarchy seemed to be largely influenced by his concept of a King as God among the people. King Birendra was compelled to introduce cosmetic changes in the party less Panchayat system, considered immutable, under the pressure of the students movement and subject it to the test of a popular referendum in 1980. However, even after, he was able to retain intact his prerogative to rule by peremptory command, through the reinforcement of party lessness as the basis for the functioning of even a legislature elected on the basis of universal adult suffrage.

It has been assumed that over a period of thirty years the monarchical party less Panchayat rule has developed a political culture made up of political orientations 'appropriate to the political order'. But the powers-that-be viewed the situation not as one of creating or encouraging new orientations, but of perpetuating old ones. The people were even denied legal freedom to evolve mass political parties or organizations to stimulate popular participation and mobilization for development purposes. Ultimately the monarch or the Crown, in whom the Panchayat system both in theory and practice vests all power and also complete responsibility for development, might be held solely responsible for the stagnation and lack of progress, with drastic consequences for the institution of monarchy itself.

During the past three decades of the royal Panchayati regime, it had also become fashionable in Nepal to reinforce the plea for 'party lessness' by arguing that Nepal's geographical location between two big countries with different social systems had made it imperative for Nepal not to have parties advocating either system because parties can be easily influenced by foreign money and inducements. Although the argument may appear to be ingenious on the surface, it undermines the very basis of Nepal's nationalism, ignores the basic right and freedom of the Nepali people as an independent nation to evolve a political system of their own choice, and shows lack of faith in their integrity. In the present-day world, there are many examples of small states situated between two ideologically antagonistic neighbours, which have developed parties as effective instruments of national stability and progress and have survived as independent nations. As to the question of political parties being readily influenced by foreign money, the simple answer is that individuals who do not have to account for their behaviour to many people can be more easily and cheaply bought than the leaders of mass organizations in which there are several groups competing for power and influence.

Nepal had experience with the non-party Panchayat rule under the 'King's direct leadership' for almost three decades. The form in which the regime has been advocated by its most vociferous and ardent supporters had the effect of making the King or the institution he represents bear all responsibility for the success or failure of the policies of successive governments during the Panchayati decades.

Samuel P. Huntington in his perceptive article 'The Political Modernization of Traditional Monarchies', published in *Daedalus*, Journal of the American Academy of Arts and Science, has visualized four possibilities for modernising traditional monarchies: (i) Invest the political system with just enough power to make it bearable to the monarch; (ii) Draw on both traditional and popular sources of authority; (iii) Centralize power and concurrently try to modernize society; (iv) Stop or retard the process of modernizing. However, the conclusion he has reached in this article is that there is no future for traditional monarchs on a long term or permanent basis unless they gradually and consciously transform themselves into modern constitutional monarchies as those of the United Kingdom, Holland, Belgium and the Scandinavian countries.

History demonstrates that the transition from absolute monarchs to anything like a broad-based government has been brought about either by revolution or gradual evolution over a long period of time. This transition in several instances has resulted in a transfer of power to an autocratic oligarchy of a military type rather than to a popularly based constitutional government. What happened with Nepal's Shah monarchy in 1846, the Ottoman empire in 1908 or in Thailand following the revolution of 1932 may be cited as examples. Egypt furnishes yet another instance of direct takeover by a military junta from a monarch in 1952. Although military oligarchies represent a slight broadening of the base of power and provide for relatively increased participation, they have never been able to secure the cooperation of a diversity of social groups. Nor has it been possible for such regimes to avoid violence and suppression, both in effecting the transition and also thereafter. The circumstances surrounding the transfer of power from the monarchy to a military oligarchy in Iraq in 1958 and the bloodshed and violence in its aftermath could be cited as a prime example.

The evolution of the political process in Nepal should be of great interest to students of comparative political modernization. In the course of a little more than two hundred years, Nepal has witnessed various forms of political transformation in a remarkable sequence. The transition from the absolute Shah monarchy, remarkable for the original unification of the country during the 1767-1806 period, to the Rana family oligarchy of a military type took place in 1846. The erosion of royal power and prerogatives was a gradual process, largely the result of the passing of power to minors and a succession of weak and vacillating regent queens during the first half of the nineteenth century. The 1951 revolution marked a change from the Rana family oligarchy to a sort of constitutional monarchy with a multiparty system. But after the first ever general election of 1959 in Nepal, the political scene changed to a single dominant party system. The net result of this was that with the exception of the main parliamentary opposition party, the Gorkha Parishad, together with the Communist Party, all other minor parties, rendered politically ineffective as a result of their poor showing at the polls, looked to the King to be salvaged. Then after a brief experiment with a parliamentary monarchy for eighteen months came the royal takeover, which put the clock back to the absolute Shah monarchy as it existed before 1846.

The Shah dynasty has since encountered several attempts at armed uprisings against it during the past three decades, such as the abortive pro-democracy struggle and armed raids of 1961-62 organized by General Subarma Shamsher of the Nepali Congress and his followers from their base of self-imposed exile in India; the unsuccessful armed revolution from 1969 till 1975 initiated by B.P. Koirala from India as his base after his release from an eight year long detention as the first-ever elected Prime Minister of Nepal; and finally, the explosion of bombs in Kathmandu on 20 June 1985 and at other townships in Nepal immediately before and after it, for which Ram Raja Prasad Singh, formerly an advocate of Nepal's Supreme Court and a former member of Nepal's Panchayati legislature, claimed full responsibility on behalf of his political party, Janabadi Morcha (The People's Front), as its President. This is the only party which had openly advocated the abolition of the monarchy.

The Royal regime has also coped with a peaceful and non-violent movement for the restoration of political parties and human rights in the spring of 1985. Though the movement was initially launched by the Nepali Congress, several Communist factions also joined it on their own. Although quite a few thousand workers of the Nepali Congress and various factions of the Communist Party of Nepal and other political activists had courted imprisonment, the movement failed in its attempt to persuade the government servants to boycott work and was eventually withdrawn on the plea that the bomb blasts in June had damaged its prospects.

Last but not the least in both scope and intensity came the recent broad-based peaceful and non-violent movement launched by the Nepali Congress and the United Left Front from 18 February 1990 with the active participation of all other democratic and left forces and members of the professional and educated classes and the intelligentsia in general. That very day some forty year ago, King Tribhuvan in his historic proclamation of 7 Falgun 2007 V.S. (corresponding to 18 February 1951) expressed his desire and resolve that the 'Government of our people be carried on henceforth according to a democratic constitution prepared by a constituent assembly elected by them.' However, after his son and grandson, King Mahendra and King Birendra, had, each in his own way, backed out of King Tribhuvan's solemn commitment, the seventh of Falgun of the lunar calendar of the Vikram era, observed as Democracy Day every year, was reduced to a mere formality devoid of any meaning and purpose to the people. It was being celebrated merely as any other routine official function, participated in mainly by the civil and military government personnel in their prescribed uniforms for the meetings and processions held on the occasion.

But December Day acquired renewed significance and vitality in 1992 as the mass movement for the restoration of democracy and human rights was also launched on that day, this time with a clear and ringing message to King Tribhbuvan's grandson, King Birendra Bikram Shah Dev - 'We want democracy', 'We want human rights'.

Thousands of demonstrators had assembled after 1pm on 18 February 1990 around Kathmandu's New Road or Juddha Road, named after the hereditary Rana Prime Minister, Juddha Shamsher. He had the distinction of being the great-grandfather of the present King and Queen of Nepal but had also acquired lasting ignominy by making martyrs of four of Nepal's most celebrated patriots and freedom fighters. The road branching off in four different directions from the pedestal of his statue at the New Road crossroads are ironically named after those four martyrs. That day the pro-democracy demonstration held up for some time the routine official procession mainly consisting of black-jacketed civil servants and military troops in uniform and also accompanied by hundreds of people brought from across the Valley in hired trucks. Prime Minister Marich Man Singh and Home Minister Niranjan Thapa rode in a carriage at the head of procession through the streets after the riot police had cleared the streets. But both of them were seen using towels and water to soothe the stinging eyes as the gas still lingered in the air. They were subsequently forced to abandon their carriage and seek shelter within the ranks of the police and military personnel.

As most of the middle level leaders had long been imprisoned and some of them had gone underground and even the top leaders of the pro-democracy movement including Ganesh Man Singh and Nepali Congress Acting President Krishna Prasad Bhattrai along with leftist leaders such as Sahana Pradhan and Bishnu Bahadur Manadhar had already been placed under house arrest or sent to prison, very few leaders were available on hand on 18 February 1990 to control and guide the action of the enraged crowd consisting mainly of students and other anti-government protesters. As the mob showered stones on the official processionists, the police retaliated by throwing the stones back at them, while groups of people shouting anti-Panchayat slogans disappeared down alleyways in Kathmandu.

The pro-democracy agitation mainly spearheaded by students spread far and wide. The central district of Chitawan witnessed mass protests and demonstrations on an unprecedented scale. No official celebration of Democracy Day could take place there as there was a virtual collapse of administration at Narayan Ghat and Bharatpur, notwithstanding the police firing which resulted in more than a dozen deaths. Several vehicles and petrol pumps were set on fire by enraged mobs. Several dead bodies were seen in the outskirts of the forests adjoining the road to Hetandu where several motor vehicles were set ablaze and encounters took place between the police and angry mobs.

Even at the scenic township of Pokhara, where the King and the Queen of Nepal were sojourning at their lakeside castle in the course of their inspection tour of the western region, two buses were set on fire. This could not be prevented, despite the fact that Pokhara had been heavily guarded by the police and the army ever since 12 February. On that day 518 students, including 100 girls, were rounded up when they took out a peaceful procession to rejoice the release of the veteran African nationalist leader Nelson Mandela. The excesses committed by the armed police in the girls hostel on that occasion had already been internationally condemned following adequate verification and confirmation by neutral and independent observers and witnesses.

On 19 February, the second day of the movement, there was a general strike throughout the country. At least eleven people were shot dead at Bhaktapur, one of the three sister towns of the Kathmandu Valley. The people there had all along borne a festering grievance against the Marich

Man Shreshtha government because it had falsely implicated Narayan Man Bijiche, the acknowledged leader of Bhaktapur town, Gobinda Duwal, a sitting member of Nepal's National Legislature from Bhaktapur, and the mayor and the deputy-mayor of the town along with dozens of other prominent citizens. The Government headed by Marich Man Singh had refused to release them on bail and held them in detention since August 1988. There was probably an exchange of stones between the inhabitants of Bhaktapur and the riot police as elsewhere, but the authorities once again chose to feed fat into the old grudge of the Bhaktapur people by firing the prohibited First World War bullets on unarmed mobs. For days and nights the gallant people of Bhaktapur continued their protest undaunted, even taking out torchlight processions until the police were forced to withdraw and leave them in peace as in the sister town of Patan which had subsequently followed in Bhaktapur's footsteps.

On 20 February lawyers did not attend the courts throughout the country in moral support of the pro-democracy movement. 25 February witnessed another successful general strike. The lawyers' boycott of the courts was followed a few days later by a token strike of doctors. University teachers staged a pen-down strike on 27 February. By the end of February thousands had been arrested and several people had been killed. According to the opposition between thirty and fifty people were killed and at least a thousand people were arrested. Those arrested were kept in overcrowded and extremely cold godowns without food and clothes. The names of detainees were kept a secret with the result that families and relatives were denied access to them. Some people did not even know the whereabouts of their family members, whether they were under detention, or killed, or injured. Beatings and physical torture were the rule rather than the exception. Some detainees were released after severe beatings with their limbs broken.

For a while towards the end had it had begun to appear as though the movement was going to peter out. However, some people were simply amazed that a peaceful and non-violent movement had sustained so long. The moral support of international human rights organizations such as Human Rights Watch, Asia Watch and Amnesty International along with that of Socialist International and other international organizations had a lot to do with it. Besides this, support of democratic India including all political parties was solidly entrenched behind the pro-democracy movement in Nepal.

As the movement had not reached the critical mass for explosion, the best was yet to be seen. The mass upsurge came as a surprise in response to a call for action by Dr buran Bhattarai as Spokesman of the United National People's Movement (apparently outside the main fold of the alliance between the Nepali Congress and the United Leftist Front) on 6 April in the wake of the royal proclamation of the name of the new Prime Minister, Lokendra Bahadur Chand, in the morning following the dismissal of the Marich Man Government the previous day. At least 200,000 people who were assembled in the open air theatre on the parade ground at the heart of Kathmandu on 6 April 1990 heard their leaders in open defiance of the authorities and their regulations. Most of the media men who had gone to Kathmandu to cover the movement during the opening days had returned disappointed that they did not see any mass action in the streets as in Eastern Europe. But when the mass upsurge did actually appear they were not there to cover it. A section of this large assemblage raised anti-Panchayat and anti-King slogans and started moving towards the main gate of the Royal Palace. No sooner had they reached King Mahendra's statue at the head of the Durbar Marga the riot police and the Royal military guards opened fire on them indiscriminately: Quite a few died and many more were injured. Another section of the enraged crowd pressing to approach the western gate of the Royal Palace from the Thamel side was fired upon in front of the SAARC Secretariat gate. There was firing upon the crowd surging ahead along the Kantipath towards the same destination. Not less than one hundred people were shot dead on Friday, 6 April 1990, turning it into the bloodiest day in the history of Nepal. The following day also there was firing because of the defiance by the people of the government's curfew and orders issued to the army to shoot at sight.

The number of those killed as a result of firing on 6th and 7th April in the Kathmandu Valley must have reached a figure of five hundred to six hundred because even the then Prime Minister, Lokendra Bahadur Chand, parried the question when specific figures of deaths were mentioned by correspondents. Dozens of truck loads of bodies were reportedly transported to the exclusive military cremation grounds for mass cremation. Even bodies of those who had died in the hospitals as a result of bullet wounds were not handed over to their relatives. Under the circumstances the precise number of deaths on those days will never be known.

After these tragic killings, King Birendra, in consultation with the opposition leaders, lifted the 30-year-old ban on political parties on 8th April. But his newly appointed Cabinet began to stall on the implementation of the popular 8-point charter of demands which was as follows:

1. As the National Panchayat and the present Government, formed under the Party less Constitution have become inconsistent under the new dispensation announced on 8 April, which removed Party lessness and lifted the ban on all political parties, we demand immediate dissolution of these bodies.

2. All the articles, clauses and sub-clauses of the present Constitution of Nepal, which are incompatible with the changed Multiparty Policy prevailing in the country today, both in form and spirit, should be repealed immediately.

3. Such bodies of the Panchayats from the district to the village levels must now be disbanded making such arrangements as are necessary to conduct urgent public business.

4. All movable and immovable properties belonging to different levels of Panchayat and Class Organizations be nationalized forthwith.

5. All political prisoners, held during or before the movement, including those charged with the intention of political revenge, should be released immediately.

6. All the families of those killed during the present movement should be respectfully compensated and those injured should be provided treatment and financial assistance.

7. The Constitution Reforms Commission should be constituted with just representation from both the Nepali Congress and the United Left Front.

8. Independent enquiry should be conducted on the atrocities perpetrated during the popular movement and the guilty should be punished.

Though the meeting of the supreme leader of the movement, Ganesh Man Singh, with King Birendra on 13 April raised some hopes of agreement between the King and the opposition, they proved to be short-lived. Reluctantly undertaken talks between the new Prime Minister and his Panchayati team on the one hand and the opposition team of negotiators consisting of second-rank leaders on 15 April failed to produce any agreement on the implementation of the 8-point charter of demands. The Government side negotiators had to be detained by the slogan-shouting crowds till the small hours of the morning on 16 April before the King agreed to implement most of the major demands at the second meeting with Ganesh Man Singh the same evening. On 17 April the King proclaimed dissolution of the Rashtriya Panchayat, the Panchayat Policy and the Investigation Committee and offered Prime ministership to K.P. Bhataarai on the recommendation of Ganesh Man Singh, which was duly seconded by the Congress Party and the United Leftist Front. Thus, after three decades, the so-called party less Panchayat system, serving as a cloak for the exercise of near-absolute power by the King had come to an end.

But the question for the future is whether the Nepali monarchy will voluntarily give up its right to rule by peremptory command based on traditional legitimacy and move forward to share power with the people by recognizing the fact that in democracy, sovereignty after all resides in the people. Will the Nepali King after forty years once again make a sincere and honest move this time to respect his grandfather's solemn commitment to the people of Nepal that they will be free to draw up the constitution which they want to live under? If the Nepali King endorses his grandfather's solemn commitment to the people in some form or the other and endeavours sincerely to fulfil it, Nepal may have stable and ordered progress as a nation. The people of Nepal should be able to evolve, in due course, a viable political structure on a trial and error basis by learning from their own experience and that of others. Such a course of action alone can ensure not only the permanent interests of the people but also those of the monarchy in Nepal.

Aditya Adhikari

"The 12-Point Pact is key to consolidation of Democracy in Nepal" - DP Tripathi

D.P. Tripathi, Editor-in-Chief, Think India, and General Secretary of the Nationalist Congress Party (NCP) of India, has remained engaged with Nepal since his student days. In what follows is the first hand account of how he along with Sitaram Yechury of the CPI(M) worked to facilitate the alliance of Nepal's mainstream political parties and the Maoists against monarchy which he shared in an interview with Aditya Adhikari of *The Kathmandu Post* during his visit to Kathmandu in January 2009.

Q: How did you get in touch with Nepalese politicians?

A: We have always been associated with the Nepalese people's struggle for democracy. During our student days, we used to meet the great Mr. B.P. Koirala. In 1990, when the major struggle for democracy was launched, we were there, along with the former Prime Minister of India Chandra Shekhar, at Ganesh Man Singhji's house. I came as a special envoy of Rajiv Gandhi and brought special letters for Ganesh Man Singh and Krishna Prasad Bhattarai. I had said that it wouldn't take more than 90 days for the struggle to succeed. It succeeded in 60 days.

In 2005, we did something that had never happened in India in support of Nepal. In February, King Gyanendra dismissed the government and put in place an authoritarian regime. I took the initiative to coordinate with the major political parties of India to form the Nepal Democracy Solidarity Committee, India. The late comrade Harkishan Singh Surjeet became the chairman of the committee and I was made secretary general. The left parties, the Congress, in fact all political parties of India except the BJP, were part of that committee. The job of that committee was to support the struggle of the Nepalese people. We came to attend various conferences here at Kathmandu. The first one was in July 2005, it was organised by the Nepali Congress, led by Girija Babu (Girija Prasad Koirala commonly known as G. P. Koirala who became Prime Minister of Nepal four times). Addressing the conference, I said, "I am speaking on behalf of the Government of India, to support the democratic struggle of the Nepalese people." I could say that as our party was a constituent of the UPA (United Progressive Alliance) government at the centre in India. I meant to send a message to the King.

Later, as you may know, I came on a fact-finding mission with Sitaram Yechury. We were attacked, stones were thrown at us. But the best thing that happened was when the parliament was reconvened in April 2006 - for the first time in the history of India-Nepal relationship a standing ovation was given by the Nepalese parliament to the two Indians - Sitaram Yechury and me. They acknowledged our support and solidarity for their democratic struggle.

Q: When did your engagement with the Maoists begin?

A: Baburam Bhattarai was closely associated with us since our student days at Jawaharlal Nehru University (JNU) in New Delhi. I met Prachanda much later. The meeting with the Maoists began with Ram Karki "Partho". I had been telling the government of India, even before meeting the Maoists, that we should try and help in facilitating their engagement with Democracy and not treat them as terrorists or enemies. The attitude of the government of India at that time was not very positive. In the meantime, the meetings began. I met Prachanda in Delhi. Actually, Prachanda met Sitaram Yechury at my residence in Vasant Kunj in March 2006. The first task before us was formation of the Seven Party Alliance in Nepal. The other major challenge was to facilitate the 12-point understanding of November 2005. That is the basis of all future developments. Even today, I think the 12-point understanding is the key to the consolidation of democracy in Nepal. Unfortunately, they (Nepal's political leaders) haven't been able to implement it. I told the Prime Minister that the need is to implement it, not talk about it.

Q: Was it difficult to convince some sections of the Indian establishment? The intelligence agencies, for example?

A: It was. In the beginning it was very difficult to convince them that there is a democratic struggle going on in Nepal, and the Maoists are not terrorists but a political force and they should be treated as such. But I must say that the Indian Prime Minister Manmohan Singh was very positive on this point. When I had a discussion with him, he told me, "If all these parties including the Maoists are giving up arms and becoming part of Democracy, India must support that. India needs a peaceful, democratic, stable Nepal. But how can you be sure that the Maoists will give up arms?" I said, "The point is that the government of India must not create impediments for the mainstreaming of all these diverse political parties in Nepal. Our job should be supporting." So initially it was difficult, but thanks to the Prime Minister of India, it was ultimately accepted that we should support the democratic process in Nepal.

Q: Because the Maoists were staying in India, there were always suspicions here that sections of the Indian establishment were using them. Do you think that was true?

A: That is completely false. We faced so much trouble in trying to support the Nepalese Maoists. Our establishment was initially not agreeable at all, they were quite hostile to the Maoists. And we were in minority. Among the important political leaders of India, there were only two - Chandra Shekhar and Harkishan Singh Surjeet - who said, "We are ready to talk to the Nepalese Maoists, and we are ready to go and meet them wherever they want." No other Indian leader was ready to do this. It is absolutely baseless to say that the Maoists were supported by the Indian establishment just because they were underground in India. We were also underground in Nepal during Emergency in India in 1975-1977. I was telling someone today that we always underrate the impact of Nepal on India. During many struggles - 1857 Revolt, the Quit India Movement (1942), the Emergency - people from India went to Nepal to take shelter.

Q: There is a perception that the Indian establishment has become cold towards the Maoists recently. Is this true?

A: The basic thing is that we will support the Democratic process. But there are two things that I want to say quite categorically. One, they will have to frame the constitution within the time -frame they have decided. Second, the government of today has to think about economic development, of the prosperity of the people. People have expectations. These will have to be met.

Q: The Maoists have tried to develop relations with China. Has this caused concern in India?

A: It doesn't cause me any concern. My answer to that question is their names are Pushpa Kamal Dahal and Baburam Bhattarai, which is more akin to Indian than to Chinese names. That is very important to me. The people of Nepal are culturally more close towards us. There is a bit of a problem with the Indian establishment. They have to be more cooperative. It should treat Nepal as an independent country and that should be respected. That should be the guiding principle for the Indian establishment. But this hasn't happened.

Q: Will the Indian establishment's support to Nepal change if the BJP comes back to power in the next election?

A : First, the BJP will not come back to power. Second, even if they do, I don't think there will be any change. When I told Rajnath Singh that he should meet the Maoists, he accepted. In India, we have reached a position where, though we have difference of opinion, we can communicate. If I tell a political leader in India, please do this in Nepal, they will accept it. Because they know I have done some work on Nepal, that I know the place. Even the BJP will accept it. I told the BJP to control Yogi Adityanath (BJP Member of Parliament, head priest of Gorakhnath Math in Gorakhpur, and supporter of the Nepali monarchy). Rajnath Singh telephoned him and told him not to indulge in any nonsense in Nepal. He told him, "You have the Gorakhnath temple, do whatever you wish with it, but don't get involved in Nepal."

Katak Malla

Nepal-India-China
Learning and Unlearning of Diplomatic Conduct

Nepal's foreign policy education is designed in the primary school curriculum, the implementation of which is seemingly resulted into unwanted consequences. At their early stage children are taught if not indoctrinated that "Nepal is a small country situated between the two giant states", namely China and India. Whether it is intentional or not, such education at early childhood has resulted in negative consequences, i.e. diplomatic deficits, lack of skill and undermining of potential diplomatic capabilities. Apparently, Nepal's foreign policy actors have become the victims of their upbringing, and continue to be affected by beliefs or suffer form a weak nation syndrome and therefore either prefer to be subordinate to the powerful ones, or lack capabilities of dealing with the two powerful neighbours in particular.

Unlike small power's perceived or real weakness, the powerful nations suffer from a deeper (hyper) power psychosis, believing that they can control some countries by force and others by favour, relying in most cases on the military force. These states seem to forget the sense of history of nation-states that power is a shifting phenomenon, powerful empire rises and falls, and enmity between nations does not last forever. Primarily, they seem to ignore the idea that global common citizenry is increasingly becoming important, breaking the narrow national discourse. The perceived weakness of small powers and deeper psychosis of super or major powers can be overcome if education is recognised not only as a means of learning of new knowledge, innovation and creativity, but also as unlearning of wrong beliefs and practices. In other words, there is a need to unlearn the practice of hegemony of power, dominance and control of other people, in other's territory, to control resources.

Unlike Nepal, China and India seem to suffer from big power superiority complex in regional context. The modern Chinese foreign policy was designed and practiced by Mao, and that policy continues to date, known as "Five Finger policy" which includes Nepal along with Ladakh, Bhutan, Sikkim and Arunachal Pradesh concerning the territorial issues. To counter the Chinese geo-political game, India has developed a policy of "Greater India." Among the so-called five fingers, Sikkim was annexed by India as is the case of Tibet by China. Bhutan is within the Indian sphere of influence, parts of Ladakh and Arunachal remain disputed territories since the 1962 China-India war. Although China and India were the victims of the colonial empires and their struggle for independence symbolise anti-colonial struggles, the "Five Finger" and "Greater India" policies are the legacy of the colonial mindset. Despite their attempts for the improvement of the bilateral relations, China and India continue to compete with each other economically and militarily.

It is not only the China-India relation, but also the many other international issues, including mutual respect and dignity, that are issues of concern for Nepal's diplomacy discourse. This means that the very idea of education of diplomacy as well as discourse as a whole have to be reviewed as to what is to be learned and what ought to be unlearned, e.g. to unlearn that my nation and culture is superior than others and not to trying to rule others.

This approach to learning and unlearning diplomatic conduct can help implement the idea of peaceful coexistence in Nepal-India-China (NIC) context as well as world at large.

In advancing an approach to learning and unlearning of diplomatic conduct, the basis of my arguments is grounded on the very idea of self-interest. One of the vital interests of any state is to create or maintain respect on the international stage. States use various means to achieve their interests, including cooperation, confrontation, threats, persuasion, sanctions, or military force, etcetera. However, in the practice of international relations, the evidence suggests that states command more respect by practicing reciprocal respect than by the use of other means. Those states which place mutual respect and dignity above all become the benchmarks that serve as models for other states. This is a form of self-interest based diplomacy, not only because of the respect aspect but also because of the negative repercussions in the long term though some states calculate that the short-term benefit from the domination is worth the trouble. The inter-governmental organisations notable among them the UN helps to enhance the fulfilment of the mutual respect of the member states; for examples, shaping the very structure of modern relations between nations (e.g. decolonization and elimination of apartheid), promoting methods and means for dispute settlements, strengthening consultation and cooperation, and supporting regional and national efforts of global common concerns. With this background, the present paper discusses legend and lessons of diplomatic deficiency of Nepal, and the role of its intellectuals.

Nepal's diplomatic deficiency: legend and lessons

Foreign policy is known to be the reflection of national interests, the fulfilment of which demands sound strategies and skilled diplomats. Diplomacy is an art, a vocation and a project, influencing others for the fulfilment of one's own national interest. Such art, vocation and project do vary from one State to another, depending on the geo-political situation and the military as well as the economic strength. A few, but important, questions arise concerning Nepal's current diplomatic approach, or lack thereof: Is there any lesson to learn from Nepal's past diplomats? Are there such diplomats in Nepal, who understand the art of diplomacy and service as vocation, rather than just reaching a position? And, above all does the country have such projects? If not, a serious discussion on diplomacy must start, the sooner the better. Nepal's location, size and state of economic development do not prevent her from adopting an independent foreign policy, and claiming the just principle of international law, resisting the big power bullying or opposing foreign interference in internal politics. In doing so, the political house of the country must be kept in order. Currently, some groups in Nepal are whipping up nationalistic feelings against the foreign involvement in the internal politics, and others are openly becoming aligned with the foreign powers to suppress their domestic opponents. "National consensus" seems to be the key word of Nepal's current political leaders, but who is preventing the political leaders (including the former king), to make a joint declaration opposing foreign interference?

Diplomatic wisdom of a legendary statesman Rishikesh Shaha is worth repeating in the present context: "Foreign policy, however successful, cannot itself deliver the goods to the people, nor can it alone achieve the positive end of nationalism." Thus, the interests of the people must be at the heart of national and international policy. In this, a distinction must be made between the interests of the people, whom governments in Nepal and the neighbouring countries claim to represent, and their policies which, more often than not, contradict the people's interests. One of the main reasons for failing to make this distinction is the fundamental failure or lack of democratic systems in the region.

Rishikesh Shaha's courage is also noteworthy for Nepal's career diplomats as well as policy makers. Shaha stood up against all odds to the then Soviet leader Nikita Khrushchev from the rostrum of the General Assembly to tell him that "he had no right banging his shoe on his desk and thereby showing disrespect for an organization that belonged first of all to small nations." When I met Shaha for the last time in the late 1990s, he said that he made both friends and adversaries by challenging the Soviet leader, at home and abroad. Shaha was admired in the diplomatic circles. Nonetheless, he was called back from his position never to return to the diplomatic service but his diplomatic career continued as a writer, and he remained as one and the only person influencing Nepal's foreign policy during his time.

In addition to the enhancement of Nepal's honour at the UN, Rishikesh Shaha's statesmanship was considered only second to the then Indian Prime Minister Jawaharlal Nehru in promoting the cause of the Non-Alignment Movement (which is currently going through a crisis of definition and direction). Time Magazine (24 Oct. 1960) wrote that the most effective work to make "neutrality" respectable "has often been done by second-echelon diplomats...Nepal's Rishikesh Shaha...". Shaha may have been somewhat politically controversial, but remains as a legendary statesman of small power diplomacy.

Unlike the powerful States' diplomacy, the small power diplomacy depends upon the adherence to just principles and the use of diplomatic wisdom and courage, more so in times of crisis. Just as in the colonial times, the control of resources and lives of other people remains the objective of powerful States. When needed, powerful States in the name of diplomacy often use threats, persuasion, sanctions or force as well as overt and covert internal political operations, ultimately in some cases leading to change (or restoration) of the political regime in weaker States.

Except for a few honourable exceptions, the European diplomacy to Nepal continues to serve as a "carrot" to the "stick" of the US diplomacy. The Chinese and the Indian diplomats are openly engaged with Nepal's internal politics so much that they look as if they are the Nepalese super political class. On the other hand, Nepal's diplomacy abroad, primarily seeking foreign aid, is becoming less significant since the donors themselves are residentially present in Kathmandu not necessarily to address Nepal's needs, but to execute the donor's interest. The internal political interference by foreign diplomats is illegal according to the basic principle of international law. Such diplomacy is being practiced, forming and/or toppling the governments. Now it is time for the foreign diplomats either to abide by the classic norms of diplomacy, keeping themselves aloof from internal matters, or to let Nepal's ambassadors abroad have the same right in the respective host countries. After all, reciprocity is the golden rule of diplomacy, i.e. either the foreign diplomats have to "shut-up" or Nepal's diplomats have to "put-up" their rights. Both the Indian and the Chinese foreign policy makers must recognise this reality and renounce the policy that David Van Preach describes as "Dragon and Serpent" towards Nepal.

Neutrality is the strength of small power diplomacy, especially in Nepal's condition. But is Nepal's geographic location so complex or its diplomatic leadership that stupid, or both? Which of them is the problem or the solution in the relations with the northern and southern neighbours? The country's geo-location serves as a natural defense or détente for its northern and southern neighbours, and has been described with a misleading metaphor: "Yam between the two rocks." The Nepalese politicians and diplomats continue to act as waiters, pleasing the masters at the South Bloc, New Delhi, or the Northern Lower Block, China Resources Building, Beijing. Nepal's foreign policy makers (somebody may also wonder if there are any) continue to suffer from the "Yam-syndrome" or the small nation-inferiority complex. This has contributed to the current policy of submission and sense of resignation to the situation, without critically assessing Nepal's strengths and weaknesses.

There can be no match between Nepal and China or between Nepal and India in terms of power configuration, e.g., territory, population and economic and military strength. Nonetheless, the mutual benefit is apparent in the triangular relations. Nearly thirty million people of Nepal are a considerable strength of the nation. Nepal has become a large market for the Chinese apples, garments and electronic equipments. Some might also remember that in the late 1980s China explored its arms market in Nepal. Traditionally, Nepal has also been a market as well as a resource for the Indian economy, ranging from water resources to the outsourcing of the Gorkha army.

So, what is lacking in Nepal is diplomatic education, wisdom and courage? One of the first steps to fill the void would be that the past and present rulers of Nepal, including political party leaders, must make a joint declaration against foreign interference, committing to sort out the internal political differences of diplomacy through genuine national reconciliation. Failure to do so would be considered as the historical betrayal to the nation. Given the involvement of the two giant neighbors in the internal politics of Nepal, the rest of the international community must take note that China and India will be held responsible for any resurgence of political conflict in the country.

Diplomacy and the Role of Intellectuals

Currently, NIC relations are chaotic and contradictory to the normal assumption that the three political regimes want to live in peaceful co-existence. A chaotic triangle has arisen, I would argue, in most part because the regimes of the three countries have clearly failed to represent the interests of their people, as demonstrated by the fruitlessness of their diplomacy. With a specific distinction between the "people" and "government" in mind, I am using the term "regime" because "governments" are duty bound to respect its own people and observe the law and those who fail to follow the rules of non-interference are by definition known as "regimes". This distinction applies whether it is in Nepal or elsewhere, including China. Some of the issues that illustrate this point are: What is the point in writing about the relations? What is "India-bashing" and how should the "one China policy" be observed?

One writes for discourse and not for obedience, for dialogue and not for promotion of official positions or to have a career in the corridors of power. Writing about diplomacy is not about conforming to the expectations of power-holders or academics, but to argue and counter argue for the betterment of the discourse. To further this cause, accountability is essential and private and public views are ought to be consistent.

The role of intellectuals, I believe, is to interprét reality, deconstruct and reconstruct discourse. It is not the fault of the discourse in itself, if someone's interpretation does not fit in the views of one or the other group of people or political parties. Consider the case of John Kenneth Galbraith, one of the giant public intellectuals, who was the US ambassador to India in the 1960s. His critics called him a communist sympathizer because he asserted that the US war against Vietnam was contrary to the interests of the United States. Galbraith's opposition to unregulated capitalism, which was in line with his sense of purpose "to help powerless people", led him to be branded as a "dissident".

What is India-bashing? Mahatma Gandhi's ideals of self-rule and local democracy have now become universal values, and who would not want those Indian values to be respected in India and abroad alike? The idea of peaceful coexistence in international relations as argued by Nehru is equally universal, but do the current regimes have lived up to the ideals. The Nepal-India relations, I would argue, go beyond history; it is one people intersected by modern borders of states. In the political sense, no self-respecting Nepali can ever forget Rammanohar Lohia who went to prison in India for the cause of Nepal's democracy.

Given these links between Indians and Nepalis, isn't it within the bounds of friendship to have healthy discussions about sensitive issues without being labelled an India-basher? For example, if one brings up the issue of the dignity of Nepali labourers in India and their contribution to the economy there, it seems that the reaction among some Indian and

Nepali élites is to counter-argue that India provides employment opportunities to millions of Nepali workers. How do these polemics enhance the discourse, and especially the cooperation that has characterised the relationship between Nepal and India over the centuries?

Regarding "One China" policy, it will be foolish to suggest that China should not be an integrated nation state. But in reality there are at least three Chinas in existence: Taiwan, Hong Kong and mainland China. The Taiwan government is almost independent and relatively democratic, with its own military and diplomatic relations around the world. Hong Kong is semi-autonomous, an unspoken exception that mainland China has accepted. These contradictions are clearly contrary to the "One China" policy. Why doesn't this toleration of multiple identities in China apply to Tibet? Self-rule and democracy for all the existing Chinese entities under "One China" would make sense rather than imposing the "One China" policy on Nepal. China's long record of trade and development assistance to Nepal is a testament to the two countries' friendship. Nepal's contributions to China over the past centuries include philosophy and architecture, among others.

Nepal has been a meeting and mixing centre of the ancient Chinese and Indian civilisations. These bonds should be the basis for genuine discussion of sensitive issues. The lesson for the genuine NIC relations is that we must learn how to become critical friends and not phony allies. Writers who are truly interested in furthering public discourse ought not be afraid of allegations and of being branded as one thing or another. The discourse on NIC relations will continue and it is up to us how it progresses.

Dhruba Kumar

Dateline Nepal: Managing the Peace

Introduction

Nepal's peace process is at the crossroads. Initiative towards peace is faltering as a consequence of divergence rather than convergence of interests between the political parties. The peace accord signed in November 2006 between the Seven Party Alliance (SPA) government and the CPN (Maoist) is virtually abandoned. The crucial agenda of the 'integration and management of the arms and armies' is deadlocked. The Maoists' combatants in the cantonments are waiting for their merger in the security forces since last four years. The Nepal Army has resisted the proposed integration of the guerrillas fearing an infringement on the institutional sanctity of the armed forces. In the absence of any concrete decision the problem is sticking. The peace process would be incomplete unless this challenge is resolved. The national predicament remains 'two armies, one state' and two competitive ideologies of communism and liberalism set against each other for governing the state. Nepal is now a nation with two states of mind.

The context

Although the crowning moment for Nepal was the successful conclusion of the CA elections on 10 April 2008, the objective reality is that all the state apparatuses remain intact. Nothing except the monarchy crashed. The military, the police, and the bureaucracy continue to function uninterrupted; the politicians of the past regime have renewed their legitimacy with the success of the *Jan Andolan-II* which led to the formation of the Maoist-led coalition government with the popular mandate of constitution making and peace building. Their withdrawal from the government on 4 May 2009, however, turned the tide of optimism into pessimism as politics took a belligerent course in inter-party interactions with the breakdown of fragile consensus. It was unexpected for the Maoists to be "ousted from power" (*Kantipur* 24 May 2009). Thus the Maoists pursuit of the single agenda to regain the lost power again under their leadership in the government as the largest party of the CA, but their inability to ascertain the magic number of 301 majorities in the legislative-parliament has defeated the momentum for peace and stability.

The Maoist leadership has pugnaciously accused certain foreign powers of conspiring against the Prachanda regime in Nepal. Except from an instinctively populist or leftist manner, the Maoists' leadership though, did not present any defining direction departing from the (mis)rule of its predecessor governments. The spectacular rise of Prachanda as a 'dramatis personnae' and his charisma faded sharply and dissolved in the political theatre of the absurd. Prachanda as a prime minister emerged as the most unpredictable executive who failed to even initiate the process of implementing the policy priority related to the commitment on integration and management of the Maoists' combatants. It was not the intransigence of the political opposition that impeded the peace process; it was but the Maoists' inability to convince and take other parties into confidence that stagnate the real issue around which the peace process revolves.

The situation is thus catastrophic. Notwithstanding mellowing and moderation in rhetoric, the Maoists are perceptually concerned with their ideological pursuit of *satta kabja*. The extremists among them are firing salvos for popular uprising for state seizure, whereas the apparently moderates are pursuing *salami* tactics - chasing state power within the framework of electoral politics first and then continuing to fight against the remnants of the so called regressive and reactionary regime. In substance, the difference in the objective of both the extremists and the moderates is paper thin and transparent. State power is central to the Maoists, despite the Leninist extinction, and their rendition remains 'grabbing' not 'smashing' the state.

The situation, as a result, has become more complicated in the competitive political environment than it was during the period of insurrectionary violence. The state is presently government-less with the 16th round of voting in the legislative-parliament failing to elect the prime minister. The state is budget-less as well, and verging towards collapse.

The Maoists opposed the caretaker government from presenting budget in the parliament. The financial crisis has exposed the vulnerability of the state. The situation was not so even when the state was in emergency and involved in violent forays against the Maoists. The failure of crisis management then had disrupted democracy with a loss of more than 16,278 people's lines, including 1,775 police and 978 army personal killed, disappeared and disabled, and whereabouts of over 1,221 commoners yet unknown (Kathmandu Post 22 September 2009; INSEC 2010).

Proliferation of small arms and emergence of some 109 armed groups presently are both a symptom and a cause of increased public insecurity. Consequently, violence remains at unacceptably high level featuring grievous transition to democracy. Data show some 1,284 people were killed and there were 2,100 abductions between 2006 and 2009, maximally committed by the emergent armed groups (Kathmandu Post, 22 September 2009). The politics of policing under the Special Security Plan of the government since August 2009 has led to 58 "encounter killings" in the Nepal Terai (Rising Nepal 4 March 2010). As impunity prevails, extrajudicial killings by the state has become 'judicious solution' to political violence. Distrust of policing and concern for personal safety has led to increase in private security establishments. This also signifies the case of the failure of conflict management, contravening the settlement of disputes between political parties and resulting into weakening of the state's capacity to deliver services to the citizenry. State capacity remains fuzzy in the absence of democratic accountability. Increase in both crime and corruption is therefore the consequence of the inefficacy of the state.

Shattered Economy

Meanwhile, national economy slides down to a situation in which hunger, scarcity and diseases have become common features for people living in the mid-and-far western Nepal. Chronic food crisis is reflection of Nepal becoming a food importing from being a food exporting country till 1970s. The youth bulge which is the essence of the economic productivity has become burdensome for the country to cope with employment challenges. Of the 400,000 job seekers entering the labour market per annum hardly 15 per cent are absorbed indigenously. Data presented by the Central

Bureau of Statistics in 2009 indicate that some 49.9 per cent of urban population is either totally unemployed or partially employed or underemployed or engaged in underpaid works. Of these 7.5 per cent population is totally unemployed in the urban areas. The rate of the use of the manpower between the age of 20 and 24 is 46 per cent in comparison to 39 per cent use of manpower of 25-29 age groups. The regular rush of youths for employment on foreign labour contracts can be observed and estimated with the crowd assembled at the passport section of the Foreign Ministry and the Airlines' counter at the Tribhuvan International Airport. The remittance they send back comprising 23 per cent of national GDP sustains consumerism at home. Conversely, an increasing number of commercial banks, shopping malls, flourishing casinos and motor vehicle showrooms in Kathmandu present an aura of thriving urban economy significantly indicating the widening rural-urban gap the progenitor of conflict. For an overwhelming majority of the Nepali population their preoccupation is to stay alive. Nepal is one of the most impoverished and least developed countries in the world with 0.509 Human Development Index in the year 2006 (UNDP 2009). Despite the government's claim of decreasing poverty level to 25 per cent (NPC 2010), the finding of an independent study suggests that 65 per cent Nepalese are below poverty line (OPHI 2010). Even though the data on decline in poverty is believed, income inequality has widened as increase in Gini coefficient from 0.34 to 0.41 indicates (CBS, et.al 2006). Accompanying this is disastrous public insecurity, double digit inflation and political uncertainty creating a situation where implementation of reforms is very difficult.

Nepal has lived with an artificially induced economic phenomenon with aid and trade by becoming an import regime since long. Aid sustains the elitist articulation of economic development even to the extent of bridging trade imbalance. Increasing imports and decreasing exports are signs of economic ruin. Imports of consumer luxuries, including branded motor vehicles and petroleum products to oil the superficial veneer of the urban life style have become unsustainable by the primary exports of the illiterate, undervalued and unskilled manpower from rural Nepal. Petroleum products, gold and vehicles are top three import items in Nepal (Kathmandu Post, 9 September 2010a). Energy that fuels industries and other economic activities is scarce reaching over 16-hours regular load-shedding although electrification has over a century's history in Nepal. Deficit finance has become unpalatable despite the increase in both domestic and foreign debts (GON 2010). Thus the country is invalid economically. Over a decade of insurgency has swamped whatever industrial and commercial potentialities the country had. The continued extortions and threats of closure by trade unions have run down industries and encouraged capital flight although some are still struggling to survive. Political instability has discouraged any renewal efforts. This scenario has debilitating effect on FDI of which India remains the largest investor in Nepal.

The shattered economy is further victimized by manifold increase in corruption. Peculiar interrelationship between a rise in revenue and government spending increasing the level of corruption is evident in Nepal. The prevalent culture of impunity has impeded law to take its course. Nepal's tarnished image is reflected in its pathetic slide down to 146 positions in 2010 from143 position in 2009 and far below from 121 ranking in 2008 out of 180 countries on the corruption perception index (CPI) developed by the Transparency International. Nepal has become more corrupt than before falling from 2.7 to 2.3 point in 2009 and further down to 2.2 point in 2010. In the measuring scale of 10 the latest score indicates a situation of growing corruption problem under democracy. A country measuring below 3 point is considered rampantly corrupt. State fragility is nowhere ascertained more concretely than in failure to control corruption under governments led by communist parties in Nepal. Evidently, corruption is eating up the vitals of national economy; fragility deepens in the absence of political will, thus, the urgency of a rethinking on the issue does not exist. It is not economic austerity that would correct the deepening economic malaise; it is necessary to control political gangsterism in order to enable the economy to deliver. State fragility is compounded further by lawlessness caused by political meddling. Law enforcing institutions should, thus, be left without political interference making judiciary free of political influence. The prevalence of rule of law is indispensable for consolidating democracy based in defence of human rights. The trampling of the human rights, instead, has become the 'best practice' pointing towards the institutional inefficacy of the state.

Picking up the Pieces

Among the many complicated issues facing the state, three are in absolute priority that could be ignored on its own peril. Crucial to the peace process to bear fruition is the amelioration of the conflicting interests between the stakeholders, particularly on the sensitive issue of integration and rehabilitation of the guerrillas living in the cantonments. The second is resettlement and rehabilitation of the displaced people and their return to normalcy. The third is the process of constitution making pursued seriously for enhancing the prospect of peace and stability. These issues, though, interrelated to determining the future of the post-monarchical Nepal, have become controversial between the political parties involved in the statecraft.

The first issue relates to the security sensitivity of the state and the objective of the Maoists as a party to the conflict. Except for discharging 4,008 disqualified, including 2,973 under-aged Maoist combatants from all the 7 main and 21 satellite cantonments, any progress in settling the challenge of integration is yet to be made. Second, the rehabilitation of the internally displaced people (IDPs) as the victim of violence has proceeded under the Nepal Peace Fund with substantial assistance from rich donors. But the fund was largely misused by the political parties in power resulting into injustice to the real victim of violence. The Local Peace Committees are indulgent in misappropriation of relief fund through political compromise. Such a practice has discouraged the actual victims of conflict to return to their place of origins for fear of discrimination and reprisal. The demand for establishing Truth and Reconciliation and Disappearance Commissions has continued for providing social justice to displaced, dislocated and physical victims of conflict.

Third, the constitution making process by the elected representatives has been the core of the struggle of the people for transforming Nepal into a democratic republic. The Maoists had propagated the elections to the CA as foundational objective of their insurgency. But, as the Maoists have preferred to draft the national constitution to their liking and on their own terms (Bhattarai, 2009), the process is now nipped in the bud. The High-Level Task Force led by the Maoist Chairman Prachanda is still quibbling on inserting the term "People's War" in the Preamble of the Constitution and on the question of compulsory military training to 18-year old citizens. Despite the fact that the legitimacy of the Task Force has already been questioned by the Chairman of the Constitutional Committee of the CA, Nilamber Acharya claiming its decisions will not be compulsory for the CA to implement, the Task Force has continued to function as a political gambit (*Kantipur*, 21 October 2010a). It has collectively decided, for example, on crucial issues related to independent judiciary, citizenship and vernacular Nepali as official language by upholding the multilingual policy.

The nature of the peace process was strongly motivated by dynamics of negotiations shaped by internal developments after the *Jan Andolan-II*. The essence of Comprehensive Peace Agreement (CPA) signed on 21 November 2006 is the power sharing between the contracting parties. It should be mentioned that the peace negotiation and agreement arrived at was not between the rivals; it was, but, between the parties who jointly struggled against autocratic monarchy and succeeded to bring about regime change in Nepal. This unique quality of peace agreement did not, however, sustain both general and specific issues inherent in it. In general terms, the CPA refrained from pursuing strategies to evolve a situation where the culture of impunity would be discouraged and the rule of law prevail to curb violence and anarchy providing social justice by upholding human rights of the citizenry. Along with the transitional justice, the CPA, on the other hand, is yet to deal seriously with specific issues like the return of the seized property, integration and rehabilitation of the Maoists' combatants to resolve the gnawing challenge posed by "two armies, one state" and democratizing and professionalizing the armed forces (GON 2006).

Two agreements signed recently by the contending parties have refreshingly reiterated to abide by the past commitments in pursuit of the peace process. First, the 'Three point agreement' signed by the top leaders of three major political parties on 28 May 2010 recommitted themselves to implement the prior commitments 'to carry on the historical responsibility of making new constitution' (point-1) followed by the extension of the term of the CA for one more year for drafting the constitution (point-2) and immediate resignation of the incumbent prime minister to clear the way for the formation of a government based on national consensus (point-3) (Kantipur, 29 May 2010b). Second, following the extension of the tenure of the CA and resignation of the prime minister but without implementing the 'prior commitments' simply described as a 'preamble' to the agreement by the Maoists, the political leaders tied their hands again by signing a 'four point agreement' that reads as:

"We, embracing past agreements and creating an environment of trust, have agreed to the following points, in order to take the peace process to a logical conclusion:

1. To give final shape to all documents prepared by the Special Committee for forwarding the peace process by reaching agreement on them as soon as possible and implementing them.
2. To bring the Maoist combatants under the Special Committee without delay and share all details about the Maoist combatants with the Committee.
3. To take up the remaining tasks of the peace process from September 17 and complete them basically by January 14, 2011.
4. To extend the term of UNMIN for the last time for a period of four months, under the current mandate (Republica, 14 September 2010).

As mentioned in point-4, UNMIN's presence by invitation for monitoring the peace process has become controversial since the beginning of 2007, albeit extension of its term for the 7th time. Its last term was extended by the UN Security Council on 15 September for 4 months as requested by the government and the Maoists in a consensus letter to the Secretary-General. The UNMIN will stay in Nepal till 15 January 2011. As per the point-2, the chain of command of the Maoists' guerrillas in the cantonment has shifted to the Special Committee in principle with understanding on transforming the Technical Committee to a Secretariat by adding four new members from security sector and the Maoists party. But the task is becoming more complicated as the Maoists again defied their commitment.

The recent disclosure about the 'secret understanding' between the Prime Minister and the Maoist Chairman on 27 June leading to the resignation of the Prime Minister on 30 June 2010 again proves the unrelenting Maoists' hypocrisy. They agreed on the terms of engagement by integrating 5,000 guerrillas in army, police and armed police force and confining the rest in separate camp providing attractive package without putting them under the Special Committee. They had also agreed to complete the task of integration during the tenure of the UNMIN within the 4-months and promulgate a democratic constitution by January 2011. However, the Maoists' urge to form a government under their leadership first and taking up the pieces through consensus later has destroyed the peace process (Nagarik, 5 July 2010). Nepal thus faces the dilemmas of peace building in the absence of credible leaders as peace building understandably is the "implementation of peace agreement" (Jarstad 2008:32). But the CPA has itself become a matter of scathing criticism for some like the Defence Minister becoming a nuisance in the cabinet (Republica, 8 October 2009). Belligerency and hate speech of political leaders targeting each other and punctuated by the rhetoric of the state seizure have presented a paranoid situation in the society. Consideration of military option even by the prime minister against the Maoists' mischief (Kathmandu Post, 28 April 2010b) has expressed ultimate despair with possible breakdown of the peace process. Timothy Sisk argues, "peace building should be based on durable termination of war" by introducing democracy "as a way to move the theatre of conflict off the battlefield and into the institutions and processes of politics" (Sisk 2008:239).

The CPA, being the framework arrangement for integrating the Maoist guerrillas, has dispensed the responsibility to the Interim Council of Ministers to supervise, integrate and rehabilitate the Maoist combatants (GON 2006). On integration, the agreement on the "Monitoring of the Management of Arms and Armies 2006" uses the term "possible integration into the security forces" provided that the ex-combatants "fulfill the standard norms"(Peace Secretariat 2006:12). Similarly, Article 146 of the Interim Constitution 2007 has stipulated that the council of ministers would form a Special Committee comprising the members of major political parties represented at the Constituent assembly to "supervise, integrate and rehabilitate the combatants of the Maoists Army". The "Arms Monitoring" agreement is explicit in suggesting "Only those Maoists combatants" registered properly at "cantonment sites" will be "eligible for possible integration" into the "security forces" provided they "fulfill the standard norms" implying the recruitment procedure of the Nepali Army.

Yet the problem stands as before. First, no meeting point has been made on the exact number of guerrillas to be integrated in the four wings of security forces. Second, there is absence of consensus on the proposed formation of a separate security institution to accommodate Maoists' guerrillas as an alternative. Third, the government's position on integration of guerrillas in three categories (i) joining the security forces; (ii) joining the mother party; and (iii) return to civil life with the provision of appropriate incentives up to Rs. 375,000 compensation with more than 60 package proposal is not acceptable to the Maoists. They have countered it by demanding Rs. 2 million for each guerrilla returning to political and civil life with rehabilitation package.

The Maoists have used guerrillas as bargaining chips. Linking the integration issue with the formation of government, they have proposed to maintain maximum flexibility on integration in case of other parties' acceptance of government under their party's leadership and vice versa. Their proposed framework for integration is (i) establishing an agency alike industrial security force comprising 7 to 8 thousand combatants; (ii) establishing around 15,000 strong border security force constituting 50 per cent manpower from the army, police and armed police force; and (iii) group merger of some 7-8 thousand combatants in police, armed police force along with at least 3,000 combatants in the army making separate units. However, the Maoists have refrained from acceding to the eligibility norms of the military recruitment while enlisting in the army (Kantipur, 11 July 2010).

In their counterproposals, the NC and the CPN (UML) have argued for (i) determining the number of combatants for merger and separating them from others to be rehabilitated within three weeks; (ii) surrendering all weapons to the government; (iii) lifting the dual security system provided to the Maoists leaders; (iv) returning seized property to their rightful owners within two weeks; and (v) ending the works related to rehabilitation and enlisting in the security forces within four months (Kantipur, 16 and 17 July 2010).

Meanwhile, the leak of a 60-week work plan on "integration and rehabilitation" submitted by the UNMIN to stakeholders has drawn the UNMIN into fresh controversy for overstepping its mandate. When political parties have been contending and contemplating on different options for resolving the merger and rehabilitation issue, the 'non-paper' created an uproar in the government, involving the prime minister, the defence minister, the peace and reconstruction minister and even the army chief in a row. UNMIN is accused of conniving with the Maoists and trying to extend its stay in Nepal. It was stringently argued that since there is no "two sides in the conflict", any rationale for extending UNMIN's term would be unpropitious (Pokharel 2010). Fortunately, the controversy did not led to the non-renewal of the UNMIN's term as understanding prevailed and the controversy died down with the 4-month extension of the UNMIN's term in Nepal.

The integration issue is again wrapped by controversy and lapsed into hibernation. The controversy in question was caused by the news of the visit to China by three of the guerrilla commanders from the cantonments taking leave of absence without the knowledge of the Special Committee. This case again draws the monitoring practice of UNMIN into question that responded with ignorance about the China visit of the guerrilla commanders. Next, the understanding that was forged to establish the secretariat constituting the 12-members Technical Committee is yet to be completed with the representation of one additional Maoist member since the last meeting in 30 September 2010. This has interrupted the integration process from moving ahead.

Conclusion

Thus the outcome of the momentous change with the assertion of a republican order is not encouraging. The promise of "permanent peace" identified with the Maoists' commitment to "full democracy" underpinning the 12-point understanding of 22 November 2005 and CPA of 21 November 2006 as the crucial outcome of that understanding is now under critical scrutiny (Republica, 8 October 2009). Central to this test is the issue of the integration of the Maoists' combatants in the security forces. The visiting Undersecretary-General of the United Nations for Political Affairs B. Lynn Pascoe has reminded his interlocutors of two things: first, the stakeholders in Nepal should be anxious about integration and rehabilitation of the combatants in the cantonments rather than the continuity of the UNMIN. Second, if the political leadership fails to agree to build consensus other forces may emerge to take control of the situation that could be extremely dangerous (Pascoe 2010).

The 'secret rendezvous' of the leaders of three major political parties at a resort in Kathmandu between 5 and 6 November 2010 reportedly ended with the signing of a four point understanding to observe the prior commitments and continue the talks for final outcome on constitution making and the peace process. They assembled again on 10 November at another resort and emerged with "constructive consensus" to continue the talks (Kantipur ,11 November 2010). This simply turns out to be another political gimmick at the nation's expenses. As the participants later disclosed, the two days talks focused on the four alternatives proposed by the Maoists on the formation of government either on their leadership or on rotation or on collective with chairmanship or the Maoists in opposition. The caveat however is that except from proposition one and four the other two are beyond the purview of Interim Constitution 2007. Though all the three parties presumably consider the proposal to rule the country on rotation, they themselves would like to be the first choice to be seated in power. But none agrees.

No agreements are self-implementing. Mutual compliance is required to implement the agreements. The Maoists abide by their electoral majority in the CA but nothing else. They feel this majority has conferred on them an invincible legitimacy to form government under their leadership. They have consistently argued that the precondition for peace and constitution making is their leadership of the government. Contrary is the view of the other political parties within and outside the CA. Their precondition for the Maoists' leadership of the government is renouncing violence along with the final decision on integration of the combatants and adherence to the democratic constitution making. Dithering on these views has continued the deadlock. The implication of this uncongenial situation created by the policy positions of three major political parties have to be examined to understand the nation's travails. Political leaders have, indeed, destroyed their own state in order to exert power and influence with personalized patronage. Their claims to electoral legitimacy has led the four years of boiling peace coming in the wake of over a decade of violent conflict to spill giving vent to spoilers of the process. The possibility for realigning these two conditions through an honest bargain nevertheless exists to avert the impending.

References

Bhattarai, Baburam (2009): "Ekkaishaun satapadiko krantiko karyadisha," *Naya Patrika*, 29 and 30 January.

CBS, et.al (2006): "Resilience Amidst Conflict: An Assessment of Poverty in *Nepal 1995-96 and 2003-04*, CBS/The World Bank/ DFID/ ADB, Kathmandu.

GON (2010): *Economic Survey Fiscal Year* 2009/10, Government of Nepal/Ministry of Finance (Vol. I), Kathmandu.

GON (2006): "Bistrit shanti samjhouta", *Kantipur Daily*, 22 November.

INSEC (2010): *Conflict Victim's Profile*, Informal Sector Service Centre, Kathmandu.

Jarstad, Anna K., (2008), "Dilemmas of War-to-Democracy Transitions: Theories and Concepts," in Anna K. Jarstad and Timothy D. Sisk (eds), *From War to Democracy: Dilemmas of Peace building*, Cambridge University Press, Cambridge.

Jowitt, Ken (1992): *New World Disorder: The Leninist Extinction*, : University of California Press, Berkeley, CA.

Kantipur (2010a): "Karyadalko haishiyat rajnitik", 21 October.

Kantipur (2010b): " Yesto chha teen dalko sahamati patra", 29 May.

Kantipur (2010c): "Maobadiko tin mahine samayojan prastav", 11 July.

Kantipur (2010d)): "Ladaku byabyasthapanbare kangress ra a-maleko prastav" and "Kangressko char mahine samayojana karyayojana", 16 and 17 July.

Kantipur (2009), "Sattabata bahirinuparla bhanne sochenko thiyeaun: Mohan Vaidya

'Kiran'", 24 May.

Kathmandu Post (2010a): "Oil, gold, vehicles top Nepal import list", 9 September.

Kathmandu Post (2010b): "Govt tells army to brace itself", 28 April.

Kathmandu Post (2009): "Nepal still a killing field", 22 September.

Nagarik (2010): "Nepal-Dahal 'Gopya Sahamati' alpatra", 5 July.

NPC (2010): "Nepal Millennium Development Goals: Progress Report", National Planning Commission, Kathmandu.

OPHI (2010): *Country Briefing: Multidimensional Poverty Index (MPI) At a Glance*, Oxford Department of International Development, Queen Elizabeth House, University of Oxford, Oxford, July, http://ophi.qeh.ox.ac.uk www.ophi.org.uk

Pascoe, B. Lynn (2010), "Shanti prakriyama pragati nabhaye missionka laagi kharcha garna sakinna", *Kantipur Daily*, 20 October, (An Interview).

Peace Secretariat (2006): "Agreement on Monitoring of the Management of Arms and Armies, 8 December 2006", Kathmandu.

Pokharel, Rajan (2010), "UNMIN hand-in glove with Maoists, claim NA," *Himalayan Times*, 26 August.

Rising Nepal (2010): "Special security plan to be bolstered," 4 March.

Republica 14 September 2010.

Republica (2009): "Defence Minister wants CPA reviewed," 8 October.

Sisk, Timothy D. (2008): "Peace Building as Democratization: Findings and Recommendations," in Anna K. Jarstad and Timothy D. Sisk (eds.), From War to *Democracy: Dilemmas of Peace Building*, Cambridge University Press, Cambridge.

UNDP (2009): "Nepal: Human Development Report 2009: State Transformation and Human Development", United Nations Development Programme, Kathmandu.

Prashant Jha

Nepal: Departure of UNMIN and the Peace Process

Nepali politics has entered an uncharted and dangerous territory after the departure of the United Nations Mission in Nepal (UNMIN) on January 15. UNMIN's exit has come amidst growing apprehension that Nepal may not meet its extended deadline of writing the Constitution by May 28. While a new process to elect a Prime Minister will begin soon, its outcome remains uncertain. All formal structures of the 2006 political framework suddenly appear fragile.

UNMIN has been an integral component of Nepal's peace agreements. For the past four years, it has monitored 19,000-plus combatants and 3,000-plus weapons of the Maoist People's Liberation Army (PLA) and a limited number of personnel and arms of the Nepal Army (NA); chaired the Joint Monitoring Coordination Committee (JMCC) that acts as a mechanism to resolve disputes between the NA and the PLA; and has been a symbolic deterrent against the resumption of violence.

Despite Maoist pressure, the Madhav Nepal-led caretaker government refused to request the U.N. Security Council to extend UNMIN's term once again. But its exit will leave a vacuum, for there are no mutually acceptable, alternative arrangements on a range of issues.

Who will do the monitoring? The government says the statutory all-party special committee will take over UNMIN's responsibilities as per a past agreement. The Maoists, however, are pushing alternative ideas a joint political mechanism, joint teams of the NA and the PLA, or a civil society mechanism.

Who will be monitored? The government insists that there is no need to monitor the NA anymore as the context has changed, while the Maoists argue that the same arrangement applies to both armies in accordance with the Agreement on the Monitoring of the Management of Arms and Armies.

What happens to the arms? The government has asked UNMIN to hand over the Maoist weapons, Maoists have said 'no', and UNMIN has taken the position that the arms will be handed over to the party which owns them in this case, the Maoists.

Who will resolve the disputes on the code of conduct and its violations? UNMIN did so in JMCC quietly and efficiently out of media glare but no alternative neutral mechanism is in place yet.

The impact goes well beyond the technical aspects, about which the parties may well find an agreement at the last minute. UNMIN's absence will increase the possibility of even a small incident spiralling out of control. The Maoists have already said this takes the country back to a 'ceasefire' situation. UNMIN leaves at a time when the most complex task of this process integration and rehabilitation of the former combatants has not even started. Its expertise and good offices could have played an important role in guiding the process. Peace has held in Nepal because Nepali actors, including the Nepal Army and the Maoists, have behaved with restraint and responsibility, but UNMIN's exit will make this task more difficult.

Why has UNMIN been pushed out?

When it was invited in 2006, UNMIN was an insurance policy for the Maoists. The former rebels saw it as giving the peace process international legitimacy; the leadership also had a sense of personal security with UNMIN around at a time when entering open politics was a big gamble. The other parties saw UNMIN's presence as useful too it kept a check on the Maoist military apparatus as well as the NA, whose loyalties were suspect given its backing for the royal coup. The U.N.'s credibility was high and its human rights mission played an enabling role in the 2006 people's movement. India was reluctant to allow U.N. presence in the neighbourhood but then gave into the wishes of the Nepali parties after realising that there was no other way to take the peace process forward.

What has changed since then is the balance of power. From working with the Maoists and being wary of the NA, the older parties, especially the Nepali Congress and the Communist Party of Nepal (Unified Marxist Leninist), now see the NA as an ally and are deeply suspicious of the Maoists' intentions and their commitment to democracy. UNMIN began to be viewed as providing a "safety blanket" to the former rebels for, it treated them as a 50 per cent stakeholder in the peace process and recognised their army. The NA has always been furious with UNMIN for "equating the NA and the PLA," and was lobbying hard to be removed from UNMIN's monitoring. India's old suspicion about other international actors in its 'backyard' persisted.

In the beginning, New Delhi worked hard to ensure that UNMIN had a limited and weak mandate but more recently it has been lobbying with other international capitals, and now with fellow members in the Security Council, to wrap up the mission. Washington and London were happy to follow the Indian lead on Nepal, even though the Secretary-General in his report stated conditions for UNMIN's departure were not optimal.

This formidable coalition of India, the U.S. and the U.K. internationally and the non-Maoist parties and the Nepal Army domestically argues that UNMIN's presence allows the Maoists to drag on the peace process; its exit will remove a safety valve and bring pressure on them, in turn, forcing them to "reform" and "disarm." But this appears more like wishful thinking which ignores the roots of the present crisis. UNMIN's exit and the larger Indian policy may well end up making the Maoists even more insecure and reluctant to let go of their coercive apparatus.

Misplaced policy

Pushing UNMIN out is in line with India's broader Nepal policy, the key tenet of which is to isolate the Maoists and exclude them from the formal power structure as the only way of democratising them. Indian officials believe that the Maoists have used the peace process only "tactically;" harbour authoritarian ambitions and cannot be allowed back to power until they undergo a "course correction," which would include giving up the PLA. Otherwise, it is argued, they would consolidate power and subvert all democratic institutions, and it would be impossible to dislodge them.

To this end, India has invested enormous political capital in galvanising the anti-Maoist forces together, and ensuring that Prachanda did not get to the majority mark in the prime ministerial elections. There is a section in both New Delhi and Kathmandu which believes that like UNMIN, the Constituent Assembly, where the Maoists command 40 per cent of the seats, is another "safety blanket" for the former rebels. This school tried hard to ensure that the CA did not get an extension last May. They are now hoping for its dissolution by the May 28 constitutional deadline, in order to "isolate" the Maoists from the only formal state structure in which they have space the legislature.

The problem with this approach is that it only strengthens the dogmatic branch within the Maoist party, and underestimates the intensity of the conflict Nepal will be engulfed in if the constitutional process fails.

It is true that the Maoists have dragged their feet on the integration and rehabilitation of the former combatants, which makes the other parties insecure about their democratic commitment. At the same time, the Maoists are insecure too for, they are being asked to surrender a major source of power, largely on the Nepal Army's terms, while in the Opposition. The hardliners within the party are quick to point out how "bourgeoisie democracy" is a sham as the largest party cannot form a government, how "Indian expansionists and Nepali reactionaries" have ganged up on them and are conspiring to dissolve the CA, and how the party should not give up the PLA at such a time reminding the cadres of the Mao dictum, "without the army, people have nothing."

The reluctance of the non-Maoist parties to share power, the Maoist dogma, and India's hardline approach all feed on one another and have contributed to mutual insecurities and belligerence on all sides, limiting the space for compromise. The Nepali Congress' withdrawal from the prime ministerial race, and the imminent initiation of a new process to elect a Prime Minister, have opened up one final opportunity to reengineer the consensus needed to push the peace and constitutional process forward.

India must shun aiding the polarisation and play a constructive role in facilitating a deal on power-sharing and the peace process, in which the Maoists will be accommodated without their coercive apparatus. This is a prerequisite for the drafting of Constitution and preventing the collapse of Nepal's ambitious experiment in political transformation.

Aditya Adhikari

Nepal's Constituent Assembly
A Conflict between Opposing World Views

The Constituent Assembly (CA) and the constitution it is meant to draft have in the Nepali popular mind been imbued with an extraordinary degree of significance. During the 2006 popular uprising against the monarchy, the political parties explained to the public that the popular movement underway heralded the beginning of a process that would culminate in a constitution drafted together by the older parliamentary parties and the Maoists and would lead to a stable peace. As the exuberance of the uprising subsided and the country's troubles returned political conflict between the major parties, simmering revolts based on culture or ethnicity and a general breakdown of law and order the public was led to believe that these troubles would disappear after elections to the CA. During the two years following the success of the movement against direct rule by the monarchy May 2006 to April 2008 all political struggles were focused on these elections: on the nature of the electoral system, on calculations based on what it would take for each party to be victorious.

Since May 2008, when the CA sat for the first time, popular discourse has presented the outcome of deliberations of the body as absolutely crucial to the future of the country. The constitution that the body will eventually promulgate, it is held, will sweep away all the sources of exploitation and discrimination that large sections of the population have been suffering from for centuries, will allow all citizens to exercise autonomous and direct democracy within their domains and thus allow for the harmonious and prosperous development of society.

Over the past two years, however, it has become clear that intractable differences persist between the major political parties over, among other things, the nature of the new constitution. Unable to resolve their differences and promulgate a constitution on schedule, the parties came to a last-minute agreement on May 28, 2010 the date the CA's term was set to expire to extend the term of the body by a year. Over six months have elapsed since this date but there has been little progress in resolving the differences.

This has led to great public cynicism that is regularly expressed in private conversations across the country and amplified by the media. "None of the parties are really interested in drafting the constitution," the refrain goes. "All they are interested in is undermining their rivals and emerging as the most powerful political party." There is some truth to this way of thinking. The constitution drafting process has been hampered by power games between the various political actors. The older parliamentary parties feel that the Maoists have become too powerful and that they are intent on establishing permanent control over the state apparatus. The Maoists in turn feel that the parliamentary parties are intent on marginalizing them and their agenda. The struggle for power between the two sides is manifested through conflicts on issues such as power sharing and government formation, and the future of Maoist combatants. Much of the energy of leaders of all parties is being spent on such issues, and as a result inadequate attention is being paid to the constitution drafting process.

This is not the whole story, however. Some progress has been made. The CA formed 11 committees soon after it came into existence. Seven of these committees were entrusted with the task to draft concept papers on various facets of the constitution such as fundamental rights and directive principles, the form of governance to be adopted and state restructuring (federalism). These committees, each consisting of members from all the large political parties and a wide array of the smaller ones, did sit together to deliberate and made attempts to reach resolution on difficult issues. In a large number of cases, however, the disagreements ran deep and could not be resolved. In each committee, the positions that commanded most of the votes were acknowledged in the concept paper; the positions that received fewer votes were registered as "notes of dissent."

Since then, a high-level task force that includes the top leaders of each major political party has been formed. Its task is to deliberate and resolve the disagreements that exist. 210 points of contention have been identified. Some 100 of them have been resolved so far. The numbers, however, are deceptive. The parties are nowhere close to reaching agreement. The issues on which agreement has been reached are relatively trivial and related to the more peripheral aspects of the constitution. The difficult issues have not been tackled yet.

Almost all of the disagreements have the Maoists on one side and the older parliamentary parties - the Nepali Congress and the CPN-UML - on the other. There are a number of smaller parties that have particular views of their own on some minor issues, but overall they are lined up in support of one of the two major sides. On all issues, the Maoists accuse the traditional parties of seeking to preserve the status quo. The Nepali Congress and the UML, on the other hand, accuse the Maoists of seeking to impose an authoritarian state on Nepal.

It is necessary to take a look at the disagreements in the CA in order to understand as to why they appear so intractable. While discussion of all the disagreements is beyond the scope of this article, it is possible to make a broad sense of the constitutional debate in Nepal through a discussion of the disagreements over the most important issues: the nature of the executive, legislature and judiciary and of the federal provinces and their demarcation.

The Executive

The Maoists maintain that Nepal requires a presidential system, where the president will occupy the positions of both head of state and head of government. The president is to be directly elected and is to select a council of ministers from all parties according to the proportion of seats they hold in the legislature. The Maoists hold that such a system is necessary in order to bring a degree of stability to governance in Nepal.

According to their argument, the parliamentary system that has existed in Nepal for the past two decades is inherently highly unstable. For most of Nepal's recent history, no single party has commanded a majority in parliament and all governments that have thus been formed have required coalitions of a number of parties. Rapidly shifting political alignments have meant that these coalitions last for a very short periods of time. Government turnover is thus extraordinarily high. Nepal, as a result, has been deprived of governments that have been able to act as agents of change and implement long-term policy. Rather, those who gain positions of power, understanding that their tenure in office is likely to be short, have spent most of their efforts on remaining in power for as long as possible and on enriching themselves.

Further, the provision for separate heads of state and of government in a parliamentary system, by allowing for a division of supreme authority over the state, also, according to the Maoists, creates problems. In such a situation, the head of state is provided with the opportunity to expand his or her power over that of the elected government. This was seen very clearly when the monarch, constitutionally the head of state, exploited ambiguous provisions in the 1990 constitution to first dissolve the parliament in 2002 and later directly take over executive power in 2005.

Replacing the parliamentary system with the presidential one, the Maoists hold, will solve all such problems. In a system where president is directly elected, it will not be easy to get rid of governments as easily as when the head of government is under the control of the legislature. This will bring an end to the instability that has existed so far and enable governments to think in terms of long-term planning and policy implementation. And by investing the president with the authority of both the head of state and of government, it will be possible to avoid problems arising from a division of supreme state authority.

The Nepali Congress, in particular, is strongly opposed to the Maoist position and has been demanding that Nepal continue with an executive system closely similar to the one that has existed for the past two decades. The Congress holds that there will be too great a concentration of power in a presidential system along the lines that the Maoists have proposed. A president in such a system will be largely unaccountable to the legislature or the public. Even if he or she performs highly objectionable actions, there will be few mechanisms to remove him or her from office. Similarly, the current provisions for the head of state separate from the head of government are necessary, according to the Congress, to act as a check upon attempts by the head of government to expand his or her power. The Maoist model, where the heads of state and government are one and the same, and the president is directly elected and is not dependent on the legislature, will lead in the direction of authoritarianism.

The Legislature

The Maoists have been insisting that the constitution must make it categorical that the legislature will be unicameral and not include any provision for an opposition. In their opinion, a House of Representatives (HoR) consisting of lawmakers elected directly should be allowed to work unhindered as it represents the will of the people. There is therefore no need for an upper house, which can only hamper the functioning of the HoR. And, in the Maoist opinion, it is necessary to ensure that conflict is avoided in the legislature. Therefore, they state, there will be no provision for an opposition. Rather, all parties in the legislature will be represented in government in proportion to the number of seats they occupy in that body.

The Nepali Congress and the CPN-UML, arguing from a liberal democratic standpoint, are firmly against both these positions. They argue that checks and balances lie at the essence of every democracy. An unchecked unicameral legislature will allow the majority to take decisions that ride roughshod over the rights of the minority. An upper house is necessary to act as a dampener on the passions of the lower house and to protect the minority. Similarly, the legislature requires an opposition present in it to check the unrestrained ambitions of the majority that is in power. Without provisions for an opposition, the smaller parties can only stand idly by as the larger parties take decisions that go against the interests of those sections of society represented by the former.

The Judiciary

The Maoists argue that so far in Nepal's history, the judiciary has failed to provide justice and have been wholly unaccountable to the wider population; it is thus necessary to subject it to greater public control and scrutiny. They have thus recommended that a Special Judicial Committee, consisting of members of the legislature be formed. This committee will recommend appointments to positions of the chief justice and other judges of the Supreme Court and after approval of the legislature, the president will ratify this recommendation. Bringing appointments under the control of the legislature (and thus of the people, which this body represents) is, according to the Maoists, a method of ensuring that the judiciary becomes more responsive and accountable. Further, the Maoists argue, the Special Judicial Committee under the legislature should also have the ultimate power to interpret the constitution and all federal laws.

The Nepali Congress and the UML, as can readily be imagined, are vehemently opposed to the Maoist position on the judiciary. It is a basic tenet of democracy, they argue, that there exist a separation of power between the three major organs of the state: executive, legislature and judiciary. The job of the legislature is to create laws; that of the judiciary to interpret them. If, as the Maoists desire, the legislature is allowed to impose its control over the judiciary, the latter will lose all its independence. If the legislature is allowed to both create and interpret laws, it will have too great a power, which it will utilize in an unrestrained and arbitrary direction. In other words, the Maoist provisions on the judiciary, if implemented will lead to the tyranny of the party that is dominant. In order to preserve the independence of the judiciary, it is necessary that appointments to the Supreme and other courts be made by a Judicial Council that is independent of the legislature. And, similarly, the courts should have the ultimate right to interpret the constitution and the laws, not the legislature.

Federalism

The arguments employed in the dispute over the federal system to be adopted are somewhat different from the ones brought to bear over the executive, legislature and judiciary. According to the Maoists, the various marginalized caste, cultural, linguistic, regional and ethnic groups of Nepal have for centuries been oppressed by a unitary state controlled by the upper-caste Hindu elite. As Lenin argued with reference to the countries in early twentieth-century Eastern Europe, the Maoists once believed that for a period of time all such oppressed groups (which they refer to as "nationalities") need to be granted full autonomy, including the right to self-determination.

The party's current position on federalism is a direct outgrowth of this Leninist position. As oppression historically took place along ethnic and cultural lines, it is argued, federalism is necessary to grant these oppressed groups the rights they have not been allowed to exercise so far. Federal provinces should thus be delineated based on areas where particular ethnic, cultural or caste groups are numerically dominant and should be named after them. These groups should be allowed "special rights" (in access to natural resources or over state power in the province, for example) over the other groups that live in the province. And each province should be granted the right to self-determination (according to the concept paper on state restructuring, however, this right, in Nepal, will not include the right to secession.)

The Maoists have the support of many cultural and ethnic groups that have historically been discriminated against by the Nepali state. The Nepali Congress and the UML, therefore, have had to accept the demand for federalism. But the latter two parties openly continue to be vehemently against federalism based on ethnicity or culture. They maintain that there is no area in Nepal where a particular cultural group is in majority. To allow a particular group "special rights" is to ensure their dominance over other groups in the province. This, it is claimed, is opposed to democratic values, according to which all groups and individuals should be provided with equal opportunities. Further, the Congress and the UML believe that the Maoist delineation of provinces, based primarily on the identity of the groups that live there, is not economically viable as some provinces have a minuscule amount of resources whereas some have a substantial amount. The non-Maoist parties thus propose that the delineation of provinces be placed in the hands of a technocratic committee consisting of economists and geographers. The attempt here is also to depoliticize the federalism debate and to prevent Nepali politics from descending into an excessive focus on identity, which, the older parliamentary parties believe, can only lead to ethnic strife and violence.

Opposing world views

From the outline presented here, it is clear that the debate in the CA is one between two entirely opposing world views. The Maoist world view holds that the parliamentary system, or, more generally, the liberal democratic one, has significant flaws that led to highly detrimental outcomes when implanted in a poor and highly unequal country like Nepal. In particular, it is believed, parliamentary democracy in this country weakened the power of the state. Consumed by factional struggles, it was unable to implement any coherent policy. It therefore needs to be replaced by a system in which the state is substantially stronger, where those in power are granted far more authority than they have been previously so that they can implement the serious reform that Nepal greatly needs. Further, the parliamentary system, besides being captured by the elites, removed all restrictions on the actions of individuals. This meant that the rich could more or less secede from the state, go in search of private advantage in other lands without any concern for those in the nation who have been left behind. The Maoist proposals on the constitution are indicative of a vision desirous of swift and far reaching changes to society. Hence the provisions for a very powerful executive that can act more or less unconstrained by the legislature and judiciary, and those for an immediate redistribution of power to those who have historically been marginalized.

The world view held by the Nepali Congress and the UML is one that is entirely opposed to that of the Maoists but more in consonance with the global ideology upheld by the Western democracies in particular. These two parties were the chief participants in the Nepali democratic experiment of the 1990s. In reality, they see little reason to modify the parliamentary system in any substantial way; the only reason they did so was because they were able to get the Maoists to give up their war against the state only by agreeing to the abolition of the monarchy and elections to the CA. For these parties, questions of redistribution or of effective public policy implementation are secondary. What is primary is the right of each individual to pursue his or her own ends without constraint as long as they do not directly conflict with those of another. That there is a great degree of inequality in Nepali society is recognized, but radical redistribution is feared. It could lead to a degree of unacceptable violence against the elite, it is thought, and to other negative consequences that are currently not possible to foresee. Better then, this line of thought goes, to allow for gradual change. There is an underlying belief here, one largely left unexamined, that the provision of individual freedom will by itself gradually lead to a more prosperous and egalitarian society.

When the Maoists signed the 12-point agreement in 2005, some in the older parliamentary parties thought that by agreeing to multi-party competition the hardline communists had accepted all the values of liberal democracy. Over the past four years it has been revealed, in the CA as well as in other forums, that this has not been the case. The Maoists are committed to elections and competition with other parties, this is not in doubt. They have stated this much in their presentations to the CA as well as in internal party documents. But from the constitutional arrangements that they desire, it is clear that what they envisage is a system that is radically different from what the other parties perceive as a democracy. These alternate visions of Nepali society continue to compete in the CA and on the streets and it is by no means clear what kind of hybrid of the two will emerge when and if the constitution is finally drafted.

Nabindra Raj Joshi

Ganesh Man Singh's Ideology and Future of Democracy

The ideas and commitment that Ganesh Man Singh, the Supreme Commander of popular movement, 1990 had expressed during his lifetime in favor of people's supremacy is still fresh in my memory. The ideas and thoughts of Ganesh Man who fought unwaveringly for democracy, people's supremacy and human rights till the last moments of his life have become a source of inspiration for the new generation.

We need to draw an inspiration from the thoughts of legendary leader Ganesh Man who was an epitome of struggle and sacrifice, who was well known for championing the cause of value and honesty based politics, and make a pledge today to safeguard democracy and human rights. After the success of popular movement of 1990, Ganesh Man used to say 'Political struggle has ended. Now we need to focus on economic revolution so as to establish an egalitarian society.' He always fought for political stability, socio-economic transformation, establishment of an egalitarian society and good governance. He always raised his voice against corruption and political anomalies.

In essence, people's welfare was upper most in Ganesh Man's mind for which he fought till the last moments of his life. Had the Nepali Congress and government embraced his thoughts in post 1990 period, the country perhaps would not have to see bad days that we are faced with today. Unfortunately, the NC and the government did not pay heed to Ganesh Man's clarion call. Had the NC embraced his ideas, the party would not have been week as it is today. Hence, his thoughts on democracy, political stability, transformation of state and good governance are more relevant and worthy today. In the later years of his life, Ganesh Man was deeply pained by the fact that his own party for which he made all kinds of sacrifices and of which he was a founder member had been negating his thoughts. It was in this backdrop that he decided to rise above the party line and play the role of a statesman. He quit the NC and the party politics for safeguarding democracy and people's rights. For Ganesh Man democracy was both the ultimate political goal and also the way of life. Therefore, he never compromised on democracy. Mid term election of 1995 produced a hung parliament. Greed of Power took such an ugly shape that it invited all sorts of anomalies in the parliament. Members of parliament were offered huge sum of money to vote for a particular Prime Ministerial candidate. In view of winning parliamentarians' favour, the government gave a huge tax exemption to MPs which earned the nickname of Pajero culture. Ganesh Man was very upset with this increasing trend of political and social aberration. One day, he called a group of young leaders at his Chaksibari residence to share his thoughts on political corruption. He urged the young leaders to fight political and social aberrations. He used other public forums as well to vent his ire against corrupt practices. He was a staunch supporter of democracy and people's supremacy.

Some dismissed his thoughts saying they were merely a rant on his own party and the government, but his thoughts were not against the party and the government, they were against political anomalies and in favour of democracy, people and the rule of law. He had indeed played the role of a statesman. In today's complicated political transition, Nepal needs Ganesh Man Singh like democratic, people oriented, true nationalist leaders, but unfortunately none of today's leaders are like him. Maoist leaders Pushpa Kamal Dahal and Babu Ram Bhattarai who joined political mainstream after ten years' armed rebellion against the state had told in an interview given to Kantipur and Kathmandu Post four years ageo that they would follow the path of Gandhi and Ganesh Man and they themselves would not join the government. But the men who pledged to follow the ideals of Gandhi and Ganesh Man not only ruled the country but massively abused the power. Now they are clamouring to establish People's Republic which has already been proved to be a failed political system in the 20 th century. Are Dahal and Bhattarai following the path of Gandhi and Gnaesh Man or following the footsteps of Stalin and Pol Pot? Dahal and Bhattarai have ignored not only people's sentiment but they have also abused the names of respected personalities like Gandhi and Ganesh Man.

If anybody wants to become Ganesh Man, then they should not espouse violence and dictatorship but they should commit themselves to democracy and they should work to protect people's rights. Dahal and Bhattarai need to pursue the politics of sacrifice and not the politics of power. They also need to put people at the centre stage and play the role of statesmen by rising above the party politics. There is hardly any other example where an institution is named after a leader during his/her own life time. Ganesh Man Singh Adhyan Pratishtan was established with the help of some democratic personalities and intellectuals. The main objective of the academy was to raise hell against bad governance. It also aims to defend democratic ideals and people's rights. There was a moment when some people including a few leaders from within the NC criticized the Pratishtan (academy). Thereafter, all of us who were associated with the academy went to meet Ganesh Man to discuss the issue. He told us that we should not be discouraged by such negative comments and should continue to champion the cause of democratic ethos, values and people's supremacy.

Ganesh Man Singh's life and ideals have left a deep impact on me and it is because of his inspiration I have been championing the cause of democracy, rule of law and people's democracy until now and I am committed to do the same in future. It was because of his inspiration that I became active in politics since early age. I had an opportunity to work under his guidance and therefore I had a kind of familial relations with him. He discussed with me not only politics but also his family matters. He took me to Syangja district when our party was staging a Satyagraha (hunger strike). He addressed the party cadres until midnight and then told them 'I am tired. I am going to sleep. Now Nabindra would tell you the rest of the things that I want to tell you.'

I am mentioning this not to highlight how deeply he trusted me but to show how deeply he trusted party cadres. We are faced with a more challenging situation now and therefore we need to be active to safeguard democracy and people's supremacy by embracing the ideals of thoughts of Ganesh Man. Will today's leaders learn from the story of Ganesh Man's struggle and commitment to the politics of value and will they be able to safeguard democracy?

Subodh Raj Pyakurel & Dipendra Prasad Pant

Ongoing Transition in Nepal

The Challenges ahead and the Human Rights concern

Introduction

There have been regime changes in Nepal on several occasions through uprisings and organized popular movements. The power shifts from the Rana oligarchy to the king and the political parties, especially the liberal Nepali Congress in 1951, the defeat of the party-less Panchayat regime introduced by King Mahendra and its replacement by parties in 1990 and the extirpation of the authoritarian king Gyanendra in 2006 were experienced in the country while being propped up by the people.

Following the formal end of a decade long armed insurgency waged by the Maoists against the state on 22 November 2006, Nepal is undergoing a transition from the authoritarian past to democracy.[1] The transition to democracy is full of problems and complexities involving various factors and actors. Nepal's present transition to democracy has also been equally complex; primarily because of the multiplicity of discourses that has surrounded it. The chasm between the political parties has widened. The myopic and shortsighted political society has hyped the change as an end itself. Neither of the big parties is without internal tensions and contradictions. The Janus-faced Maoists, since its entry into peaceful democratic mainstream has adopted a deceitful policy by portraying one set of feelings and acting under the influence of ulterior another.

---

[1]Many believe that Nepal is in transition to democracy; however our contention in the ensuing pages tries to state that Nepal's transition is likely to head more towards uncertainty rather than democracy.

Furthermore, political stalemate in the country has been protracted unnecessarily and undesirably increasing the chances that such stalemate will ultimately polarize the parties as the groups that subvert or co-opt the transition. In addition, the present transition is compelled to proceed while being intertwined with the ethnic, nationalist, regional, radical as well as religious discourses and it also has the convoluted task of taking the incompatible political forces of the past together. In this context, this write-up discusses the present transition and human rights situation in Nepal, taking multiple aspects like the negotiated peace process and subsequent problems, crimes, the failure to keep commitments, neighboring countries and the possible constraints to improve the human rights situation in the country into account.

Negotiated peace and the post-conflict problems of the parties

The transition to democracy in Nepal, actually, had begun through the Comprehensive Peace Agreement to embark a shared future leaving behind the sheer divisions of the past. It is pertinent to quote Bloomfield here in this regard:

> A negotiated peace may open up the possibility of a process designed through negotiation between equals. In this case, though one side may pressure amnesty for its members and supporters as the price of its agreement to support existence while the other is pursuing justice and punishment as the price of its support. Lacking absolute control, neither side will achieve its goal in this. (Bloomfield: 2003)

Developing in line with the view of Bloomfield, the present transition to democracy has been the peace versus justice controversy. The UCPN Maoist wants blanket amnesty for its violations and offenses committed in the course of the war or afterwards putting forth its logic that it has adopted a democratic course. And, the other political parties[2] want the violations

[2]Other political parties' implies differently in the pre and post Constituent Assembly (CA) election contexts. Before the election it referred to the major seven political parties and at present this refers to about two dozens out of 27 political parties having representation in the CA.

and offenses committed by the Maoists in course of the war or afterwards to be punished and the Maoists shun organizational structure like that of a warring party.

To reconcile, a society has to move from a divided past to a shared future. But, post-conflict Nepal has remained divided. The political leaders do not have any motivation for building future to ensure that the past doesn't return. Responsible actors in the country have been unable to manage the issues that create social division and make democracy defunct. As per Bloomfield (2003), a set of fair procedure for peacefully handling the issues that divide a society (the political and social structures of governance) and a set of working relationship between the groups involved are necessary for a functioning democracy.[3] Nepal has failed to establish and consolidate a dual foundation for a functioning democracy. To quote the UN, "in many cases, including Nepal and Pakistan recently, crises of legitimacy have prompted transitions from authoritarian states. But consolidating democratic practices has proven more difficult... although negotiated power sharing may avoid or help end conflict, cycles of protest and repression may follow."[4]

Passing through the transition towards consolidating democracy by building congenial relation among the major political parties is full of challenges almost insurmountable for the political parties. So, questions have started to be raised as to whether or not Nepal has embarked on a safe and democratic transition.

Looking into the present transition of Nepal through the benchmarks that are required to exist in a post-conflict country, we have ample space to doubt that the present transition will certainly lead to democratic consolidation. It is believed that negotiation of peace from above and peace

[3]Working relationship among the political parties has been badly deteriorated. Failure of the parties to elect a new Prime Minister for the 16th time, prolonging the country's political crisis and putting the nation at risk of running out of money is the worst example of deteriorated working relation among the political parties in Nepal. At a time when the public services, like schools, government hospitals and governmental offices were almost running out of budget, new budget has been presented through ordinance whereas there is legitimate legislative parliament in the country for bringing budget.

[4]Human Development Report 2010, page 69.

building form below have to function effectively in a post-conflict country. However, the peace negotiation has been breached, either by transgressing the letter and spirit of the already signed agreements or by not fulfilling the obligations arising from the agreements.[5]

At the grassroots level, there have been continued killings, beatings and unabated feuds over the local resources, administrative control and power politics, especially among the youth wings of the political parties. Thereby, challenging the incipient peace building effort and the achievements to date. As per the INSEC data base 2732 persons have been beaten and 66 persons have been killed in between 22 November 2006 to 31 December 2009. The data below, however, is exclusive of the beatings and killings by the other political, semi-political and armed groups that are not considered as the main political forces in terms of the 12-Point Understanding and the Comprehensive Peace Agreement.

Table 1. The Incidents of Beating in between 22 November 2006 to 31 December 2009 and the Perpetrators

Beatings

Perpetrators	**Total**
ANFSU	20
ANNISU (Revolutionary)	157
CPN (UML)	82
Maoists	1314
MJF	121
Nepal Students Union	11
Nepali Congress	129
Rastriya Jana Morcha	29
V C Force	3
Young Communist League	788
Youth Force	78
Grand Total	**2732**

Table 2. The Incidents of Killing in between 22 November 2006 to 31 December2009 and the Perpetrators

Killings

Perpetrators	**Total**
CPN (UML)	1
Maoists	22
MJF	31
Young Communist League	10
Youth Force	2
Grand Total	**66**

This shows that breaching the negotiations signed at the central level and giving continuity to the anti-peace building activities at the local level has put the transition period of Nepal in jeopardy. Political forces seem to have been distracted from the prime duty of writing the constitution and their failure to act sincerely as the democratic transition demands. The post-conflict situation of a country demands peace and reconciliation as an immediate task and the development as the long term strategy. However, expecting the convergence of the political parties has been a distant dream given the present inter-party relations in the country.

In what are nowadays termed 'post conflict societies' the pattern is generally that the warring sides negotiate a settlement in the form of new structures for governance. Almost always these structures are democratic, so former enemies often having a long history of violence between them find themselves faced with the task of implementing the new negotiated structures for the future management of their differences on a minimally cooperative basis. One of the biggest obstacles to such cooperation is that, because of the violence of the past, their relations are based on antagonism, distrust, disrespect and quite possibly, hurt and hatred.[6] This political philosophy and international experience also unfailingly applies to the non-cooperation and the intensifying distrust among the political parties in Nepal now. Similarly, the current political ambiance in Nepal is the result of an interplay of the overriding issues the parties agreed to earlier[7] at a time when the king overplayed his hand by usurping power. The agreements, it seems now, were not reached in the parties' own volition taking the Nepali people as the centre of agreements, rather, the party politics and interests were at the center. To be more specific, internecine party politics and the detrimental effects the parties had during the armed conflict against each other has repelled them now, rather than attracting them to reconcile.

Reconciliation has not been easy in Nepal. The disqualified discharges and the ex-combatants who are not registered in the camp and are working as political cadres have posed difficulty to reconciliation. Of the 4008

---

[6]Hachhethu, et al. 2008. page 11

[7]12 point understanding was the base for the political parties, depending on which the king finally was extirpated from the power.

disqualified combatants discharged so far, it's still unknown how many of them have returned to their place of origin and are in interaction with the victims they perpetrated. Many full-fledged ex-Maoist combatants are still under the hold of the Maoist party as full-fledged political cadres and are living a collective life. However, sooner or later, they will have to return to their community of origin. This home coming could become a source of re-traumatization for the surviving victims if no explicit measures with respect to reintegration are taken and a reconciling environment at the grassroots level are created.

"Reconciliation involves the creation of the social space where both truth and forgiveness are validated and joined together, rather than being forced into an encounter in which one must win out over the other or envisioned as fragmented and separated parts (Lederach: 1997)." The problem in Nepal is that the parties, especially the UCPN Maoist, want to prevail over others rather than moving ahead hand in hand with other political parties making truth and forgiveness compatible.

Besides, post-conflict Nepal is full of many other challenges despite the fact that it has made progress very sluggishly over time. 'The establishment of broadly representative nature of the CA and the discharge of 4,008 disqualified Maoist combatants offer a glimmer of hope. Still, the state's response to proliferating non-state armed actors, ethnic armies, militant youth wings of various political parties and identity based social movements is highly skewed, not systemic. As a result, a deadlock in the centre and high dynamics at the periphery continue to serve as bottlenecks to focus on long term vision of peace, constitutional state, good governance and an early recovery from human recession.' (Dahal: 2010)

Harig high dynamics at the periphery is the underlying cause of the entire problems in Nepal. A decade long armed conflict was the result of these very dynamics. However, the deadlock in the centre, a result of the excessive yen of the political parties, has debarred a solution to these complex problems, whereas especially the Maoist party has attempted its utmost to lead the government at any cost. If we agree that radical ideology and the people's discontent, especially that of the minorities, were at play during the climactic point when the Maoists started the war against the state, the

Maoists' naked struggle for power and control over the ethnicities is not unnatural because 'Conflicts which used to have strong ideological dimensions or which expressed deep popular or minority discontents have tended over the years to degenerate into naked struggles for power ... or to control the ethnic and national identity of the state." (Luckham, 2003:21)

At a macro level, Nepal's post-conflict order has been hampered by indecision, dilemma and disputes between dichotomies. To quote Dahal (2010), 'the dilemma between conflict management and conflict resolution (also transformation), dissolution of feudal land system versus recognition to property rights, provision of social security versus weak tax base of the state to subsidize welfare benefits, commitment to universal values of democracy versus old political culture of patronage, rights-based discourse on democratization versus increasing militarization of society, constitutionalism versus popular sovereignty, realistic policies versus populist trap etc expose the obvious gaps between promise and practice of Nepalese political leadership"

Transition and crimes in Nepal

International experience shows that crimes pose a threat to the post-conflict situation of a country. Nepal isn't an exception in this regard. As per the database of INSEC, a total of 1713 persons have been killed in between 22 November 2006 (the date of signing the Comprehensive Peace Agreement) to 5 November 2010 where 1313 persons were killed in the Terai districts alone. Of the total killed, 152 persons were killed by the state and 155 persons were killed by the Maoists and their affiliated organizations. Similarly, during the period a total of 2359 persons were been abducted whereas 1433 have been abducted in the Terai districts.

Very seriously, crimes have been badly politicized and politics has been criminalized. The line between political activities and criminal activities is increasingly blurring. Felons have not been punished due to politicization of crimes and criminalization of politics. Not a single criminal behind serious crimes has been prosecuted in spite of the courts', the Supreme

Court included, orders to prosecute.[8]

The incumbent government has implemented a Special Security Plan with special focus on peace and security situation in the Tarai region as per the government's commitment to end the culture of impunity, protect human rights and fulfill the desire of the people to live peacefully by improving the law and order situation in the country.[9] Viewing in terms of the number of crimes in the country, the plan has been relatively efficacious. 551, 541 and 473 persons were killed in 2007, 2008 and 2009 respectively. Only 126 persons have been killed in between 1 January 2010 to 5 Nov 2010. This shows a decreasing trend of killing in the country but it is not commendable.

Nepal has many problems regarding security situation in the country. The army is bound to be confined in the barracks due to the CPA; the role of the Armed Police Force is unclear as to the general peace and security situation in the country[10] and the Nepal Police has been used as a political tool and crimes have been politicized often providing political protection to certain criminal activities. Similarly, lack of logistic resources, inadequate specialized training and public distrust in the police have been collectively responsible for the weak security situation in the country. Apart from this, police has been the victim of the vulnerability of the transitional phase on the matters of utilizing full capabilities in the course of maintaining peace and security in the country.

---

[8]The apex court had forwarded the text of its January 3 verdict on September 5 to Okhaldhunga court for prompt execution of the verdict that slapped a 20-year jail term on Balkrishna Dhungel, the Unified CPN-Maoist Constituent Assembly member and ordered confiscation of his property for killing Ujjan Shrestha in 1998. Dhungel has not been arrested yet. Similarly, District Court of Kavre issued an arrest warrant against the four accused including Major Niranjan Basnet on 31 January 2008 for their involvement in killing Maina Sunar. District Court of Kavre on 13 September 2009 ordered the Nepal Army to suspend Major Niranjan Basnet in accordance with Section 66 (3) of the Army Act 2063. Despite the arrest and suspension order of Kavre District Court, the accused continued his service with full protection from Nepal Army. Instead of giving effect to the court's orders, he was deployed to the UN Mission in Chad. Later he was vetted and repatriated to Nepal. Mr Basnet has not been prosecuted. These are the exemplary cases only.

[9]See Nepalnews.com, 22 October, 2009 for detailed explanation of the Minster for Home Affairs on need of implementing Special Security Plan .

[10]For further detail see 'Public Report 2007 on the Findings of Nepal Police- Civil Society Dialogue", United States Institute of Peace, Washington DC

So, it will be really difficult for the government to normalize the situation. Worry still exists that Nepal will fail towards delivering the basic services needed to ensure human security, respect for human rights and maintain law and order in the country slowly. Crimes and insecurity are still likely to erode the nominal gains made in establishing a culture of human rights and respect for the rule of law. Checking and improving these entire situations is directly connected with political parties but, 'we are in transition' is often the response from the responsible political parties as if democratic accountability and the rule of law are luxuries that can be postponed until order and security are restored.

Failure to keep the commitments

The Comprehensive Peace Agreement was an ideal mechanism agreed upon by the major political parties. It was a base and opportunity towards establishing a democratic set up, respecting human rights and reconciling the opposite warring forces in the country. The provisions in the agreement had encompassed all the urgent issues to be acted upon to strengthen democracy. The agreement was human rights-friendly as well. It was correctly thought at the time of reaching the agreement that the situation of human rights situation in the country largely depends on the implementation or non-implementation of the Comprehensive Peace Agreement.

However, its implementation is very disappointing. No concrete steps have been taken towards management of armies and arms.[11] Although there have been discussions for 3 years, the integration and rehabilitation of the Maoist combatants is yet to be made a reality. Even the seemingly less complicated process of rehabilitating the disqualified Maoists combatants (including 2,973 minors) took a considerably long time to begin. Point 4.7 of the agreement states, 'Both sides shall not recruit additional military forces or shall not transport arms and ammunition and explosives or conduct military activities against each other…' but the Nepal Army (NA) issued a recruitment appeal in October 2008 creating a huge controversy. The NA

[11]Point 4.4 of the CPA states that the Interim Council of Ministers shall work to supervise, integrate and rehabilitate the Maoist combatants.

claimed that it was only filling its vacant positions.[12] However, this was disputed by the UCPN-Maoist. Similarly, PLA combatants have been arrested on numerous occasions for carrying weapons outside the Maoist army cantonments.[13] Although, no further incidents of recruitment from either side are recorded afterwards, this episode has shown the failure of the stakeholders to stick to the agreements and has created political debates and turbulence at the same time.

The phenomenon of enforced disappearances has been widespread in Nepal, particularly during the decade long insurgency. According to the United Nations Working Group on Enforced and Involuntary Disappearances, during the armed conflict, Nepal recorded the highest number of enforced or involuntary disappearances in the world. According to INSEC's database 1,006 persons disappeared between February 1996 and November 2006. Yet, no concrete steps have been taken to investigate or make public the status of the disappeared despite the commitments made by both sides.[14] Hundreds of cases of the disappeared during the conflict have not been properly clarified or investigated still.[15] Despite the continued promises and commitments from the government, a Disappearances Commission is yet to be formed. The Disappearances (Crime

[12]INSEC has been monitoring the peace process based on the CPA. As per its monitoring report Commitment vs. Reality, the issue was brought to the Supreme Court and during the hearing on March 8, 2009, the PLA also decided to begin recruitment, in order to fill positions which were vacant after UNMIN disqualified PLA personnel. The Court issued interim orders to both the NA and the PLA ordering them to stop the recruitment process. In its final verdict, the Court held that the NA must not carry out any recruitment. Again on April 19, 2010 Nepal Army opened its recruitment process for 271 positions in 40 different technical positions.. And, finally, the Supreme Court (SC) refused to issue a stay order against the recruitment drive initiated by Nepal Army, on May 12, 2010.

[13]INSEC'S Monitoring Report 2010 -Commitment vs. Reality 2010

[14]Point 5.2.3 of the CPA deals with ceasefire and states - both sides agree to make public the information about the real name, surname and address of the people who were disappeared by both sides and who were killed during the war and to inform also the family about it within 60 days from the date on which this Accord has been signed. Similarly, the point 7.3.2 of the agreement deals with right to life and mentions- both sides shall, respecting fully the individual's right to freedom and security, not keep anyone under arbitrary or illegal detention, kidnap or take as hostage. Both sides agree to make public the status of every disappeared person and held as captive and inform the matter related there to their family members, legal advisors and other authorized persons.

[15]See INSEC's, 'Impaired Accountability: State of Disappearances in Nepal Brief Assessment of Implementation of UN WGEID Recommendations', August 2008.

and Punishment) Bill that was promulgated as an Ordinance on February 10, 2009 drew huge criticism as it did not comply with international standards or the Supreme Court guidelines. The government tabled the Bill on Offences and Punishment of Disappearance, 2066 at the legislature parliament on April 20, 2010 for the investigation of persons abducted and disappeared during the Maoist Conflict.

Although both sides agreed not to keep anyone under arbitrary detention, kidnap or take anyone as hostage, this provision is widely violated by the UCPN-M cadres by abducting people. From the date of signing of the CPA to August 2010, INSEC has recorded 772 cases of abductions by them. The draft Truth and Reconciliation Bill issued by the Government in July 2007 was widely criticized for not meeting international standards. Furthermore, there has been little effort by the Government to prioritize the reform of the Bill to ensure a credible and effective Truth and Reconciliation Commission.

Similarly, the commitment to form a National Peace and Rehabilitation Commission hasn't been fulfilled. Thus, the constant assurances to set up the two Commissions, intended to support the victims of conflict as mentioned in the Comprehensive Peace Agreement, haven't materialized. In spite of the directives given by the Supreme Court in April 2007 and the recommendations made by the UN Committee on Economic, Social and Cultural Rights to prioritize special programs for Kamaiyas, as of July 2009, out of 27,000 freed Kamaiyas some 9,600 are yet to be rehabilitated. Promises of a separate Landless Commission to solve the problems of the landless people in Nepal are yet to materialize.

The adoption of a policy to introduce a scientific land reform program by ending feudal land ownership and a policy to provide land and other economic and social security to the economically backward classes including landless, bonded labors and pastoral farmers are provided for in the CPA. 'Land reform' has always been embedded with and has been the catchphrase of the political parties while in struggle for a democratic set up but establishing the land reform commissions, just to make defunct after achieving power has been the trend. So, demand for land reform and a distribution policy are not new in Nepal. However, reform is now termed

Scientific Land Reform. The late 1950's governing administrations of all political hues had pronounced land to the tiller redistribution necessary to abolish feudalism and advance economic transformation. Yet they have persistently failed to achieve these objectives.[16]

Should the neighbors be responsible, should the peace process further protract?

Nepal's democratic transition has been perceived by many to link with neighbouring countries as well. Because of the conjuncture with the neighbouring big countries, which have the capacity to influence the global politico-economic powers, Nepal's situation, to some extent, will certainly be affected by them. Our national consensus, interest and diplomatic aptitude are of paramount importance in the matters of getting benefits from the neighbours especially in this phase of transition. The tendency of the responsible political party to receive benefits by drawing the neighbors into controversy is unfortunate. If we want the neighbours to act as per our vulnerability, we also have to be able to understand their concerns. "While Nepal anticipates its two immediate and powerful neighbours India and China to understand the vulnerability of a small country and respect its independence, sovereignty and territorial integrity, it is in the national interest of Nepal to become sensitive to the security concerns of its big neighbors and take appropriate measures to prevent and curb all kinds of hostile operations against them.'[17]

---

[16]See Willy, Chapagain and Sharma's overview in the findings of a scoping study on land reform for DFID Nepal, 2008. As per the research Nepal's formal land reform started since 1951 and many attempts have been there afterwards. However, these attempts either have gone ineffective of led to formation of commissions which could not come up with any concrete way to reform and got defunct with the political system change of even in the change of governance. Interim Constitution pledges compensation for land losses due to enforcement of a scientific land reform 'by doing away with the feudal land ownership', special socio-economic security programmes including positive discrimination for landless squatters, bonded labor & tillers, women and disadvantaged groups. Notably also ruled that no case could be brought as to whether these actions implemented or not (Art. 36). The three Year Interim Plan defines scientific land reform, lists 20 broad targets (e.g. including irrigation) including establishment of a High Level Land Commission, 50% discount on transaction fees when land purchased by woman or member of a deprived class land to 200,000 landless, rehabilitation support for 13,244 freed Kamaiyas, plan to relocate Guthi land administration to districts etc. Several land reform Commissions have also been formed but have failed to yield result.

[17]In 'Defining National Interest in an Emerging Nation-State: Challenges Ahead, by Dr. Mohan Lohani (Paper presented by the author at a CSAS/KAF Seminar held in Kathmandu, October 21, 2009).

In retrospect, however, there have always been disputes among the political actors in Nepal regarding the perception of the neighboring countries. Similarly, the neighbors too perceived Nepal differently during different situations. However, it seems that especially after the peace process started, the relation between Nepal and the neighboring countries has started to thaw with internally and externally volatile dynamics. There has been a hectic amount of diplomatic activities and exchanges of visits[18] but the expressions of diplomatic and political concerns by the countries provide space to doubt that we will have a normal relation with the close neighbors. It seems that the cold war mindset has revived to haunt the political actors especially the Maoists. If this is true, the Cold War mind-set of Nepal that perceives India and China as opposing forces will be detrimental for Nepal because the result of such a mindset will never be for regional ties, economic interdependence, diplomatic exchanges, mutual benefits and coexistence. Political actors now are not aware of the fact that Nepal has right to deepen its relationship with its neighbors but one relationship does not have to come at the cost of the other. If only Nepal can realize this and act accordingly, we will be able to manage the transition to democracy successfully. And, the failure of the political parties to conclude the ongoing peace process as per the spirit of the CPA will cause the level of trust placed in the parties to plummet.

Fulfilling the long existing popular expectations: still a distant dream

The failure of the changed political system of 1990 to meet the high expectations of the Nepalis bred a brooding sense about their future and aggravated discontent simultaneously, ultimately setting the stage for armed conflict. The armed conflict that swept across the country, beginning in 1996, was seen as a response to poverty, injustice, regional disparity and other structural deficiencies and ill-management. "The change of political system in 1990 brought about high hopes and expectations in the people

[18]Chinese Foreign Minister Yang Jiechi's arrival to Nepal on 2 Dec after several days of Indian Foreign Minister Pranab Mukhherjee's visit to Nepal in Dec 2008, PM Puspa Kamal Dahal's two visits to China; one as the Prime Minister and another as the Chief of the Party, visits of Nepal's President and the Vice President to China, the visit of the commanders of the Maoist combatants and also a top level representation of the Chinese Communist Party at the General Convention of the Madhesijanadhikar Forum in Birganj etc.

that in the new polity there would be, among others, no political prejudice, no nepotistic administration of opportunities and no centralization of power...politics was criminalized with frauds and rigging in elections and political opposition was silenced with the abuse of state administration and bureaucracy" (Karki and Kattel: 2007)

The violation of human rights in the country was a routine during the Panchayat regime. Especially towards the end of the 80's, it got even more dismal.[19] However, the restoration of democracy provided sufficient ground for the political actors in the steering seat of governance to work for a better human rights situation in the country and to proceed by accepting the human rights approach to development. The actors failed to do so. The economy was left at the mercy of unbridled market competition, minimizing the role of the state to regulate and control whereas two things- redistribution of wealth, power and status of the individual, groups and community in a just manner for the societal good; and the human rights approach to development and social justice were of high importance.

At a time when Nepal was in need to boost the rural and agrarian economy, targeting the low income classes who were finding it increasingly difficult to survive, the state couldn't be an active development partner and honest implementing agent. The liberal economic policies adopted from the last years of the Panchayat regime, especially since the restoration of democracy in 1990, incorporated liberalization, privatization and structural adjustment. The Nepali Congress led governments prioritized this. Development became asymmetrical, a large portion of investment, mostly from the foreign resources mainly as loans, benefited especially a small section of the population in the urban areas adding affluence to an already rich class. As a result, the Maoists led insurgency received space and support to rouse the people in the rural areas and minority sectors.

---

[19]Public Security Act, Organizations Control Act and Treason Act were in action to curb the anti- palace and pro-democratic activities. A trifling fault could be interpreted as an offense deserving punishment. As an absurd instance of punishment Bhup Nidhi Pant, the journalist and lawyer in Pokhara was arrested twice in six months and charged with treason on both occasion. His first 'crime' was to publish king's photo with black ink smeared around the face and second was to misspell Queen Aishworya's name in vernacular Nepali. For more detail see the book "Nepalese Political Behavior" by Ole Borre, Sushil R Pandey and Chitra K Tiwari, page 23.

As the insurgency intensified, the adopted development practices turned further inefficacious and the social dynamics that were waiting for the equitable treatment became more complex worsening the security and human rights situation in the country. The post CA election strategy of the Maoists now affirms that they are endeavoring to fill up the vacuum appeared in the country following the exit of the authoritarian monarchy from the state affairs. Their activities have posed problems to solve the long existing socio-economic problems and human rights concerns. Hence, except the political changes and the constitutional assertion for the problems created by the social dynamics, no progress has been made so far. Nepal is undergoing transition without initiating any concrete steps against the problems that existed in the country once they surfaced in the 1990s. So, if the government fails to solve these problems prudently, rights situation in the country will go even worse in the near future.

Nepal's democratic struggle and popular participation in the struggle has always been propelled by the demand of humanitarian governance that requires social justice as the benchmark in a concrete sense. By the time Nepal saw the unprecedented mass uprising in 2006 these issues were vociferously demanded. Democratic governance, rule of law, social justice, good governance and respect of human rights, elimination of region, caste, class and sex based inequalities, among others, were the demands during the uprising. But, parties have undermined the demands even after the establishment of Loktantra in the country.

Long-run move and the constraints to speed up

To borrow the words from Amartya Sen, "the world has moved on since 1990". So has Nepal since that year compared to the sluggish development prior to 1990.[20] We have to acknowledge that Nepal has come a long way in the long run. According to the Human Development Report 2010, Nepal ranked 138th in terms of the HDI rank with 0.428 HDI value. It is very encouraging for us that Nepal has stood first in terms of HDI improvement rank. The HDI (Human Development Index) value change

---

[20]In introduction to Human Development Report 2010, 20th Anniversary Edition.

is also encouraging.[21] Sectors like communication, forests and education are improving. "That Nepal is one of the fastest movers in the Human Development Index (HDI) since 1970 is perhaps surprising in light of the country's difficult circumstances and record of conflict...the gap between Nepal's life expectancy and the world average has narrowed by 87 percent over the past forty years. By contrast economic growth was modest and, and the lack of jobs many Nepalese to seek opportunities abroad."[22]

What has been achieved can equally be attributed to the INGO (International Non-Government Organisation) development practices; this has led to a heightened sense of human rights among the people and an increase in local participation. Often, the private sector and the governmental authorities understand human development and human rights in isolation oblivious to the fact that human development focuses on individual and group empowerment; and human rights, on structural safeguards. Human rights and human development have much in common but it seems that Nepal has failed to understand this fact even though it is a state party to many international conventions and protocols that have given legal status to the normative claims of human rights. To quote the Human Development Report 1994, "Human security is a child who didn't die, a disease that didn't spread, a job that was not cut, an ethnic tension that didn't explode in violence, a dissident who was not silenced. Human security is not a concern with weapons- it is a concern with human life and dignity."[23]The failure to understand this has posed problems in our efforts to establish human rights based development approach in Nepal.

Political uncertainty is and will be the main problem in Nepal. Even if politics takes an order towards democratic consolidation in a dramatic way, the route towards consolidating democracy is full of constraints. Basically, corruption, human rights violation, crimes and the consequences of the possible natural disasters caused by the global climate change will

---

[21] According to Human Development Report 2010 there has been continuous increase in HDI value. In the years 1980, 1990, 1995, 2000, 2005, 2009 and 2010 there were 0.210, 0.316, 0.344, 0.375, 0.400, 0.423, 0.428 HDI values respectively.

[22] Human Development Report 2010, page 54.

[23] For further detail see Human Development Report 1994, page 22

be the prime factors for our socio-political and economic retardation and underachievement. Transparency International (TI), the global coalition against corruption, has ranked Nepal 146th out of 178 countries surveyed in the Corruption Perception Index (CPI) 2010, making it one of the most corrupt countries in the world. Nepal slipped three positions down this year. Last year, Nepal was ranked 143rd.[24] In terms of human rights violation Nepal has the score 4, in the UN designed score range from 1-5 where less score means better human rights situation in a country.

Similarly, reports prepared by watchdogs like the Commission for the Investigation of Abuse of Authority (CIAA) have shown that in the absence of elected representatives, a large amount of government budget allocated to local bodies has been misused with the involvement of a handful of local political leaders and civil servants.[25] The report says that rampant bribery, cartels and other corrupt practices undermine competition and contribute to massive loss of resources for development in Nepal. Officials at the Ministry of Local Development here concede that only 75 to 80 per cent of the total development budget Rs 22 billion received in the last fiscal year has been spent and a large amount of the spent funds is unaccounted for.[26] In the name of forging consensus, the budget allocated for the local bodies either has been frozen or unaccounted for. There has been no political representation at the local bodies for a long time. Political parties have not expressed any worries about to the vacuum in local governance.

It is highly likely that possible calamities and their consequences and the failure of the government to protect natural assets will increase the probability of the further degradation of the situation in the country. Nepal reporter to the BBC News has, to take an example in this context, revealed through a field investigation in the western part of Nepal that Nepal faces massive deforestation, mainly because of corrupt bureaucracy fuelled by prolonged political instability. The study shows that several routes are being used to illegally transport logs across the border into Indian territories. As India takes steps to protect its forests in the fight against climate change,

---

[24]The TI's Corruption Perception Index (CPI)-2010 released globally on 26 October 2010.

[25]The Kathmandu Post 26 October, 2010.

[26]ibid.

timber smuggling from Nepal is on the rise, say the Nepali conservationists and officials.[27]

Similarly, a report prepared jointly by the United Nations Environment Programme (UNEP), the Centre for International Climate and Environmental Research (CICERO) and the International Centre for Integrated Mountain Development (ICIMOD), following a two-year pilot assessment, states that Nepal, which is normally known for its water abundance has experienced extreme droughts, some lasting for years.[28] The arrhythmic climatic features, droughts and floods experienced in the country in the recent years indicate that Nepal is one of the countries to be badly affected by the global climate change.

Conclusion

Nepal is undergoing a transition from its authoritarian past; however, it can't be taken for granted that the transition will go towards democracy. Looking at the present transition of Nepal through the benchmarks required in a post-conflict country, one can not be assured that the peace process will surely succeed. To reconcile, a society has to move from a divided past to a shared future. But, post conflict Nepal has remained divided. Both truth and forgiveness are not validated and joined together but hatred, aggression; distrust and non-cooperation have engulfed the political actors. This has been the prime hindrance against establishing political order in Nepal. Breaching the negotiations and giving continuity to the anti-peace building activities has put the transition period at jeopardy.

Nepali society has not been demilitarized. Although the CPA provided the basis for demilitarizing Nepali society, no concrete steps have been taken towards this end. It seems that militarism is only momentarily dormant. Crimes have replaced militaristic violence. The CPA, idealistically, is human rights-friendly as well. However, its implementation is very disappointing and so is the human rights situation in the country. The parties have failed to stick to the already signed treaties and accords. The

---

[27]For more detail see Nepal's Forests 'Being Stripped by Indian Timber Demand' By Navin Singh Khadka Environment reporter, BBC News, Nepal accessed on November 21, 2010.

[28]Climate Change: Threatening Survival of Himalayan Communities, UN Report 11 December 2009

political actors are oriented towards producing more fissures rather than resolving the existing problems and precluding emergence of further problems. Even after a long period of striking the peace accord fear still looms large that parties might undo the ongoing peace process. The unnecessarily and undesirably protracted peace process hints at this danger.

It is highly likely that such a situation will erode the nominal gains made in establishing the base for the culture of human rights and respect for the rule of law. Checking and improving these entire unwanted situations is directly connected with political parties but their naked struggle for power has underrated and shadowed the burning issues at hand. Political uncertainty will be the main problem in Nepal. Even if politics takes a shift towards democratic consolidation, the course towards consolidating democracy is not free from restraints. Basically, corruption, human rights violations, crimes and the consequences of possible natural disasters caused by the global climate change will be the prime factors for our socio-political and economic retardation and the degraded human rights situation in the country.

References

Baral, Lok R. (ed.) (2006): *Nepal: Quest for Democracy*, Adroit Publishers, New Delhi.

Bloomfield, David (2003): "Reconciliation: An Introduction" in David Bloomfield, Teresa Barnes and Lue Huysle (eds.) *Reconciliation after* Violent Conflict: *A Handbook*, International Institute for Democracy and Electoral Assistance, Stockholm.

Dahal, Dev R. (2010): "Post-Conflict Peace-Building in Nepal: A Perspective from Civil Society", *Nepalese Journal of Public Policy and Governance*, Vol. xxvi (3), page 3.

Hachhethu, Krishna. et al. (2008): *Nepal in Transition: A Study on the State of Democracy*, International Institute for Democracy and Electoral Assistance (International IDEA), Stockholm.

Karki,Arjun and Mukunda Kattel (2007): "Options for Peace Building in Nepal" in Kailash Pyakurel, Kathryn March and Bipin Acharya (eds.) *Nepal in Conflict: Theoretical Understandings, Conflict Resolution, Conflict Transformation and Peace Building*, SASON (Sociological/ Anthropological Society of Nepal), Kathmandu.

Khan, Irene et al. (2010), *The Unheard Truth: Poverty and Human Rights*, Viva Books, New Delhi.

Lederach, John P. (1997): "Building Peace: Understanding Reconciliation" in *Divided Societies*, United States Institute of Peace, Washington D.C.

Luckham, Robin (2003): "Democratic Strategies for Security in Transition and Conflict in Gavin Cawthra and Robin Luckham, (eds.) Transition to Democracy: Governing Insecurity.London: Zed Books Limited.

Mkandawire. T. (1999): "Crisis Management and the Making of 'Choiceless Democracy' in Richard Joseph (ed.) *State Conflict and Democracy in Africa*, Boulder Co: Lynne Reinner.

Sharma, Shankar P. (1997): "Market-Led Development Strategy in Nepal" in Krishna B Bhattachan and Chaitanya Mishra (eds.) *Development Practices in Nepal*, Kirtipur: Tribhuvan University, Central Department of Sociology and Anthropology and FES, Germany.

Sklar, R.(1987): *Development Democracy: Comparative Studies in Society and History.*

Wily, Liz A. Devendra Chapagain, and Shiva Sharma (2008), *Land Reform in Nepal: Where is it coming from and where is it going?*, Nepal: DFID.

BR Deepak

China in Nepal

What is at stake for India?

Nirupama Rao, the Foreign Secretary of India, is slated to visit Nepal from January 18, 2011. She is expected to assess the halted peace process in Nepal and discuss issues of common concern with the caretaker Nepali Prime Minister and other senior government officials, as well as the leader of opposition Maoist Party, Pushpa Kamal Dahal Prachanda. She would also attempt to pull out the jittery relations from the quagmire, which nose-dived in October 2010 in the aftermath of the Unified Maoist party cadres hurling several pairs of shoes at the Indian ambassador to Nepal, Rakesh Sood. China would be watching each and every word of the Indian diplomat while she is in Nepal as it is considered the principal weight behind the Maoists.

In order to get a better understanding of the present contours of the increasing footprints of the Chinese in Nepal and their implications to India, it is pertinent to review the historical background of this triangle, especially the events that took place in the 19th and 20th centuries, for they impacted the entire geo-political situation in these three countries, and the legacy continues to affect us even today.

India-China-Nepal in retrospect

In the early 18th century, Nepal was under the rule of various chieftains whose governance and culture were highly influenced by Tibet. During the 1760s, the Gurkhas conquered these chieftain states and emerged so strong that they began to threaten the surrounding kingdoms including Tibet. Their expansion resulted in overrunning many Tibetan territories in 1788.[1] The Gurkha action against Tibet, which was a tributary state (fushu guo stated in Chinese historical documents) of China, enraged the Chinese emperor Qianlong (1736-1795) who in turn dispatched forces against Nepal in 1791-92 and reduced Nepal to the status of yet another vassal in China's periphery. Nepal was forced to send tribute to China once in every five years.[2]

When expanded south, the Gurkhas met a deadlier foe, the British. The confrontation culminated in the Anglo-Nepalese War of 1814-1816. The war was precipitated by the Nepalese invasion of Sikkim. Nepal being a tributary of China dispatched envoys to Tibet and requested for help but the request went in vein. According to Wang (1998:4), China at this point of time was weak and helpless. However, if we go back into the history of China, Qianlong's era (1735-95) was the golden era of Chinese power and glory. This period saw the Chinese reserves increasing to 70 million taels (Hsu 1995: 430). The Anglo-Nepalese War took place just 20 years after Qianlong's retirement, during Jiaqing's (1896-1820) reign. Moreover, the opium trade during this period was also favourable to the Chinese, for between 1800 and1810, some 26 million taels of silver had flown into China (Hsu 1995:168). The balance of power remained in China's favour throughout Jiaqing's reign. Therefore we can surmise that China was still in a strong position. But, why did it not help Nepal?

The principal reason why China did not agree to the Nepalese request was its distance from China as well as its tiny stature. The attitude of the Qing government towards Nepal was that the "Gurkhas were bullies and insatiably avaricious and were to be held responsible for fomenting trouble and instability in the south-western frontiers (Lu 1996: 57)." The Nepalese once again requested Qing for help and threatened to throw their allegiance to the British. This irked the Chinese emperor and he rebuked Nepal: "if you throw your allegiance to the British, then you would not be entitled to send tributes to the Celestial Empire ... As regards dealing with the tribes outside our frontiers, the Celestial Empire will not extend militarily assistance to any of the warring side. The Celestial Empire is least bothered if your country concludes peace or goes to war with the British, approach as or eventually throws your allegiance to the British (Zhang 1983: 386)."

It was in the light of these developments that Nepal in 1815 concluded the Treaty of Sugauli with the British, in 1815 which was ratified on March

4, 1816. Nepal had to cede Kumaon, Garhwal and some Tarai areas to the British, besides being reduced to a British protectorate. However, Nepal was allowed to send tribute missions to China. The last mission it sent to China was in the year 1908, at the fag end of the Qing dynasty. Nevertheless, due to the border problems with Tibet, the Tibeto-Nepalese War was fought between 1854 and 1856. In 1856 a peace treaty was concluded which was grossly in favour of Nepal. However, in the treaty Nepal agreed to pay their respect as before to the Chinese emperor. The Tibetan agreed to pay a sum of 10,000 rupees annually to the Gurkha government. The Nepalese also offered military protection to Tibet in the event it is invaded by other states. They also acquired residency and trading rights in Lhasa from the Tibetan government.[3]

The Nepalese conquest of Tibet and stationing of a permanent resident at Lhasa is pointer to the fact that China had a very loose control over Tibet, and that Tibet was in full control of its internal and external affairs. Though the Chinese might say that China was weak and a victim of Opium Wars, it can be argued that China could have protested and demanded the withdrawal of Nepalese Resident, which it did not, and the Nepalese Resident remained in Lhasa even after the fall of the Qing dynasty. By the middle of the 19th century the Ranas captured the political power in Nepal. The British guaranteed Nepalese independence and won the Ranas' loyalty.

During the early 20th Century, in recognition of the contribution of Nepal during World War I, the "treaty of perpetual peace and friendship," which recognised the independent status of Nepal and upgraded the British resident to an envoy was signed in Kathmandu on 21 December, 1923 between the Great Britain and Nepal. It was the 1923 treaty that governed the Anglo-Nepalese relations prior to the Indian independence; the treaty was replaced with the 'India and Nepal Treaty of Peace and Friendship' concluded on July 31, 1950 which allows free movement of people and goods between India and Nepal. In recent years, the treaty has generated a lot of heat in various quarters in Nepal and has been very unpopular, for it is believed that the treaty impinges upon the sovereignty of Nepal.

China's interests in Nepal

Indo-Nepal relations were excellent during King Tribhuvan's reign; however, the equation changed after his death in 1955. His son, King Mahendra, amidst the deteriorating Sino-Indian relations dismissed the Nepali Congress Government in 1960. The move was considered by India as undemocratic and essentially anti-India. China seized the opportunity and went on to develop "special relations" with Nepal and accused India of 'expansionism' and 'hegemonism.' According to Brigadier Abdul Hafiz (Chen 1995:281; Ranganathan and Khanna 2000:110), Director General of the Bangladesh Institute for International and Strategic Studies, China lauded Nepal's "struggle" to preserve its "independence and sovereignty" and gradually became an important factor in Nepal's economic and international relations both. In 1960, China and Nepal signed a peace and friendship treaty and also signed the border agreement and the construction of Kathmandu-Tibet highway a year later. China's another interest in Nepal was to flush out the Tibetan guerrillas who were operating from Mustang Area in Nepal with the help of CIA. Citing Yang Gongsu, Garver (2001:148) also reports about a joint Nepalese-People Liberation Army (PLA) operation against the Tibetan insurgents/refugees in the area in 1960. However, Shakya (1999:360-64) posits that King Mahendra was still sympathetic towards the Tibetans. In 1969, the Crown Prince Birendra even met the new leader, Gyatho Wangdu in Mustang camp. After the death of Mahendra in 1972, his son Birendra continued the equidistance policy of his father. He became the first foreign dignitary to visit Tibet in 1976. Two years later Deng Xiaoping visited Nepal. Brigadier Abdul Hafiz (Chen 1995:281) remarks that as with other south Asian countries, Beijing's efforts were directed towards cultivation of "special relations" with Nepal, too.

With the improvement in Sino-india relations during the 1970s, and given the close socio-economic and geographical proximity of Nepal with India, China probably saw the futility of excessive courting of Nepal. This was evident when India imposed economic sanctions and closed 13 of the 15 transit points on Indo-Nepal border in 1989. India was annoyed when it learnt that Nepal was purchasing Chinese arms. China attempted to salvage Nepal by transporting some goods for some time, but could not subside the increasing social unrest and cost of goods in Nepal. Moreover, with the change of political command and initiation of economic liberalization, China itself talked less of 'hegemonism' and 'expansionism' albeit its literature pertaining to India meant for domestic consumption is still full of such cold war era jargons and anti-India rhetoric. During Zhao Ziyang's 1981 visit to Nepal, though the Chinese supported the Nepalese proposal of turning Nepal into a Zone of Peace, he also talked but talked about promoting cooperation among developing countries. China herself adopted a policy of equidistance towards Nepal and India. In November, during his visit to Nepal, Li Peng expressed China's inability to extend substantial support, advising the Nepalese leaders to peacefully resolve their differences with India (Chen 1995: 282).

China's 'excessive' courting of Nepal and India's stakes

It was perhaps for its international image that China denounced the Maoist Insurgency in Nepal during the Monarchy. It repeatedly stated that Mao's China had nothing to do with the Maoists in Nepal and India; instead, the latter were misusing the name of their helmsman. However, when Maoists formed the government and Pushpa Kamal Dahal, also known as Prachanda, was sworn in as Prime Minister, the first country he visited was China. He was 'invited' to attend the closing ceremony of Olympic Games in 2008. The visit lasted for five days and the special bonding between the Maoists and China was visible. There are people who argue that China is not only courting the Nepalese Maoists, but also rendering political as well material support to the Indian Maoist whose ultimate aim is to overthrow the parliamentary democracy through an armed struggle (Singh 2010).

It is the Maoists, who have been making every hue and cry over the 1950 treaty and have vociferously advocated for scrapping of the treaty. The sheer political capital of the Maoists, and the anti-China Tibetan protests in March 2008 in various parts of Tibet including Sichuan, underscored the importance of Nepal to China, for Nepal has a sizeable Tibetan community, of 20,000, according to one of the representatives of the Dalai Lama. In fact, all Tibetans who escaped Tibet, had to register at the office of UNHCR office in Nepal before entering India. It was perhaps for first time in the history of Nepal that brute force was used by the

Maoist supported Nepalese government to suppress the anti-China protests of the Tibetan émigré in 2008, which also revealed the close relationship between the Maoists and China.

It seems that with the deterioration of Indo-Nepal relations, Nepal has sought a countervailing force in China. We have mentioned of the 1989 episode; in 2005, China further supplied arms to King Gyanendra; in the same year, Nepal voiced for the inclusion of China into SAARC irrespective of the fact that India had expressed its reservations for China's entry; in September 2008, China invited Nepalese Defence Minister Ram Bahadur Thapa as an observer to the military exercise 'Warrior 2008', and during his meeting with China's Defence Minister Liang Guanglie, China announced a military aid package of USD 1.3 million to Nepal. In December 2008, Lieutenant General Ma Xiaotan of the PLA pledged USD 2.6 million in non-lethal military aid to Nepal during his Nepal visit. It could be discerned that there is a close bonhomie between the two sides. Conversely, in 2007 when India sent non-lethal military assistance to Nepal, it created a furore with the Maoists lodging vigorous protests and accusing New Delhi of trying to sabotage the peace process. Politically, even as Prachanda called for the revision of 1950 Treaty, Nepal accepted the draft of a 'Peace and Friendship Treaty' submitted and proposed by Hu Zhengyue, Assistant Chinese Foreign Affairs Minister during his Nepal visit in April 2009. It may also be mentioned that Nepal is reluctant to sign the Extradition Treaty proposed by India in 2008, thus ignoring India's concerns over terrorists having links in Nepal.

Besides deepening political and military ties, the proliferation of China Study Centres (CNC) across Nepal has also generated lot of interest and apprehensions in India. According to Samanta (2008) "the CNC which started as a benign China-supported informal civil society group in 2000 to promote cultural interaction is growing in membership and has become an effective tool to promote the Chinese perspective on key issues concerning Nepal." The centres have increased to over two dozens of branches by now, most of these operating from the Tarai region of Nepal. Upendra Gautam (2009), the general Secretary of the CNCs Nepal, attempted to allay the Indian apprehensions by asserting that the Centres were established "with a view to promoting and further strengthening friendly ties between Nepal and China at the people to people level, and firmly upholds the principle of Panchasheel in inter-state relations."

Another apprehension of the Indian government in Nepal is the reconstruction of the Nepal-China highway by China. As mentioned in previous sections, the highway was built in 1958 and opened to traffic in 1965. It starts from Lhasa, capital city of Tibet Autonomous Region and ends in Kathmandu, capital city of Nepal with a total length of 900 kilometres. Of the total length only 100 kilometres is in Nepal. The renovation is expected to consume a whopping 800 million RMB (about 100 million USD), and is likely to be completed in 2010. This would be another milestone for China after the completion of Qinghai-Tibet railway. China predicts rapid border trade development with neighboring countries, especially in South Asia and sees these projects as extremely important overland channels to communicate with South Asia. Besides, China also handed over the Zhangmu-Kathmandu optical fibre cable project to Nepal in 2008. China is also helping Nepal in the construction of the Melamchi Water Supply Project. The Project will improve the health and well-being of the people in Kathmandu Valley by alleviating the critical water stress in the region, where 1 million urban dwellers receive piped water for only two hours every two days. The project is budgeted at 294.4 million USD and is expected to be completed by 2014. It is believed that China has invested millions of dollars in Nepal's hydroelectricity projects as well.

Conclusion

It is obvious that both India and China have had enjoyed close historical ties with Nepal. China's ties with Nepal resulted from its patronage of Tibet. However, with the deterioration in sino-indian relations, China not only courted Nepal, but also other countries in India's vicinity. In the same vein, India's neighbours looked for a countervailing force in China. Moreover, with China's increasing economic muscle and political clout, its political, economic and diplomatic assertiveness has become increasingly visible. Of late, its engagement with Nepal and other countries surrounding us has been multi-dimensional and designed to diminish the Indian influence in South Asia both in short run and long run. Why China has been able to change the perceptions of the people in the subcontinent favourable to China calls for introspection, and requires corrective and immediate measures, for India cannot afford to take its historical and cultural ties with Nepal and other countries for granted.

It could also be discerned that there is a flurry of diplomatic as well as economic activities between China and Nepal. Last year alone, an unprecedented 38 Chinese delegations visited Nepal. In such a backdrop, getting paranoid over China's investment in the developmental projects such as China-Nepal Boda Hospital in Kathmandu, Zhangmu-Kathmandu optical fibre project, Melamchi Water Supply and many others is not an answer. On the contrary, we must ask ourselves, why has Nepal and other countries in the subcontinent gone to China? Have we looked after the vital interests of these nations? Have we sensitised ourselves to the 'threat' they perceive from us? Is the issue of our Border Security Forces harassing the Nepalese in Tarai region being addressed or not? Are we being considerate when the Nepalis talk about getting unfair deal or being cheated while negotiating treaties with them? Will the Kosi Treaty (1954) and the Gandak Treaty (1959) cast its shadow over future collaborations with Nepal? These are some of the issues we need to address while approaching Nepal, as well as when we talk of China's increasing presence in Nepal.

Given China's military and other quasi-military projects in Nepal, Sri Lanka, Bangladesh, Myanmar and Pakistan, it is amply clear that China has consistently followed the strategy of pinning India to the subcontinent, and has used our differences with countries in our vicinity to their own advantage with a lethal statecraft. However, the question we must ask ourselves is, do we have the capabilities to undertake the projects the Chinese companies are taking in our vicinity, or is it because of the sloppiness of our government as well as private sector to avail such opportunities in our neighbourhood? As far as China's infrastructural development projects in our vicinity are concerned, these may generate multiplier effects and pave way for trade and commerce for Indian companies as well. However, China also must be careful in inciting anti-India rhetoric in these countries as well as to its own domestic audience, for this may prove the 'string of pearls' thesis of containing India true, and force India to move closer to the United States as well other countries and regions that are antagonistic to China. Therefore, India and China need to work closely in their shared neighbourhood on the issues of security, including the maritime security as most of the Shipping Lines of Communication run through the Indian Ocean.

References

Chen, Hefeng , Wang, Hongyu, Du, Youkang and Shen Dingli (eds.)(1995),"China and South Asian Relations in the 1990s", Sichuan People's Publishing House, Chengdu. Garver, John W. (2001), "The protracted contest: Sino-Indian rivalry in the twentieth century", University of Washington Press, Seattle.

Gautam, Upendra (2009), "China Study Center - Nepal rebukes Indian allegations", Telegraphnepal.com, July 21, 2009 (accessed November 29, 2010)

Hogg, Charu Lata (2010), 'China, India and Nepal: Intrigue on Top of the World' in The *World Today*, vol 66 (6), June 2010.

Hsu, Immanuel. C (1995), The Rise of Modern China, Oxford University Press, New York. Lu, Zhaoyi (ed.)(1996), "British India and China's South-western Border: 1774-1911", Chinese Academy of Social Sciences Publication, Beijing.

Malhotra, Jyoti (2010), 'Prachanda's loss throws open India-China rivalry', in Business *Standard*, September 9, 2010.

Ranganathan, C. V. and Khanna, Vinod (2000), "India and China: The Way Ahead After "Mao's India War", Har Anand Publications Pvt. Ltd., New Delhi.

Samanta, Pranab Dahal (2008), "Pro-China centres, calling for reduced ties with Delhi, sprout along Nepal border with India", *Indian Express*, February 11, 2008 (accessed November 29, 2010).

Shakya, Tsering (1999), "The Dragon in the Land of Snow: A History of Modern Tibet Since 1947", Pimlico, London.

Singh, RSN (2010), 'Maoists: China's proxy soldiers' in *Indian Defence Review*, vol 25 (3), July-September 2010 (published IDR online on October 6, 2010).

Zhang, Qiqin (1983), "Documentary Collection of Tibetan Affairs During Qing Dynasty", Tibetan Studies Editorial Division, Lahsa.

Pramod Dhakal

Nepalese Diaspora

How they matter in Education and Knowledge Translation

Context

Nepal, as poor as it is known from the eyes of statistics, has been presented with an opportunity to rebuild itself. The country is emerging out of a decade-long armed conflict fuelled primarily by social and economic disparities and is in the process of writing a new constitution and national reconciliation. While Nepal is seeking help from Nepalese Diaspora from around the world in the rebuilding process, it is important to see how Diaspora will matter to Nepal in the days to come. Because research has proven education as the largest single contributor to solving the problems of poverty, income gap, gender inequality, ethnic inequality, and inequality in well-being, this article attempts to see the role of Diaspora in the field of education and knowledge. Perspectives presented here are contemplative and the burden to prove, disprove, add, or reduce the ideas presented here is left to educationists and researchers. Diaspora in Early Education and Now

As countries of Indian subcontinent were being absorbed in British India, places linguistically and culturally connected to present day Nepal got separated by political boundaries. Thus people who were freely connected previously became the early Diaspora. In the last few decades many Nepalis have migrated all over the world in search of education, work, or better living conditions. The Diaspora today is more educated, empowered, and ever more conscious of its identity. Accordingly its impact on scientific, educational and technological aspiration of Nepal is also shifting.

Until the first half of the 20th century, ordinary Nepalis were forbidden from attending formal schools. Education became slowly accessible to them since the fall of Rana regime in 1950. Value of Diaspora scholars became apparent when people built schools in various parts of Nepal and teachers for those schools came from Banaras, Haridwar, Darjeeling and other centres of learning in India. These Diaspora had a significant role in uplifting the state of basic education as well as the social and political consciousness in Nepal. Diaspora-Nepal relationship has however undergone a change in recent times due to the circumstances that are beyond Nepal's control.

Decades ago, the Diaspora scholars were happy to return to Nepal as the standard of living in Nepal was no inferior to its neighbouring countries. The new Diaspora is now scattered all over the world in countries more developed than Nepal. Even those who are now living in India enjoy superior material standard of living and better educational opportunities than in Nepal. In near future, it is unlikely that Diaspora Nepalese will ever return to Nepal, except for the negligible few. In this context it has become important to know how Diaspora population can be of significant utility to their native places.

Tackling the Shift in Society and Economy: Technology is not only being used by people but is also affecting people's attitudes, work patterns, and social dynamics. Telephone, television, radio, processed food, and other products of technologies are altering tastes, habits, agricultural outputs, and ways things are done. While the effects of consumption are altering the face of Nepal, much is yet to be done in producing something tangible to convert import-only scenario into import-export scenario. And that requires a massive effort in knowledge exchange and collaboration with the world.

Closing Educational and Technological Gap: Unlike in the past, people expect employable, professional, and practical skills out of education. Yet offerings made by institutions become obsolete quickly with the rapid advancement of practices, tools, technologies and new knowledge. Consequently, today's student must be in pursuit of lifelong learning to remain afloat in the marketplace.

People in Nepal are also becoming increasingly more vulnerable to job loss as agriculture is occupying increasingly smaller portion of the economy. Thus, simultaneously advancing their education and career is a forced imperative for many Nepalese. And meeting such accelerated demand for advanced education from all frontiers has become a monumental challenge to Nepal. Finding necessary budget and full spectrum of highly qualified educators in all required fields is almost impossible without international cooperation in education.

Some decades ago, Nepal had a shortage of teachers in Mathematics, English and Science, but today such shortage has shifted to other emerging fields in which the country holds no indigenous expertise. Therefore, the new Diaspora that has gained proficiency in science, technology, and other emerging disciplines holds some keys to meeting that need.

Unless the least developed countries also conquer technology, it wouldn't be an exaggeration to say that they will be conquered by the countries rich in technology. The poor countries, therefore, have little alternative than turning to their Diaspora to acquire open-knowledge and technology with which they can build their own new knowledge and technologies. Thus Diaspora scholarship is more important to less developed countries than to the developed ones.

Increasing the Size of Our Thoughts: A person who grows in a small confine of space with simple and a small number of problems to solve possesses much less amount of knowledge compared to the person exposed to wider varieties of information and presented with larger number of problems of varying complexities. Therefore, larger the size and complexities of problems one attempts to solve, greater would be the knowledge acquired in the process by that person.

Diaspora population faces one set of problems and problem-context at its native place and another set of problems and problem-context in its adopted lands. It also gets to mingle with people who are solving complex technical, scientific, societal, and philosophical problems. Therefore, its approach to problem solving would be largely influenced by a wider context it is exposed with. Therefore, they would have the opportunity to significantly increase the size of their thoughts from what they would have had if they stayed in the first context only.

Proving Quality in Education: The level of craftsmanship and intellectual performance of Diaspora population directly impacts the perception on the quality of education they receive in their native place. Therefore, the dignity, honour and acceptance of their native institution would be directly tied to the quality and consistency of the performance of the Diaspora in their adopted land. They are the ones who can popularize home institutions to people around the world through their superior performance in professional accreditation and licensing examinations and work performances.

In sum, the Diaspora presents an indispensable utility to the countries of their nativity in the field of knowledge, science, technology and education. And before discussing how the Diaspora potential can be harnessed to the advantages of the developing countries, it is important to discuss the changing context of knowledge acquisition and production.

Shifting Nature of Education and Knowledge Production: Moral to Economy to Emotional-Equilibrium: While education at one time attempted to create an obedient and moral man, it did not allow questioning of the values that were passed on as "inviolable truths and norms". For example, Dalits were not allowed to study books in Nepal and India. Later education, and that of our time, focused on making us free thinking and practical people, thereby offering lives of material plenty and intellectual freedom. Yet the material progress could not lead to moral progress and emotional equilibrium. Today humanity is eager for practical, ethical, and emotionally enlightened people. And education is the most potent tool to achieve that societal goal.

Oral to Paper to Electronics: While early education relied on oral transmission of ideas, the birth of printing press gave rise to mass publication of books, self-interpreted reading, preservation of intellectual gains, and birth of Enlightenment in Europe and elsewhere. Today many educationally least developed countries are poised to jump directly from oral traditions to electronic transfer and rendering of writings and other knowledge content. On-line and interactive learning tools and techniques are altering the way teaching, learning, and knowledge production are done. Technology assisted learning is going to be the way of the future.

Preservation-of-Tradition to Reciprocity to Collaboration: For long, education was limited among religious clergies, who worked to ensure strict adherence to traditionally established values. Later, students from wealthy families gained knowledge from their teachers in return for secrecy, loyalty, fees, or other in-kind favours to teachers. A teacher was viewed as a source of knowledge and facilitator and manager of learning for his students. In reciprocity, he gained status and wealth. Today, students are increasingly becoming independent learners who collaborate with one another and with the teachers. With massive encroachment of technology and information in daily lives of people, this trend is sure to continue. In such a scenario, the role of students is not only to understand the existing knowledge but also to produce knowledge in the process of learning.

Equality to Disparity to Equality: Some influential ancient scholarship advocated equality of all humans. Hindu text Gita wrote: "The most educated of persons, a cow, an elephant, a dog, or a wretched person, are to be viewed in equal reverence by a learned person.[5.18]" Later, we accepted superiority of one species over another, one race over another, one gender over another, and one person over another. Likewise, we went on to thinking that an entrepreneur should be permitted to accumulate any amount of wealth. To ensure that it happened, patenting was introduced to protect intellectual property. Again, this has raised a question of ethicality of unlimited accumulation, far too exceeding the contributions made by the individual, and most importantly the ethicality of hiding knowledge. Thus the open source movement was born which is making contribution in flattening the disparity in knowledge by offering free and open source operating systems, software applications, knowledge references, and learning materials. Today, the debate between the worthiness and societal utility of proprietary and patented use of knowledge versus sharing of knowledge has intensified. New ways are needed to compensate for the purpose served by patenting, knowledge hiding, and contractual thinking so that we could achieve openness and equality in knowledge production and transmission.

Archiving to Translation to Flow of Knowledge: There was a time when we excessively revered knowledge that was already produced and did not care much for its further production and proliferation. In the post-printing age, we were busy archiving knowledge in papers and books. Then we emphasized the concept of technology transfer and knowledge transfer, which gained much popularity within different branches of a single organization but could not give the same comfort in inter-organizational and inter-country context.

Recently the Canadian Institute of Health Research introduced a new term "knowledge translation" to mean "the exchange, synthesis and ethically-sound application of knowledge within a complex system of interactions among researchers and users" [search web]. Today we are concerned with how that information from one context can be synthesized and translated into another context in an ethically sound way. This approach also keeps its significance in international collaboration in knowledge endeavours, especially to make education grounded in the learning context of learners of various parts of the world and various parts of the same country and the same economy.

Then an important issue immediately associated with knowledge translation is of making public knowledge accessible to people around the world. Concern for the future would be on how we could let the knowledge flow freely for all humanity to enjoy while amply rewarding the knowledge producers.

Memorization to Analysis to Synthesis: There was a time when we used education as a platform for memorizing facts, figures, instructions and ways. The later focus has been in the work of analysis. Today we are in the age of extreme data collection and extreme data analysis. We are writing papers that refer to a lot of other papers. We are producing too much data, too many papers, and too many books. When a person finds one paragraph worth of useful information, he or she writes a long book with hundreds of pages and hundreds of references to justify the idea and to convince us. It appears as if we were to find an idea the size of a corn kernel, we would not just make popcorn out of it but a huge volume of air. Only through way of synthesizing these obfuscated ideas we will be able to re-construct the corn kernel from the air, will overcome the pain of information overload, and will prevent information from losing its relative value. It is imperative that we enter into an age of synthesis with urgency. In developing countries where most of the population is unable to synthesize higher knowledge, massive support is required in the field of knowledge translation and synthesis.

One-to-one Learning to Mass Learning to On-line Learning: In early days, rich people hired personal tutors to satisfy their learning needs. Then came an age of mass education where the entire young population received compulsory education that was designed, funded and delivered by the state. With the advent of on-line learning and distance education, the future of education is once again being altered significantly. In future, learning would have some significant characteristics like (1) lifelong learning, (2) on-time learning, (3) distance learning, (4) choices in learning, (5) lateral and cooperative learning, (6) personalization in learning, and (7) technology enhanced and interactive learning.

In sum, it could be said that all countries are in need to acquire knowledge from around the world, but such need is far greater in poorer countries. That is the income gap between rich and poor countries is too huge for poorer countries to be able to attract their Diaspora backing; so the plans and policies to utilize Diaspora knowledge and potential should be accordingly developed. The next section delves on the ways of harnessing Diaspora knowledge, talent and skills.

How can diaspora knowledge be harnessed?

When interacting with Diaspora population, one can invariably hear one recurring message. "I am willing to give back if conditions are right." They say, they would even return if there exist right opportunities and environment for their return. Then the question comes, how can materially, technologically, and scientifically poor countries create environment acceptable to scientists, technologists, and educators that are habituated to salaries, lifestyles, and intellectual opportunities that are offered to them by already advanced countries? How would we create a condition that is conducive to creating the condition demanded by the Diaspora knowledge producers? These questions are not that easy to answer.

Nevertheless, significant amount of knowledge, education, and skills could be gained if there is an institutional approach and thrust for harnessing Diaspora knowledge and skills. While a separate ministry or agency to look at Diaspora matter could be justifiable, the most immediate impact could be realized through open and distance universities and institutionally promoted distance collaboration mechanisms. Successes achieved in small scale collaborations could then give rise to collaborations in more ambitious and complex endeavours. In that light, some potential avenues for harnessing Diaspora knowledge and skills are discussed in this section.

Understanding the Search for Unique Advantages: Even the Diaspora that has landed in developed countries would be in the quest for specific professional or knowledge advantages over other competitors. He or she has to constantly compete for opportunities. In the process, he or she is in search of an economical access to high quality professional knowledge and education. Therefore, it is in their own advantage to have access to institutions that add unique values to their portfolio. Sometimes, being able to take the same programme as one offered at their adopted country but at a much reduced cost can also be of significant advantage. Sometimes, new immigrants would be in advantage to be able to pass adopted countries' professional licensing examinations from their native countries before they make the actual move. Therefore, even the Diaspora has much to gain from educational developments in their native places. Given a proper institutional framework, Diaspora among themselves can become teachers, students, and facilitators for such causes. In the process the native country can also benefit with the exchange of knowledge.

Offering Access to New Opportunities: Today we are moving from an age of exploration of Moon and Mars to of DNA and other puzzles of lives. We are more so in search of biological puzzles and biological information than manufacturing of larger and faster rockets. We are moving away from the technology of mass manufacturing to molecular engineering and nanotechnology, away from mass movement of goods to mass movement of knowledge, from material development into moral development, and from single lab research to collaborative research. Therefore, the quest is on to find knowledge treasures from all cultures, philosophies, and biological matters of the world. Search of cures for diseases, improvements of varieties and nutritional content of foods, and discovery of new synthetic materials are going to be found in species of plants and animals from around the world. Being conversant in both the offering of their adopted places and native places, Diaspora are best placed to exploit this unique opportunity in the quest of knowledge and the benefits to be derived from it. Thus countries could offer opportunities for scientific collaboration for mutual benefits.

Letting to Discover the Self: An increasing number of people are moving from less-urban to more-urban places and more-advanced countries in search of opportunities. Though the more urban places they move their importance as individuals steadily decreases, but their mass identity built by collectively delivering increasing progress becomes greater. A poor Nepali may become advanced Canadian at the expense of his personal identity. "But seated deep inside each of us is a person that is reluctant to accept oneself as an anonymous member of human species." Therefore, the Diaspora often ponders on his achievements and losses, and hopes to find his or her lost self in the land that they were attached throughout their formative years. A sizable number might want to compensate for their emotional isolation by becoming a willing participant in ethically doable knowledge endeavours that would be meaningful to the place they left in return for visibility and feeling of importance.

Understanding the Causes of Non-Return: Despite good intentions, it is not practicable for most people to return to their native country. That is due to a number of personal and professional reasons, which include educational opportunities for children, health and medical reasons, issues of building pensionable retirement, opinion of family members, and fear of instability and uncertainty in native land, particularly in the case of poor countries. It is so rarely that a professionally established person gives up everything and returns. A daring young person in the beginning phase of a career is more likely to return for entrepreneurial pursuit than an established professional. Therefore, it is better for a country to make institutions with plans, policies and programmes to utilize what the Diaspora people know from where they live and what they do without any need to return to their native places. Since all researchers around the world are seeking new opportunities for creative endeavours, being able to inculcate collaboration in problem solving and research should outweigh the issue of physical return.

Presenting Raw Data for Analysis and Synthesis: A country can collect raw data on many frontiers of its society, natural environment, resources, economy, and so on. Such data could be put in a public domain and the Diaspora and international scholars could be given access to do the analysis in the areas of their expertise on those data and publish their findings. This would contribute to rapid advancement of knowledge. They could also be asked to synthesize the knowledge derived from all the analyses that would be done. In the process, the contributors could make scholarly gain of their own; some may even earn higher degrees and professional advancements through such work. Such works would help both the Diaspora and the native country.

Presenting Numerous but Small Scale Problems: It is always possible to break large or complex problems into a set of numerous small problems. When sets of numerous but small problems are presented to the Diaspora, much could be derived from the collection of individual contributions especially when it comes to the pursuit of building knowledge and education. For example, instead of asking the Diaspora to write about the flora and fauna of Nepal, it is possible to select the most common 100 trees, 100 shrubs, 100 grass, 100 insects, 100 animals and so on and put their pictures and videos with empty Wiki-like blank pages with a challenge to the Diaspora and international scholars to write about them. Similarly a book can be broken into chapters. A technological problem can be broken into component parts. Curriculum for delivering technical education in health, agriculture, and other areas based on indigenous environment and resources could be broken into numerous learning modules. In a short span of time, a large amount of knowledge could be built in that manner in a transparent and ethical way.

In general, many problems can be solved through scholarly collaboration or only by Diaspora enthusiasts given such problems are defined clearly. When applying this technique, much knowledge and understanding can be achieved on the natural and artificial resources of the country. Knowing about what one has is a necessary step in finding what can be done. When possibilities are revealed, there would be scholars from around the world who would be interested in scholarly and other technological collaborations. It is equivalent to building the highly sophisticated Linux operating system by writing its code again and again to the perfection by collaborating with enthusiasts from around the world. An open environment to compete and be recognized for the contribution of solutions can accelerate the contributions. In all this, some institutional approach is required to aggregate the pieces of knowledge and to construct a larger body of knowledge that can positively transform the society and economy.

Hiring as Professors, Tutors, Researchers, and Program Developers:

Diaspora scholars could be recruited as professors and tutors of distance learning universities and colleges in the areas of their expertise. In doing that they would not only make knowledge contribution to their native place but also earn supplementary income during their spare time. They can also fulfil the knowledge need in emerging areas in which there may be lack of expertise in the country. Besides, a small number of Diaspora could return and serve as full-time staff.

The Diaspora community could be asked to build programmess that other Diaspora need. For example, many people of trades and professions with verified skills and licensing requirements in countries around the world could be offered courses and accredited programmes, which can also be useful to countries hosting the institutions first in generating income and secondly in educating their own native population in those fields.

Exploring and Connecting with International Scholars: Diaspora scholars could be the best ambassadors for a country in establishing connections for knowledge pursuits. They can help establish connections with professional associations, philanthropic organizations, research institutions, universities and colleges and individual scholars. Such inter linkages can help research and education pursuits including in the establishment of universities, colleges and research institutions.

Utilizing a Common Thread: Solving problems of their native place can sometimes help inspire and unify the Diaspora like no other issue. For example, the initiative for Open University of Nepal has noticeably excited Diaspora Nepalese because it has great potential to engage them in understanding and solving the educational, research, and technological needs of Nepal, their common binding thread. Many such galvanizing and common issues could be pursued to inspire Diaspora contributions.

Conclusion

Importance of Diaspora in the endeavours of knowledge and education is extremely important for developing countries. A country should use variety of means to tap its Diaspora knowledge and intellectual capacity as it may be impracticable for them to return to their native country for the purpose of providing knowledge services. That the presence of technology in people's lives has become a matter of fact, the plans in knowledge acquisition, translation, synthesis and production should not ignore the technology equation. At a time when the differences in the standard of living between countries are remarkably large, it is prudent to utilize Diaspora potential from where they live and from what they do using distance education and distance collaboration approaches fostered through institutions made specifically to promote such cooperation and collaboration.

Uddhab Pd. Pyakurel

Some Reflections on Nepal-India Relations in the context of Nepali Nationalism

Benedict Anderson in his book "Imagined Communities: Reflections on the Origin and Spread of Nationalism" rightly points out that the terms 'nation', 'nationality' and 'nationalism' all have proved notoriously difficult to define[1]. The difficulty arises due to the fact that many old nations, which once believed to be fully consolidated, find themselves challenged by 'sub-nationalism' within their borders. Such a trend of emerging 'sub-nationalism' within a nation is defined by Anderson as 'nation-ness'[2]. Whether is it nationalism or nation-ness, these, according to him, are cultural artifacts of a particular kind, and we need to consider carefully three basic things[3] to understand them properly[4].

Nation is an imagined political community, i.e. imagined as both inherently limited and sovereign[5]. It is imagined because the members of even the smallest nation will never know most of their fellow-members, meet them, or even hear of them, yet in the minds of each lives the image of their communion[6]. For Anderson, the nation is imagined as *limited*, as

---

[1]Benedict Anderson, Imagined Communities: Reflections on the Origin and Spread of Nationalism. London: Verso. 2006 (new edition). p. 3.

[2]He states that "nation-ness is the most universally legitimate value in the political life of our time," for details. See Benedict Anderson, Imagined Communities: Reflections on the Origin and Spread of Nationalism. London: Verso. 2006. p. 3.

[3]A) how they have come into historical being, b) in what ways their meanings have changed over time, and , c) why, today, they command such profound emotional legitimacy.

[4]Anderson, op.cit. p. 4.

[5]Anderson, op.cit. p.6.

[6]Hugh Seton-Watson, Nation and States: An Enquiry into the Origins of Nation and the Politics of Nationalism. Boulder: Westview press. 1977.

sovereign and as a *community*[7].

However, nationalism is basically considered as a collective state of mind or consciousness in which people believe their primary duty and loyalty is to the nation-state. According to the Cultural Dictionary (online), nationalism often implies national superiority and glorifies various national virtues. Thus, love of the nation may be the overemphasized concern with national self-interest to the exclusion of the rights of other nations.

In fact, the concept of nationalism has been popularized as a necessary aspect for citizens of a country to identify themselves as belonging to a nation, that is, a large group of people who have something in common. The realization that they might possess a common history, religion, language or race also aided people in forming a national identity. When both a common identity and a formal authority structure over a large territory (i.e., the state) exist, then nationalism becomes possible. However, the idea basically grew in the world when there was rise of centralized monarchies, which placed people under one rule and eliminated feudalism, and made this possible.

In the case of Nepal, too, nationalism is a phenomenon which was initially driven by feudal monarchs; and it is obvious that the concept has inbuilt political characteristics. As elsewhere in the world, Nepal too has been suffering from the 'politicized' nationalism. Also, there are people of formerly feudal monarch ruled countries, who are yet to get rid of the political nature of nationalism even after the removal of the institutions of monarchy.

Talking about the history of Nepali nationalism, it can be traced back to 1769 when King Prithvi Narayan Shah 'unified' some of the principalities and adopted 'Nepal' as the name of the country and made 'Kathmandu' its capital. In fact, Nepali nationalism was basically an initiative taken by the King. As Anderson views nationalism as cultural artifacts[8], King Prithvi 'conquered' various small states and tried to project "Nepali Nationalism" as a common identity by making 'Nepali' the common language and 'Hinduism' the common religion for his 'subjects.'

---

[8]Anderson, op.cit. p. 4.

He made a sentimental statement with the pride of a leader of Nepali nationalism: "Mero Sano Dukha Le Arjyako Muluk Hoina, Sabailai Chetana Bhaya" (the nation has come into existence as a result of my great sacrifice, all should acknowledge the fact). Stating Nepal as a 'yam' sandwiched between two stones (China and India), he tried to make his people aware of the possible 'encroachment' by the two big neighbours. That is why he closed Nepal to all foreign merchants[9].

However, his successors could not follow him as far as his idea of nationalism was concerned. Nepal witnessed its greatest military setback just 40 years after King Prithvi's death at Almora (in Kumaon) at the hands of the British force backed by local Kumaoni troops. Subsequently, Nepal accepted its loss in various wars with humiliation, and had to sign treaties such as Sugauli Treaty with British India in 1816 and Betrawati Treaty with China in 1849. The principal reason behind the continued losses was the internal power struggle within the palace. The most surprising fact was that his successors in the later days started presuming upon not only good offices from either of the two neighbours to remain in power in the country, but also started using foreign territories for their political gain.

The trend of using good offices of external power for internal politics increased when there was internal conflict among the ruling classes, and it was further strengthened when the Rana Regime assumed power in Nepal in 1846 and the British in India became powerful. Nepal signed a treaty with East India Company in 1801 consenting to allow a British representative to reside in Nepal as envoy. In return, the British agreed to keep the ex-King Rana Bahadur Shah "in honourable custody in Banaras and restrain his activities and movements."[10] More than that, the Nepali political elites not only "continued their animated negotiations over the distribution of power and patronage in Nepal" in the presence of the agent, Mr. Knox, but also asked him to play various roles and settle Nepal's domestic

---

[9]Ludwig F. Stiller, S.J. *Nepal: Growth of a Nation*. Kathmandu: Human Resource Development Research Center, 1993.p.22.

[10]Ramjee Prasad Parajuli, *The Democratic Transition in Nepal*. Boston: Rowman & Littlefield Publishers, INC, 2000.

problems[11]. It was the turning point in the political history of Nepal after which the British India entered into Nepali domestic affairs with its 'personal preference.' Also, an illusion got popularized in Nepal along with the entry of the British that external backing was a necessity to remain in power in Kathmandu.

The British presence in Nepal after the Sugauli Treaty divided the ruling class (the forum of ruling class at that time was called the Court) into pro-British and anti-British faction.[12] It was Janga Bahadur Rana, the founder of the Rana family rule, who frequently visited the office of the British resident in Kathmandu while he was not recognized as the Prime Minister of Nepal by the British on the ground that he had obtained power through "inhumane and reprehensible" means[13]. It is believed that Jung Bahadur felt uneasy working as Prime Minister without the recognition of the Governor General of East India Company, though it was "unnecessary."[14] He also spent more than a year in Britain during his premiership, just to exhibit his loyalty towards the Great Britain. Recalling all this, what one can conclude is that seeking foreign support to remain in power is not a new phenomenon for the Nepali ruling class, though they always wanted others to recognize Nepal as an 'independent' country. That is why time and again they tried to use words such as 'independent' and 'sovereign' in each and every treaty and agreement signed with other countries.

As regards their relations with India, the Nepali ruling class tried to apply two opposite strategies simultaneously first, they sought the support of British India for their existence in power, and while doing so they never behaved in the spirit of rulers of an independent country; and second, they encouraged people and officials "to beat their drums" against the British in the past, and against India now. It has been the common practice for Nepali rulers, as it was followed by Bhimsen Thapa too, though he was accredited by the British as the only statesman in the subcontinent who could

---

[11]Stiller,op.cit. p.41.

[12]Parajuli, op.cit. p. 31.

[13]Ibid.

[14]Stiller, op. cit. p.82.

understand the company's intention and methods.[15] According to Stiller, Thapa did so to build up the army morale.[16] He had a very tough time in convincing his army to support the British Military during the Anglo-Burmese War in 1824 as his army was still contemplating the British Army as an enemy. All the rulers after Bhimsen Thapa have continued to follow more or less the similar ambivalent strategy as far as Nepal's foreign policy is concerned.

Nepal's relation with independent India

Researchers face difficulties while trying to follow the practices and paradigms of Nepal-India relations. The difficulty is due to the non-availability of data and evidences. While every letter from the Indian side along with notes based on each one-to-one conversation is available, there is hardly anything available on record about the similar documents in Nepal. Since no one from Nepal has ever opposed or questioned the authenticity of the published information from India, a researcher therefore per force has to rely on the data mostly made available from the Indian side to analyze the trend.

Nepal-India relations underwent a paradigm shift after India became independent. Many drastic changes could be observed from the Indian side in dealing with Nepal compared to how British India dealt with Nepal. Now, the question arises as to why India became more sensitive towards Nepal than the British in India? There are two palpable reasons for that first, the rise of Communism in China, and second, the increased Chinese involvement and interest towards its southern counterpart. Moreover, an independent and democratic India had to work with the people of Nepal as the leadership of India was very much aware of the contribution of pro-democracy people of Nepal to Indian freedom struggle. Also, Independent India had no option but to extend its willingness to work with the people of Nepal in its struggle for democracy as it had to reduce the anti-East India Company feeling which was prevalent on a big scale.

No doubt, India tried its best to engage with the then Rana rulers

---

[15]Stiller, op. cit. p. 60.

[16]Stiller, op. cit. p. 63.

too, but in a cautious manner - on the one hand India tried to show its willingness to work with the Ranas, on the other it lingered over the proposal of the Ranas to sign a fresh treaty. It seems that India did pretty well by delaying the signing of the proposed treaty prepared by the Ranas because had India agreed to sign the treaty drafted and forwarded by the Ranas, it would have been a major set back to the struggle for democracy in Nepal as India had to stop the people of Nepal from using its territory for launching movements against the Rana oligarchic rule as per the proposed treaty. It was Nehru who tried to push the Rana rulers to accept political reforms being demanded by the people of Nepal. In a letter to Sri Prakash, Nehru wrote:

> The Prime Minister of Nepal, Maharaja Padma Shamsher Jung Bahadur Rana, has asked us to send him someone of high degree to advise him about constitutional reform in his country...he has not made the request officially to us but in a friendly way to me personally. I think we should respond to this friendly gesture and give him such help as we can (Nehru's letter to Sri Prakash May 13, 1947).[17]

The above quote reveals two important facts. One is about the Nepali leadership's ambivalent attitude towards Indian leadership, and another is about Nehru's interest to see politically reformed Nepali society. One can easily guess from Nehru's letter that Padma Shamsher had asked for advice from India to overcome the prevalent crisis. It is also clear from the above quote that Nepal tried to build its relation with independent India not in changed manner, but in the same manner as it had its relations with the British India. Here, one can argue that Nepal-India relations could have gone beyond the colonial legacy had Nepal understood the willingness of independent India.

It was indeed very difficult for the Indian leadership to extend its uncritical support to the Rana oligarchic political system as "the shadow of colonial rule in India had made Indians strong supporters of democracy

[17]Avtar Singh Bhasin, *Nepal-India, Nepal-China Relations: Documents 1947-June*. (5 volumes). New Delhi: Geetika Publishers. 2005. pp. 36.

and freedom." However, even in a difficult situation like this, Nehru tried to find a "middle way" to accommodate both the Ranas and the pro-democracy forces under a reformed political system. While talking to Nepali Congress delegates led by Matrika Prasad Koirala, Nehru once disclosed India's primary concern for Nepal. He said, "you know that other nations are eager to exploit her (Nepal) to their benefit, but India must not give this chance."[18] Also, on September 11, 1954, he wrote to the King of Nepal: "Independence and Progress: Indeed the two are connected in many ways because without progress no strength can be built up and no country can function with real independence.[19]" Nehru's interest in Nepal's political reform and his willingness to work with Nepal show that he genuinely wanted to bring both the countries together in terms of development and social transformation. While reading Nehru's letters sent on various occasions to Nepali leaderships, and his notes on Nepal, one can easily discern that he was favourably inclined to Nepal's independent identity and progress. Speaking before the parliament on March 17, 1950, Nehru stated, "We have accordingly advised the Government of Nepal, in all earnestness, to bring themselves into line with democratic forces that are stirring in the world today." Also, when Mohan Shamsher did not show his interest in pursuing political reforms in Nepal, Nehru sent a strong message to him; but while doing so, he did not forget to recognize Nepal as an independent country. He wrote to Mohan Shamsher on June 9, 1949:

> As a government, it is not our business to interfere in the domestic policies in Nepal. Nepal is an independent country, friendly to us and having our friendship, I wish her and her people well. But in this complicated and related world, it is difficult and almost impossible for any country to ignore what is happening in another adjoining country.[21]

---

[18]Discussion between Jawahar Lal Nehru and representatives of the Nepali National Congress, May 28, 1947, in Avtar Singh Bhasin, *Nepal-India, Nepal-China Relations: Documents 1947*

Jawaharlal Nehru, India's Foreign Policy: Select Speeches (September 1945-April 1961). 1971. pp.147.

[19]June. (5 volumes). New Delhi: Geetika Publishers. 2005. pp. 42.

[20]Ibid p. 353.

[21]Avtar Singh Bhasin, *Nepal-India, Nepal-China Relations: Documents 1947-June*. (5 volumes). New Delhi: Geetika Publishers. 2005. pp.70

While analysing Nehru's engagement with Nepal-India relations, one can argue that Nepal could have capitalized on Nehru's best wishes for its progress and prosperity, but Nepali leadership took Indian sentiment in a different manner. The following statement of a former Prime Minister, Tanka Prasad Acharya, proves that Nepali leadership, in fact, tried to play with Indian sentiment by using its rival, China. Acharya states:

> I directed the local newspaper *Samaj* to print a rumour that China was going to give millions of rupees to Nepal as aid...the paper said that China was giving twenty-four million rupees. It said that Russia was also giving us money. This flustered the Americans (obviously Indian as America used to see Nepal through Indian eye), as I intended it to.[22]

His intention was to provoke India and America against China. He was, in fact, given the opportunity to be the Prime Minister by King Mahendra who was not happy with the Indian intention and interest to strengthen democratic system in Nepal. And, eventually King Mahendra not only took over power through coup d'état in 1960 and imposed his authoritarian rule in Nepal but also tried to play 'China card' against India.

Whatever could be the causes, Nepal-India relations have been in a difficult mode in recent years, even though both the countries acknowledge that they have "special relations." As Rose writes, the rulers of Nepal usually have perceived India as the more dangerous of its neighbours, whereas China has been considered as too distant - both in physical and cultural terms - to threaten the country's independence, but close enough to serve as a potential source of support[23]. This attitude of the Nepali rulers was guided by three basic reasons. The first and foremost was that Nepali rulers, who wanted to keep the Nepali subjects under their control, had nothing to share with the people except anti-Indianism. B.P. Koirala rightly stated

[22]James F. Fisher. *Living Martyrs: Individuals and Revolution in Nepal.* Delhi: Oxford University Press. 1998. pp. 171.

[23]Leo E. Rose, *Nepal: Strategy for Survival.* Bombay: Oxford University Press. 1971.

that Nepali Nationalism seems to have nothing except anti-Indianism[24]. All the political forces - right from monarchy to most of the leftist parties - which wanted to rule Nepal in an authoritarian way, tried to popularize anti-Indianism in Nepal in the name of nationalism. Though Ramachandran[25] argues that anti-Indianism in Nepal is a necessity to subsume Nepal's "separate identity," the Nepalese rulers did so due to the fact that they perceived a threat coming from democratic India in case they imposed any undemocratic rule in Nepal. When they found that India was becoming more sensitive towards its northern neighbours, the Nepalese rulers tried to distance themselves from India and come closer to China, which was "neither feasible nor attractive."[26] The trend became more emphasised after India became independent. Interestingly, most of the Nepali political forces still follow the similar tendency when they want to side-step democracy and establish a kind of authoritarianism, they start playing the 'China card'. On many occasions, both the rightists and leftists in Nepal joined hands to propagate anti-Indianism.

Regarding the response of the Nepali side to the changed context with independent India, Nepal tried not to change its stance but to continue as it had in the past with British India. In other words, the Nepali leadership neither tried to change their behaviour nor did they change their expectations from its southern neighbour. One of the most vital concerns of the then Nepali ruling class, especially for the Ranas, was to let India accept Nepal's sovereignty and independent status as did the British through the treaty of friendship in 1823. That is why Rana rulers proposed to sign the new Peace and Friendship Treaty just after India became independent. In the later days, the Nepalese started dealing Nepal-India relations at the level of bureaucracy and this trend seems to be increasing after 1990. Why the Nepalese preferred this option was that they felt it easier to deal with bureaucracy as it is considered as a "permanent institution of governance". More so, they opt for it as they are aware of the fact that

---

[24]For details, see Uddhab Pyakurel, "Rastriyatako Kasima 1950 Treaty" (1950 treaty in the context of Nationalism), Kantipur, February 24, 2010

[25]Shastri Ramachandran, "Nepal as Seen from India" IIC Quarterly, Vol.30 (2), Monsoon 2003.pp. 95.

[26]Rose, op.cit. p. 288

only the bureaucracy could help them to fulfil their petty interests such as admission of their children in Indian schools and colleges, facilitation of their 'illness' trips, and other similar requirements. That is how Nepal is losing its strength to deal with it friendly neighbor - India - on a moral ground. Also, it is losing its ground to maintain the Nepal-India relations at a political level. Nepalese political parties have to understand the limitation of bureaucracy; it unlike political parties and their leaders has nothing to do with any radical/progressive agenda. It is the institution only to run the system. It seems that the newly established political forces like United Communist Party of Nepal-Maoist and some other Madhesi parties hardly have any relations at the political level with India.

Also, Indian civil society blames that the Nepali political parties and leaders use India just as ladder to capture power in Kathmandu; once they are in power they forget to continue such relations. That is why it has been a difficult task to work together and strengthen people-to-people relations between the countries.

To summarise, I find two major problems while going through the history of Indo-Nepal relations. These are:

1. Double standard of Nepali leaders and ambivalent write-ups

As mentioned in the earlier sections, Nepali leaders have kept up with their double standard in their attitude and expectations from India. On the one hand, they seem ready to compromise everything before their Indian counterparts just to reveal their loyalty to the latter, and on the other, they use every opportunity to encourage men and officials to beat their drums against India. Such an attempt of Nepal's earlier ruling class was to boost up army morale, and now they do it show their 'nationalist' facade to their cadres.

According to Pradip Giri, "freedom to press and freedom of expression have been used to popularize the Nepali nationalism after 1950."[27] It is true that people can express their views freely only when there is democracy. And evidences show that Nepali nationalism got expanded in a different

[27]Personal interaction with author on December 23, 2010.

way along with the emergence of democracy in Nepal after 1950. B.P. Koirala can be a case study to exemplify while relating democracy and emergence of nationalism. It was B.P. Koirala who, being one of the good friends of India, also had to make ambivalent speeches many times while talking about Nepal-India relations. It was due to the situation in which anti-India sentiments became much popular among a sizeable section of Nepalese. And, even a democratic leadership could fear a threat of not securing votes of the people if he/she goes beyond public sentiment. That must be the background of the argument of Ramachandran[28] who talks about India's realization that a democratic Nepal would be harder to tackle than the earlier governments which were autocratic in nature.

2. Patronizing behavior from Indian elites

Nepali politicians and others sometimes share their bitter experiences while dealing with India. According to them, Indian elites try to patronize Nepalese by considering their identity same to that of Indians. We often hear a sentence "Nepal aur India to eki hai, kuchh pharak nahi hai" (There is no difference between Nepal and India). But the Nepalese take offence at such attitude of the Indians. For them, Nepalese and Indians are similar, but are two separate identities. Though Indians interpret it in good sense, it is viewed quite differently by the Nepali public.

Some Recommendations

1. The first and foremost remedy to strengthen Nepal-India relations could be that there should be consensus in Nepal in terms of its foreign policy in general, and Indian policy in particular. Generally, foreign policy is the subject of consensus elsewhere. In other countries, one sees political battles among the political parties on various issues, but they do not have differences of opinion in terms of foreign policy. No matter whether the Labour Party or Conservative Party is in the government, the foreign policy of Britain would be the same. A similar trend exists in the USA and other countries, including in India. Hence Nepali political parties have to decide their foreign policy in a unanimous way. They should come up with a resolution

---

[28]Shastri Ramachandran, "Nepal as Seen from India" IIC Quarterly, Vol.30 (2), Mansoon 2003.pp. 93.

whether they need Indian good office for settling their internal political matters. If they need Indian good offices, for that also they should stop double toning. If not, they should simply request India and other foreign countries for assisting as per the national plan.

Evidences show that the situation becomes more complicated once Nepal wants Indian backing or witness for settling its internal political matters. It is obvious that no power, either internal or external, can play a neutral role as each one has its preference and bias. Even if one tries his best not to be preferential or biased against anybody, he cannot preserve the interest of all actors in an equal manner. In this situation, there is high chance of making it controversial. And, those who are not satisfied with the outcome of the initiatives, can always term it as 'intervention.' And, others would welcome the initiatives if it had come as per their interest. Indians, in my opinion, have been suffering from this kind of problem in Nepal. They want to help Nepal as per Nepalis' requests. Once the action materializes, one party will be happy and make celebration. In the meantime, another party will be terming the help as 'intervention' and start protesting in public. And, while making a consensual foreign policy, all political parties {if not possible, at least the Maoist (negative nationalist), Nepali Congress (positive nationalist) and Madhesi (pro-India)}should come up with a new policy to deal with India. If so, that would be a stable one as it would cover interests of most of the segments of the Nepali society.

2. Political parties and groups in Nepal should also stop indoctrinating their cadres with anti-Indianism. Nepalis have every right to keep their reservations about India's policy towards Nepal by using a proper channel, if they feel it is against their interest. But they have to differentiate Indian people and the Government of India while pursuing their reservation. And, misusing/abusing the Indian flag and its other national symbols would be a blunder which not only damages the Nepal-India relations, but also provokes Indian citizens to react against Nepal and Nepalese.

What we can see is that anti-Indianism in Nepal is increasing and political parties are being instrumental in doing so. If we do not stop the present anti-Indianism in Nepal, Nepalis working in India are likely to be the worst sufferers. Till today, hardly any anti-Nepali protest is seen in

India though there are big anti-India protests in Nepal with abuse of Indian's national symbols. We should salute the patience and tolerance of Indian people as they keep quiet even after they hear of a talk about "Balkanizing India". But we should not take such patience and wisdom of Indian citizens for granted. While discussing with Indians about Nepal-India relations, we sense that we (Nepalese) have to be sensitive to Indian people's values and principles too. "It is impossible for a patriot Indian to be patient always against each and every strange stand against India," one Indian shared with me. An Indian socialist activist shared with me an interesting discussion that he had with an Indian pro-Maoist on Nepal-India relations. According to him, his pro-Maoist friend was arguing about the impossibility for Nepalese to be anti-Indian. But his reply was that "our security establishment along with military personnel are not so unhistorical...it was Nepal, in the past, who collaborated with the British imperialists and fought with its 9,000 soldiers against Indian soldiers of the first independence struggle of India."

3. Also, Nepal-India relations would improve if both the sides try to understand each others' sensitivity, i.e, both the sides should be polite in speech, language and gesture. No doubt, India has every right to pursue its security interest, as national interest is the very essence of a foreign policy. It should focus on its own interest and also come up with a concrete proposal of what it can offer to Nepal on a reciprocal basis.

4. More effective compliance and judicious implementation of the 1950 treaty would be another remedy. Both, Nepal and India have to form one special cell to look after security and other issues of the citizens of the neighbour--Nepalese in India, and Indians in Nepal. Also, there should be a joint body to monitor and discuss the reports of both the special cells, and come up with an integrated policy to reduce anti-neighbourhood feelings. It has become necessary because of the fact that both the nationalities - Nepalese working in India, and Indians working in Nepal - are now living in a fearful environment. The fear is the outcome of some past incidents in which innocent people were made to suffer by the local authorities. Nepalese who are working in India often express grievances that they have been facing various problems such as difficulties in opening bank accounts, etc. Also, they face problems in India when only few Indian institutions

accept citizenship certificates issued by Nepal government for its citizens as identity proof. Though the government as such has no policy to torture Nepalese in India and vice versa in Nepal, it happens as per the interest of local authorities as many of Nepali and Indians are unknown about the 1950 treaty provisions which treat citizens of both the countries as equal. But the blame is always put on to the country as a whole though it is not involved.

5. Another remedy would come from economic benefits. India should not take it seriously even if there is trade deficit between Nepal and India. If some trade deficit exists between the two countries, it hardly matters for the Indian economy. Myron Weiner's claim seems to be appropriate to be mentioned here. According to him, "India is thus like a huge lorry with a dozen or more tyres; a puncture in one or two tyres does not throw the lorry into the ditch."[29] But some experienced politicians and bureaucrats from Nepal state that Indian political leadership seems to be ready to offer tax relaxation on goods and items which go to Nepal but that cannot be implemented when the file comes down to the bureaucrats. Why it happens is because of the fact that there are business communities on the Indian side who lobby with the government to save their interest. Then government officials start looking for options to save one's business interest in the name of controlling the balance deficit. However, if India wants a good trade relation with Nepal and Nepalese, it should not impose tax on those goods which will be imported into Nepal from India. Nepalese provides a huge number of cheap labourers for the growth of the Indian economy and that should be reciprocated by exempting tax on the goods made in India.

---

[29]Myron Weiner, *The Indian Paradox: Essays in Indian Politics*. New Delhi: Sage. 1989. pp. 36. cited in Lok Raj Baral "Nepal-India Security Relations: Global and Regional Context." An unpublished paper presented in a seminar on 60th year of 1950 Treaty of Peace and Friendship organized by Nepal Center for Contemporary Studies (NCCS) in collaboration with the Embassy of India, Nepal in Kathmandu from September 11-13, 2010.

Indra Adhikari

Nepal: Democratization of Military and Institutionalization of Democracy

"The Nepalese soldiers are at all times, and under all circumstances, most singularly obedient to the "powers-that-be", and they obey the constituted authority be it Raja, Rani, Prince or Ministers most unhesitatingly, and without any reference to the duty required or its consequences."[1]

By character, military organization can never be democratic, if we define democracy in military as in multi-party system that accepts or recognizes the opposition as a key component of the system. It is always a highly centralized administrative mechanism practicing through a single control and command system with full acceptance of hierarchical arrangement among the ranks and files within the organization. But it does not mean that such 'distinct organizational discipline' and its nature of specialization for resolving the crisis by force make a military undemocratic. Military can be understood as democratic, if it: (i) follows the legitimate order of the legitimate authority as per the constitution; (ii) internalizes the international law where the state is one of the signatories; and (iii) respects the norms and values of human rights with its specialized skill, capability and minimal/less "use of its authority of 'monopoly of violence"[2]as far as possible. Democratization of military can be contextualized in the case of Nepal by making it socially more inclusive,

---

[1] Henry Ambrose Oldfield, *Sketches from Nepal*, Vol. I London: W.H. Allen and Co, 1980,p.349, as given in Rishikesh Shaha, Politics in Nepal 1980-1990, Kathmandu: Ratna Pustak Bhandar, 1990, p24.

[2] Hans Born, "Democratic Control of Armed Forces: Relevence, Issues and Research Agenda", in Giuseppe Caforio (ed.), *Handbook of the Sociology of the Military*, New York: Kluwer Academic and Plenum Publishers 2003.

organizationally transparent, and functionally accountable and responsible.[3] Thus, the role of military in politics and its level of professionalism itself indicate the status of democracy in a particular country. For, good civil-military relation and democratic oversights of military have a symbiotic relationship and work co-relatively in deepening and strengthening democracy. All these requisites are not only deeply influenced by the national history, sentiments and traditions, but also depend on relationship of military with the spheres of power, politics, economy, modern science and technology, culture and history. It is determined by public opinion towards defence and foreign policy of the regime and certain action of the military for such policy etc.

Military and democracy in the history of Nepal

In South Asia, no other countries except India and Sri Lanka are stable democracies where the military is under the civilian control. In Sri Lanka, particularly during the ethnic war, military might have played an important role in taking crucial decisions, but on the whole the established constitutional order continued to prevail.[4] In the case of Nepal, founder of military is also founder of the greater Nepal and its direct use under the command and control of the king without compartmentalizing the responsibility of the public, administrative, civilian and military authority created the character of the civil-military relation.[5] Then, the character of the National Army (NA) can be described as being (1) loyal to the de-facto ruler, (2) controlled and commanded by the strongest having vision and mission in making military policies and tactic and professional/corporate enhancement. Among other qualities for commanding the Nepali army, a

---

[3]Indra Adhikari, Basis of Recruitment in Nepal Army, The Rising Nepal, see in, http://www.gorkhapatra.org.np/detail.php?article_id=7517&cat_id=7

[4]Stephen P. Cohen, *The Pakistan Army*, London: University of California Press 1984.; StephenP. Cohen, *The Indian Army*: Its contribution to the Development of a Nation, New Delhi: Oxford University Press, 2004; K.Subrahmanyam, "Military and Governance" in V. A. Pai Panandikar (ed.), *Problems of Governance in South Asia*, New Delhi: Kanark Publishers Pvt.Ltd, 2002; Husain Haqqani, *Pakistan: Between Mosque and Military*, Karachi: Vanguard Books, 2005.

[5]Ludwig F. Stiller, *The Rise of the House of Gorkha: A Study in the Unification of Nepal: 1768-1816*,Ranchi: Patna Jesuit Society, 1975,(first edition in 1973). P.N. Shah, *Dibya Upadesh*, Narahari Nath Yogi (ed.), Kathmandu: 2016 B.S. 1960; M.C. Regmi, *Imperial Gorkha: An Account of Gorkhali Rule in Kumaun (1791-1815)*, Delhi: Adroit Publishers,1999.

ruler should possess the capacity to be recognized as capable and strong, should be able to look into the interest of the army.[6]

Thus, whoever wanted power in Nepal found the military as the best constituency. It put both civil and military fields under the command of the power wielders even after 1990, despite the lip service paid to the kings who lost power due to internal conflicts during the rule of the Shah dynasty. The civilian leaders like Bhimsen Thapa, Mathbar Singh Thapa and Jang Bahadur Rana became powerful leaders in the history of Nepal by taking military in their confidence and involving it for their political gain, i.e. removing their potential threats from the political scene by using it. The Nepal Army stood by Jang Bahadur Rana during and after the Kot and Bhandarkhal Massacre of 1846 in his struggle against the 'plenipotentiary queen', Rajyalaxmi, and subsequently in Alau massacre also against King Rajendra in 1847.[7] Even during the Rana oligarchy, the army stood by the strongest members irrespective of the rule of succession made by the founder of the system.[8] Similarly, the army stood as a shield of the Rana government during the armed insurrection by Nepali Congress (NC) in Nepal and did everything in its power to crush the popular armed uprising even after King Tribhuvan had shown his sympathy for the popular democratic force. The same army, after the king was restored to his position by securing the throne as a result of the tripartite agreement between the Rana, the King and NC for the 1951 political change, prompted the king and newly appointed Home Minister, B.P. Koirala to keep a distance from the pro-Ranas forces. While the armed police force, Raksha Dal, formed from the liberation army of NC, revolted against the NC government of the day, the army again came to the rescue of the government. Contrary to the incident, the army stood firmly by King Mahendra, when he decided

---

[6]Rishikesh Shaha, *Politics in Nepal 1980-1990: Referendum, Stalemate and Triumph of People Power,* New Delhi: Manohar, 1990; Rishikesh Shaha, Modern Nepal: A Political History 1769-1955, Vol. I, 1762-1885, New Delhi: Manohar 1990; Rishikesh Shah, Three Decades and Two *Kinas (1960-1990): Eclipse of Nepal's Partyless Monarchic Rule*, New Delhi: Sterling Publishers Pvt Ltd. 1990.

[7]Baburam Acharya, *Aba Yasto kahilyae Nahos (Never Again)*, Kathmandu: Sri Krishna Acharya, 2004.

[8]Krishna Kant Adhikari, *Nepal Under Jang Bahadur: 1846-1877*, Vol.1, Kathmandu: Buku, 1984; Adrin Server, *Nepal Under Rana*, New Delhi: Oxford and IBH Publishing Co. 1993.

to impose the state of emergency and dissolved parliament on 15 December 1960, imprisoned the first elected Prime Minister of Nepal, B.P Koirala and his cabinet colleagues.[9] During 1960-1990 and 2002-2006 the Royal Nepal Army stood as a defender of the institution of monarchy.

The military, however, found no rationale to support the leaders of the government having neither the power to exert the state authority nor the agenda that made the military men benefit personally and organizationally. In case of good civil-military tie, it could only make the king suspicious of politicians. On the basis of the military, the kings tried to be assertive. Hence, the Kings invariably became the major power centre. Monarchy as a traditional institution also added its authority besides being the head of the army. The resignation of Home Minister Govinda Raj Jyosi in 2000 and Prime Minister G.P. Koirala in 2001 also proved how the elected government failed to implement its policy to curb the Maoist insurgency because of the non-cooperation of military under the direction of the king.[10]

Nepal Army like most militaries of the world obeys the state authority in real and de-facto sense of the word. The logic can be proved by the attitude of the military in responding to the Irst and IInd Mass Movements in 1990 and 2006, respectively, and to the interim governments formed thereafter. Yet, neither authoritarian ruler nor government before 1990 and after 2002 could be saved by the Nepal Army, though it had been badly used by the ruler of the day for the safety of the imposed system. The question raised here is whether the NA accepts the political change as claimed by the military commanders. Nepal Army, like most armies of the world, is neither against nor in favour of democracy and the representative government. This is proved by the reaction of a commander of NA who commented "how many soldiers (mera ketaharu) under me should be lost for fulfilling the interest of a greedy man (King Gyanendra)." It seems that

[9]Lok Raj Baral, *Oppositional Politics in Nepal* (Second Edition), Kathmandu: Himal Books, 2006a; R.S. Chauhan, *The Political Development in Nepal 1950-70: Conflict between Tradition and Modernity*, New Delhi: Associated Publishing House, 1971; Anirudha Gupta, *Politics in Nepal: A study of Post-Rana Political Development and Party Politics*, New Delhi: Allied Publishers Pvt. Ltd., 1964; Anirudha Gupta, *Politics in Nepal: 1950-60*, Delhi: Kalinga Publications, 1993, (originally published in 1963).

[10]Joshi, Govinda Raj (2000), "Press Statement of the Home Minister", 29 September.

the main concern of the military is its professional and corporate interest. It can support any government if the government assures either status quo or advancement of the military, by softly applying the relative benefit theory. In Nepal, its orientation, socialization, and institutionalization process does not allow direct military intervention in politics. But it always prefers to work in tandem with authoritarian forms of government mainly because representative governments, as military understands, not only limits its role firmly within defense activities except rare consultation for the policy-making and implementation arena, but also controls its commandeer sources.[11]

Most representative governments give higher priority to investment in the social service sector for assuring human security rather than in strengthening armed forces, which may in the long-run challenge the democratic system itself, if the state faces the crisis of leadership for long under the new and fragile democracy. The rationale is that without developing the source of 'soft power' of the state quality population, investment in strengthening the military capability (an instrument of hard power) may be proved unproductive investment for security of the people and the state. More importantly, the ambition of making a highly professional and large-sized army can be a source of foreign intervention for a poor and developing country like Nepal, which has to be dependent on the other countries not only for professionalization and modernization of the army, but also on its institutional sustainability. It makes the country more vulnerable in terms of losing secretes having strategically and diplomatically high value in the area of politics and military. Similarly, external dimensions also expand the role of military. The way American Ambassador visited the military regional Headquarters in 2004 and Indian especial envoy stayed in Military Quarters in 2006 show how the foreign powers play in the country by making military as an instrument. Also, the Royal Nepal Army (RNA) which could hardly brief security situation of the country to the Prime Minister and concerned committee in the Parliament, briefed the US Assistance Secretary, Cristina Rocca, in 2003 at RNA Headquarters about the security situation and military policy to

[11]Indra Adhikari, *Military-Democracy Interface in Nepal: 1990-2002*, M.Phil Dissertation, submitted to the Jawaharlal Nehru University, New Delhi, 2006.

control it.[12]

Prospect of democratization of military: an overview

Thus, successful reforms also require a long-term policy vision, driven by political leadership. The military should be steadily removed from non-military responsibilities, such as rural development, domestic intelligence, policing and giving political appointment that erodes the distinct role of military as a defence force, allowing it to be indulgent in political conflict. Moreover, "democratic empowerment" of civilian authority is equally important for achieving competency in managing military intelligently and responsibly. It can be done by staffing expertise in defense ministry, foreign intelligence bureau and legislative oversight committee, etc. It, however, takes time to adopt the new structure of authority as well as to develop confidence and trust between it and the civil-military elites. Any form of violent protest, ethnic secessionist movements, and religious fundamentalism that can provoke the military for intervening the politics, should be solved through peaceful accommodation for stabilizing democracy.[13] If democracy is institutionalized and developed more economically, the conflicting social groups and military itself become more viable partners of the representative government.

The separation of power is one of the key principles of democratization of all the organs of the government. The army which came under the civilian command after 2006 needs to work in close coordination and cooperation of executive, legislative and judicial organs respecting the theory of check and balance. The Proper system and channel should be developed between the Chief of the Army Staff (COAS), Defense Minister, Prime Minister and the President. The main obstacle for good civil-military relation during the 1990s was the old modus-operandi followed by the new leadership. The Palace had the de-facto control of Royal Nepal Army (RNA) and the COAS was required to be in good rapport with it, thus bypassing the

---

[12]Indra Adhikari, "Political Security and Legitimacy", *The Kathmandu Post*, 2 July, 2005; Indra Adhikari, "Nepal: Contextualization of comprehensive security", *The Kathmandu Post*, 4 January 2004.

[13]D.L. Bland "An Unified Theory of Civil-Military Relations", *Armed Forces and Society*, Vol. 26, No.1.; Thomas Carothers "The End of the Transition Paradigm", in *Journal of Democracy*, Vol 13, No.1, 2002.

defense ministry.[14] Naturally, RNA had a strong control over the national security issue even under the civilian government, as the government leaders considered the RNA as the exclusive domain of the Palace and refrained from raising any question concerning the institution. Therefore, the elected governments were neither able to amend the Military Act of 1960, nor make a security policy. The Prime Ministers invariably tried to develop rapport with the COAS bypassing the Ministry, but the control of the military lay with the king rather than with the government regardless of its nature elected or nominated. Theoretically, the post-1990 governments were more powerful than those of the royal regime prior to 1990. In actual practice, however, the old relationship of the palace with the army continued. Thus, haunted by the "ghost of the palace" or guided by the petty interest for being in power, parties' leaders did not care for changing the military structure. For them, it was a "sensitive" area which could hardly be changed without the approval of the King even constitutionally.

It can be found that the major problem of non-cooperation of the military to civil governments and its half-hearted involvement in actions were the dual command system including personality and power clash of the non-professional authorities of RNA the King and the Prime Minister. The developing activities and relation between the civil and military, and Prime Minister and President after 2008 showed that the political scenario and system have been changed but the attitude and mindset of the leadership is the same. This logic has been proved by the constitutional ambiguity even in the interim constitution that has created parallel power centres as head of the Council of Minister and head of the state, i.e., PM and President respectively. Both are elected by the same institution Constituent Assembly (which also acts as parliament), using a similar method of election. Somehow, the Prime Minister under the constitution is really in a pitiable condition, since he can neither choose cabinet members under him nor take a decision on any important issue without getting

[14]Indra, Adhikari "Chhuttai Rakshamantri" (Demand for Separate Defense Minister), *Kantipur Daily*, 2008;, Geja Sharma Wagle "National Security Policy and Role of National Security Council", in Rajan Bhattarai and Rosy Cave (eds.), *Changing Security Dynamics in Nepal: A Collection of Essays*, Kathmandu: National Institutute for Policy Studies and Saferworld, 2009; Dhruba Kumar, "Political Transition and Constitution Making: The Military Dimension", *Nepali Journal of Contemporary Studies*, Kathmandu: Vol. IX, No.1 March, 2009.

prior approval of the coalition partners of the government.[15]

Most civilian leaders hardly try to understand the rationale of democratic control, but politicize the military in the name of 'civilian supremacy over military' ignoring structural constrains and customary evidences. Military seems independent, while civil authorities are divided into civilian authority and coalition partner in the cabinet, and largest parties and oppositions in parliament in this regard. The practices led ultimately to either "subjective control"[16] or military dominance in politics. The conflict between General Rukmangad Katuwal and Pushpa Kamal Dahal Cabinet in 2009 in Nepal was outcome of such practices of "Civilian Supremacy." Even most of the so called democratic leaders prefer more 'loyal army' rather than professional one, such attitudes also lead to the subjective control over military which ultimately, one or the other way, threatens the process of democratization.

The constitutional head of the state under the parliamentary democracy, if other partners of the government do not agree on a particular issue, can defy or nullify the decision of the PM as "the guardian of the constitution" showing the cause of violation of the constitutional provision that dictates the government to solve major issues in consensus. The decision taken by the Maoist-led government to suspend the then COAS, General Rukmangad Katuwal, and the step taken by the President against the decision of the Dahal Cabinet, is one outcome of such constitutional ambiguity. The Parliament became an eyewitness to the power conflict between the PM and President that led the country towards establishing yet another form of constitutional authoritarianism. The idea, strategy and modus operandi adopted by both the civilian leaders have adversely affected the role of military under the newly established political system. The precedent against the spirit of "objective control" of the army was not new in the history of Nepal. Several leaders in the government before and after 1990 resigned from the post because of the confrontation between the civilian and military leaders. Yet, struggle for recovery of their political

---

[15]Government of Nepal *The Interim Constitution of Nepal-2063*, (The third and the Fourth amendments), Kathmandu: Ministry of Law, Justice and Parliamentary Affairs, 2008.

[16]Samuel P. Huntington, *The Soldier and the State: The Theory and Politics of Civil-Military Relation*, Cambridge: Harvard University Press, 1957.

image and life remained unsolved.[17] What is more worrisome today is that the same old pattern is likely to be repeated by making military more powerful for determining the dynamics of politics in the country. Such primacy gained by the Nepal Army is only due to the mutual threat perceptions developed by the major political parties in the post-Constituent Assembly election 2008.

"Civilian supremacy" gives the democratically elected government unquestioned authority over all policy arena including the goals, organization and implementation of national defense. But it does not mean that it is above the constitutional arrangement, i.e. rule of law, which is the main spirit of democracy. Even the duly taken decision should go by proper channel while it is in the process of implementation. The immaturity was shown by the then government led by Puspa Kamal Dahal in 2009, while taking the decision of suspending the COAS. It not only ignored the cooperation of its coalition partners but also annoyed the President by not adhering to the procedures required for sending its decision to the latter. Other twenty-two parties also forgot their experience of the past when the king turned to be more assertive after the 1990 change (while the opposition party in parliament and faction of Prime Minister's own party went to the palace for seeking the grace of the king for their opposition steps).[18] Their request to the President to take steps against the Prime Minister's decision to sack the COAS was contrary to the system of parliamentary democracy. Action and reaction of the parties in government and parliament on the Katuwal suspension issue has shown that no party has a clear stand on its own agenda. It seemed that all are engaged in fulfilling their short-term petty interests. As a result, the government headed by the Maoists (the largest party) collapsed following the resignation of the prime minister on the issue of violation of civilian control over the army. Political parties are now divided. The Maoist, now Unified Communist Party of Nepal (Maoist)/

---

[17]Indra Adhikari, *Democratization of Nepali Polity: The Role of Military, 1990-2007*, Ph.D Thesis submitted to Jawaharlal Nehru University, New Delhi, 2010.

[18]Krishna P. Khanal, "Parliament and Governance" in Lok Raj Baral (ed.), *Nepal: Political Parties and Parliament*, New Delhi: Adroit Publishers, 2004; Krishna Hachhethu, "Parties in Parliament: Role of Prime Minister" in Lok Raj Baral (ed.), *Nepal: Political Parties and Parliament*, New Delhi: Adroit Publishers, 2004.

UCPN (Maoist), is engaged in politics of opposition. The constitution-making and peace process have become uncertain. The main beneficiaries are the traditional and regressive elements including the military. Such uncertainty and political mess have provided an opportunity to the external powers that are bent on enlarging their own influence in Nepal.

The political system, environment, situation and people's expectation have changed but the mindset of the political leaders remains the same, hence the problem of adaptation to the changes.[19] Halfhearted involvement of political parties in the peace process and their compulsion to follow every radical agenda without any serious homework has also created hurdles for institutionalizing democracy. Similarly, the shortsightedness of the parliamentary political leaders to integrate the "qualified" Maoists' combatants into security agencies[20] and dishonesty of the Maoists not to adopt the parliamentary system of government have created mutual threat perceptions and distrust among them. It ultimately made them more self-centred and devoid of any vision for the consolidation of democracy. The Maoist official stand that recognizes the NC as a major enemy and the CPN(UML) as an opportunistic party[21] have further widened the gap between the three major forces of Nepali politics.

Problems of Institutionalization of democracy and the Military

The nature of problem in civil-military relation is very complex as both the society and the military are changing in a very peculiar way. The role of political parties, backbone of democracy, is also equally important for changing the civil-society-military complexity to cooperative relation in

---

[19]Lok Raj Baral, "Nepal in 2000: Discourse of Democratic Consolidation ", *Asian Survey*, Vol. 41, No. 1, 2001;, Lok Raj Baral "Nepal: Governance, Defense and Development", *RCSS Policy Studies, special issue on Governance and Defense Spending: Views from South Asia*, Vol. 21, 2001, Krishna Hachhethu, "Legitimacy Crisis of Nepali Monarchy", *Economic and Political Weekly*, 19 May, 2007.

[20]12 point Understanding Between Parties and the Maoists, 22 November 2005 in Uddhab Pyåkurel, *Maoists Movement in Nepal: A sociological Perspective*, New Delhi: Adroit, 2007. Comprehensive Peace Accord between the Government and the Maoists, 2006; Agreement on Monitoring of Management of Arms and Armies between the Government and the Maoists, 2006, 8-point agreement between the SPA and the CPN (Maoist), Government of Nepal/PMO, 16 July 2006.(www.gorkhapatra.org.np as given in Nepal Update (2007), Kathmandu NCCS, January-April, Annex ii,

[21]CPN Maoists, The Maoist's resolution passed in Kharipati, Bhaktapur, December, 2008.

more broader and liberal ways. Experiences of different states in the world show that without good triangular relations among society, civil government and the military, there can be no socio-political harmony for maintaining political stability and democratization.

Radicalization of society, militarization of political parties and ruining the authority of the government are the major source of threats to initiating democratization process. The non-Maoist political parties themselves began to militarize their parties instead of discouraging the past conflict. They rationalized their initiatives for the defense of the cadre of their own parties. The involvement of the Young Communist League (YCL), a sister organization of the Maoist, in criminal activities and formation of similar other 14 forces such as the Youth Force by CPN (UML) for countering the YCL have promoted the trends of human rights violation and impunity in the country. Such trends provided political shelter to the wrong doers or criminals are evident in the failure of the state.[22] As a result, democratic culture is fast eroding together with the emergence of criminal gangs and armed groups in Tarai and in other parts of the country. The parties that have indulged in the power game can hardly forge any consensus on tackling such violent trends. A serious question can be raised here as to how democratic culture can be developed if the whole society and polity is being affected by the spurt of violence and anarchist trends in the protection and provocation of major political parties. Guided by the tit-for-tat policy against the Maoist offences, most political parties who have some sort of influence in the country have formed the militant or semi-militant organizations.(see the details in the table given below.)

---

[22]Adams Brad, "India Is Protecting Nepal Army" an interview taken with him (Asia director of Human Rights Watch (HRW)) by Kiran Chapagain, *My Republica*, 3 November: 2009 http://myrepublica.com/portal/index.php?action=news_details&news_id=10954

Table 1 : Main militant groups formed by the political parties/groups

Ser No	S.N. Youth Organisations	Mother Organisations	Geographical Influence
1	Young Communist League	UCPN (Maoist)	All over the country
2	Youth Force	CPN (UML)	All over the country
3	OBC Regiment	Pichhada Varga Mahasangh	Central Terai region
4	Madhesi Youth Force	Madhesi Janaadhikar Forum (MJF)	Eastern, Central and Mid Western Terai regions
5	Security Brigade (Rakshya Bahini)	Nepal Sadbhawana Party (Rajendra Mahato)	Central and Mid Western regions
6	Madhesi Commando	Nepal Sadbhawana Party	Central and Mid Western regions
7	Kirat Limbuwan Volunteers	Pallo Kirat Limbuwan Rastriya Manth	Eastern region
8	Terai Madhes Sewa Surakshya Sangh	Terai Madhes Loktantrik Party	Mid Western and Western regions
9	Tharu Sena	Tharuhat Swayatta Parishad	Certain Districts of Mid Western and Western regions (for e.g., Dang, Kapilbastu and Bardiy
10	Khas Kshetri Unity Society	Khas-Kshetri Unity Society	Some regions
11	Limbuwan Volunteers and Limbuwan Liberation Army	Sanghiya Loktantrik Rastriya Manch / Limbuwan Rajya Parishad	Eastern region
12	Madhesi Raksha Bahini	Sadbhawana Party	Some of the Terai districts
13	Janasurakshya Bal	CPN-Maoists	Some districts
14	All Nepal Democratic Youth Organisation	Rastriya Janamorcha Party	Mid Western and Western regions
15	Chure Bhawar Shanti Sena	Chure Bhawar Ekta Samaj Party	Central and Mid Western regions

Source: Indra Adhikari, " Conflict Transformation: A Nepali Case" a presented paper in a seminar, "Conflict Transformation and the Challenge of Peace" organized by Department of International Relation, University of Karachi in collaboration with Hanns Seidel Foundation of Islamabad, Karachi on 6-7 December 2010.

These development tend to promote conflict and violence that automatically vitalize the role of the military in society and polity, since the last weapons of national defense ultimately remains with the institution of military. The experience of Pakistan, unlike India ,shows that the social conflict and violence in the transitional period, and inability of political leaders to manage it politically created fertile ground for military's intervention and it's long term sustenance in politics.[23] In Nepal the government's modus operandi to deal with the movement groups further helped in increasing the influence of the armed and semi-armed groups. Its attitude of not recognizing the opposition and turn a deaf year towards the voices that rose through peaceful means helped to adopt the means of violence by the movement groups. Thus many peaceful movements were compelled to be converted into violent mode. This led to believe that only violent means can get the attention of the government and, hence unprecedented increase in extra-constitutional mode of struggle that reached more than a hundred in number.[24] If the government fails to address the demand of such groups through democratic means, then ultimately the military will be the only means to manage the conflict, hence more vitalizing role of the military rather than limiting it.

Excessive partyization in the society and polity by "filling up posts with parties' members and hangers-on" and involvement of political parties in institutionalizing the politics of bhagbanda (distribution of share) at every level and in each sector as per their share in the power structure has further damaged the democratic prospect.[25] Such practices as a whole showed the contradiction exists not only between the expectations and experiences of the people but also between the word and action of the leaders in government. It has thus created adverse consequences for the peace process. The ministry created for promoting peace and reconstruction of the state has almost turned into a partisan ministry. Neither the commission as framed in the Interim Constitution for Truth and

---

[23]See, Husain Haqqani, *Pakistan: Between Mosque and Military*, Karachi: Vanguard Books, 2005.

[24]Indra Adhikari and Uddhab Pyakurel, "Internal Conflict in Nepal after the Comprehensive Peace Agreement (CPA)", paper presented in a seminar organized by Banaras Hindu University, 5-8 March 2010.

[25]Indra Adhikari, "Tri. Vi. Ra Rajniti" (Tribhuban University and the Politics), *Kantipur Daily*, 2 August 2009. Lok Raj Baral, ".."Republica 2 November 2009.

Reconciliation is formed so that the real victims of the conflict could be identified and provided justice. How the inability of political leader in government in transitional period to identify the real victims and address their problem timely and amicably gives the ground to politically more ambitious military leader is proved by the engagements of military leader in non-military affairs. The memorandum submitted by the victims to the former COAS, General Rukmangad Katuwal at his residence is one of such examples. The victims through memorandum requested the COAS to reappoint them in the respective posts in the institutions in which they were working before they left the job under the pressure of the then insurgent, the Maoist.

The political parties in democracy are key players. Their role is vital for systemic stability and institutionalization, despite their competition. The confrontational attitudes of the leadership and their engagement in making the charges at each other at very low level for fulfilling their petty interests are the major challenges of maintaining political stability in Nepal even after 2006. Additionally, attempts to use the military by the civil leaders in government for their political gain or against the interest of opposition are dangerous trends to vitalize the role of military in politics. The best example of such trends is the anti-United Nations Mission in Nepal chorus. It was more ridiculous when the Prime Minister give an advice to the COAS, Chhatra Man Gurung to lobby against the extension of UNMIN tenure, as it has been supervising and monitoring the activities of Nepal Army and the Maoists ex-combatants under their own request. Civil leaders mostly either charges the military while they are incompetent to handle it, or make the military man lead crucial non-military issue while they fail to do so. The former Defense Minister Ram Bahadur Thapa charged the senior most officers of Nepal Army of acting under direction of foreign power, but Prime Minister Madhab Kumar Nepal used it for lobbing against the UNMIN stay in Nepal. The civil leaders themselves are initiating politicized role of military, since there is no other traditional institution like the monarchy to blamed for creating such situation. The people see them now as the major culprits for promoting/provoking the military and stalling democratic development and peace process.

In addition, the division of political forces on the basis of ideology is another challenge for democratization. Maoists' consistent claim for "capturing the state" and others reactions of 'tit for tat' treatment vis-a-vis the Maoists, have put them at the loggerheads.. The differences between the two forces on most issues, including the civilian supremacy over military, are also guided by their subjective interpretations. The Maoist dictum, for example, accepts the army as an extension of party that reflects the will of the people (people as defined by the Maoists are constituted by only the leaders, cadres and sympathizers supporting for the cause of the communist party),[26] is not acceptable to others who take it as an "apolitical"[27] institution. The Maoist view and action plans seems to annoy the military institutionally as it tried to polarize the political forces into pro and anti-NA and ex-PLA. Such polarization ultimately vitalized the importance and influence of military in politics that made the issue of democratization of army more complicated. Nor did such division between the civilian parties on military matters help to establish the civilian supremacy over the army. Nobody is unaware that one of the key causes of the good civil-military tie[28] between the Interim Government formed under G.P. Koirala in 2006 and the institution of military was the political unity on the military matter. Koirala, the most unsuccessful Prime minister after 1990 because of non-cooperation of military, succeeded to establish "the best civil-military relation" after Jana-Andolan-II because of the legitimacy of his leadership during and after the Andolan and absolute support to the government under his leadership form the major political forces of the country.

Similarly, the commitment of the Maoists to return the confiscated individual and institutional property to the owners and disband the parallel organizations created during the insurgency could not be fulfilled sincerely. Such commitments, among many other utterances, remain unfulfilled creating more mistrust among the political forces indicating a pessimistic scenario for institutionalization of democracy as envisaged by the 2006 movement. The Maoist's reluctance to settle the Ex-combatants and their threats to go back again to 'armed revolt' for establishing "People's Republic"

[26]Abi Narayan Chamlagai, "Maoists Insurgency: An Ideological Diagnosis" in Lok Raj Baral, *Nepal: Facets of Maoists Insurgency*, New Delhi: Adroit Publishers, 2006, p23.

[27] Samuel E. Finer, *The Man on Horseback: The Role of Military in Politics*, London: Pall Mall Press, 1962.

[28]Indra Adhikari, "Emerging Civil-Military Ties", *The Kathmandu Post*, 5 July, 2008.

makes other reluctant to initiating the democratization of Nepal Army, as they think that the Nepal Army is the only institution to prevent such threat, and secure themselves and the system established by the Jana Andolan-II.

Conclusion

Military reform is one of the major issues, without which the process of institutionalization of democracy may be remote. The rationale of the existing armed forces, keeping the existing geopolitical reality, state capacity and national experiences in mind, should be justified in Nepal where army has not fought external war for defending the sovereignty after 1816 but has always been used against the elected government and democracy. Hence, adequate attention should be paid for establishing a system of democratic control of armed forces while writing the new constitution rather than limiting it in a bureaucratic system of appointment of COAS, control, mobilization and management of the army. Such an arrangement can be made possible by convincing military officers that expanding civilian control does not compromise the nation's security, institutional prestige and integrity of the military.

Likewise, the regime's performance in the field of politics and economy and capacity of political institutionalization through strengthening bureaucracy, institutionalizing all organs of the government, electoral system and political parties, and assuring accountability of rule of law are also required for consolidating democracy. Thus, a gap between the commitment and performance of the leaders in the party and the government, and the trends of the formation of the government including the people having no popular mandate, is against the spirit of the representative democracy. The government formed by such wrong tendency has less legitimacy that can hardly control command and oversight the military, since professional military always prefers to obey the legitimate order by the legitimate authority. Thus some sort of consensus among the major political parties regarding the key issues of governance and national defence is a must to overcome the major challenges posed against democratization of military and institutionalization of democracy in Nepal.

Manoj Dahal

Krishna Prasad Bhattarai :A Political leader with the saintly qualities

A politician can hardly be called a saint in our contemporary politics. The two terminologies contradict each other. But Nepal's former Prime Minister Krishna Prasad Bhattarai was called a Saint Leader, a title he earned in the esteem of the people after his rigorous trial and tested statesmanship. If a longer stint in power is a parameter of success in politics, he was probably a failure. But if power becomes secondary, and a person stands for his conviction with courage and commitment, and refuses to compromise on values, and if at all these virtues count, Bhattarai, often referred as '*Kishunjee*' was a rare species in contemporary politics.

Out of 87 years he lived, he spent 14 years in prison, for opposing authoritarianism of different forms, and for crusading for democracy, but always refusing to accept any condition for his release. All through, he lived a simple and virtuous life as an ardent disciple of Mahatma Gandhi. He was probably the only leader in South Asia who despite having been the Prime Minister of his country twice, died without a house of his own.

Kishunjee was perhaps least bothered about how he will be judged during and after his life time, but he moved on in his one way, doing what he thought was his duty. Gandhi's once said he was unsuccessful in his final days of life because he could not stop India's partition. Society may be viewing a person differently, but how one introspects is equally important.

Kishunjee tried to emulate Gandhi in many ways. He believed in the peaceful means for establishing democracy. But when he joined a violent movement in the late 40s and to overthrow the Rana oligarchy that was ruling the country for 104 years, he apparently followed the party dictate, and not his conscience, a fact that he has repeated and regretted many times. While the Nepali Congress succeeded in overthrowing the oligarchy, the fight for democracy ended there.

Bhattarai's campaign continued ceaselessly another 30 years beginning December 1960 when King Mahendra dismissed the parliament he was presiding and put top leaders of the Nepali Congress including BP Koirala, Ganeshman Singh and *Kishunjee* behind bars. In fact, Bhattarai continued to be in incarceration for nearly 14 years with brief releases in between, BP and Singh were released in 1968, after which they went to India on political exile. Bhattarai chose not to sign any paper or accept any condition for his release, and also different with his leaders on the question of living inside the jail in Nepal, or going to India on exile. "Going out of Nepal may get us support from other countries, but that will not be free from strings," Bhattarai often used to say in public, and has narrated in his prison diary. In other words, like Gandhi lived and fought for India's struggle for freedom continuously from inside since 1915, Bhattarai chose his own territory as the base for his politics.

A democrat can not have two standards. Democracy is both passion and commitment for such people. That is why Bhattarai got involved first in the freedom struggle in India when he was barely 15, and a student in Varanasi. That was also the time, when he could see Gandhi both as an individual and a phenomenon, a mass leader and a great human being who could easily connect with that mass. Clear vision, clear mind and dedication to the cause come what may, that is what Gandhi meant to him and he tried to be that through out. Being honest to the self and to the country with no duality in thoughts and character was something that Bhattarai was.

Bhattarai would often scribble in his diary—in fact in many pages—that he wrote in the prison between 1961 and 63 that he was perhaps not cut out to be in politics. The rot in politics, its use for self-interest than as a means for service to the nation and nation building was a clearly visible trend in politics in the country. Yes, he never quit it, but always remained different from most of the contemporary politicians who followed politics of power and for power. A committed revolutionary may not always make a good administrator or a leader, especially if one follows the Gandhian value in politics which discourages disparity between words and deeds. *Kishunjee* was part of the democratic movement that successfully overthrew the Rana regime, and became a speaker at the age of 34 when Nepal had first elected Parliament.

He was chosen for the post as Nepali Congress leader and Prime Minister BP Koirala saw in Bhattarai enough ability to mediate between democratic forces and the monarchy then. Nepali Congress, especially BP and King Mahendra, both with clear vision about how the country should move forward, unfortunately could not reconcile at that point and the King, in pursuit of his ambition, staged a coup and took over.

But with return of BP Koirala and Ganeshman Singh from exile in India in December 1976, and their call that monarchy –that represents Nepali nationalism, and Nepali Congress, representing democratic forces, must join hands together to save the country, became the new political philosophy and guide line for future politics. BP even said that his and the King's neck were tied together implying that another dies naturally if one is hung.

This was exactly, the philosophy that *Kishunjee* believed in. He wanted the king to be patriot, pro-people and not some one hankering for power and he believed such a monarchy will be a unique symbol of national unity some that Nepal would need for foreseeable future. As Working President of the Party in 1985—three years after BP was dead and gone—Bhattarai led peaceful *satyagraha* in the country for restoration of democracy. But almost in line with what Gandhi did in Chauri Chaura after pro-independence elements burnt the police post there, Bhattarai also called off the movement indefinitely as Ramraja Prasad Singh bombed hotel, public place and the legislature targeting civilians there. Bhattarai said succumbing to 'cowardly violence' was something he would not go for, and instead suspend the peaceful movement for the time being.

But ultimately, the movement for democracy succeeded, although in a different form, five years later. Nepali Congress and the Communist Parties joined hands for the first time to restore democracy in 1990, and that took the form of a powerful mass movement enjoying sufficient backing from the international community. That was also a phase when Communism suffered the worst set-back following the disintegration of the Soviet Union.

Ganeshman was the leader of the successful movement, but when he was invited by King Birendra to head the government with the responsibility to draft the new constitution and hold the general election within a year, he suggested that the responsibility should go to Bhattarai. The King complied. And Bhattarai ensured that Nepal got one of the best constitutions with all democratic and fundamental rights guaranteed. He was also able to hold the second general elections in May 1991, after 33 years, proving that he was both honest and committed towards democracy. A prolonged transition, and rule under interim constitution for longer period or beyond the mandate will push the country into anarchy.

Bhattarai never deviated from his ideology and idealism till the last moment. A man who suffered imprisonment under monarchy for the longest period in the country also stood firmly against the Nepali Congress and the Maoists when they abolished monarchy and switched over to federal system. "This will disintegrate the country," he said in his letter written to the GP Koirala, president of the Nepali Congress during its general convention. When Koirala refused to take Bhattarai seriously, he severed his more than six decade long association with the Party. He said Nepali Congress was formed on solid principle that it would pursue policy of multi-party democracy and constitutional monarchy, and with that given up 'I see no useful purpose in continuing in it'. Bhattarai never went back to his word, but the Nepali Congress under Sushil Koirala, gave a broader hint that the Party would be following the ideals and politics set by Bhattarai in the years to come. The Nepali Congress is getting weaker, but what it does in future is still uncertain. There is a section in the party today which believes G P's pro-Maoist policy has brought to an end what BP, GM Singh, KP and the Nepali Congress believed in, and for democracy to prevail, NC must review its post 2006 policies.

There are many who believe Bhattarai died a defeated man in March, 2011 but his prolonged indisposition did not dilute the courage of conviction he was known for.

I had not interacted with him closely until I got an opportunity to discuss about his autobiography 'Mero Ma' (Me and My own) that he was keen to have published. The book was full of interesting anecdotes and experiences that he encountered in Banaras, the place he was born in, and grew and later when he came to Nepal for good and became one of its most respected politicians. My meetings with him became almost a regular affair then, and luckily, his autobiography was published on his birthday (Jan 1, 2011), that turned out to be his last one. He would talk about life, spirituality and many experiences he had, and had the knack to explain it in a livid and intense way. He was above hatred towards any one, and his belief in accumulated 'karma' guiding this life, perhaps made him so forgiving.

"Why did you not go along with your leader BP asked you to accompany him to India and launch the movement from there?" Bhattarai's answer would be simple. "If we fight for democracy from India, Indian interest will come into the movement and in that we will be pushing China far away. Nepal should always have a balanced and role of equal-distance with India and China."

Simple by his nature and life style Bhattarai is most possibly the single former Prime Minister in the world who died without a home of his own. He always lived in rented accommodation, or that provided by his admirer. Towards the end of his life, the state provided him an 'Ashram' that is in the process of being converted into a Trust to promote his social, spiritual and constructive views.

A man known for sharp wits and sense of humor, Bhattarai would even not spare himself.

"You were the Prime Minister, and yet you lost the election?" BBC's Mark Tully asked him when he lost a by-election in 1993. "How else could I have proved that the election was free and fair?" He would often say he is going to be the Prime Minister again.

But when an author asked him, "do you have a wish to become the Prime Minister again?" His answer was different, "I have higher purpose in life than to be a Prime Minister. I want to meet god in my life time." Gandhi often talked about 'higher laws' or law of conscience, and saw the service of the humanity as the means to realize god. For Bhattarai, politics was simply a means, and his ultimate aim of life remained unchanged.

In the contemporary politics, politics and politicians are normally hated. It's largely because of politics bereft of values, and its growing distance from the people. The pursuit of politics of power is a visible trend in the region today. That is probably the reason why even the 'condolences' and mourning on the passing away of leaders who have occupied key positions during their life time, becomes a routine rituals.

But when a leader with distinct philosophy and character passes away, he is debated equally intensely and ceaselessly after death. That is why BP is discussed and debated today. And Bhattarai, despite his own party disowning his policy favouring "constitutional monarchy and mult-party democracy'" is being seen, debated and respected even after death as a leader or a statesman who will simply not follow an emerging tide. He stood against it, because for him politics was guided by conviction and commitment, and not by impulsive approach or lust for power.

For someone, who became Party's General Secretary at the age 22 and then rose to be the Prime Minister of the country twice, first in 1990 and then in 1999, to preserve those values, and not barter that with power all along is a remarkable phenomenon. Interestingly, *Kishunjee* had differences with his leaders including BP and GM Singh many times during their long association and crusade for democracy. But as a democrat committed to the cause, he will not hesitate to follow the party line after making his point 'loud and clear'. But that never soured his relationship with any of his leaders. Only time, he reacted sharply and declared his 'dissociation' from the Party was when Nepali Congress under GP Koirala switched to – pro republic and pro-federal policy without discussing the issue in the party intensely in 2005. Bhattarai, Gandhian and votary of peaceful means in politics was not comfortable with Nepali Congress that he headed for 20 years since 1976—when B P and Ganeshman Singh returned from exile—suddenly followed the radical policies of the Maoists that had led armed insurgency in the country for a decade since 1996. BP-G M Singh and Bhattarai's policy are in favour of national reconciliation to consolidate democracy and nationalism. In fact, B P and Singh also gave up their earlier view that an armed revolution (declared in 1973) was not the proper means to seek political change in Nepal, and agreed to endorse Bhattarai's line of peaceful means on their return to the country.

Making false promises against his conviction was not in his nature, something the current day politics will demand. That explains why he lost first three elections he contested, first in 1958, 1991 and 1993. Bhattarai was the mixture of three different personalities. Though he never got married he was a family man who always enjoyed with people around him, who always had love and was passionate towards his people. Second, he was a political leader with the strong conviction and honesty, and was some one who treated each single penny of the treasury with utmost transparency.

He entered Baluatar, Prime Minister's official residence with an aluminum trunk, a *surahi* (a water pot made of soil) and an umbrella. On completion of his tenure, he walked out with no added property. "With him gone, can we be any longer in politics," the much talked about Cartoon by Rabin Sayami said which showed umbrella and *surahi* in conversation, that depicted a lot about the simplicity, honesty and conviction of a Gandhian.

Hari Bansh Jha

Madhesh and Madheshias of Nepal

Background

Of Nepal's three ecological regions, the flat land of Madhesh covers 23 per cent of the total land area of the country (147,181 sq. kms). The normal length of Madhesh is 800 kilometers; while its width varies between 25 to 32 kms. Width of this region is comparatively larger in the east and smaller in the west. The region called *Bhitri Madhesh* (inner Madhesh) consisting of flat land north of Siwalik or Churiya range consisting of Chitwan and Dang Deukhari bordering India is also a part of the Madhesh. Thus, the boundary of the Madhesh starts from the foothills of the Siwalik or Churiya range of the Himalayas in the north and extends upto the Indian border in the south. Of the 75 districts in Nepal, 20 districts including Jhapa, Morang, Sunsari, Saptari, Siraha, Dhanusha, Mahottari, Sarlahi, Rautahat, Bara, Parsa, Chitwan, Nawalparasi, Rupandehi, Kapilvastu, Dang, Banke, Bardiya, Kailali and Kanchanpur are located in the Madhesh.

Population

Table 1 shows that Nepal's total population in 2001 was 23 million; of which 49 per cent of the total people resided in the Madhesh and the remaining 44 per cent and 7 per cent people lived in the hill and mountain regions respectively. Anomalies in the distribution of population are quite distinct as 49 per cent of the population lived on land that constituted only 23 per cent of the total land area of the country; whereas 51 per cent population lived on land forming 77 per cent of the total land area. Because of the population pressure, the density of population in the Madhesh was 330 per sq. km.; which was 167 per sq. km. in the hills and 33 per sq. km. in the mountain.

Table No. 1:Population in the Ecological Regions

Ecological Regions	Male Population	Female Population	Total	%	Area in Sq. Km. in %	Density of Population per sq. km.
Madhesh	5,710,059	5,502,394	11,212,453	49	23	330
Hill	5,016,802	5,234,309	10,251,111	44	42	167
Mountain	837,060	850,799	1,687,859	7	35	33
Total	11,563,921	11,587,502	23,151,423	100	147,181	157

Source: CBS: Population Census 2001: National Report

Growth Rate of Population

Table 2 shows that the average annual growth of population in Nepal was 2.25 per cent in 2001. At the regional level, the average annual growth of population was highest (2.62 per cent) in the Madhesh followed by the same in the hills (1.97 per cent) and in the mountain (1.57 per cent).

Table No 2:Average Annual Population Growth in 2001

Ecological Regions	Average Annual Growth %
Madhesh	2.62
Hills	1.97
Mountain	1.57
Total	2.25

Source: Agriculture Sector in the Ninth Plan 2003

Population Composition

The composition of population in the Madhesh changed partly due to the migration of population from hills and partly due to the immigration of population from outside the country. As the table 3 shows, the hill population in the Madhesh formed merely 6 per cent during 1952-54, which shot up spectacularly to 43 per cent in 1981. Though marginally, it showed a declining trend thereafter as it formed 40 per cent in 1991 and 37 per cent in 2001. Surprisingly, the rate of growth of hill population in the Madhesh recorded a growth of 1,868 per cent between 1952-54 and 1981. During the same period, however, the rate of growth of Madheshi population was merely 67 per cent. This spectacular growth in the hill population in the Madhesh was mainly on account of various incentives provided to them for settlement in the region.

Table 3:Population Growth Trend in the Madhesh

Year	Hill Population in Madhesh 1	Rate of Growth of Population 2	Madheshi Population in Madhesh 3	Rate of Growth of Population 4	Total 5	Rate of Growth of Population 6	% of Hill Population in Madhesh (1 as % of 5) 7
1952/54	142	-	2,246	-	2,388		6
1981	2,795	1,868	3,762	67	6,557		43
1991	3,444	23	5,262	40	8,706		40
2001	4,120	20	7,092	34	11,212		37

Source: http://demrepubnepal.blogspot.com/2006/02/govind-shah-social-inclusion-of.html

Composition of Madheshi Population

Among the total Madheshi people in the Madhesh region, altogether 59 caste/ethnic groups have been identified. The following table shows that out of the total population of Madheshi caste/ethnic groups consisting 7,256,384, the Tharus share 21.13 per cent followed by the Muslims (13.38 per cent), Yadav (12.33 per cent) and Teli (4.19 per cent). Only these four groups form 51 per cent of the total Madhesh population.

Other Madheshi caste groups include Chamar/Harijan/Ram (3.71 per cent), Koiri (3.46 per cent), Kurmi (2.93 per cent), Dhanuk (2.59 per cent), Musahar (2.37 per cent), Dusadh/Paswan/Pasi (2.18 per cent), Sonar (1.99 per cent), Kewat (1.88 per cent), Brahman (1.85 per cent), Baniya (1.74 per cent), Mallah (1.60 per cent), Kalwar (1.59 per cent), Hajam/Thakur (1.35 per cent), Kanu (1.35 per cent), Rajbanshi (1.32 per cent), Sudi (1.24 per cent), Lohar (1.14 per cent), Tatma (1.05 per cent), Khatwe (1.03 per cent) and Dhobi (1.01 per cent).

Those Madheshi caste/ethnic groups whose share is less than 1 per cent in the Madhesh are Nuniya, Kumhar, Danuwar, Haluwai, Rajput, Kayastha, Badhae, Santhal/Sattar, Jhangar/Dhagar, Bantar, Barae, Kahar, Gangai, Lodha, Rajbhar, Bin/Binda, Bhediyar/Gaderi, Nurang, Tajpuriya, Chidimar, Mali, Bengali, Dom, Kamar, Meche, Halkhor, Punjabi/Sikh, Kisan, Koche, Dhuniya, Jaine and Munda, Kuswadiya/Patharkata.

Table 4: Composition of Madheshi Caste/Ethnic Groups

Sr. No.	Identified Madhesh/Madheshi Caste/Ethnic Groups	Total	Madhesh
1	Tharu	1,533,879	21.13
2.	Muslim	971,056	13.38
3.	Yadav	895,423	12.33
4.	Teli	304,536	4.19
5.	Chamar/Harijan/Ram	269,661	3.71
6.	Koiri	251,274	3.46
7.	Kurmi	212,842	2.93
8.	Dhanuk	188,150	2.59
9.	Musahar	172,434	2.37
10.	Dusadh/Paswan/Pasi	158,526	2.18
11.	Sonar	145,088	1.99
12.	Kewat	136,953	1.88
13.	Brahman(Madhesh)	134,496	1.85

14.	Baniya	126,971	1.74
15.	Mallah	115,986	1.60
16.	Kalwar	115,606	1.59
17.	Hajam/Thakur	98,169	1.35
18.	Kanu	95,826	1.32
19.	Rajbanshi	95,812	1.32
20.	Sudi	89,846	1.24
21.	Lohar	82,637	1.14
22.	Tatma	76,512	1.05
23.	Khatwe	74,972	1.03
24.	Dhobi	73,413	1.01
25.	Nuniya	66,873	0.92
26.	Kumhar	54,413	0.74
27.	Danuwar	53,229	0.73
28.	Haluwai	50,583	0.69
29.	Rajput	48,454	0.66
30.	Kayastha	46,071	0.63
31.	Badhae	45,975	0.63
32.	Marwadi	43,971	0.60
33.	Santhal/Sattar	42,698	0.58
34.	Jhangar/Dhagar	41,764	0.57
35.	Bantar	35,839	0.49
36.	Barae	35,434	0.48
37.	Kahar	34,531	0.47
38.	Gangai	31,318	0.43

39.	Lodha	24,738	0.34
40.	Rajbhar	24,263	0.33
41.	Dhimal	19,537	0.26
42.	Bing/Binda	18,720	0.25
43.	Bhediyar/Gaderi	17,729	0.24
44.	Nurang	17,522	0.24
45.	Tajpuriya	13,215	0.18
46.	Chidimar	12,296	0.16
47.	Mali	11,390	0.15
48.	Bengali	9,860	0.13
49.	Dom	8,931	0.12
50.	Kamar	8,761	0.12
51.	Meche	3,763	0.05
52.	Halkhor	3,621	0.04
53.	Punjabi/Sikh	3,054	0.04
54.	Kisan	2,876	0.03
55.	Koche	1,429	0.02
56.	Dhunia	1,231	0.02
57.	Jaine	1,015	0.01
58.	Munda	660	0.00
59.	Kuswadiya/Patharkata	552	0.00
	Total	**7,256,384**	**100.00**

Source: Central Bureau of Statistics

Social and Economic Exclusion

The local Madheshis constitute nearly two-thirds of the total population in the Madhesh. However, they have not been brought into the national mainstream due to the lack of adequate representation in political, administrative, judiciary and various other state organs.

The Madheshis have been discriminated all through the history of Nepal. Employment was denied to them overtly and in other government services covertly. Besides, much of the land possessed by these people was taken away in the name of *Birta, Jagir, Rajguthi, Devguthi* and land reforms. Such land was distributed among the feudal lords, priests, courtiers, government employees and Hindu Gods and Goddesses of the hill region.[2]

The exclusion policy of the state forced many of these people to live a degraded life. Nearly 41 per cent of Muslims and 79 per cent of Musahars are landless. Also, 79 per cent of the Dalits, 68 per cent of the Muslims, 54 per cent of indigenous Janajatis and 42 per cent of mid-caste population in the region are illiterate. Literacy rate among the Dalit and Muslim women is as low as 11 per cent and it is still worse in the case of Musahars (7 per cent).

Human Development

Table 5 indicates that the Madhehi population living in the Madhesh have per capita income (NRs. 6,911) lower than that of average Nepalis of NRs. 7,673. They are behind the other dominant communities of Nepal like the Brahmin, Chhetri and Newar in all such indicators as adult literacy, mean years of schooling, educational attainment, human development index (HDI) and also in ratio to HDI Nepal. They are also behind the marginalised community like the Janajati in the adult literacy rate.

---

[2] Govind Neupane, "Madheshis: Colonial subjects or masters of their own destiny" in http://www.nepalresearch.com/coup_2005/papers/neupane_060826.pdf

Table 5: Human Development by Caste and Ethnicity

Categories	Brahmin	Chhetri	Newar	Madheshi	Janajati	Dalit	Nepal
Life expectancy	60.8	56.03	62.2	58.4	53.0	50.3	55.0
Adult literacy rate	58.00%	42.00%	54.80-%	27.50%	35.20%	23.80%	36.27%
Mean years of schooling	4.4647	2.786	4.370	1.700	2.021	1.228	2.254
Per capita income (NRs.)	9921	7744	11953	6911	6607	4940	7673
Per capita income US$ (PPP)	1533	1197	1848	1068	1021	764	1186
Life expectancy index	0.957	0.522	0.620	0.557	0.467	0.422	0.500
Educational attainment index	0.490	0.342	0.462	0.221	0.280	0.186	0.295
Income index	0.237	0.181	0.289	0.160	0.152	0.110	0.179
Human development index (HDI)	0.441	0.348	0.457	0.313	0.299	0.239	0.325
Ratio to HDI Nepal = 100	135.87	107.3	140.73	96.28	92.21	73.62	100.00

Source: State Building in Nepal: Creating a Functional State

Share in Governance

Table 6 indicates that the Madheshis with nearly one-third of Nepal's total population have only 7.6 per cent positions in court against 77 per cent of the Brahmin/Chhetri caste. Their share in constitutional bodies is only 12 per cent against 56 per cent of the Brahmin/Chhetri caste. In public administration, their share is only 3.7 per cent against 77.6 per cent of Brahmin/Chhetri caste and 17.6 per cent of Newars caste. Similarly, their share in cabinet, party leadership, civil society leadership and other such areas is far from satisfactory.

Table 6:Integrated National Index of Governance (In percentage)

Categories	Brahmin/ Chhetri	Newar	Madheshi	Janajatii	Dalit	Other	Total Integrated National Index of Governance
Court	77.0	13.6	7.6	1.7	0.0	0.0	235
Constitutional bodies	56.0	24.0	12.0	2.8	0.0	0.0	25
Cabinet	62.5	9.4	15.6	12.5	0.0	0.0	32
Parliament	60.0	7.6	17.4	13.6	1.5	0.0	265
Public administration	77.6	17.6	3.7	1.2	0.0	0.0	245
Party leadership	58.8	10.9	15.8	15.2	0.0	0.0	165
Leadership: local elected bodies	55.5	15.7	16.2	12.0	0.0	0.0	191
Leadership: commerce and industry	16.7	47.6	35.7	0.0	0.0	0.0	42
Leadership: educational arena	77.3	11.3	7.2	2.1	1.0	1.0	97
Leadership: cultural arena	69.1	17.1	0.0	4.9	0.0	0.0	123
Science/ Technology	58.1	29.0	9.7	3.2	0.0	0.0	62
Civil Society Leadership	75.9	14.8	7.4	1.9	0.0	0.0	54
Average %	66.5	15.2	11.2	7.1	0.3	1.0	
Population %	31.6	5.6	30.9	22.2	8.7	1.0	
Difference from population %	+34.9	+9.6	-19.7	-15.1	-8.4	-1.0	

Source: State Building in Nepal: Creating a Functional State

Citizenship

Since the political change in 1960, the government of Nepal has remained conservative in granting citizenship certificates even to the genuine Nepalese. Nevertheless, the government formed after 2006 April movement declared 1990 as the cut-off year and exhibited rare courage to provide citizenship to some 2.6 million eligible Nepalese citizens before the CA election in 2008. Yet due to certain complex rules and regulations and other bottlenecks, nearly 1 million to 2.4 million people in the country are still devoid of citizenship certificates. Amidst such a situation, the recommendation made by the Fundamental Rights and Directive Principles Committee of the Constituent Assembly to impose the clause in which a foreigner marrying the Nepalese would have to wait for 15-long years to qualify for naturalized Nepalese citizenship might prove regressive, particularly in the case of Madhesh where cross-border marriage among Nepalese and Indian border inhabitants is most common and is a natural phenomenon.

International Migration and Remittance

Because of the lack of prospects at home, many of the people in the Madhesh region have started migrating to foreign countries for employment. Initially, they used to go to India, particularly in Punjab and Haryana states for seasonal employment. In recent years, however, there has been a significant decline in the number of migrant workers going to India from the Madhesh region for employment. The flow has largely been diverted to overseas countries i.e. countries out of Indian sub-continent. The overseas countries that are in the reach of migrant workers from the Madhesh are Saudi Arabia, Qatar, Malaysia, etc. Presently, most of the rural households in the Madhesh region have at least one member employed in a foreign country, though an empirical survey on it has never been conducted.

Interestingly, the district wise data of Nepali migrant workers show that the largest number of persons migrated to foreign countries from Dhanusha district of the Madhesh region. Of the total 75 districts, the share of migrant workers from Dhanusha district is 6.7 per cent closely followed by Jhapa (5.28 per cent), Siraha (4.78 per cent), Morang (4.24 per cent), Mahottari (3.97 per cent), Nawalparasi (3.17 per cent), Chitwan

(2.88 per cent), Tanahu (2.84 per cent), Sunsari (2.73 per cent) and Saptari (2.64 per cent).[3] More significantly, nine of the top ten districts with the highest number of migrant workers are from different districts in Madhesh.

So far, records show us that migrant workers from the Madhesh are predominantly male. But now a new trend is developing, particularly among certain sections of the indigenous women such as the Tharu and Rajbanshi communities, who have gone to work in overseas countries.

A significant portion of Nepal's US $ 1.5 billion remittance is pumped into the Madhesh but there is no official record that tells us how much. However, the *Report on the Nepal Labour Force Survey 2008* shows that the average per capita remittance amounted to Rs. 3,253 in the Madhesh, Rs. 3,718 in the hills and Rs. 1,803 in the mountain region.[4]

Larger portions of the hard-earned remittance money in the Madhesh region go for consumption expenditure. People often buy consumer items for themselves or for their family members such as radio, TV, mobile, bicycle, motorcycle, fancy clothes and food. Upon receiving money from overseas workers, the family members' frequency of visits to the town or district headquarters increase along with money spent on cinemas, restaurants and alcohol - something very alien to traditional ways.

Therefore, savings made by family members of migrant workers after cutting off expenditure is quite low, though no statistics is available on this aspect. At the national level only 6 per cent of the total remittance amount is saved. Hence, the capital formation for productive purposes is largely lacking.

More than any other sector, the agriculture in the Madhesh met a major setback due to out migration of population from this region. Because of the labour shortage, the wage rates have increased phenomenally. Also, there has been substantial increase in the prices of manures, fertilizers and agricultural tools. Other infrastructural facilities such as irrigation, rural

---

[3] The information is based on the data provided by Department of Foreign Employment of the Government of Nepal.

[4] CBS. 2009. *Report on the Nepal Labour Force Survey 2008.* Kathmandu: CBS, UNDP and ILO, p. 169.

roads and marketing channels remain to be developed. As such, very less portion of remittance is invested in the agricultural sector. At the national level, only 1 per cent of the total remittance amount was invested in the agricultural sector.[5] The case of the Madhesh region might not be much different from the national pattern.

Agriculture

Nepal's agricultural productivity was highest in South Asia in early 1960's, which turned to be the lowest one in the region by 1990's.[6] Higher agricultural productivity in Nepal was mainly due to the higher agricultural productivity in the Madhesh. Until a couple of years back the Madhesh region was called grain basket. But now even this region has turned to be food deficit area, though it accounts for 57 per cent of cereal crops and 74 per cent of cash crop production. The increased level of population together with the decline in productivity of land is largely responsible for the food deficit situation in the region. The farmers with small size of land holdings are exposed to unfavourable cost-risk return structure, higher interest rates, lower use of organic fertilizers, and unfriendly market.

Significantly, during the recent years, the climate change has started making adverse impact on agricultural production and productivity in the Madhesh region. Unexpectedly, the weather, water and environmental conditions have changed.[7] People in the region have gradually been realizing that the climate change is no more an issue of international or national concern, but it is an acute local problem. The reduced level of rainfall together with shifts in precipitation patterns, longer drought, flash floods and deficit in recharge of groundwater has started making adverse impact on the agricultural sector thereby affecting the livelihood of millions of people in the region.

---

[5] ADB, DFID and ILO. 2009. Nepal Critical Development Constraints. Mandaluyong City, Philippines, p. 89.

[6] Prakash Kharel, "Grains of Truth," in Republica, 21 October 2009.

[7] Livelihoods and Forestry Programme, 2009. *Impact of Climate change on Forests and Livelihoods: Issues and Options for Nepal.* Kathmandu: DFID, pp. 52-53.

Industries

The Madhesh region accounts for 58 per cent of total manufacturing establishments and 67 per cent of total manufacturing production. Yet, the labour unrest, power shortage, *bandh*, non-availability of raw materials in time, forced donations, and undue interference by the government authorities and certain political parties in the normal business affairs of the industries have adversely affected their productivity and production. This has overshadowed the prospect of employment opportunities, FDI and SEZs in the Madhesh. No significant effort has been made for developing pro-industrial policies and programmes for the region.

Infrastructure

Infrastructural facilities, though pre-requisite for the development, is yet to be adequately developed in the Madhesh. Education system met serious setback at all the levels. Health facilities are awfully poor. Connectivity among different Madhesh districts is a major problem due to the lack of road such as Hulaqi (Postal) Highway along the densely populated southern Madhesh region and various north-south roads in the region.

Theoretically, 80 per cent of the irrigation facilities are confined to the Madhesh, yet only 22 per cent of the farmland of the region is irrigated in the winter season and 5 per cent in the spring season. Electricity supply for the industries, agriculture and household is awfully lacking as the country produces only 600 MW out of 83,000 MW of potential to generate hydropower in the country. The loadsheding is a major problem in the region. The railway network in the region is limited. The service between Janakpur-Jaynagar sections provided by Nepal Railways Company is most disappointing. International Airport is yet to be constructed. Communication network is mostly confined to the urban areas of the Madhesh and its coverage in the rural areas is limited.

Understanding the importance of the Madhesh in Nepal's national economy, a few bilateral/multilateral agencies and INGOs have been extending cooperation for the development of infrastructural facilities and human resources in this region. Among all such aid and assistance to the development of the region, Indian co-operation in the Madhesh is unique both in terms of volume and coverage as it is solely guided by the motive of making the region self-reliant, vibrant, prosperous and modern in sectors related to the development of roads, airports, railways, communications, education, health, industry, urbanization or cultural promotion.

Cross Border Relations

Cross border economic activities are part of the life of the people living in two sides of Nepal-India border region. Most of these people meet the demand for goods needed for private consumption, business and social activities from the nearby border market and haat bazaars. Due to the open border between Nepal and India, the border inhabitants have greatly benefited from education, health, employment, tourism and several other sectors.

Thousands of Indian tourists visit the Nepalese bordering areas for pilgrimage, recreation and shopping. The Madhesh region attracts the religious Hindu tourists from across the border in India. Janakpur is the major pilgrimage centre as it is the birthplace of Sita. Similarly, Lumbini, the birthplace of Lord Buddha, is the pilgrimage centre for the Buddhists.

There is a great potentiality for the development of different sectors of the border region through the active cooperation between the government authorities of Nepal and India, which, however, is lacking so far. In the absence of high level Border Authority, planning, programming, execution and monitoring of the development projects are not taking place effectively. The need for such a body has been acutely felt in the recent years due to massive interest of Nepalese and Indian governments for the development of different infrastructural facilities in the border region of the respective countries.

Conclusion

Asymmetrical relations between Kathmandu and the Madhesh in terms of development opportunities have posed as a big challenge. Being in the centre, Kathmandu controls the entire distribution and allocation of national resources, which accentuated and reinforced the inequalities between the centre and the periphery causing exploitation and neglect of the Madhesh in various sectors such as educational institutions, health facilities, transportation, communication, electrification and several other public works. As a result, people in the region are extremely poor. Many of the problems of the Madhesh are due to the faulty policies and programmes of the planners, policy makers and the government. This is also due to the fact that there is no separate planning for the development of the Madhesh. As such, the government and the donor agencies have shown less of interest in making adequate investment in infrastructural projects in the Madhesh despite higher level of Internal Rate of Return (IRR) in most of the projects. In view of the importance of Madhesh in Nepal's national economy, any neglect of this region in development opportunities and resource allocation could affect the growth of national economy.

As such, it is in the national interest that the socio-economic conditions of Madhesh and the Madheshi people are improved in Nepal. For this, all possible efforts should be made by the concerned units to introduce drought tolerant, less water demanding crop varieties and climate change adaptive cropping practices in the Madhesh region to mitigate the impact of climate change on the agricultural sector and increase the production and productivity of agricultural land. The Madhesh-based rivers should be tamed for the purpose of flood control and also for irrigating land in the region.

Conducive environment needs to be created in the Madhesh for addressing labour problems. Problem of energy crisis has to be resolved and also law and order situation has to be substantially improved. The products of the manufacturing establishments should be linked to market within the country and also across the border and to the third countries.

The exclusion policy of the state towards the Madheshis has to be stopped through affirmative actions; for which empowerment process has to be initiated partly through literacy, education and economic upliftment programmes and partly by promoting their due participation in various state organs on the priority basis. To make the Nepalese society more coherent, peaceful and prosperous, it is necessary that all those who have failed to receive citizenship certificates due to one or the other reason should be encouraged to acquire it.

Nepal needs to prioritize the entire Madhesh region by investing in infrastructural projects like road, irrigation, railways, transportation, communication and other needed sectors. Any investment in the Madhesh in some of these sectors will have multiplier effect on the national economy as this region is the engine of Nepal's growth.

The planners, policy makers and governments of Nepal and India need to execute common action programs to develop the border region. Also, the government and concerned bodies in Nepal need to adopt suitable policies to tame the donor agencies and INGOs working in the Madhesh region in a way that they are able to channelize their resources in activities aimed at poverty eradication and also for promoting the use the remittance earned by the people of this region in productive activities rather than on mere consumption.

Milestones

1. Time Line: Nepal
2. Treaty of Peace and Friendship between the Government of India and the Government of Nepal, July 31, 1950
3. The Twelve Point Understanding between the Seven Party Alliance and Maoists, November 22, 2005
4. The Comprehensive Peace Agreement concluded between the Government of Nepal and theCommunist Party of Nepal (Maoist), November 21,2006
5. The Seven Point-pacts signed between CPN-UML President Jhalnath Khanal & Unified CPN-Maoist President Pushpa Kamal Dahal. It was first revealed on February 5,2011
6. The Five point deal signed by the heads of three major political parties (The Maoist, Nepali Congress and the UML) on May 28,2011

Time Line : Nepal

A Chronology of key events:

1768 - Gurkha ruler Prithvi Narayan Shah conquers Kathmandu and lays foundations for unified kingdom.

1792 - Nepalese expansion halted by defeat at hands of Chinese in Tibet.

1801- A treaty signed with East India Company which for the first time allowed British Residents to reside in Nepal

1814-16 - Anglo-Nepalese War; culminates in treaty (Sugauli Treaty) which establishes Nepal's current boundaries.

1846 - Nepal falls under sway of hereditary chief ministers known as Ranas, who dominate the monarchy and cut off country from outside world.

1923 - Treaty with Britain affirms Nepal's sovereignty.

1950 - Treaty (Peace and Friendship) with India

1950 - Anti-Rana forces based in India form alliance with monarch.

1951 - End of Rana rule. Sovereignty of crown restored and anti-Rana rebels in Nepalese Congress Party form government.

1952 - Beginning of Absolute monarchy

1955 - Nepal joins the United Nations.

1955 - King Tribhuwan dies, King Mahendra ascends throne.

1959 - Multi-party constitution adopted; first parliamentary election; Nepali Congress Party wins elections with 2/3 majority; BP Koirala elected as the Prime Minister of Nepal.

1960 - King Mahendra seizes control and suspends parliament, constitution and party politics; B. P. Koirala and other leaders arrested.

1962 - New constitution provides for non-party system of councils known as "panchayat" under which king exercises sole power.

1963 - First elections to Rastrya Panchayat.

1972 - King Mahendra dies, succeeded by Birendra.

1980 - Constitutional referendum follows agitation for reform. Small majority favours keeping existing panchayat system. King agrees to allow direct elections to national assembly - but on a non-party basis.

1985 - NCP begins civil disobedience campaign for restoration of multi-party system.

1986 - New elections of National Panchayat.

1989 - Trade and transit dispute with India leads to border blockade by Delhi resulting in worsening economic situation.

1990 - Pro-democracy agitation co-ordinated by NCP and leftist groups. Street protests suppressed by security forces resulting in deaths and mass arrests. King Birendra eventually bows to pressure and agrees to new democratic constitution.

Multi-party politics

1990 - Interim Government under the premiership of NCP leader Krishna Prasad Bhattarai

1991 - Nepali Congress Party wins first democratic elections. Girija Prasad Koirala becomes prime minister.

Political instability

1994 - Koirala's government defeated in no-confidence motion. New elections lead to formation of Communist government.

1995 - Communist government dissolved.

1996 - Nepal Communist Party (Maoist) begins insurrection in rural areas aimed at abolishing monarch and establishing people's republic, sparking a conflict that would drag on for over a decade.

1997 - Prime Minister Sher Bahadur Deuba loses no-confidence vote, ushering in period of increased political instability, with frequent changes of prime minister.

2000 - GP Koirala returns as prime minister, heading the ninth government in 10 years.

2001 1 June - King Birendra, Queen Aishwarya and other close relatives killed in shooting spree by drunken Crown Prince Dipendra, who then shoots himself.

2001 14 June - Prince Gyanendra crowned King of Nepal after Dipendra dies of his injuries.

2001 July - Maoist rebels step up campaign of violence. Prime Minister GP Koirala quits over the violence; succeeded by Sher Bahadur Deuba.

2001 November - Maoists end four-month old truce with government, declare peace talks with government failed. Launch coordinated attacks on army and police posts.

2001 November - State of emergency declared after more than 100 people are killed in four days of violence. King Gyanendra orders army to crush the Maoist rebels. Many hundreds are killed in rebel and government operations in the following months.

2002 May - Parliament dissolved, fresh elections called amid political confrontation over extending the state of emergency. Sher Bahadur Deuba heads interim government, renews emergency.

2002 October - King Gyanendra dismisses Deuba and indefinitely puts off elections set for November. Lokendra Bahadur Chand appointed as PM.

2003 January - Rebels, government declare ceasefire.

2003 May-June - Lokendra Bahadur Chand resigns as PM; king appoints his own nominee Surya Bahadur Thapa as new premier.

End of truce

2003 August - Rebels pull out of peace talks with government and end seven-month truce. The following months see resurgence of violence and frequent clashes between students/activists and police.

2004 April - Nepal joins the World Trade Organisation (WTO).

2004 May - Royalist Prime Minister Surya Bahadur Thapa resigns following weeks of street protests by opposition groups.

2004 June - King Gyanendra reappoints Sher Bahadur Deuba as prime minister with the task of holding elections.

Direct power

2005 1 February - King Gyanendra dismisses Prime Minister Deuba and his government, declares a state of emergency and assumes direct power, citing the need to defeat Maoist rebels.

2005 30 April - King lifts the state of emergency amid international pressure.

2005 November - Maoist rebels and main opposition parties agree on a programme intended to restore democracy.

2006 April - King Gyanendra agrees to reinstate parliament following weeks of violent strikes and protests against direct royal rule. GP Koirala is appointed as prime minister. Maoist rebels call a three-month cease fire.

2006 May - Parliament votes unanimously to curtail the king's political powers. The government and Maoist rebels begin peace talks, the first in nearly three years.

2006 16 June - Rebel leader Prachanda and PM Koirala hold talks - the first such meeting between the two sides - and agree that the Maoists should be brought into an interim government.

2006 November - The government and Maoists sign a peace accord, the Comprehensive Peace Agreement (CPA), declaring a formal end to a 10-year rebel insurgency. The rebels are to join a transitional government and their weapons will be placed under UN supervision.

2007 January - Maoist leaders enter parliament under the terms of a temporary constitution. Violent ethnic protests erupt in the south-east; demonstrators demand autonomy for the region.

Maoists join government

2007 April - Former Maoist rebels join interim government, a move that takes them into the political mainstream.

2007 May - Elections for a constituent assembly pushed back to November.

2007 September - Maoists quit interim government to press demand for monarchy to be scrapped. This forces the postponement of November's constituent assembly elections.

2007 October - UN Secretary-General Ban Ki-moon urges Nepal's parties to sink their differences to save the peace process.

2007 December - Parliament approves abolition of monarchy as part of peace deal with Maoists, who agree to re-join government.

2008 January - A series of bomb blasts kill and injure dozens in the southern Terai plains. Groups there have been demanding regional autonomy.

2008 April - Elections to Constituent Assembly; Former Maoist rebels win the largest bloc of seats in elections to the new constituent assembly, but fail to achieve an outright majority.

2008 May - Nepal becomes a republic.

2008 June - Maoist ministers resign from the cabinet in a row over who should be the next head of state.

2008 July - Ram Baran Yadav becomes Nepal's first President.

2008 August - Maoist leader Prachanda forms coalition government, with Nepali Congress going into opposition.

2009 May - Prime Minister Prachanda resigns in protest against "unconstitutional and undemocratic" move by President Yadav to block the sacking of the army chief.

2009 May : Veteran Communist leader Madhav Kumar Nepal named new Prime Minister.

2010 May - Governing coalition and Maoist opposition agree to extend deadline for drafting of new constitution to May 2011.

2010 June - PM Madhav Kumar Nepal resigns, following prolonged pressure on him from Maoists to step down.

Treaty of Peace and Friendship signed between the Government of India and the Government of Nepal

(Kathmandu, July 31,1950)

THE Government of India and the Government of Nepal, recognising the ancient ties which have happily existed between the two countries for centuries;

DESIRING still further to strengthen and develop these ties and to perpetuate peace between the two countries;

HAVE resolved therefore to enter into a Treaty of Peace and Friendship with each other and have, for this purpose, appointed as their plenipotentiaries the following persons, namely,

The Government of India :

His Excellency Shri Chandreshwar Prasad Narain Singh,
Ambassador of India in Nepal.

The Government of Nepal :

Maharaja Mohun Shamsher Jang Bahadur Rana,
Prime Minister and Supreme Commande'r-in-Chief of Nepal,

WHO, having examined each other's credentials and found them good and in due form

HAVE agreed as follows :

Article I

There shall be everlasting peace and friendship between the Government of India and the Government of Nepal. The two Governments agree mutually to acknowledge and respect the complete sovereignty, territorial integrity and independence of each other.

Article II

The two Governments hereby undertake to inform each other of any serious friction or misunderstanding with any neighbouring state likely to cause any breach in the friendly relations subsisting between the two Governments.

Article III

In order to establish and maintain the relations referred to in Article I the two Governments agree to continue diplomatic relations with each other by means of representatives with such staff as is necessary for the due performance of their functions.

The representatives and such of their staff as may be agreed upon shall enjoy such diplomatic privileges and immunities as are customarily granted by international law on a reciprocal basis : Provided that in no case shall these be less than those granted to persons of a similar status of any other State having diplomatic relations with either Government.

Article IV

The two Governments agree to appoint Consuls-General, Consuls, Vice-Consuls and other consular agents, who shall reside in towns, ports and other places in each Other's territory as may be agreed to.

Consuls-General, Consuls, Vice-Consuls and consular agents shall be provided with exequaturs or other valid authorization of their appointment. Such exequatur or authorization is liable to be withdrawn by the country which issued it, if considered necessary. The reasons for the withdrawal shall be indicated wherever possible.

The persons mentioned above shall enjoy on a reciprocal basis all the rights, privileges, exemptions and immunities that are accorded to persons of corresponding status of any other state.

Article V

The Government of Nepal shall be free to import, from or through the territory of India, arms, ammunition or warlike material and equipment necessary for the security of Nepal. The procedure for giving effect to this arrangement shall be worked out by the two Governments acting in consultation.

Article VI

Each Government undertakes, in token of the neighbourly friendship between India and Nepal, to give to the nationals of the other, in its territory, national treatment with regard to participation in industrial and economic development of such territory and to the grant of concessions and contracts relating to such development.

Article VII

The Governments of India and Nepal agree to grant, on a reciprocal basis, to the nationals of one country in the territories of the other the same privileges in the matter of residence, ownership of property, participation in trade and commerce, movement and other privileges of a similar nature.

Article VIII

So far as matters dealt with herein are concerned, this Treaty cancels all previous treaties, agreements and arrangements entered into on behalf of India between the British Government and the Government of Nepal.

Article IX

This treaty shall come into force from the date of signature by both Governments.

Article X

This Treaty shall remain in force until it is terminated by either party by giving one Year's notice.

DONE in duplicate at Kathmandu this 31st day of July, 1950.

sd/-	sd/-
CHANDRESHWAR PRASAD SINGH	MOHA SHAMSHER NARAIN JANG BAHADUR RANA
For the Government of India	For the Government of Nepal

At a Press Conference in New Delhi on 3rd December 1959 Prime Minister Jawaharlal Nehru for the first time disclosed that letters were exchanged along with the signing of the Treaty which were kept secret. Though these letters have not been officially made public, they have since appeared in a number of texts and are reproduced below - Editor

Letter From the Ambassador of India to the Prime Minister of Nepal

KATHMANDU

Dated the 31st July, 1950

YOUR HIGHNESS,

In the course of our discussion of the Treaties of Peace and Friendship and of Trade and Commerce1 which have been happily concluded between the Government of India and the Government of Nepal, we agreed that certain matters of details be regulated by an exchange of letters. In pursuance of this understanding, it is hereby agreed between the two Governments :

1. Neither Government shall tolerate any threat to the security of the other by a foreign aggressor. To deal with any such threat, the two Governments shall consult with each other and devise effective countermeasures.

2. Any arms, ammunition or warlike material and equipment necessary for the security of Nepal that the Government of Nepal may import through the territory of India shall be so imported with the assistance and agreement of the Government of India. The Government of India will take steps for the smooth and expeditious transport of such arms and ammunition through India.

3. In regard to Article 6 of the Treaty of Peace and Friendship which provides for national treatment, the Government of India recognize that it may be necessary for some time to come to afford the Nepalese nationals in Nepal protection from unrestricted competition. The nature and extent of this protection will be determined as and when required by mutual

agreement between the two Governments.

4. If the Government of Nepal should decide to seek foreign assistance in regard to the development of the natural resources of, or of any industrial project in Nepal, the Government of Nepal shall give first preference to the Government or the nationals of India, as the case may be, provided that the terms offered by the Government of India or Indian nationals, as the case may be, are not less favourable to Nepal than the terms offered by any other foreign Government or by other foreign nationals.

Nothing in the foregoing provision. shall apply to assistance that the Government of Nepal may seek from the United nations organization or any of its specialized agencies.

5. Both Governments agree not to employ any foreigners whose activity may be prejudicial to the security of the other. Either Government may make representations to the other in this behalf, as and when occasion requires.

Please accept your Highness, the assurances of my highest consideration.

Sd/-

CHANDRESHWAR PRASAD NARAIN SINGH

Ambassador Extraordinary and plenipotentiary

of India at the Court of Nepal.

To

His Highness Mohan Shamsher Jang Bahadur Rana,
Maharaja, Prime Minister and Supreme Commander-in-Chief
of Nepal.

Letter from the Prime Minister of Nepal to the Ambassador of India

KATHMANDU

Dated the 31th July 1950

EXCELLENCY,

In the course of our discussion of the Treaties of peace and Friendship and of Trade and commerce which have been happily concluded between the Government of India and the Government of Nepal we agreed that certain , of details be regulated by an exchange of letters. In pursuance of this understanding, it is hereby agreed between the two Governments:

1. Neither Government shall tolerate any threat to the security of the other by a foreign aggressor. To deal with any such threat, the two Governments shall consult with each other and devise effective countermeasures.

2. Any arms, ammunition or warlike material and equipment necessary for the security of Nepal that the Government of Nepal may import through the territory of India shall be so imported with the assistance and agreement of the Government of India. The Government of India will take steps for the smooth and expeditious transpor1olsucharmSandammunitionthroughlndia.

3. In regard to Article 6 of the Treaty of Peace and Friendship which provides for national treatment, the Government of India recognize that it may be necessary for some time to come to afford the Nepalese nationals in Nepal protection from unrestricted competition. The nature and extent of this protection will be determined as and when required by mutual agreement between the two Governments'

4. lf the Government of Nepal should decide to seek foreign assistance in regard to the development of the natural resources of, or of any industrial project in Nepal, the Government of Nepal shall give first preference to the Government or the nationals of India, as the case may be, provided

that the terms offered by the Government of India or Indian nationals, as the case may be, are not less favourable to Nepal than the terms offered by any other Foreign Government or by other foreign nationals.

Nothing in the foregoing provision shall apply to assistance that the Government of Nepal may seek from the united Nations organization or any of its specialized agencies.

5. Both Governments agree not to employ any foreigners whose activity may be prejudicial to the security of the other. Either Government may make representations to the other in this behalf, as and when occasion requires'

Please accept Excellency, the assurances of my highest consideration.

Sd/-

MOHAN SHAMSHER JANG BAHADUR RANA,

Maharaja, Prime Minister and
Supreme Commander-in-Chief of Nepal

To

His Excellency Shri Chandreshwar Prasad Narain Singh,
Ambassador Extraordinary and Plenipotentiary of India at the
Court of Nepal,
Indian Embassy, Kathmandu.

Twelve-point Understanding between Seven Party Alliance and Communist Party of Nepal (Maoists)

Nov 22, 2005 (unofficial Translation)

The long struggle between absolute monarchy and democracy in Nepal has now reached a very grave and new turn. Establishing peace by resolving the 10-years old armed conflict through a forward-looking political outlet has become the need of today. Therefore, implementing the concept of absolute democracy through a forward-looking restructuring of the state has become an inevitable need to solve the problems related to class, caste, gender, region etc. of all sectors including political, economic, social and cultural, bringing autocratic monarchy to an end and establishing absolute democracy. We make public that, against this existing backdrop and reference in the country, the following understanding has been reached between the SPA and the CPN (Maoist) through different methods of talks.

Points of Understanding

1. At present all Nepalese desire peace, democracy, prosperity, social progress and independent and sovereign Nepal. To achieve this goal, we fully agree that the autocratic monarchy is the main obstacle. We are in clear agreement that peace and prosperity of the country is quite impossible without ending autocracy and establishing absolute democracy. Hence, all anti-regressive forces have come to an agreement to focus their attack against the autocratic monarchy independently, and bring it to an end by intensifying the ongoing democratic movement across the country.

2. The seven-party alliance is fully convinced that sovereignty and executive right of the people can be reestablished through the reinstatement of parliament (on the basis of people's movement); formation of all-party government with full executive power; talks with the Maoists and election to the constituent assembly. Whereas CPN-M believes that people's

sovereignty can be established through formation of an interim government formed after a national conference of agitating democratic forces, which will oversee the election to the constituent assembly [This is the only point of divergence, so to speak, between the seven-party alliance and the rebels]. Both of us agree to continue negotiation and dialogue to reach common agreement in these procedural issues. However, we have agreed that people's movement is the only way to attain our agreed goals.

3. The nation has demanded constructive end of the present armed conflict and establishment of a lasting peace. Thus, we are fully committed to end autocratic monarchy and establish lasting peace through election to constituent assembly. In this regard, the CPN-M expresses its commitment to move into new peaceful political line. After bringing the autocratic monarchy to an end, we have agreed that the arms of both the Royal Nepalese Army and the Maoists will be supervised by the United Nations or a dependable international body to ensure free and fair election to the constituent assembly. Both parties have also agreed to accept the results of the elections. We also expect an involvement of a credible international community in the dialogue process.

4. CPN-M has expressed firm commitment to acceptance of competitive multiparty system, fundamental rights of the people, human rights, and rule of law and democratic principles and values and to act accordingly.

5. CPN-M has agreed to create conducive atmosphere to allow all leaders and cadres affiliated to other democratic forces and common people, who were displaced from home during the conflict, to return to their respective places with full respect. The Maoists have also agreed to return the houses and physical properties of people and party cadres seized unjustifiably. People will be allowed to take part in political activities without any hindrance.

6. CPN-M has also agreed to criticize itself for its past mistakes and has expressed commitment not to repeat them in future.

7. Parties will introspect on their past mistakes and they have expressed commitment not to repeat such mistakes in future.

8. During the peace process human rights principles and freedom of press

will be fully respected.

9. The municipal and parliamentary polls which have been pushed forward with the malicious intention of deceiving people and the international community, and to legitimize the king's autocratic and unconstitutional rule will be boycotted and made unsuccessful.

10. People, representatives of people and political parties are the real bulwark of nationalism. We are committed to protecting our independence, national unity and sovereignty, and safeguarding geographical integrity. It is our responsibility to maintain cordial relationship with all nations in the world--especially with our neighbors, India and China-- based on the principle of peaceful co-existence. We appeal to all patriotic Nepalis to be wary of the Mandale brand of nationalism preached by the monarch and his sycophants to protect their rule and interest. We also appeal to the Nepali people and international community to provide help to our Loktantrik movement.

11. We also appeal to all people, civil society members, professional communities, various sister organizations, journalists and intellectuals to participate actively in the people's peaceful movement launched under the common agreement based on democracy, peace, prosperity, social transformation, and the nation's sovereignty.

12. The parties and Maoists have also agreed to probe into past incidents and take action against the guilty. In future, if any problem occurs among political parties, the concerned high level leaders shall discuss and settle the issues amicably through dialogue.

Peace Agreement concluded between the Government of Nepal and the Communist Party of Nepal (Maoist)

November 21, 2006 (unofficial Translation)

Preamble

Respecting the popular mandate in favour of democracy, peace and progress expressed through repeated historic struggles and people's movements from the pre-1951 era to date;

Reaffirming total commitment to the 12-point understanding and the 8-point agreement concluded between the Seven Political Parties and the CPN (Maoist) and the 25-point codes of conduct agreed between the Government of Nepal and the CPN (Maoist), all agreements, understandings, codes of conduct concluded between the Government of Nepal and the CPN (Maoist) as well as the decisions of the Summit Meeting of the Seven-Party Alliance and the CPN (Maoist) adopted on November 8, 2006 and letters of similar spirit sent to the United Nations by the Government of Nepal and the Maoists;

Pledging for forward-looking restructuring of the state by resolving the prevailing problems related to class, ethnicity, regional and gender differences;

Reiterating commitments to competitive multiparty democratic system, civil liberties, fundamental rights, human rights, complete press freedom and all other democratic norms and values including the concept of rule of law;

Remaining committed to the Universal Declaration of Human Rights 1948, international humanitarian laws and the fundamental principles and basic principles and norms related to human rights;

Guaranteeing the fundamental right of the Nepali people to participate in a free and fair Constituent Assembly election in an environment free from fear;

Keeping democracy, peace, prosperity, forward looking economic and social transformation as well as independence, integrity, sovereignty and dignity of the country at the centre;

Expressing confidence to implement the commitment of holding the election to the Constituent Assembly in a free and fair manner within June 15, 2007;

Declaring the beginning of a new chapter of peaceful collaboration by ending the armed conflict plaguing the country since 1996 on the basis of political consensus reached between the two parties to ensure the sovereignty of the Nepali people, forward looking political resolution, democratic restructuring of the state and economic-social and cultural transformation through the Constituent Assembly;

The Government of Nepal and CPN (Maoist) hereby conclude this Comprehensive Peace Agreement with commitments to convert the present ceasefire into lasting peace.

1. Preliminary

1.1. The name of this agreement is "Comprehensive Peace Agreement 2006". In short the agreement shall be called Peace Agreement.

1.2. The agreement shall come into force with effect from today through public declaration by the Government and the Maoists.

1.3. Both the sides shall give necessary directives to all agencies under their control for immediate implementation of this agreement and to abide by it and implement it and get it implemented.

1.4. All the agreements, understandings, and codes of conduct and decisions reached among the seven political parties, the government and Maoist sides as included in the annex shall be an integral part of this agreement.

1.5. The understandings and agreements that may be reached hereafter as necessary for the implementation of this agreement shall also be the integral part of this agreement.

2. Definition: Unless the subject and context mean otherwise, in this agreement:

(a) "Ceasefire" means the banning of all forms of aggressions, kidnappings, disappearances, taking into custody, aimed at each other between the Government of Nepal and the CPN (Maoist),as well as mobilization, strengthening of the armed forces, and their aggressive and violent acts, spread of social disharmony in any manner including acts of incitement and instigation.

(b) "Interim Constitution" means the "Interim Constitution of Nepal 2006" to be adopted and remained in force until drafting and enforcement of the new constitution by Constituent Assembly.

(c) "Interim Council of Ministers" means "Interim Council of Ministers" to be constituted in accordance with the Interim Constitution.

(d) "Both the sides" means the Government of Nepal and the Communist Party of Nepal (Maoist).

(e) "Prevailing Laws" means Interim Constitution of Nepal 2006 and existing Nepal Laws not inconsistent with it. But this definition shall not interfere with the legal arrangement existing before the enforcement of the Interim Constitution 2006.

(f) "Verification" means the subject of verification and true record keeping of military, combatants and arms by the United Nations.

3. Political-Economic-Social Transformation and Conflict Management

Both the parties are in agreement to pursue the following policy and program for political-economic and social transformation and to affirmatively resolve existing conflict in the country:

3.1. To ensure forward moving political, economic and social transformation on the basis of decisions made in summit meeting between Seven Political Parties and CPN (Maoist) held on November 8, 2006 (Annex-6).

3.2. To constitute Interim Legislature - Parliament as per the Interim Constitution, to have the elections to Constituent Assembly held by the Interim Government in a free and fair manner within June 15, 2006 and to practically guarantee sovereignty inherent in the Nepali people.

3.3. No state powers shall remain with the king. The properties owned by the late King Birendra, the late Queen Aishwarya and their family members shall be brought under the control of the Government of Nepal and used in the interest of the nation through a trust. All properties (such as palaces at various places, forests and National Parks, heritages of historical and archaeological significance etc.) acquired by King Gyanendra in his monarchical capacity shall be nationalised. The issue of whether to continue or scrap the institution of monarchy shall be decided by a simple majority of the Constituent Assembly in its first meeting.

3.4. To pursue a political system that fully complies with the universally accepted fundamental human rights, competitive multiparty democratic system, sovereignty inherent in the people and the supremacy of the people, constitutional check and balance, rule of law, social justice and equality, independent judiciary, periodic elections, monitoring by civil society, complete press freedom, people's right to information, transparency and accountability in the activities of political parties, people's participation and the concepts of impartial, competent, and fair administration.

3.5. In order to end discriminations based on class, ethnicity, language, gender, culture, religion and region and to address the problems of women, Dalit, indigenous people, ethnic minorities (Janajatis), Terai communities (Madheshis), oppressed, neglected and minority communities and the backward areas by deconstructing the current centralised and unitary structure, the state shall be restructured in an inclusive, democratic and forward looking manner.

3.6. A common minimum program for socio-economic transformation in order to end all forms of feudalism shall be prepared and implemented on the basis of mutual understanding.

3.7. Policies shall be formulated to implement a scientific land reform program by doing away with the feudal land ownership practice.

3.8. Policies to protect and promote national industries and resources shall be followed.

3.9. Policies shall be undertaken to establish the rights of all the citizens to education, health, shelter, employment and food security.

3.10. Policies shall be pursued to provide land and socio-economic security to backward communities like the landless squatters, bonded labourers, tillers, bonded domestics, bonded cattle-tenders and such other groups.

3.11. Policies shall be adopted to take strict actions against those who, occupying governmental positions of benefit, have amassed huge properties through corruption.

3.12. A common development concept shall be adopted for the socio-economic transformation of the country and for making the country advanced and economically prosperous in a just manner within a short span of time.

3.13. Policies shall be followed for ensuring the professional rights of workers and increasing investment for the promotion of industries, trade, export etc. in order to significantly enhance employment and income generating opportunities.

4. Management of Army and Arms

The following shall be done in order for holding the election to the Constituent Assembly in a peaceful and fair environment free from fear and for the democratisation and restructuring of the Army in line with the spirit of the 12-point understanding, 8-point agreement, 25-point code of conduct, the 5-point letters sent to the United Nations and the decisions of the Summit Meeting of the Seven-Party Alliance and the CPN (Maoist) reached on November 8, 2006:

Relating to the Maoist army

4.1. As per the commitments expressed in the letters sent to the United Nations by the Government of Nepal and the Maoists on August 9, 2006, the combatants of the Maoist army shall be confined to the following temporary cantonments. The United Nations shall verify and monitor them. The main cantonments shall be located in the following places:

1. Kailali, 2. Surkhet, 3. Rolpa, 4. Palpa, 5. Kabhre,

6. Sindhuli, 7. Ilam.

There shall be three smaller camps located in the periphery of each of these main cantonments.

4.2. All the arms and ammunitions shall be securely stored within the cantonments except those needed for providing security to the cantonments after the Maoist combatants are sent to the cantonments. The arms and ammunitions shall be locked with a single padlock and the side concerned shall keep the key to it. For the UN to monitor it, a device with siren as well as recording facility shall be installed during the process of padlocking. The UN shall make necessary inspections of the stored arms in the presence of the party concerned. Technical details in this regard including camera monitoring shall be as per the agreement among the United Nations, the CPN (Maoist) and the Government of Nepal.

4.3. Once the Maoist combatants are confined to the cantonments, the Government of Nepal shall take care of their ration as well as other arrangements necessary.

4.4. The Interim Cabinet shall constitute a Special Committee to carry out monitoring, adjustment and rehabilitation of the Maoist combatants.

4.5. Security arrangements for the Maoist leaders shall be made with the consent of the Government of Nepal.

Relating to the Nepali Army

4.6.The Nepali Army shall be confined to the barracks as per the commitments made in the letters sent to the United Nations. Non-use of its arms for or against either side shall be guaranteed. Like number of arms as those stored by the Maoist Army shall be safely stored also by the Nepali Army. These arms shall be locked with a single padlock and the party concerned shall keep the key to it. For the UN to monitor it, a device with siren as well as recording facility shall be installed during the process of padlocking. The UN shall make necessary inspections of the stored arms in the presence of the party concerned. Technical details in this regard including camera monitoring shall be as per the agreement among the United Nations, the Government of Nepal and the CPN (Maoist).

4.7.The Council of Ministers shall control, mobilise and manage the Nepali Army in accordance with the new Military Act. The Interim Council of Ministers shall prepare and implement the detailed action plan for the democratisation of the Nepali Army on the basis of political consensus and the suggestions of the committee concerned of the Interim Legislature. This includes, among other things, right-sizing, democratic restructuring reflecting the national and inclusive character and imparting training to the Nepali Army on the values of democracy and human rights.

4.8.Such functions as border security and security of the conservation areas, National Parks, banks, airports, powerhouses, telephone towers, central secretariat and the distinguished personalities hitherto being carried out by the Nepali Army shall continue.

5. Cease-Fire

5.1. Ending of military action and mobilisation of armed personnel:

5.1.1.Both sides express commitments to refrain from carrying out following activities:

a. Direct or indirect use of any type of weapon or acts of attack against each other.

b. Searching or confiscating weapons belonging to the other side with or without weapons at the place where the arms have been stored as per the understanding reached between both sides.

c. Acts rendering harm to or mental pressure on any individuals.

d. Acts of setting up ambush targeting each other.

e. Acts of murder and violence.

f. Acts of kidnappings / detentions / imprisonments / disappearances.

g. Acts rendering loss to public/private/governmental or military properties.

h. Arial attacks or bombings.

i. Mining and sabotage.

j. Spying military activities of each other.

5.1.2. Neither side shall recruit additional troops, transport arms, ammunitions and explosives and conduct military activities against each other.

However, the Interim Government may deploy the security forces for patrolling, searching and confiscating for the prevention of illegal trafficking of the arms and explosive materials and parts and/or raw materials thereof at the international borders or customs points.

5.1.3. No individual or group shall carry any illegal arms, ammunitions and explosives while travelling.

5.1.4. Both sides shall assist each other by providing information as regards the location sketches and storage of ambushes and landmines used during the war time within 30 days and by defusing and destroying them within 60 days.

5.1.5.Armies of neither side shall be present with arms and in combat fatigue in any civil assembly, political meetings and public programmes.

5.1.6.The Nepal Police and the Armed Police Force shall continue the task of maintaining lawful arrangements and peace and order as well as that of criminal investigation in line with the norms and spirit of the people's movement and the peace accord and as per the prevailing laws.

5.1.7.Both sides shall issue circulars to their respective armed bodies or personnel imposing restrictions on using the term 'enemy' while addressing or making any other dealings with the armed personnel of the other side.

5.1.8.Both sides agree to keep records and return immediately the government, public and private buildings, land and other property seized, locked up or forbidden for use during the armed conflict.

5.2 Measures for the Normalization of Situation:

5.2.1.Forced and unlawful collection of donations in cash or kind and illegal collection of tax shall not be allowed.

5.2.2.Both sides agree to make public the status of the people under their respective custodies and release them within 15 days.

5.2.3.Both sides agree to make public within 60 days of the signing of the agreement the correct and full names and addresses of the people who 'disappeared' or were killed during the conflict and convey such details to the family members.

5.2.4.Both sides agree to constitute a National Peace and Rehabilitation Commission and carry out works through it for the normalization of the difficult situation that arose as a result of the armed conflict, maintain peace in the society and run relief and rehabilitation activities for the victims of conflict and those displaced.

5.2.5.Both sides agree to set up with mutual consent a High-level Truth and Reconciliation Commission in order to probe into those involved in serious violation of human rights and crime against humanity in course of the armed conflict for creating an atmosphere for reconciliation in the society.

5.2.6. Both sides pledge to abandon all types of wars, attacks, counter-attacks, violence and counter-violence in the country with a commitment to ensure democracy, peace and forward-looking transformation of the Nepali society. The two sides also agree to cooperate with each other for bringing about peace and maintaining law and order.

5.2.7. Both sides guarantee to withdraw political accusations, claims, complaints and cases under-consideration against various individuals and to instantly make public the status of those detained and release them immediately.

5.2.8. Both sides express commitment to allow without any political prejudice the people displaced during the armed conflict to return voluntarily to their respective places of ancestral or former residence, to reconstruct the infrastructure destroyed as a result of the conflict and to honourably rehabilitate and reintegrate the displaced people into the society.

5.2.9. Both sides agree to take individual and collective responsibility for resolving any problem arising in the aforementioned context on the basis of mutual agreement including with the support of all political parties, civil society and local organizations, and for creating an atmosphere conducive to the normalization of mutual relations and reconciliation.

5.2.10. Both sides express commitment not to discriminate against or exert any kind of pressure on any member of a family on the basis involvement with one or the other side.

5.2.11. Both sides agree not to raise any obstacle and not to allow the creation of any kind of obstruction to the employees of the Government of Nepal and other Public Bodies in the freedom of movement throughout the country, in the discharge of their duties and in carrying out their functions thus facilitating them in their work.

5.2.12. Both sides agree to allow unrestricted lawful movement throughout the State of Nepal to the personnel of the United Nations, International Donor Community, Diplomatic Missions based in Nepal, National and International Non-Governmental Organizations, Press Community, Human Rights Activists, Election Observers and foreign tourists.

5.2.13. Both sides are committed to organizing publicity programs in a decent and respectable manner.

6. End of conflict

6.1. On the basis of the historic decisions reached between the Seven Political Parties and the CPN (Maoist) on November 8, 2006, we hereby declare that the armed conflict ongoing in the country since 1996 has been brought to an end and that the current cease-fire between the Government and the Maoists has been made permanent.

6.2. The decisions of the meeting of the summit leaders of the Seven Political Parties and the CPN (Maoist) held on November 8, 2006 shall be the main policy foundation for long-term peace.

6.3. Following the confinement of the Nepali Army to the barracks and the combatants of the Maoist Army to the temporary cantonments, possession and display of arms and intimidation as well as use of violence and arms in any manner contravening the existing understandings and agreements and prevailing laws shall be punishable under law.

6.4. Armies of both the sides shall not be allowed to campaign or work for or against any side. However, they shall not be deprived of their voting right.

7. Compliance to Human Rights, Fundamental Rights and Humanitarian Laws

While remaining committed to the Universal Declaration of Human Rights,

1948, the International Humanitarian Laws and the fundamental principles and values of human rights, both the sides agree as follows:

7.1. Human Rights:

7.1.1. Both sides reiterate their commitment to the respect and protection of human rights and the international humanitarian laws and agree that no individual shall be discriminated on the basis of colour, gender, language, religion, age, race, nationality or social origin, property, disability, birth and other status and thought or belief.

7.1.2. Both sides agree to create an atmosphere where the Nepali people can enjoy their civil, political, economic, social and cultural rights and are committed to ensuring that such rights are not violated under any circumstances in the future.

7.1.3. Both sides express their commitment that impartial investigation shall be carried out and lawful action would be taken against individuals responsible for obstructions in the exercise of the rights contained in the agreement and guarantee not to encourage impunity. Apart from this, they shall also guarantee the right to relief of the families of victims of conflict, torture and disappearance.

7.1.4. Both sides shall refrain from inflicting torture, kidnapping and coercing the ordinary people to any work, and shall take necessary actions to discourage such acts.

7.1.5. Both sides shall respect the social, cultural and religious sensitivities, and the protection of religious sites and beliefs of any individual based on the values and norms of secularism,

7.2. Right to Life:

7.2.1. Both sides respect and protect the fundamental right to life of any individual. No individual shall be deprived of this fundamental right and no law that provides capital punishment shall be enacted.

7.3. Right to Individual Dignity, Freedom and Movement

7.3.1. Both sides respect and protect the right to individual dignity. In this connection, no person including those deprived of the enjoyment of freedom under law shall be subjected to torture or any other cruel, inhuman or degrading behaviour or punishment. The citizen's lawful right to privacy shall be respected.

7.3.2.Both sides shall fully respect the individual's right to freedom and security, shall not keep anyone under arbitrary or illegal detention, and shall not kidnap or hold anybody captive in a like manner. Both sides agree to make public the status of every individual disappeared and held captive and provide such information to their family members, legal counsel, and any other authorized persons.

7.3.3.Both sides shall respect and protect the citizens' right to freedom of movement and the right to choose the location of one's residence in a manner acceptable under prevailing laws, and express their commitments to respect the right of individuals and families displaced during the conflict to return to their original places of residence or to settle in any other places of their choice.

7.4. Civil and Political Rights

7.4.1.Both sides are committed to respect individual freedom of speech, expression, association and peaceful assembly and right against exploitation.

7.4.2.Both sides respect the right of every citizen to participate directly or through one's nominated representative in issues of public concern, to vote, to be elected to public office and to enjoy equal opportunities for public employment.

7.4.3. Both sides are committed to respect the individual right to be informed.

7.5. Economic and Social Rights

7.5.1.Both sides are committed to respect and protect the individual's right to livelihood through employment of their choice or acceptance.

7.5.2. Both sides are committed to respect and guarantee the right to food security of all the people. They assure that there shall be no interference in the use, transportation and distribution of food items, food products and food grains.

7.5.3. Both sides accept the fact that the citizens' right to health should be respected and protected. Both sides shall not obstruct the supply of medicines and health related assistance and campaigns, and express commitment to provide medical treatment to those injured in course of the conflict and to work for their rehabilitation.

7.5.4. With the realization of the fact that the right to education to all should be guaranteed and respected, both sides are committed to maintaining a congenial academic environment in educational institutions. Both sides agree to guarantee that the right to education shall not be violated. They agree to immediately put an end to such activities as capturing educational institutions and using them, abducting teachers and students, holding them captives, causing them to disappear, and not to set up army barracks in a way that would adversely impact schools and hospitals.

7.5.5. Both sides agree that the private property of any individual shall not be seized or usurped unlawfully.

7.5.6. Both sides believe in the fact that industrial production should continue, the right to collective bargaining and social security in the industrial establishments should be respected and the establishment and workers should be encouraged to seek peaceful settlement of any disputes between them without disturbing the industrial climate of the country, and respect the standards of work as determined by the International Labour Organization.

7.6. Rights of Women and Children

7.6.1. Both sides fully agree to special protection of the rights of women and children, to immediately stop all types of violence against women and children, including child labour as well as sexual exploitation and abuse, and not to conscript or use children who are aged 18 or below in the armed force. Children thus affected shall be rescued immediately and appropriate assistance as may be needed shall be provided for their rehabilitation.

7.7. Right to Individual Liberty

7.7.1. Both sides agree to enforce and cause to be enforced the freedom of thought and opinion, freedom of expression and publication, freedom of peaceful assembly without arms, freedom of movement, freedom of choice of profession or occupation, freedom of acquisition, ownership and disposal of property, freedom to participate in peaceful political activities, the right to equality before law and a just legal system.

8. Differences Settlement and Implementation Mechanism

8.1. Both sides agree to take individual as well as collective responsibility for not repeating the mistakes committed in the past and making correction gradually in the future.

8.2. The National Peace and Rehabilitation Commission may set up necessary mechanisms for the success of the peace campaign. The constitution and working procedure of the Commission shall be as determined by the Interim Council of Ministers.

8.3. Both sides are committed to settle all kinds of issues and mutual differences, current or that may arise in future, through mutual talks, understanding, consensus and dialogue.

8.4. Both sides express their commitments that the Interim Council of Ministers may constitute and determine the working procedures of the National Peace and Rehabilitation Commission, the Truth and Reconciliation Commission, the High-Level State Restructuring Recommendation Commission and other mechanisms as may be necessary for the implementation of this Agreement, the Interim Constitution and all the decisions, agreements and understandings reached between the Seven Parties or the Government of Nepal and the CPN (Maoist).

9. Implementation and Monitoring

Both sides agree to make the following arrangements for the implementation of the understandings contained in this agreement and for their follow-up:

9.1. Both sides agree to give continuity to the task of monitoring of the human rights provisions mentioned in this agreement by the United Nations Office of the High Commissioner for Human Rights, Nepal.

9.2. Both sides agree to the monitoring of the management of arms and the armies by the United Nations Mission in Nepal as per the provisions of the five-point letters sent earlier to the UN and those of the present agreement and agree to facilitate the process.

9.3. Both sides agree to have the United Nations observe the election to the Constituent Assembly.

9.4. The National Human Rights Commission shall also carry out responsibilities related to the monitoring of human rights as mentioned in this agreement together with the responsibility assigned to it as per the laws. While carrying out its functions, the Commission may liaison with and seek assistance from national as well as international human rights related organizations.

9.5. Both sides agree to receive the reports submitted by the above-mentioned bodies, to provide requisite information to them, and to implement their suggestions and recommendations on the basis of discussions and consensus.

10. Miscellaneous

10.1. Pursuant to the essence of the decisions of November 8 and the spirit of the peace agreement, both sides agree not to run any structure, including those parallel to the government, in any areas of government or state apparatus.

10.2. Both sides agree to sign additional supplementary agreements as may be necessary for the implementation of the present agreement.

10.3. This agreement may be amended any time with the consent of both sides. In case an amendment is desired, both sides agree to provide a notice in writing to the other side. Pursuant to such a notice, amendments may be made to the agreement with the consent of both sides. The provisions to be covered by such an amendment shall not be inferior to universally accepted norms of international human rights, standards of international humanitarian laws and the core spirit of the establishment of peace.

10.4.If any dispute arises in the interpretation of this agreement, a joint mechanism comprising both sides shall make the interpretation as per the spirit of the preamble and the documents annexed to this agreement, and such interpretation shall be final.

10.5.The concept and existence of the 'two sides' as mentioned in this agreement shall automatically come to an end after the constitution of the Interim Legislature -Parliament. Thereafter, all the responsibility of implementing the obligations mentioned in this agreement shall be as per the arrangements made by the Interim Council of Ministers. It shall be the duty and responsibility of all political parties to extend cooperation in the compliance and implementation of the agreement.

10.6.At a time when the entire country is focused on the principal campaign of the election to the Constituent Assembly, we sincerely request to all to have their problems and demands resolved through talks and dialogue and to contribute to the election of the Constituent Assembly and to the maintenance of law and order.

10.7.We sincerely appeal to the civil society, the professional groups, the class organizations, the media, the intellectuals and the entire Nepali people to actively participate and make successful the historic campaign of building a new democratic Nepal and establishing lasting peace through the election of the Constituent Assembly thus ending the armed conflict.

10.8.We sincerely request the international community including all friendly countries and the United Nations to extend support to Nepal in the campaign of establishing a full-fledged democracy and lasting peace.

Having realized the responsibility towards the future of the country and the people, and remaining fully committed to this Comprehensive Peace Agreement, we, on behalf of the Government of Nepal and the Communist Party of Nepal (Maoist), hereby sign this comprehensive peace agreement and make it public.

Prachanda Chairman Communist Party of Nepal (Maoist)	Girija Prasad Koirala Prime Minister Government of Nepal

Signed on November 21, 2006

The Seven Point-pacts signed between CPN-UML President Jhalnath Khanal & Unified CPN-Maoist President Pushpa Kamal Dahal. It was first rrevealed on

February 5,2011

1. The two Parties vow to strengthen inclusive democracy and establish Political and social system geared towards socialism while adhering to the pillars of national independence, indivisibility and sovereignty to create an independent economy through socio-economic transformation.

2. Agree to write a new constitution to institutionalise republic federalism uprooting all forms of feudalism, thus strengthening inclusive democracy and national independence.

3. Pledge to take the peace process to a logicla end by executiing all tasks related to integration, rehabilitation and voluntary retirement of Maoist combatants. We also agree to form a separate force for Maoist combatants or an alternative force cobining the PLA and other security forces.

4. Agree to constitute a joint government. A high-level mechanism will be formed to assist in the governance. The mechanism will be led by the chiefs of the signatory parties on a rotational basis. A new government will be formed by including as many parties as possible. The sharing of important ministries, including home and defence, will be done in an appropriate and respectable manner. Top leaders of the two parties will take the responsibilty for the same.

5. Minimum Common Programme of the new govenment and code of conduct will be formulated and enforced.

6. The two parties will lead the future government on a rotational basis based on mutual understanding and long term cooperation.

7. It is hereby agreed that the UCPN (Maoist) will vote for the UML candidate in the prime ministerial election.

The Five Point deal signed by the heads of three major political parties (The Maoist, Nepali Congress and the UML) on

May 28, 2011

We the Political parties have reached the following agreement today, May 28,2011

1. To complete the basic tasks of the peace process within three months
2. To prepare the first draft of the constitution from the Constituent Assembly (CA) within three months
3. To implement effectively the various past agreements reached with the Madhesi Front, including the one to make the Nepal Army (NA) an inclusive institution
4. To extend the CA term by three months
5. The Prime minister to resign and pave the way for the formation of a consensus national unity government

Contributors

LATE BP KOIRALA was the first democratically elected Prime Minister of Nepal.

LATE HARIDEV SHARMA was a Socialist thinker. He also served as Director at Jawaharlal Nehru Memorial Museum and Library, New Delhi.

SD MUNI is a Visiting Research Professor, Institute of South Asian Studies, Singapore. He is also the former Ambassador of India to Lao People's Democratic Republic.

NARAHARI ACHARYA is a Member of Constituent Assembly and central committee member of Nepali Congress. He is also the former Minister of Parliamentary Affairs, Govt of Nepal.

ANAND SWAROOP VERMA is a senior journalist and Editor, Samkaleen Teesri Duniya, New Delhi.

BC UPRETI is the Director, South Asia Studies Centre, University of Rajasthan, Jaipur.

PRADEEP GYANWALI is a Member of Constituent Assembly and politburo member of Communist Party of Nepal (UML).

BIMAL PRASAD, is the former Professor at School of International Studies, Jawaharlal Nehru University, New Delhi and former Ambassador of India to Nepal.

PUSHPESH PANT is a Professor, Centre for International Politics, Organisation and Disarmament, School of International Studies, Jawaharlal Nehru University, New Delhi.

HARI KISHORE SINGH is the Vice Chairman, Bihar State Planning Board, and Chairman, AN Sinha Institute of Social Studies, Patna, Bihar. He is also the former Minister of State, Department of External Affairs, Government of India, New Delhi.

LOK RAJ BARAL is a Professor and Executive Chairman, Nepal Centre for Contemporary Studies, Kathmandu. He is also the former Ambassador of

Nepal to India.

LATE RISHIKESH SHAHA was the Foreign Minister of Nepal and a celebrated human rights activist.

ADITYA ADHIKARI is an Opinion Editor, *The Kathmandu Post*, Kathmandu.

KATAK MALLA teaches legal issues of environment, constitutional and civil rights and social justice as a guest lecturer in universities in Nepal, Sweden and Finland.

DHRUBA KUMAR is a Professor of Political Science at Centre for Nepal & Asian Studies, Tribhuvan University, Kathmandu.

PRASHANT JHA is an eminent Nepali journalist based in Kathmandu.

NABINDRA RAJ JOSHI is a member of Legislative Parliament of Nepal and the Chairman of Ganeshman Singh Foundation.

SUBODH RAJ PYAKUREL is the Chairperson of FORUM-ASIA, Bangkok, Thailand.

DIPENDRA PRASAD PANT works as an Editor of '*Informal*', a Kathmandu based quarterly publication on Human Rights & Social Justice.

BR DEEPAK, Managing Editor, Think India Quarterly, is the Associate Professor, Centre of Chinese and Southeast Asian Studies, Jawaharlal Nehru University, New Delhi.

PRAMOD DHAKAL is the Executive Director, Canada Foundation for Nepal, Kathmandu. He is also former Faculty Member of Tribhuvan University, Kathmandu.

UDDHAB PD. PYAKUREL is a Research Scholar at Centre for the Study of Social Systems, Jawaharlal Nehru University, New Delhi.

INDRA ADHIKARI completed her Phd at School of International Studies, Jawaharlal Nehru University, New Delhi and is working as SAARC visiting fellow at IDSA, New Delhi.

MANOJ DAHAL is associated with a Nepali National Daily, *NAGARIK* as the Editor, News Desk.

HARI BANSH JHA is a Professor of Economics and Executive Director of Centre for Economic and Technical Studies in Nepal.

Acknowledgements

For knowledge about Nepal, I must acknowledge the contributions of many political leaders (both from India and Nepal) and a number of my Nepalese friends. Nepal as a country is of special significance for India and the world. This endeavour through a book is to present the various dimensions of the Nepalese society, and its politics and history.

We are grateful to the members of the Editorial Advisory Board of Think India Quarterly, Chairman Vichar Nyas Foundation and all the authors who have written in the special issue on Nepal (October-December 2010). Since most of the articles in the book are taken from the special issue of Think India Quarterly on Nepal, we are grateful to all those who helped us in bringing out the issue. Our special thanks are due to Rt. Honourable Dr. Rambaran Yadav, the first President of the Republic of Nepal who kindly consented to release our special issue on Nepal in New Delhi on 31 January 2011.

My grateful memories go back to the great leaders of Nepal Mr. BP Koirala, Mr. Ganesh Man Singh, Comrade Madan Bhandari, Ms Shailaja Acharya, Mr. GP Koirala and Mr. KP Bhattarai who played historic roles in the shaping of the modern Nepal. The story of real friendship between India and Nepal will not be complete without remembering the great friends of Nepal Mr. Chandrashekhar, Comrade Harkishen Singh Surjeet and Surendra Mohan. Their affection has been our great strength.

The book would not have been possible without the help of my dear friend Mr. Pradip Giri, Honourable Member of Parliament of Nepal, Mr. Uddhab Pyakurel and my very old friend Mr. Anand Swaroop Verma.

We are indebted to the untiring efforts of our publisher Brigadier P.K. Vij and his team members.

- D. P. Tripathi

New Delhi

Index

U

V

W

Y

Z